MIDDLE ENGLISH SURVEY

MIDDLE ENGLISH SURVEY
Critical Essays

EDITED BY

Edward Vasta

UNIVERSITY OF NOTRE DAME PRESS

Notre Dame   London

To My Wife

EDITOR'S NOTE

I WAS LED TO UNDERTAKE THIS ANTHOLOGY BY THE GROWING scarcity of medievalists in our colleges, resulting from a scarcity of interest among students, and the consequent necessity of displaying for students the meaningfulness of Middle English literature. Hopefully, the fifteen essays collected here on nine major works and genre (excluding Chaucer) will help to bring those studying independently or in the classroom to a vital confrontation with the literature. These essays have been selected from among those that seem to me conducive to such a confrontation. They have not been chosen as providing introductory information, as representing various critical approaches, as exhausting their subjects, as typifying predominant interpretations, or as having conspicuously influenced scholarship, although all of them belong in various of these categories. Rather they have been chosen because they seem fundamentally educative: they seem effectively to lead into literary aspects of the works and also to inspire further inquiry.

These essays have been edited, furthermore, with a view to stimulating interest among undergraduate as well as graduate students. Whenever possible, quotations have been checked and corrected against the originals; the Middle English spelling, wherever used, has been retained; and except for the first essay, an abridgement of a chapter from Professor Manning's book on the lyric, all essays are reproduced uncut in their text and notes. The graduate student, therefore, and the professional scholar as well, may deal with these essays in the confident knowledge that they are complete and accurate as originally published. In addition, brief supplementary bibliographies are provided, listing related studies not already cited in the notes.

For undergraduates, all terms and quotations in Middle English and foreign languages are translated, both in the notes and the text, if they have seemed likely to be at all troublesome. The translations are as literal as the sense will allow, and thus may be used as a kind of running gloss rather than as substitutes for the original. Wherever an author has indicated preferred meanings, these meanings have been adopted in the translations so that they may be as faithful to the author's argument as possible. In most cases, however, if the texture of a quotation does not demand otherwise, the "thou" form of the pronoun is translated "you" in order to avoid the clumsiness of the "-est" ending of the related verbs. Since my intention in translating has been to remove impediments to a student's involvement with the literature, I have preferred to translate too much rather than too little.

In the course of assembling this anthology I have benefited from the assistance of many. Professor Mortimer J. Donovan has been more than generous with his time, his effort, and his knowledge. Professor John P. Turley has allowed me liberal use of his time and his expert knowledge of Latin. I owe thanks as well to Professor Richard J. Schoeck, Professor Jerome Taylor, Professor Robert W. Ackerman, and Reverend Paul E. Beichner, C.S.C., all of whom have given me both encouragement and counsel.

I am especially grateful, finally, to the authors whose contributions constitute this anthology, and to their publishers for permissions.

E.V.

Notre Dame, Indiana
March 28, 1965

CONTENTS

ix

ANALOGY AND IMAGERY

Stephen Manning

TO A DEGREE THAT MANY MODERNS CANNOT APPRECIATE, THE medieval world was theocentric. It was theocentric spatially and temporally—i.e., in the realm of nature and in the realm of history. Nature was a theophany; it was the visible garment of divinity; it was, as Emile Mâle points out,

a book written by the hand of God in which every creature is a word charged with meaning. The ignorant see the forms—the mysterious letters—understanding nothing of their meaning, but the wise pass from the visible to the invisible, and in reading nature read the thoughts of God. True knowledge, then, consists not only in the study of things in themselves—the outward forms—but in penetrating to the inner meaning intended by God for our instruction, for in the words of Honorius of Autun, "every creature is a shadow of truth and life."[1]

This concept of the correspondence between the visible and the invisible, the corporeal and the spiritual, has a long history, but

Reprinted from *Wisdom and Number* by Stephen Manning by permission of University of Nebraska Press. © 1962 by the University of Nebraska Press. For other studies of medieval lyrics in general, see George Kane, "The Middle English Religious Lyrics," in *Middle English Literature* (London: Methuen & Co., 1951), pp. 104–81; and Arthur K. Moore, *The Secular Lyric in Middle English* (University of Kentucky Press, 1951).

[1] *The Gothic Image,* trans. Dora Nussey (New York, 1958), p. 29. For other examples of the concept of the book of nature, see Henri de Lubac, *Exégèse médiévale* (Paris, 1959), I, p. 124; Curtius, pp. 319–26.

in the later Middle Ages it was vitalized by St. Francis of Assísi and especially by St. Bonaventure in his celebrated doctrine of analogy.[2] When we consider the significant role of the Franciscans in shaping English spirituality and especially in shaping the course of the English lyric, the wonder is that this doctrine of analogy and its role in the symbolic interpretation of the universe inspired so few of the English religious lyrics. But if God spoke to man through nature, he spoke also through history. For the Christian, all history unites at its focal point: the Incarnation and Redemption; as Mâle says, "All leads up to Christ as all begins anew in Him" (p. 176). To read the Old Testament is to accept the events which it narrates as historical facts; to read it from the focal point of history is to interpret these facts as prophecies. The concept of a *New* Testament which abrogated the Old meant that the Old in itself had application only for the Jews and not for the Christians; exegetes, therefore, following the example of St. Paul and indeed of Christ Himself, gave the Old Testament a Christian relevance.[3] Similarly, profane history was given a Christian reference and was interpreted as reflecting the Old Testament or the New. But the Incarnation was not only the fulfillment of the old dispensation; it began the new. It embodied a set of spiritual values which affect the daily life of the Christian throughout time. It embodied a spiritual reality which was given meaning in the interior life of every Christian. The Incarnation therefore has for the Christian a profundity which transcends its historical reality. As Jean Daniélou has remarked,

The Christian faith has but one object: the mystery of Christ dead and risen. But this one only mystery subsists under different modes. It is prefigured in the Old Testament; it is realized historically in the life of Christ on earth; it is contained by way of mystery in the sacraments; it is lived mystically in souls; it is accomplished socially in the Church; it is consummated eschatologically in the kingdom of heaven. Thus the

[2] See Etienne Gilson, *La Philosophie de Saint Bonaventure,* Études de philosophie médiévale, IV (Paris, 1924), pp. 196–227.

[3] See de Lubac, *op. cit.,* I, pp. 305–28, 490–522.

2

Christian has at his disposal, for the expression of that single reality, several registers, a symbolism of several dimensions. All Christian culture consists in grasping the bonds of union that exist between the Bible and liturgy, between the Gospel and eschatology, between the mystical life and the liturgy.[4]

Thus, in history as well as in nature, behind the surface, lay the invisible reality which unified all human existence. . . .

The analogies which the Middle Ages saw between the corporeal and the spiritual levels of existence are . . . reflected in the imagery which the poets use. If we restrict imagery, as I do here, to include primarily simile, metaphor, allegory, and symbol, the poets wrote many image-less lyrics. And when we examine those that do contain imagery, we often find the images very few and insignificant in the structure of the poem as a whole. Why? Perhaps for three related reasons. First, the song and songlike lyric do not need imagery in this restricted sense to create their characteristic effects. Imagery, particularly metaphor and symbol, may bear too great an intellectual content for the songlike lyric. It suits better the insight into religious experience which these lyrics do not present. As we have observed, they tend rather to affirm the generally understood forms of religious experience. If they employ images, they find most helpful those which alliterate and those which are thoroughly conventional, for such images will not deflect attention from the sound pattern. Indeed the medievals valued imagery, not for its rich emotional overtones, but for its ability to stimulate the mind toward the supernatural. As D. W. Robertson has commented:

the function of figurative expression was not to arouse spontaneous emotional attitudes based on the personal experience of the observer, but to encourage the observer to seek an abstract pattern of philosophical significance beneath the symbolic configuration.[5]

[4] "Le Symbolisme des rites baptismaux," *Dieu vivant,* I (1945), 17, as translated by Walter J. Burghardt, "On Early Christian Exegesis," *Theological Studies,* XI (1950), 79. See also Jean Daniélou, "Les Divers sens de l'Écriture dans la tradition chrétienne primitive," *Ephemerides theologicae Lovanienses,* XXIV (1948), 119–26.

[5] Ed., Saint Augustine, *On Christian Doctrine,* Library of Liberal Arts (New York, 1958), p. xv.

This leads to a second consideration. The Franciscans, who were so influential in shaping the course of the Middle English religious lyrics, were concerned more with arousing emotional response with their poems than they were in philosophical significances. There existed, in fact, a controversy between the friars and the secular clergy over the respective emphasis given devotional poetry and allegorical poetry.[6] Poetry written under Franciscan influence definitely did not tend to use imagery to illumine familiar religious concepts; unlike that poetry which used imagery to encourage the search for abstract philosophical patterning, its concerns were more to arouse spontaneous emotional attitudes.

A third reason, not so much for the lack of imagery but for the types of imagery used, issues from the didactic purpose of many of the lyrics and the confusion in general of rhetoric and poetic. Clarity—not ambiguity—is the chief aim of the rhetorician and the teacher. He is not primarily interested in a characteristic poetic technique of striking several notes at the same time. His images therefore tend to be single-dimensional. They clarify, but they do not illumine; they restrict, but they do not simultaneously expand. Rather than being intrinsic to the thought, they merely illustrate it. Once they have served their immediate purpose, they disappear. Indeed, because they are usually single-dimensional, they can encompass only a small portion of the theme and must be dropped. One poet, in speaking of Christ on the cross, comments: "Als streme dose of þe strande, his blode gan downe glyde" [As a stream does from the brook, his blood did glide down] (XIV, No. 83, line 40). This image focuses the abundance of the bleeding and is therefore more precise and carries a stronger emotive value than a less specific statement. But there is no insight. There is no suggestion of the infinite

[6] See Charles R. Dahlberg, "The Secular Tradition in Chaucer and Jean de Meun," unpublished dissertation (Princeton, 1953), esp. pp. 127–28. For the Franciscan influence on the English lyrics, see Rossell Hope Robbins, "The Authors of the Middle English Religious Lyrics," *JEGP*, XXXIX (1940), 230–38.

rivers of grace, of the "laver of redemption," of the spiritually cleansing power of Christ's blood. The image restricts but does not expand; it therefore remains single-dimensional. This characteristic sometimes rankles when the image appears over a number of lines and is then dropped. In three instances the image takes up half the poem, then vanishes: XIV, Nos. 62 and 63; XV, No. 68. But the poet has in all three instances developed the single dimension of the image about as far as it can go, and he must either invest it with added meanings or abandon it. The rhetorician generally prefers the latter. Even more suggestive of the rhetorician is the explicit exegesis with which he invests his image, especially when he uses allegory and feels obliged to make his point perfectly clear. (In fact, the single-dimension of many similes is reminiscent of the one-to-one equation of allegory.) But this quality is not confined to allegory; the following lines referring to Christ illustrate the technique at its boldest (XIV, No. 48):

> Brother & syster he es by skyll,
> For he sayd & lered þare lare,
> Þat who-so wroght his fader will
> Brother & syster to him þai ware. (36)

> [Brother and sister he is by reason,
> for he taught that whoever performed
> the will of his Father would be
> brother and sister to him.]

Such a flat and obvious technique may contribute to the poet's realization of his theme as a whole, but it sorely limits his poem's ultimate literary worth.

Despite the influence of the song, of the Franciscans, and of the rhetoricians and preachers, we can discover some highly effective images in the religious lyrics. We can even find multivalent images reminiscent of modern use of symbolism. At this point we should recall the historical use of analogy in the Middle Ages—that perspective which viewed the events of the New Testament as reflected in the Old, as repeated in the life of the Church, as exemplifying the life of every individual soul, and as prophesying the life to come. The Middle Ages often referred collectively to these levels of interpretation as *allegory*. We would probably call it symbolism. The medievals did, however, distinguish between what we might term symbol and allegory; their terms were *allegoria in res* [allegory in the thing] and *allegoria in verbis* [allegory in the word]. The primary basis for this distinction lay in the treatment of the literal level.[7] In *allegoria in verbis* the literal level has no real significance; it is, as Dante calls it, "a beautiful lie." The literal basis of *allegoria in res,* however, lies in actual fact. This literal basis may be a thing (an eagle), a person (Adam), or an event (the Israelites crossing the Red Sea). In each instance the spiritual significance given the actual object, person, or event derives from a Christocentric view of the universe, an attempt to relate all things to the Christian life. Thus, the exegetes detected an analogy (1) between the Old and New Testamtents, applying the signification to Christ either in His own life or in the life of His Church; (2) between the corporeal and spiritual worlds, in which the corporeal indicates a course of supernatural action which the individual Christian souls follow; and/or (3) between this temporal existence, as reflected in actual history, and the life of the world to come. Basically, then, this symbolism (as we call it) works on two levels—a literal and a spiritual. The spiritual level, in turn, is capable of interpretation on three different planes, sometimes called respectively the allegorical, the tropological, and the anagogical.[8] Perhaps a clearer set of terms is Christological-ecclesiological, moral, and eschatological. We

[7] See Anthony Nemetz, "Literalness and the *Sensus Litteralis,"* *Speculum,* XXXIV (1959), 76–89. For *allegoria in res* and *in verbis,* see de Lubac, I, 493–98. For Dante's distinctions, see Charles S. Singleton, "Dante's Allegory," *Speculum,* XXV (1950), 78–86; Richard Hamilton Green, "Dante's 'Allegory of Poets' and the Mediaeval Theory of Poetic Fiction," *CL,* IX (1957), 118–28.

[8] De Lubac distinguishes a triple and a fourfold exegesis of Scripture (I, 139–57, 203), but this distinction is not necessary for our purposes. De Lubac also insists upon the importance of the literal level, pp. 425–39.

cannot insist too much on the fact that each of these levels arises from the preceding. What applies to Christ or the Church as a whole applies as well to the individual soul, for Christ or the Church is the model for the individual soul to copy. Similarly, what characterizes the life of the soul on earth foreshadows its existence in heaven. And of course all these spiritual interpretations are based on the literal fact. Such an elaborate interrelationship of values is thus not only meaningful, but coherent and unified as well. The same image may not yield all three spiritual interpretations, however; the value may fluctuate from context to context. Moreover, the particular significance which the object yields may also vary: the eagle, for example, may symbolize St. John, or Christ, or mankind—but these interpretations are not necessarily mutually exclusive. Sometimes the same object may embody opposite values: the lion may be either Christ or the devil, and both these significations may be traced to scriptural bases (Rev. [Apoc.] 5:5 and I Pet. 5:8). We must not forget that the symbolic value which the Middle Ages saw in the things of this world gave those things their worth; nature was valuable for the Christian because it reflected God, the supreme reality. As Otto von Simson has pointed out, in differentiating medieval from modern times,

For us the symbol is an image that invests physical reality with poetical meaning. For medieval man, the physical world as we understand it has no reality except as a symbol. But even the term "symbol" is misleading. For us the symbol is the subjective creation of poetic fancy; for medieval man what we would call symbol is the only objectively valid definition of reality. We find it necessary to suppress the symbolic instinct if we seek to understand the world as it is rather than as it seems. Medieval man conceived the symbolic instinct as the only reliable guide to such an understanding.[9]

Since we are thus accustomed to taking the word *symbol* as representing a poetic rather than a metaphysical reality, and since a religious symbol may or may not function as a poetic

[9] *The Gothic Cathedral*, Bollingen Series, XLVIII (New York, 1956), p. xix.

symbol, I think that for our present purposes in trying to determine the literary quality of the religious lyrics, we should maintain the usual modern distinction between allegory and symbol, and use the threefold spiritual analogy as possible connotations of either.

Allegory may be defined, according to Robin Skelton, as "an image having apparent independence within a poem, but being, in reality, dependent upon an explicit identification of it with a concept or idea." A symbol, on the other hand, is "An image, possessing great associative value, and multiplicity of meanings, which acts independently within the poem, and is not dependent upon any comparison with, or equation with, a concept or idea."[10] In other words, allegory *tends* to give a one-to-one equivalence to the image (vehicle) and the idea or person to whom it refers (tenor); symbol is generally multivalent, or at least bivalent. In allegory the image exists for the sake of the idea; it in effect substitutes for it. In symbol the image exists first as a literal, concrete object and then suggests some abstract principle(s). Varieties are possible within each classification, and Skelton has listed and named these possibilities. To avoid so much nomenclature, however, we shall simply note relevant branches without giving them specific names.

The following image clearly illustrates what a symbol is not: "The pasche lambe, þat on þe croce did clym" [The paschal lamb that on the cross did climb] (XV, No. 112, line 23). Now lambs—paschal or otherwise—do not ordinarily climb crosses. The literal meaning of this line is nonsense, and therefore does not contain a poetic symbol. Even though the paschal lamb is one of the most widespread religious symbols of Christ, it does not function here independently of its tenor and is therefore not a poetic symbol. It is instead a species of allegory—even though it has multiple connotations. This particular kind of allegory I will give a specific name, for it is a device occasionally found in rhetoric. It is a figurative epithet without the noun it de-

---

[10] *The Poetic Pattern* (Berkeley, 1956), p. 102.

scribes; the epithet appears in place of the noun. In this sense it is a kind of synecdoche since one term (the epithet) is used in place of another (the noun described). The technical name is antonomasia, but I shall call it simply figurative epithet. This same device turns up in such literally impossible lines as "When aungels brede was dampned to dede to safe oure sauls sare" [When angel's bread (i.e., Christ) was damned to death to save our sore souls] (XIV, No. 83, line 44); "And seyde che xuld bere the flour / That xulde breke the fyndes bond" [And said she (Mary) should bear the flower that should break the fiend's bond] (Greene, No. 175C, lines 7–8); "Thow art the sterre with brestis softe as sylke" [Thou (Mary) art the star with breasts soft as silk] (XV, No. 135, line 8). Each of these images has multiple connotations, but is not a poetic symbol simply because it is literally impossible. If, as in these instances, the image is conventional enough and appears only in passing, the poet can substitute such epithets for the persons without unduly upsetting his audience. And if he employs them in a conspicuous sound pattern, he is even less likely to disturb them.

The poet's failure to keep in mind the literal value of the image can become disturbing in allegory, however, for here the image has been developed, and the modern mind seizes upon the discrepancy. The first stanza of a sixteenth-century carol (Greene, No. 321) offers a familiar allegorical interpretation of John 12:24–25:

> On Cristes day, I vnderstond,
> An ere of whet of a mayd spronge,
> Thirti winter in erth to stond,
>   To make vs bred all to his pay.   (4)

> [On Christ's day, I understand,
> an ear of wheat sprang from a maid,
> thirty winters on earth to stand,
> to make us bread to his liking.]

The image is allegory, not symbol, for ears of wheat do not spring from maidens. But watch what happens in stanza two:

> This corn was repyn and layd to grownd
> Full sore beten and faste bownd
> Vnto a piler with cordes rownd;
>> At his fyngers endes the blod ran owt that day.   (8)

> [This grain was ripened and laid on the ground,
> very sorely beaten and bound fast
> to a pillar with round cords;
>> at his fingers' ends the blood ran out that day.]

Tenor and vehicle have become so identified in the poet's mind that he does not observe the properties of the vehicle as it actually exists. No wonder that the vehicle disappears completely from the last stanza! Although the sound pattern helps cover the flaw, we still object because the image extends beyond reason. We do not object because we cannot *visualize* a grain of wheat being scourged, but because the comparison between the reaped grain and the scourged Christ includes details (lines 7–8) appropriate to the latter but not to the former. Now observe line 2; here the discrepancy is not quite as glaring since *spronge* continues the image and since the thought is passed over quickly. The second stanza, though, points up the artificiality of the allegory: it is ornamental here rather than functional.

Allegory may thus be divided into two types: arbitrary and descriptive.[11] Arbitrary allegory is self-explanatory; the vehicle bears no relationship whatever to the tenor. For example, in "Ful feir flour is þe lilie" [A very fair flower is the lily] (XIII, No. 19), the vehicle is the lily which has five leaves, interpreted as charity toward God; love of neighbor; righteousness; then

> to seruen crist vid feid &
>> honden,
> to firsaken tricherie,
> prude & onde & lecherie;   (24)

[11] The terms are Helen Flanders Dunbar's; see esp. p. 476. I consider personification allegory more personification than allegory and do not discuss it. (It appears seldom in the lyrics.) See Dunbar, p. 279; but also see Robert W. Frank, "The Art of Reading Medieval Personification Allegory," *ELH*, XX (1953), 243–45.

[to serve Christ with feet and hands,
to forsake treachery,
pride, envy, and lechery;]

and finally, confession. This interpretation of the five leaves of the lily does nothing to elucidate the nature of the lily, nor on the other hand, does the nature of the five leaves of the lily have anything to do with the fivefold significance. Why not a lily with four leaves? The relation between image and signification is, in other words, purely arbitrary. The signification could be any other signification as long as it consists of five points; the choice of image could have been any image which suited a fivefold interpretation.

On the other hand, descriptive allegory contains some sort of intrinsic likeness between vehicle and tenor; it consequently exhibits some kind of interaction which makes possible an incisive comparison of tenor and vehicle. Descriptive allegory, therefore, can, at its best, penetrate directly into the theme. The poems which speak of Mary as rose are descriptive allegories, and usually they make explicit the similarities which make the comparison appropriate: beauty, excellence, love, virginity (usually when without thorns). But one of the most striking instances of this type of allegory is the opening of "Somer is comen & winter gon" [Spring has come and winter gone] (XIII, No. 54). After introducing the joyousness of spring, with the song of the birds, the poet continues:

> So stronge kare me bint,
> al wit Ioye þat is funde
> in londe,
> Al for a child (8)
> þat is so milde
> of honde.

[Strong care binds me,
with all the joy found in the land,
for a child who is mild of hand.]

> Þat child, þat is so milde & wlong
> & eke of grete munde, (12)

11

boþe in boskes & in bank
  isout me hauet a-stunde.
Ifunde he heuede me,
for an appel of a tre   (16)
    ibunde;
He brac þe bond
þat was so strong
      wit wunde.   (20)

[That child, who is so mild and proud
and also of great power,
both in bushes and bank
has sought me for a time.
He had found me,
through an apple from a tree, bound;
he broke the bond,
that was so strong,
with wounds.]

Þat child þat was so wilde &
    wlong
  to me a-lute lowe,
fram me to giwes he was sold—   (24)
  ne cuþen hey him nout
     cnowe.

[That child, who was so wild and proud,
to me bowed low,
from me to Jews he was sold—
they could not know him.]

Child here is obviously Christ, but the image is ambivalent. In one sense Jesus is a youth of noble birth, "milde / of honde" (lines 9–10), yet proud as befits his nobility, and of great power (lines 11–12). His power is shown, in fact, by His breaking the strong bond of sin by His wounds. The speaker, now Everyman, re-emphasizes that this noble youth is proud and accustomed to taking His own way (line 21); this prepares for the contrast in the following line, recalling Phil. 2:8. But *child* also has connotations here of regained youth, of regeneration, so that the image thereupon assumes definite associations with the springtime of the Redemption, the time of rebirth and renewal. Finally, that Jesus is a youth sold to the Jews reminds us of a favorite exegesis of the Old Testament story of Joseph. What makes the image so striking are these multiple connotations; the poet is emphasizing his insight into the nature of the redemptive act through the image of the child. Although the rest of the poem has many excellent touches, including a brilliant handling of variation in the sound pattern, I do not feel that it matches this opening section.

That allegorical images can have multiple connotations is, I hope, sufficiently obvious. If there is any doubt, this splendid carol should dispel it (Greene, No. 322A):

> Lully, lulley; lully, lulley;
> The fawcon hath born my mak away.
>
> He bare hym vp, he bare hym down;
> He bare hym into an orchard brown.
>
> In that orchard ther was an hall,
> That was hangid with purpill and pall. (4)
>
> And in that hall there was a bede;
> Hit was hangid with gold so rede.
>
> And yn that bed ther lythe a knyght,
> His wowndes bledyng day and nyght. (8)
>
> By that bedes side ther kneleth a may,
> And she wepeth both nyght and day.
>
> And by that beddes side ther stondith a ston,
> *Corpus Christi* wretyn thereon. (12)
>
> [Lully, lulley; lully, lulley;
> the Falcon has borne my mate away.
> He bore him up, he bore him down;
> he bore him into an orchard brown.
> In that orchard there was a hall,
> that was hung with purple and pall.
> And in that hall there was a bed;
> it was hung with gold so red.
> And in that bed there lies a knight,

13

> his wounds bleeding day and night.
> By that bedside there kneels a maid,
> and she weeps both night and day.
> And by that bedside there stands a stone,
> *Corpus Christi* written thereon.]

Lines 11–12 clearly mark this poem as allegory: the knight is Christ, Mary or Ecclesia is the *may*. We have a definite one-to-one relation. Moreover, lines 1–2 undoubtedly allude to the garden where the sepulchre was (John 19:41), with a possible further allusion to the apple tree in Eden. Now the connotations here are multiple. The poem is reminiscent of a typical ballad situation, but even more so of the Grail Legend and the myth of the dying God. (This connotation marks the poem even more strongly as allegory.) Finally, there are suggestions of the Eucharistic host and possibly a remote connection with the Mass.[12] The situation, in fact, calls to mind the Forty Hours Devotion, which commemorates the forty hours Christ spent in the tomb. During this time the Blessed Sacrament is exposed on the altar for the adoration of the faithful. This devotion, in fact, dates from the sixteenth century, the date Greene gives the MS of our poem.[13] Perhaps this poem was written in celebration of, or was inspired by, the devotion. The hall may well be the physical church; the bed, the monstrance; the may, Ecclesia; the stone, the altar stone upon which the monstrance rests. The continuous bleeding supports the Catholic dogma of the Real Presence. The stone also contributes something to this doctrine; it is traditionally a symbol of rebirth and clearly refers to the stone over the tomb which the holy women found rolled away on Easter morning. The image thus emphasizes the reality of Christ's exist-

---

[12] The poem emphasizes the doctrine of the Real Presence more than being a more or less systematized allegorizing of the Mass. If we consider Greene's B version, the hound in stanza six may be the priest at Mass, but the image makes more sense to me as the faithful who drink Christ's blood in the Eucharist.

[13] "Forty Hours Devotion," *The Catholic Encyclopedia*, VI, 151. For earlier analogues to this devotion, see Charles V. Finnegan, *Priest's Manual for the Forty Hours Devotion* (Paterson, N.J., 1958), p. 3.

ence and His divinity (since the Resurrection is considered the ultimate proof of His divinity). At any rate, the poem has nothing to do with Joseph of Arimathea, despite Annie Gilchrist's pleas and Greene's approval.[14]

The quality of this carol is, as Speirs has pointed out, a "strangely exciting" one: "One is led by steps as through a maze until one reaches the centre of the maze, the heart of the mystery."[15] The chief problem which the lyric poses is that of the refrain. Is it mere nonsense, equivalent ultimately to "Hey, nonny no"? Or does the refrain have a definite thought relationship to the rest of the poem? I prefer the latter solution since I feel that the poem is too artfully constructed to have a nonsensical refrain. Moreover, the *he* and *hym* of line 1 refer to the falcon and the mate in the refrain, so the refrain surely must have a meaning. The first thing we have to determine is the tenor of each vehicle in the refrain. "My mak" is obviously Christ; the falcon is probably death. The second thing to determine is the speaker. It may be the *may* of line 10, for the familiar lullaby suggests Mary and her Child. Or it may be Ecclesia paradoxically soothing her children, for Christ's death has once more established peace between God and man and can occasion the sense of calm and well-being connoted by the first line of the refrain. Moreover, Ecclesia daily remembers the sacrifice of Calvary through the sacrifice of the Mass. If Mary speaks the refrain, the emotional intensity of the poem increases; if Ecclesia,

---

[14] Miss Gilchrist and several others discuss the carol in *Journal of the Folk-Song Society*, IV (1910–13), 52–66, esp. pp. 55–59. Greene sums up the chief arguments, pp. 411–12. He has recently advanced a historical interpretation of his own, "The Meaning of the Corpus Christi Carol," *Medium Aevum*, XXIX (1960), 10–21, in which he argues not very convincingly that the weeping and praying "may" in the poem "startlingly" parallels the account of Catharine of Aragon's exile as told by Nicholas Harpsfield. The wounded knight is Christ in the Host, the object of Catharine's devotion from the chapel window; Catharine purportedly wept night and day, and this fact would tend to make almost any contemporary hearer identify her in the "may"; the stone refers to Catharine's weeping on the stones at Buckden.

[15] *Medieval English Poetry* (London, 1958), p. 77.

the poet shows a greater insight into the significance of the Crucifixion. I prefer the latter.

The Corpus Christi carol is, as we have seen, allegory because the knight is not a knight, but Christ. Because of the last couplet, the image does not exist independently of its signification. A symbolic image does, and this is the basic distinction between the two kinds of image. Symbols are rare in the religious lyric, and I shall illustrate them by Herebert's English translation of the "Hostis Herodis impie" (XIV, No. 12):

> Herodes, þou wykked fo, whar-of ys þy dredinge?
> And why are þou so sore agast of cristes to-cominge?
> Ne reueth he nouth erthlich god þat maketh ous
> heuene kynges.

> [Herod, thou wicked foe, whereof is thy dread?
> And why art thou so alarmed at Christ's coming?
> He robs no earthly goods, who makes us kings of
> heaven.]

> Þe kynges wenden here way and foleweden þe
> sterre, (4)
> And sothfast lyȝth wyth sterrelyth souhten vrom
> so verre,
> And sheuden wel þat he ys god in gold and stor
> and mirre.

> [The kings wended their way and followed the star,
> and true light with starlight sought from so far,
> and well showed that he is God through gold and
> incense and myrrh.]

> Crist, y-cleped heuene lomb, so com to seynt Ion
> And of hym was y-wasȝe þat sunne nadde non, (8)
> To halewen our vollouth water þat sunne hauet
> uordon.

> [Christ, called heaven's lamb, then came to Saint
> John and by him was washed so that he had no
> sin, to sanctify our baptismal water that sin had
> destroyed.]

A newe myhte he cudde þer he was at a feste:
He made vulle wyth shyr water six cannes by þe
leste,
Bote þe water turnde in-to wyn þorou crystes
oune heste.   (12)

[A new power he showed at a feast:
he made to be filled with clear water at least six
cans,
but the water turned into wine through Christ's
command.]

Wele, Louerd, boe myd þe, þat shewedest þe
to-day
Wyth þe uader and þe holy gost wythouten
ende-day.

[Glory, Lord, be with thee, who showest thee
today
with the Father and the Holy Ghost without
ending.]

On the literal level this poem speaks of the threefold manifestation (epiphany) of Christ as God. The first stanza announces
the coming of God to earth and establishes Him as a spiritual
monarch. Each of the next three stanzas presents one of these
manifestations of Christ as God: to the Magi, to the Jews at His
baptism (Mark 1:9–11), and to the Apostles at the marriage
at Cana (John 2:1–11). The final stanza translates the dox-
ology and refers to the theme of manifestation. The Latin hymn
appears in the Divine Office for the feast of the Epiphany,
which originally commemorated the other two events as well
before they were transferred to the Sundays succeeding the
Epiphany. The liturgy, in fact, contains the key to the symbolic
value. Each of these events has a spiritual significance in addition to its role in the threefold manifestation of Christ as God.
We have a basis for the symbolic interpretation in line 3 with
the reference to Christ's making us kings of heaven. The word
kings, in fact, ties the symbolic significance to the first event:
the kings (Magi) were symbols of the Gentiles, and their wor-

ship of the Child represents the calling of the Gentiles. The second event, Christ's baptism, symbolizes our own, by which we are entitled to enter heaven. The third event, the changing of water into wine, symbolizes our own transformation from a purely human nature into partakers of the divine nature through sanctifying grace and thus truly making us kings of heaven. Thus the two themes—Christ's manifestation of His divinity and our calling to and participation in His divine nature—are closely interwoven. Yet the literal theme exists independently of the symbolic (but not vice versa); it is this, in fact, which marks the poem as symbolic rather than allegorical. But are we justified in this symbolic interpretation? I contend that we are, for patristic exegeses and the liturgy itself suggest such a tropological (or moral) interpretation. If Herebert knew the liturgical original of his poem, why would he not have known its symbolic interpretation as well?[16]

In examining the relationship between a poet's use of imagery and his religious subject matter, we can easily see that to be effective, arbitrary allegory depends upon an imaginative intensity, since it offers little insight into its subject. Descriptive allegory, on the other hand, can, along with symbol, illumine the audience's generally accepted notions. But since the poet relies by and large on stock images, he runs the risk of depending upon the inherent value of the imagery to illumine, rather than modifying or extending this inherent value to suit his context. He may, in effect, handle his imagery the way he handles his formula of address plus petition—mechanically or organically.

---

[16] See the Sarum Breviary, ed. Francis Procter and Christopher Wordsworth (Canterbury, 1883), I, cccxxx; the York Missal, ed. T. Henderson, Surtees Society, LX (Durham, 1874), pp. 317–18. For elaborate and particularly relevant passages, see Ivo Carnotensis, "De Epiphania Domini," *PL*, CLXII, 574–75; pseudo-Bonaventure, *The Mirrour of the Blessed Lyf . . .* , pp. 54–55. Herebert and his sources may be using an allegorical as well as a tropological sense; some of the analogues cited stress the marriage of Christ with His Church, but what applies to the Church as a whole applies to the individual members, and this twofold interpretation is easily justified.

And if he handles it organically, he may either increase the emotional intensity with which the subject matter is usually held, or may actually penetrate the significance of his subject. The literary quality, of course, lies in direct ratio to this presentation of the subject matter.

Another aspect of the literary quality depends upon the structural use to which a poet puts his images, and in the lyrics we can detect two common structural patterns. Sometimes a poet may use multiple images, which complement or even contradict one another; sometimes he may use a basic image with multiple connotations, around which the poem moves concentrically. The former technique is often accompanied by parallelism and occasionally shows linear structure. Ordinarily the Middle English religious poets handle this technique most effectively when the poem is short and exemplifies thematic evolution, as in the following:

> He yaf himself as good felowe,
>   Whan he was boren in wre wede;
> Als good norice he bowh down lowe,
>   Whan wiht himself he wolde us fede.   (4)
> Als good schephirde upon ʒe lowe,
>   His wed he yaf for wre nede;
> In hevene as king we schulen him knowe,
>   Qwan he himself schal yiven in mede.[17]   (8)

> [He gave himself as a good fellow,
> when he was born in our clothing;
> as a good nurse he bowed down low,
> when with himself he wished to feed us.
> As a good shepherd upon the hill,
> his clothing he gave for our need;
> in heaven as king we shall know him,
> when he shall give himself in reward.]

Each of the four images represents some aspect of Christ's love for mankind; they are presented in chronological order, referring

[17] Printed in Thomas Wright and J. O. Halliwell, eds., *Reliquiae Antiquae* (London, 1843), II, 121.

to the Incarnation, the institution of the Holy Eucharist, the Crucifixion, and the union of the individual soul with Christ after death. The first image is striking; *good felowe* suggests the tone of our modern "regular guy." This colloquial tone is not at all irreverent, for it underscores the tremendous humility manifested by the Incarnation. The image of the nurse very aptly expresses Christ's giving Himself in the Eucharist; bowing down low recalls Phil. 2:8 and refers to the Incarnation as well as to the literal image of feeding. The third image reminds us that the Good Shepherd lays down His life for His sheep (John 10:15), and the poet puns upon the hill of Calvary. The last two lines carry definite sexual connotations, suggesting something like mystical union. Now although the poet has chosen four vigorous independent images, he has also interlinked them effectively. The clothing image joins lines 2 and 6 with a paradoxical twist: Christ assumed our garment so that He might give it up for our neediness. The concept of Christ's giving Himself to us joins lines 4 and 8. In the former it is as food in Holy Communion; in the latter it is as lover in final union. The juxtaposition of these two thoughts relates them notionally, and the poet seems to establish the first as a foretaste of the second. In addition to the chronological order and the interlinking of images, the poet unifies his work by the thought of the last two lines, which climax the thought structure. He has been speaking of Christ as man, but in heaven we will recognize Christ for what He is—God as well as man. This thought completes the familiar circular pattern begun in lines 1–2: God descended to become man in order that He might raise man up to Him. Admittedly, this is a minor poem, but the poet has fashioned his materials with considerable skill.

Perhaps the poem which comes closest to handling the multiple-image technique the way modern readers know it is Thomas of Hales' love ron (XIII, No. 43). The poem divides readily into halves, and its images reflect a general thematic content of nature vs. grace. The introduction sets up the *raison d'être* for the poem; the good Friar seems to be enjoying a little joke. Apparently some young lady who dedicated herself to God's service (in a general sense) requested Friar Thomas to compose for her a poem containing advice on taking a second true love (other than God, presumably). Having thus set up the circumstances, the text proceeds with the ron. In the first part (lines 9–88) the speaker contemplates the transitoriness of this world with its joys and gifts. Trust in such ephemeral love, he warns, and you place your trust wrongfully. Moreover, a true lover cannot be found in this world; truth in love lasts forever, not just until death, and this world is by nature transitory. Therefore in the second part (lines 89–192) the speaker describes, as the young lady wished, the truest and best man. But there is no "other" man involved—it is Christ Himself Whom the speaker describes. He emphasizes in this section the virtue of chastity, a treasure consigned by Christ, so that, paradoxically, by remaining chaste the girl may have a Lover Who will remain true forever. This motif of virginity is accented by the allusion in the closing lines to the Annunciation scene (lines 205–6). The theme of the inevitability of natural decay is, as we have said, the dominant theme of the first part of the poem. The author draws six images from nature to describe the lot of the earthly lover and all his attributes, and the characteristics of the world itself: the lover glides away as does a blast of wind (line 14); he fades as meadow grass (line 16); this world is as the shadow that glides away (line 32); it is as wind (line 39);[18] the lover will wither as the leaf on the bough (line 48); he has glided out of the kingdom as the blade cuts off the head from the sheaf (lines 71–72).[19] The fact that these multiple images are drawn from nature underscores the fact that it is man's nature to die. (Most of these

[18] Brown reads *aswynde,* "languish away."

[19] *The Middle English Dictionary* glosses *cleo* as "? a reaping hook." The word has proved something of a crux, but I am unaware of any more satisfactory interpretation. *Cliff* makes little sense, for it weakens the simile; the sense of rapidity which the other reading gives emphasizes the idea of transitoriness.

images also have biblical overtones, thus verifying the certainty of the comparisons.) Therefore, if we seek a true love who will remain true forever, we must seek elsewhere.

In the second part of the poem we find three other images drawn from nature, but this time the natural objects fall short of the object being compared. The girl herself, while she guards her castle, i.e., her body, is sweeter than any flower (lines 151–52) and sweeter than any spice (lines 167–68); the gem of her chastity is more precious than any other precious stones, including those of which heaven itself is constructed (lines 169–76).[20] The suggestion in these images is that the maiden of the poem is placing herself above a mere natural plane by remaining chaste, for she guards the treasure which Christ has consigned to her (line 145). Yet the fact that she will thus be (implicitly) a flower sweeter than any earthly flower, a spice sweeter than any earthly spice, and that her chastity itself is a gem more valuable than any earthly gem suggests that this is part of man's nature too. He has a soul which is immortal and therefore capable of true (i.e., eternal) love. To realize this capability, man must raise himself above the merely natural level through sanctifying grace, a gift which God freely bestows upon him (line 111) so that He may become the soul's lover. Only through this gift can man transcend his mortal nature and fulfill his potential supernaturally. Friar Thomas stresses this transcendence by presenting Christ as better than any mere earthly lover, for only He is capable of loving truly (i.e., forever). Our poet can now ask:

> Ne doþ he, mayde, on vuele dede
>   þat may cheose of two þat on,
> & he wile wiþ-vte neode
>   take þet wurse, þe betere let gon? (192)

[Does he not, maid, a foul deed
who may choose one from two,
and he will needlessly take the worse,
letting the better go?]

[20] Rev. [Apoc.] 21: 19–20; the images of the flower and spice have parallels in the Song of Songs.

He has anticipated this argument in the first part by declaring that whoever places his love in this world acts as a blind man (lines 37–38); in other words he is deliberately depriving himself of what is properly his—his eyesight. Similarly, in this second part, man deprives his soul of what is properly hers—her one true Lover—if he chooses a worldly lover. These various image-groups, then, weigh the natural (mortal) against the supernatural (eternal), or nature and God's grace, just as their respective sections contrast the worldly and the spiritual. If a modern poet wrote this poem, he might have preferred to use symbol rather than allegory (he at any rate would not have felt it necessary to explain his allegory); so might have Friar Thomas, but he wanted above all to make his meaning clear (cf. lines 161–62) and preserve this maiden for Christ. If his purpose is consequently more rhetorical than poetic, he has nonetheless created an artistic whole—to which his use of multiple images skilfully contributes.

That medieval poets sometimes used imagery which is consistent and which approximates modern use must come as a surprise to those commentators who see little else but disjointedness in medieval literature in general. Moreover, we can even find effective use of a central image other than that afforded by allegory. "Vndo þi dore, my spuse dere" [Undo thy door, my dear spouse] (XIV, No. 68), for example, makes the heart a central image which contains within itself the paradoxical theme of the poem. The poet has taken as his text Rev. [Apoc.] 3:20; his treatment shows familiarity with the traditional glosses, but he manipulates his image independently of them. The poem opens by dramatizing the image: Christ, His hair dripping with blood, knocks at the locked door of the speaker's heart, beseeching entrance. (The situation recalls Songs [Cant.] 5:2, and thus contributes heavily to the images of Christ as Lover and the soul as beloved.) Hearing Christ's plea, the speaker realizes that he has driven Him from his heart. He implores forgiveness, and resolves to open his heart to take in Christ, his true Love. In one sense, the poem is now over, but our poet adds six more lines of the speaker's reflections, which develop the basic image three ways:

> For þin herte is clouen oure loue to kecchen,
> Þi loue is chosen vs alle to fecchen;
> Min herte it þerlede ȝef i were kende,
> Þi suete loue to hauen in mende.　　　　　　　　(20)
> Perce myn herte with þi louengge,
> Þat in þe i haue my duellingge. Amen.

> [For thy heart is cleft to catch our love,
> thy love has chosen to fetch us all;
> my heart it would pierce if I were kind,
> thy sweet love to have in mind.
> Pierce my heart with thy loving,
> that in thee I have my dwelling. Amen.]

The poet reserves the ultimate paradox of his image for the last line; in the meantime he introduces to the heart image the related image of the hunt or chase (kecchen, fecchen), which restates the theme of the dramatized opening lines. The heart now becomes the bait as well as the prey. Second, these two meanings unfold more when the speaker asks that his heart be cleft with the spear of love, as Christ's was by Longinus' spear. The goal and the bait again become synonymous as the speaker's heart and Christ's become one. Finally, line 22 completes the image by the paradoxical significance of the union of the two meanings of the image; the speaker admits Christ to the dwelling place of his heart in order that he may thereby live in Christ. The union is so complete that they dwell within each other simultaneously. The thought resembles that in John 15:4–5, although the image of the heart seems less profound than that of the vine and branches. Nonetheless, the poet's penetrating development of the image strongly suggests mystical union, and he has achieved a complementary thematic and imagistic unity.

On occasion the central image is much more complex than that of the heart, as in the following highly praised and familiar instance (XIII, No. 17A):

24

For ou²¹ þat is so feir ant brist
    uelud maris stella,
bristore þen þe dai-is list,
    parens & puella, (4)
i crie þe grace of þe:
leuedi, prie þi sone for me,
    tam pia,
þat i mote come to þe, (8)
    maria.

[Before you who are so fair and bright,
    like the star of the sea,
brighter than the day's light,
    mother and maiden,
I cry for grace:
Lady, pray thy son for me,
    so gentle,
that I might come to thee, *Maria.*]

Leuedi, best of alle þing,
    rosa sine spina,
þou bere ihesu, heuene-king, (12)
    gratia diuina.
of alle þou berest þat pris,
heie quen in parais
    electa: (16)
moder milde ant maiden ec
    efecta.

[Lady, best of all things,
    rose without thorns,

---

²¹ Brown emends to *For on,* although he claims the MS "clearly" reads *ou* (XIII, p. 24). He is supported in his emendation by the reading of the Egerton MS. The second person pronoun makes better sense than the indefinite *one* because it avoids an ambiguity of reference when the poem shifts to *þe* in line 5. *Ou* is, of course, the plural form, but the singular and plural forms often shifted places about this time; see, e.g., Fernand Mossé, *A Handbook of Middle English,* trans. James A. Walker (Baltimore, 1952), p. 94. Cf. the shift from *þe* to *eu* in Thomas of Hales' love ron, line 118. *For* may be translated "before," "in the presence of." *Is* is the northern form for *arn* or *are;* to support a northern influence, cf. in the Egerton MS the form *til hym* (line 17) and the rime *sone : bone* (lines 37, 39).

you bore Jesus, king of heaven,
   divine grace.
You of all bear that prize,
high queen in paradise
   the chosen one:
mother mild and maiden *made.*]

In car ant consail þou art best,
   felix fecundata;   (20)
to alle weri þou art rest,
   mater honorata.
bi-hold tou him wid milde mod
þat for us alle scedde is blod   (24)
   in cruce;
bidde we moten come to him
   in luce.

[In care and counsel thou art best,
   happy in thy fruitfulness;
to all the weary thou are rest,
   honored mother.
Behold thou him with mild heart
that for us all shed his blood
   on the cross;
ask that we might come to him *in light.*]

Al þe world it wes fur-lorn   (28)
   þoru *eua peccatrice*
to-forn þat ihesu was iborn
   ex te genitrice;
þorou *aue* e wende awei   (32)
þe þestri nist, ant com þe dai
   salutis;
þe welle springet out of þe
   uirtutis.   (36)

[All the world was lost
   through *Eve the sinner*
until Jesus was born
   from thee, Mother;
through *ave* he turned aside
   the dark night, and came the day,
of salvation;
   the well springs from thee of *virtue.*]

Vuel þou wost he is þi sone
uentre quem portasti;
he nul nout werne þe þi bone
paruum quem lactasti.   (40)
so god ant so mild e is,
he bringet us alle in-to is blis
superni;
he hauet i-dut þe foule put   (44)
inferni.

[Well you know he is thy son,
whom you carried in your womb;
he will not refuse thee thy wish,
the little one whom you suckled.
So good and so mild he is,
he will bring us all into his bliss
of heaven;
he has shut the foul pit of *hell.*]

This poem is constructed upon two overlapping patterns: first, an image pattern of light and darkness, and second, a logic pattern, in no strict sense formal, and certainly naive, yet irrefutable in view of the strong religious faith which shapes it. This logic pattern, which reinforces and is reinforced by the image pattern, has two aspects: (1) what might be called argument from the general to the particular in the matter of Redemption, which involves a significant shift from *I* to *we*; (2) a pseudo-causal connection based upon the Mother-Son relationship. In the fourth stanza these two patterns unite and become clear. The image pattern is introduced in the opening line in *brist*, then modified by the traditional epithet *stella maris* (line 2). This simile connotes four things pertinent to the light pattern: grace, purity, a guiding light, begetter of Light. In fact, the usual interpretation of *stella maris* in the commentaries is twofold; Mary is so called first because she bore Christ (the basis of all her prerogatives) and then because she is guide to sinners.[22] The

[22] References are legion; among the lengthier discussions, see St. Peter Damian, "De Epiphania Domini" I, *PL,* CXLIV, 508; St. Bernard, "Super *Missus Est*" II, *PL,* CLXXXIII, 70; Peter Cellensis, "In Annuntiatione Dominica" III, *PL,* CCII, 714; *Old English Homilies of the Twelfth Century,* ed. Richard Morris, EETS, LIII (London, 1873), p. 161.

poet follows the usual order, devoting stanza two to her bearing Christ and stanza three to her role on behalf of mankind. A new connotation of the light image appears at the end of stanza three: heaven is light (line 27). In the fourth stanza the poet develops the fourth connotation of the light image: the birth of Christ brings the day of salvation (lines 33–34). Christ is, first of all, the Sun Whom the sea-star has brought forth.[23] Second, through Christ's birth the darkness of sin is turned away and the light of grace is brought to mankind. The light-dark pattern, then, centers on the Virgin as star of the sea, who illumines the darkness of this world and leads souls to herself (and her Son) in the light of heaven. She has these powers because she has brought forth the True Light and is thereby the light of grace in the day of salvation to the night of sin caused by Eve.[24] This rather elaborate, systematic interrelationship of images supports the logic pattern.

The speaker, then, has set up a basis for his request in Mary's role as star of the sea. He first asked for grace from Mary, who is herself full of grace and thereby "feir ant brist." In stanza two he reminds her that God gave her a special grace. Now in stanza four he reminds her that she has brought grace to all mankind. Since God has granted her so singular a grace as to become His mother yet retain her virginity, and since it was through her that grace in the form of redemption came to mankind, God will surely grant her the grace which the speaker requests. Further, since Mary brought the day of salvation to all mankind, surely she will bring it to that part of mankind for whom the speaker prays ("bidde *we* moten come to him," line 26). The poet sums up the fourth stanza with "þe welle springet out of þe/*uirtutis*." The immediate meaning of this line lies in the contrast between sin and virtue, as in a contemporary Latin hymn: "Peccatum excluditur, / Virtus introducitur" [Sin is shut out, Virtue is

---

[23] This concept is popular in Latin hymns; e.g., *AH,* XX, Nos. 27, 43, 137, 191.

[24] St. Thomas Aquinas, "In Nativitate BMV," *Opera Omnia,* ed. Petrus Fiaccadoris (New York, 1948–49), XXIV, 232.

brought in].[25] Another and more significant meaning does not emerge until the final stanza.

In the final stanza the shift in line 26 from *I* to *we* is clarified. Stanza four functions as an analogy with the request in stanza one. In the first stanza the speaker requests that Mary, by her light, lead him from the darkness of this world to the light of heaven. In stanza four he mentions an analogous situation: mankind in general was lost in the night of sin because of Eve, until Mary brought the day. The shift from *I* to *we,* then, is made in preparation for this generalization; the speaker uses a naive logic that, from a religious standpoint, possesses conviction. This logic works both independently of, and along with, the analogy developed in stanza four. First of all the poet reminds Mary that she is well aware Christ is her Son; if she is *maris stella* because she bore Christ, then surely she is *maris stella* as guide to sinners and will lead men to heaven by asking her Son for this grace. Christ, her Son, will not refuse her request, simply because He is her Son. The speaker, therefore, is confident that we shall all reach heaven (*bringet,* line 42, i.e., "will bring"), and supports his confidence by reminding Mary that Christ has shut up "þe foule put" (line 44) of hell. This of course refers to the work of the Redemption, referred to as *day* in 33–34. *Foule put* and *inferni* carry connotations of darkness, and implicit is another analogy. Just as Mary brought day and turned away night through the birth of Christ, so by the act of Redemption Christ delivered man from the darkness of hell. Therefore He will surely deliver us from the darkness of this world, through the intercession of His Mother—*stella maris.* And, by extended analogy, if He will deliver us, mankind, He will deliver me, the speaker. The psychology of the generalization here suits the quasilogical approach of the poem.

In this poem, then, unlike many other lyrics, the shift from *I*

[25] *AH,* XX, No. 158. In another Latin hymn Mary is called "origo / Virtutis" [source of Virtue] (*AH,* XLVᵃ, No. 8); in still another, "Mater virtutis et nostrae causa salutis" [Mother of virtue and cause of our salvation] (*AH,* L, No. 292).

(line 8) to *we* (line 26) is significant. In one other example the shift (although reversed) is significant:

> we mowen iheren ant
>   isen,
> leuedi, for þi muchele miste,
> þe swete blisse of heuene briste,
> seinte marie, hernde me (XIII,   (48)
>   No. 18).

> [that we may hear and see,
> Lady, through thy great power,
> the sweet bliss of bright heaven,
> Saint Mary, intercede for me.]

This speaker also argues from the general to the particular. Through Mary's might we are all entitled to heaven, and the speaker claims his right, as it were, by requesting that Mary intercede for him and thus show her might on a personal level. (*Miste* is an excellent synonym for the idea in lines 35–36, as we shall see presently.) Our poet, besides the meaningful shift from *I* to *we,* shifts also from Mary (*þe,* line 8) to Christ (*him,* line 26). The psychology involved here seems to be that Mary, the mediatrix of all grace, is the special recourse of the individual; when Christ is spoken of, it is with less assurance of personal salvation. In fact the entire argument is based upon Mary's asking her Son for the grace the speaker requests, rather than approaching Christ directly.

The poem ends rather abruptly; from the point of view of the logic pattern, however, there is nothing more to say. But it is not strange that the poem concludes with attention focused on Christ, rather than Mary; the speaker does not even recapitulate nor make a final appeal to Mary. This shift in attention from Mary to Christ is complete, and this ties in with the poet's argumentative technique of approaching Christ through Mary. But Mary is not lost sight of in the last five lines. In the first place, the speaker still addresses her, reminding her of Christ's goodness. Second, we must now go back and reread lines 35–36. *Vir-*

tue has the sense of "strength" or "power," and refers to Christ's stopping up the foul pit of hell and snatching mankind from the power of the devil. Mary, we recall, is the well from which this power has sprung (*springet,* historical present). But the present tense in line 35 can also have the sense of what we might call an "everlasting" present, and the relevance of this line depends upon its being read both as a historical present and as an ordinary present. It then becomes part of the logic pattern and rounds out the argument. If the power of God once sprang from Mary and the pit of hell was shut, then it will once again spring from Mary to keep the speaker from the darkness of hell. The reminder of Christ's achievement in lines 41–45, then, is also a reminder of Mary's participation, so that the poem concludes, not only with the image pattern, but also with the final argument in the logic pattern.*

"For ou þat is so feir ant brist" thus reflects the unity of existence which the medieval mind saw so acutely. The Incarnation has a personal meaning for the speaker; it is at the center of his own history, and the multiplicity of analogies which he summons to his support verifies his consciousness of the unity of existence. Similarly, the translation of the "Hostis Herodis impie" sees in the events of Christ's life a significance for His Church collectively and individually; His threefold epiphany symbolizes His marriage to *Ecclesia* and to *anima.* This interpretation comes direct from the liturgy, as indeed the hymn itself does. But the medievals saw other analogies not sanctioned by the liturgy; the Corpus Christi carol may have liturgical overtones, but its suggestions of the Grail myth and the dying God would automatically suggest to the Christian the ultimate reality behind all existence—God Himself. It is this attempt to pierce reality that the medieval use of imagery so clearly demonstrates. This world was very real for medieval man, but it would not last. It therefore could not be the ultimate reality. But this world was created by

---

* This careful working out of the image and logic patterns distinguishes the Trinity version from the inferior Egerton MS.

God, and God is reflected in His creation. Thus the medievals sought to perceive God—reality—in the natural world; thus the recipient of Thomas of Hales' love ron would respond immediately to the forcefulness of his use of natural images to support his theme of mutability. The fact that the medieval poet utilized traditional imagery did not mean that he was restricting the possibilities of what he could express. On the contrary, these images had a connotative richness simply because they did penetrate reality. Reality is multiple, is complex, indeed even contradictory. So also the imagery. But the ultimate reality is suprasensible, and imagery is sensible. Hence imagery can depict only fragments of that reality; hence one image must be modified by another. The danger inherent in traditional imagery for the medieval poet was not that it could express so little of his thought, but that he might rely on it too much in itself to express his thought. As with his subject matter and with forms borrowed from religious devotion, the poet could rely too much on the inherent value of his image. The best poets verify the truths inherent in their images or push the images even further into reality than they had been pushed before. "Wynter wakeneþ al my care" verifies emotionally the lesson of mutability; "Somer is comen & winter gon" places the image of the child in a context which invites multiple connotations in order to focus on the multiple spiritual significances of the Incarnation. Perhaps two questions come to mind in connection with the poets' use of imagery: Are we justified in reading all these connotations into medieval poetry? The applicability to biblical exegesis is perhaps clearer than it is to poetry explication. The second question is this: If these images are so complex, is this not attributing to the song a greater intellectual complexity than a song is able to bear? The answer to this question is our concern in the next chapter.* The answer to the first question has been the subject of

* Chapter V: "Piety and Wit," in *Wisdom and Number,* pp. 138–70. [Ed.]

much dispute.[26] But a strong argument for the unity of existence seems necessarily to include an argument for poetic as well as biblical application. Why must we contend that the medieval clerk encountered patristic exegesis in the Divine Office, in the lessons read to him during meals in the monastery, in the books he copied; that he encountered it in the art and architecture of the church wherein he worshipped; that he used this same exegesis in his sermons, in his spiritual treatises, in his Latin hymns; but that when he sat down and wrote poetry in the vernacular, he completely divested himself of such folderol? His English poetry dealt with the same spiritual reality that those other forms dealt with—a reality so great that not even all the images in the world could express it. And yet these images have their purpose: "that by tho thinges that ben visible / and that man kyndely knoweth / he be stired and rauysched to loue and desire gostly invisible thinges that he kyndely knoweth not" [that by those things that are visible and that man knows naturally he may be stirred and ravished to love and desire invisible spiritual things that he knows not naturally].[27]

---

[26] See, e.g., J. M. Campbell, "Patristic Studies and the Literature of Mediaeval England," *Speculum,* VIII (1933), 465–78; D. W. Robertson, "Historical Criticism," English Institute Essays, 1950, ed. Alan S. Downer (New York, 1951), pp. 3–31; Morton W. Bloomfield, "Symbolism in Medieval Literature," *MP,* LVI (1956), 73–81; and the essays by E. Talbot Donaldson, R. E. Kaske, and Charles Donahue in *Critical Approaches to Medieval Literature,* ed. Dorothy Bethurum (New York, 1960), pp. 1–82.

[27] Pseudo-Bonaventure, *The Mirrour of the Blessed Lyf . . . ,* p. 9.

THE OWL AND THE NIGHTINGALE
AND CHRISTIAN DIALECTIC

Douglas L. Peterson

RECENTLY, ALLEGORICAL INTERPRETATION OF *The Owl and the Nightingale* has been condemned in favor of the view that "so delightful a poem should be allowed to stand as an example of the bird fable, as a story told for its own sake, without our seeking to find in it a hidden meaning which isn't there."[1] But it is difficult to believe that a medieval poem consisting of nearly eighteen hundred lines and making precise distinctions between foreknowledge and predestination and between spiritual and carnal sin (as well as discussing Christian doctrines of repentence, atonement, and *caritas*) was conceived only as "a story told for its own sake."

Allegory was not, after all, the only means available to the medieval poet for didactic purposes. And I am convinced that the intentions embodied in *The Owl and the Nightingale* are expressly didactic—that the debate is, as an exercise in dialectics, similar in both purpose and method to Abelard's *Sic et Non*, and that by applying dialectic to the arguments advanced by the

Reprinted, by permission of author and editors, from the *Journal of English and Germanic Philology*, LV (1956), 13–26. See also Mortimer J. Donovan, "The Owl as Religious Altruist in *The Owl and the Nightingale*," *Medieval Studies*, XVIII (1956), 207–14.

[1] A. C. Baugh, "The Middle English Period" in *A Literary History of England*, ed. A. C. Baugh, et al. (New York, 1948), p. 155.

debaters, the reader is expected to arrive at a final verdict in accord with the poet's sympathies.[2] By leaving the outcome of the debate undecided, the poet has placed the reader in the rôle of judge so that he may acquire the truth for himself; and he has provided the reader with ample instructions and forewarnings which, if heeded, will lead him to the verdict intended.[3]

This is not to interpret the poem for more than it is: a debate skilfully developed within the bird fable convention. The contestants remain birds, though of course personified as spokesmen for traditions with which they had commonly come to be associated: the Nightingale with sensuality, love, and fertility; the Owl with asceticism, wisdom, and melancholy. The principal issues of the debate, as clearly set forth early in the poem, have no concealed meaning.

> & eiþer seide of oþeres custe
> þat alre-worste þat hi wuste:
> & hure & hure of oþere[s] songe
> hi holde plaiding suþe stronge.[4] (9–12)

> [And either side (spoke) of the other's character
> the worst that they knew:
> and especially of each other's song
> they held very strong disagreement.]

[2] Atkins, in a summary treatment of the historical development of the debate as a literary form, accounts for its popularity throughout the twelfth century in terms of Abelard's influence on dialectical method. Though Atkins discusses the *Sic et Non* and the method employed in it for pedagogical purposes, especially the author's refusal to provide a final reconciliation of the opposed authoritative views presented, he does not consider that *The Owl and the Nightingale* may also lack a final verdict for precisely the same reasons. (See below, Note 4.)

[3] It has been argued that since the poem was written as a plea for preferment, the poet intended no final decision in order to indicate "the depth of Nicholas' understanding of life and his wisdom in examining all sides of a question—qualities of high import for a judge." R. M. Lumiansky, "Concerning *The Owl and the Nightingale*," *PQ*, XXXII (October, 1953), 411–17.

[4] This and all subsequent quotations from the poem are from the C text in J. W. H. Atkins, *The Owl and the Nightingale*, ed. with Introduction, Texts, Notes, Translation and Glossary (Cambridge: University Press, 1922).

If attempts to recover the meaning of the poem have been generally unsuccessful, it is perhaps because we have not recognized
those medieval doctrines of logic, cosmology, and theology out
of which the poem emerged. We have not isolated the fundamental and unifying principle in terms of which every charge
and rebuttal in the debate is argued. Nor have we taken notice
of the Christian commonplaces which recur throughout the
poem.

The high praise bestowed on Nicholas by both contestants
(one of the few issues on which they are agreed) is generally
accepted as convincing if not conclusive evidence that the poem
is a "plea for preferment." It may also be interpreted literally as
a clear statement of those qualities which the poet expects the
reader to show in rendering a final verdict. The Nightingale,
after the disorderly preliminary skirmish, suggests the contest
be brought before Master Nicholas:

> he is wis and war of worde:
> he is of dome suþe gleu,
> & him is loþ eurich unþeu.
> He wot insiȝt in eche songe,
> wo singet wel, wo singet wronge:
> & he can schede vrom þe riȝte
> þat woȝe, þat þuster from þe liȝte.   (192–98)

> [he is wise and cautious of word:
> in judgment he is very prudent,
> and he loaths every vice.
> He can discern, in each song,
> who sings well and who sings wrong:
> and he can distinguish right
> from wrong, darkness from light.]

The Owl, after pondering for a time—she is aware of Nicholas'
former sympathies—agrees.

> Ich granti wel þat he us deme,
> vor þeȝ he were wile breme,
> & lof him were niȝtingale,
> & oþer wiȝte gente & smale,
> ich wot he is nu suþe acoled.

37

> Nis he vor þe noȝt afoled,
> þat he, for þine olde luue,
> me adun legge & ȝe buue:
> ne schaltu neure so him queme,
> þat he for þe fals dom deme.
> He is him ripe & fast-rede,
> ne lust him nu to none unrede:
> nu him ne lust na more pleie,
> he wile gon a riȝte weie.   (201–14)

> [I heartily grant that he judge us,
> for though he was formerly passionate,
> and loved nightingales
> and other gentle and small creatures,
> I know he is now quite cooled down.
> He is not fooled by you,
> so that for your old love
> he will put me low and you above;
> nor shall you ever so please him
> that he will judge falsely on your account.
> He is mature and steadfast of mind,
> he is no longer inclined to folly:
> no longer is he pleased to frolic,
> he will go the right way.]

In short, if the reader is to arrive at the correct verdict, he must be wise, cautious, and prudent, sufficiently qualified to judge the issues, able to distinguish truth from error, and not inclined to favor one side because of past sympathies. Finally, the Owl's closing compliment to Nicholas—that he is beyond the persuasive powers of even so eloquent a singer as the Nightingale (211–14)—can be construed as a veiled warning to the reader not to be so pleased by beautiful rhetoric as to "false dom deme."

If the praise of Nicholas applies to the judicial reader (and we need not be concerned here with theories of authorship and preferment), consider the issues to be judged and the terms in which they are argued. There is no reason for assuming that "custe" pertains only to which of the birds has "the more pleasing personality" or that "songe" pertains only to aesthetic matters.[5] Rather, the ways in which both these issues are argued show clearly that both are subordinate to a more fundamental question, one which both birds accept as decisive in determining the relative merits of "custe" and "songe": service to mankind. The judge, then, if he is concerned with sifting truth from error, will award the final verdict to the debater offering the more logical and cogent arguments in terms of service to mankind, and, by rendering his decision in those terms, he will be deciding actually which of the two birds enjoys the higher place in the hierarchy of corporeal being created for man's use. Thus the question of services to mankind also constitutes a controlling and unifying principle throughout the poem which scholarship has not recognized. Uniting seemingly unrelated phases of the debate, it restores meaning to passages previously interpreted as pure invective and makes apparent that the poet has employed a bird fable to dramatize a familiar Christian commonplace consisting of opposed and irreconcilable attitudes toward experience, the one logical and consistent with Christian ethics, the other sophistical and even heretical.

The flood of invective comprising the Nightingale's opening attacks (33–252 *et passim*) is essentially an amplification of evidence derived from traditional lore to substantiate a single, fundamental accusation—that the Owl is a monster (vnwiȝt), a mishap of nature, and therefore an unnatural being.[6] She cites the Owl's apparent deformities and unnatural activities: (1) she "tukest wroþe & vuele . . . over smale fuȝele" [angrily and evilly maltreats small birds]; (2) she is "lodlich to biholde" [loathsome to behold]; (3) she "sittest adai & fliȝ[s]t aniȝt" [sits by day and flies by night], showing by this that she is "on vnwiȝt"

---

[5] Atkins, *op. cit.*, p. lviii.

[6] The Nightingale is attacking the Owl's rightful place in a hierarchical universe by authority of the fundamental Christian doctrine of evil as deprivation, in which good is defined as that which is in accord with its own nature. See St. Augustine, *Confessions*, VII, 11–17. See also Etienne Gilson, *The Spirit of Medieval Philosophy*, trans. A. C. Downes (New York, 1936), chaps. XV–XVIII.

[a monster]; (4) she is "unclene" [unclean]; (5) she sings "aniȝt noȝt adai" [by night, not by day]; (6) her whole song is "wailawai" [wellaway], which terrifies all who hear it; and (7) she is evil because she is blind by day, keen of sight at night, and loves darkness; "vor eurich þing þat schuniet riȝt, / hit luueb þuster & hatiet liȝt" [for everything that shuns right, it loves darkness and hates light] (229–30).[7] If the Nightingale can conclusively establish that the Owl is a monster, she has won her case; for in terms of the Christian doctrine of evil as deprivation, monstrosities are "utterly without intention in the operations of nature" and are evil in relation to their natural forms "absolutely."[8] If the Owl exists "without intention" as a mishap of nature in a hierarchial universe contingent for its existence on God and created to serve man's ends, she is of no use to either God or man.

The Owl in her rebuttal goes directly to the point. She does not deny that she hides by day and is hated by the smaller birds. She is a hawk and finds night the best time to carry out her war-

[7] See Kathryn Huganir, *The Owl and the Nightingale: Sources, Date, Author* (Philadelphia, 1931), p. 51. Miss Huganir notices that the Nightingale's association of evil with darkness and good with light suggests John 3:19–20: "And this is the condemnation, that light is come into the world, and men loved darkness rather than light, because their deeds were evil. For every one that doeth evil hateth the light, neither cometh to the light, lest his deeds should be reproved." But for an interesting parallel see St. Anselm, *Dialogue on Truth,* Chapter V, "On the truth of natural action and of action which is not natural," in *Selections from Medieval Philosophers,* ed. and trans. Richard McKeon (New York, 1929), I, 158–60. Citing John 3:20–21 for Scriptural authority, Anselm discusses the doctrine which the Owl presently cites (ll. 269–77) to refute the Nightingale's charge that her unnatural actions are proof of her monstrosity.

[8] Thomas Aquinas, *Summa Contra Gentiles* in *The Basic Writings of Saint Thomas Aquinas,* ed. and trans. Anton C. Pegis (New York, 1944), II, 10–13. Though I have been unable to find an equally explicit twelfth-century statement concerning monstrosities as accidents of nature, and therefore evil absolutely with respect to species of their causal agents, Aquinas' statements appear in context as corollaries to the Augustinian doctrine of evil as deprivation. Certainly these corollaries had been defined before Aquinas summarized them.

like expeditions; and it is *natural* that the smaller birds should
hate her because of her fierce nature:

> Ich habbe bile stif & stronge,
> & gode cliuers scharp & longe,
> so hit bicumeþ to hauekes cunne;
> hit is min hiȝte, hit is mi w[u]nne,
> þat ich me draȝe to mine cunde,
> ne mai [me] no man þareuore schende:
> on me hit is wel isene,
> vor riȝt cunde ich am so kene. (269–76)

> [I have a stiff and strong bill,
> and good claws, sharp and long,
> as is proper to hawk's kin;
> it is my joy, it is my pleasure,
> that I am drawn to my kind,
> nor may any man reproach me for it:
> in me it is quite apparent
> that I am fierce through right nature.]

The Owl refers in her defense to a Christian doctrine which had
been commonplace since Augustine; and in her answer to the
charge that she can sing only of lamentation in a manner "þat
hit is grislich to ihere" [that it is grisly to hear] she develops the
familiar Christian distinction between sensual pleasure and eternal happiness. In contrast to her own song, the Owl asserts that
the Nightingale's is incessant and unvaried and that therefore
"me ne telþ of þar noȝ[t] w[u]rþ" [I see nothing worthy in it], for

> Eurich mur ȝþe mai so longe ileste
> þat ho shal liki wel unwreste. (341–42)

> [Every pleasure may last so long
> that it shall become displeasing.]

There is, however, one, all-important exception:

> Mid este þu þe miȝt ouerquaite,
> & ouerfulle makeþ wlatie:
> an eurich mureȝþe mai agon
> ȝif me hit halt eure forþ in on,
> bute one, þat is Godes riche,

> þat eure is svete & eure iliche:
> þeȝ þu nime eure o[f] þan lepe,
> hit is eure ful bi hepe.
> Wu*nder* hit is of Godes riche,
> þat eure spenþ & eu*er* is iliche.　　　(353–62)

> [You might overcram yourself with pleasure,
> and excess produces disgust:
> and every pleasure may flee
> if I persist in it,
> except one, the kingdom of God,
> that is ever sweet and unchanging:
> though you take continually from the basket,
> it is ever overflowing.
> It is a marvel of God's kingdom
> that it is always given out and always the same.]

The distinction is again orthodox. Eternal happiness is the end for which God created man; pleasures of the world are the momentary gratification of man's lower nature and are opposed to eternal happiness. If the Owl can establish that her opponent's song is but an earthly pleasure and consequently not merely of small benefit to man but actually an obstacle to be overcome in his quest for salvation, she has won her case.

The poet reveals his sympathies in the description of the Nightingale's reaction:

> Þe niȝtingale in hire þoȝte
> athold al þis, & longe þoȝte
> wat ho þaraft*er* miȝte segge:
> vor ho ne miȝte noȝt alegge
> þat þe hule hadde hire ised,
> *vor he spac boþe riȝt an red.*[9]　　　(391–96; italics mine)

---

[9] Besides recognizing the validity of the distinction made between physical pleasures and eternal happiness, the Nightingale, in dropping her charge that the Owl is monstrous, indicates that she accepts the Owl's refutation as conclusive. Thus she recognizes the validity of the doctrine on which the Owl's refutation is based: Just as "fire, when it warms, is determined for warming by that from which it has its being [its informing nature] . . . does that which it should," (Anselm, *op. cit.*, p. 159) so the Owl, when she attacks small birds and carries out her

[The Nightingale held all this in mind
and thought long about
what she then might say:
for she might not refute
what the Owl had told her,
since he spoke rightly and wisely.]

The Nightingale now realizes that somehow she must establish that her own song contributes to man's happiness and that her enemy's does not; therefore, though having failed in her attempt to prove the Owl a monster, and dismayed by the counterattack on her own song in irrefutable Christian terms (the Owl "spac boþe riȝt an red"), she attacks the content of her adversary's song. It is of misery, anger, and melancholy, heard only in the winter, and it reflects the Owl's envy of those who are able to rejoice in the pleasures of spring. Her own song, however, introduces spring and fertility and brings happiness to all creatures. She sings not "wane mon hoȝeþ of his sheue" [when man is anxious for his sheaves] (455), for there is then no need.

The Nightingale has admitted that she sings of sensual pleasures, and the Owl seizes her advantage. After pointing out that she is of service to man at a time when he is most in need of comforting, and that besides doing all she can to make people merry, she helps man to celebrate the Nativity, the Owl again identifies the Nightingale's song with those pleasures which are soon glutted through excess. It is only a song of wantonness, an unreasonable impulse soon departed when satisfied (489–522). The Nightingale has put herself in a precarious position with respect to Christian Doctrine by admitting that her song is of

---

expeditions by night, is determined by her nature and does what she should.

Moreover, the Nightingale in her charge is guilty of a faulty syllogism:

> Everything that shuns right loves darkness and
> hates light.   (229–30)
> The Owl loves darkness and hates light.
> Therefore the Owl shuns right.

The middle term, "loves darkness and hates light," has not been distributed. The poet would expect his medieval audience to recognize such an elementary and flagrant error in logic.

sensual pleasure; and the Owl has confronted her with the moral consequences of her position. The judge with the capacities ascribed earlier to Master Nicholas would not dismiss those consequences lightly.

The first stage of the debate has been concluded. The Nightingale has made her charges, and the Owl has successfully answered them. Though the Nightingale is anxious to stay on the attack by answering her opponent's charge with another allegation of her own, the Owl, appealing to the laws governing legal disputation, asserts that the Nightingale's formal plaint has been concluded and that it would be illegal for her to make a new charge; hence, she makes a countercharge of her own. It, too, is argued in terms of service to mankind: if the only thing the Nightingale can do is sing, and if her song is merely of wantonness, she is of no use to man:

> Seie me nu, þu wrecche wiȝt,
> is in þe eni oþer note
> bute þe hauest schille þrote?
> Þu nart noȝt to non oþer þinge,
> bute þu canst of chateringe:
> vor þu art lutel an unstrong,
> an nis þi regel noþing long.
> Wat dostu godes among monne?   (556–63)

> [Tell me now, you wretched creature,
> is there in you any other use
> besides having a shrill throat?
> You are (suited) to no other thing
> except you know how to chatter:
> for you are little and weak,
> and your measure is not at all long.
> What good do you do among men?]

The Owl claims that her opponent lacks beauty, size, strength, and cleanliness, and that her dietary habits are no more fastidious than her own. Her sole reason for being, her one talent, is her ability to sing, a pernicious talent since directed only toward lust. The Owl claims, on the other hand, that she "can do wel gode wike" [can perform very good services],

vor ich can loki manne wike:
an mine wike boþ wel gode,
vor ich helpe to manne uode.
Ich can nimen mus at berne,
an ek at chirche ine þe derne:
vor me is lof to Cristes huse,
to clansi hit wiþ fule muse,
ne schal þar neure come to
ful wiзt, зif ich hit mai iuo.   (604–12)

[for I can look after men's dwellings:
and my service is very good,
for I help with men's food.
I can catch mice in the barn,
and also in church in the dark:
for I love Christ's house,
to cleanse it from foul mice,
nor shall there ever come too
foul a creature if I may seize it.]

Once again the truth of the Owl's charges is underscored by
the poet's description of the Nightingale's reactions:

Þe niзtingale at þisse worde
was wel neз ut of rede iworþe,
an þoзte зorne on hire mode
зif ho oзt elles understode,
зif ho kuþe oзt bute singe,
þat miзte helpe to oþer þinge.
Herto ho moste andswere uinde,
oþer mid alle bon bihinde:
an hit is suþe strong to fiзte
aзen soþ & aзen riзte.   (659–68)

[The Nightingale at these words
was well nigh out of ideas,
and thought hard to herself
about whether she knew something else,
whether she could do something besides sing,
that might be useful in another way.
To this she must find an answer,
or withal remain behind:
and it is very hard to fight
against truth and right.]

The poet makes it clear that the Nightingale's answer must be an argument of expedience thought up on the spur of the moment, and that it must be deliberately sophistic since it must "fiȝte aȝen soþ & aȝen riȝte." It is an argument which of necessity must proceed by dissimulation and the trimming of words:

> He mot gon to al mid ginne,
> þan þe horte boþ on [w]inne:
> an þe man mot on oþer segge,
> he mot bihemmen & bilegge,
> ȝif muþ wiþute mai biwro
> þat me þe horte noȝt niso:
> an sone mai a word misreke
> þar muþ shal aȝen horte speke;
> an sone mai a word misstorte
> þar muþ shal speken aȝen horte. (669–78)

> [He must proceed with cunning,
> whose heart is set on contention:
> and the man must speak of other things,
> he must trim and dissimulate,
> if the mouth without may conceal
> what only within the heart is seen:
> for quickly may a word go astray
> when the mouth against the heart shall speak;
> for quickly may a word go wrong
> when the mouth shall speak against the heart.]

And the argument itself leaves little doubt that it is sophistry deliberately contrived, for it is founded on a familiar Christian heresy. Admitting that she possesses but one accomplishment, in contrast to the many possessed by her adversary, the Nightingale claims that her single accomplishment, since it aids man in his quest for the ultimate end for which he was created, renders those of her opponent inconsequential:

> Betere is min on þan alle þine,
> betere is o song of mine muþe
> þan al þat eure þi kun kuþe:
> an lust, ich telle þe wareuore.

Wostu to wan man was ibore?
To þare blisse of houene-rich,
þar euer is song & murȝþe iliche:
þider fundeþ eurich man
þat eni þing of gode kan.
Vorþi me singþ in holi-chirche,
an clerkes ginneþ songes wirche,
þat man iþenche bi þe songe
wider he shal, & þar bon longe:
þat he þe murȝþe ne uorȝete,
ac þarof þenche & biȝete,
an nime ȝeme of chirche steuene,
hu murie is þe blisse of houene.   (712–28)

[Better is my one thing than all yours,
better is one song from my mouth
than all your kin could ever do:
and listen, I will tell you wherefore.
Do you know to what man was born?
To the bliss of heaven,
where there is always song and mirth alike:
thither strives every man
who knows anything of good.
Therefore I sing in church,
and clerks compose songs
so that man is reminded by it
whither he goes and where he shall long remain:
so that he may not forget the mirth,
but think of it and obtain it,
and become aware, from the church's voice,
how merry is the bliss of heaven.]

She encourages men to be happy and prays that man may obtain

"þan ilke song þat euer is eche."   (742)

[that very song that is everlasting]

Not only has the Nightingale avoided consideration of the steps by which man must regain the state of grace, but having previously admitted that her song is confined to sensual pleasure, she now seems to have identified sensual pleasure with "blisse of houene-riche." The Owl is quick to attack her opponent's argument on the grounds of rhetorical sophistry:

> "Abid! abid!" þe ule seide,
> "þu gest al to mid swikelede:
> alle þine wordes þu bileist
> þat hit þincþ soþ al þat þu seist;
> alle þine wordes boþ isliked,
> an so bisemed an biliked,
> þat alle þo þat hi auoþ,
> hi weneþ þat þu segge soþ. (837–44)

> ["Stop! stop!" the Owl said,
> "you proceed with too much deceit:
> you color all your words
> so that all you say seems true;
> your words are specious
> and made so plausible and pleasing
> that everyone who accepts them
> believes they speak truth.]

The remainder of the rebuttal (854–66) is also common Christian doctrine: man can gain eternal happiness only through due atonement for his sins; singing is no substitute for the arduous task of earning salvation. Then, again contrasting her own song with the Nightingale's, the Owl claims hers is an aid to man in his quest for salvation (ll. 867–92). She sings to men "no foliot" [no foolishness], for her song is "of longinge" and "imend sumdel mid woninge" [somewhat mingled with lamentation]. Not only does she help men pure in heart, who "long for heaven," to shed tears for other men, but she helps the sinful man as well, by teaching him "þare is wo" [where woe is]. And to conclude her rebuttal, she indites the Nightingale again as the perpetrator of wantonness, this time in terms of the Christian distinction between carnal love and *caritas*:

> þu draȝst men to fleses luste,
> þat w[u]lleþ þine songes luste.
> Al þu forlost þe murȝþe of houene,
> for þarto neuestu none steuene:
> al þat þu singst is of golnesse,
> for nis on þe non holinesse,

ne wene[ð] na man for þi pipinge
þat eni preost in chir[ch]e singe.[10]   (895–902)

[you draw men to carnal lust,
who listen to your songs.
You lose completely the mirth of heaven,
for you have no voice for it:
all you sing is of wantonness,
since in you is no holiness,
nor does any man believe through your piping
that a priest sings in church.]

By now the intentions and methods of the respective debaters
should be clearly perceived. The Nightingale is not concerned
with distinguishing between right and wrong or good and evil,
as she had earlier pretended, but only with the immediate end
which is victory over her hated enemy, even if victory necessi-
tates dissimulation, the trimming of words, the deliberate striving
"aȝen soþ & aȝen riȝte," and the defending of a Christian heresy.
By the nature of her arguments as well as by the author's comments she is characterized as a cunning, sophistical rhetorician;
whereas the Owl, as both Wells and Atkins have noted, is por-
trayed as a logician.[11] Even her bitter and natural rival has on
two occasions admitted that her arguments are wisely conceived,
right, and true. And she is made to defend traditional Christian
doctrine in the best scholastic fashion, attacking her opponent's
position and defending her own with Christian dialectics. It now
becomes clear that the issue to be decided also involves the question of the validity of methods employed by the debaters: should
the verdict be awarded to the sophist who seeks an expedient
end, or to the logician who seeks to preserve the truth of Christian doctrine?

As the debate continues, the Owl attempts to reduce the Night-

---

[10] The distinction between carnal love and *caritas* is discussed at length
by Etienne Gilson in *The Mystical Theology of Saint Bernard,* trans.
A. C. Downes (New York, 1950), pp. 33–60.

[11] Atkins, *op. cit.;* J. E. Wells, *The Owl and the Nightingale* (Boston,
1907).

ingale's argument to absurdity by demanding to know why, if she pretends to teach man to sing of eternal happiness, she does not travel to places where skill in songs, religious or otherwise, is utterly lacking (903–32). Though the Nightingale is well schooled in rhetoric and wisely waits for her anger to subside (939–48), her reply is weak and openly heretical. She journeys not to the north countries because there her song would be wasted; moreover, her "riȝte stede" [proper place] is "þar louerd haueþ his loue libedde" [where a lord has his love abed], for

> Hit is mi riȝt, hit is mi laȝe,
> þa[t] to þe he[x]st ich me draȝe.[12]   (969–70)

> [It is my right, it is my law,
> that to the highest I betake myself.]

No wonder the Owl "was wroþ" [was angry] and "hire eȝen abrad" [her eyes widened]. For by identifying "þar louerd haueþ his loue ibedde" with "he[x]st," after having just claimed that her song is a constant reminder to mankind of the "blisse of houene-riche," the Nightingale identifies sexual pleasure with heavenly bliss!

The Owl's ensuing diatribe, containing the tale of the Nightingale put to death for having encouraged a wife to pursue an unlawful love, is of significance to the present discussion primarily in that it provides the Nightingale the chance to restate her charge that the Owl sings only of man's troubles and to make two new charges—that she is of service to man only when dead and that she is a hated witch.

> Ȝif þu art iworpe oþer ishote,
> þanne þu miȝt erest to note.
> Vor me þe hoþ in one rodde,
> an þu, mid þine fule codde,
> an mid þine ateliche s[w]ore,
> biwerest manne corn urom dore.
> Nis noþer noȝt, þi lif ne þi blod:
> ac þu art sh[e]ueles suþe god.

---

[12] I have accepted Atkins' reading.

Þar nowe sedes boþe isowe,
pinnuc, golfinc, rok, ne crowe
ne dar þar neuer cumen ihende,
ȝif þi buc hongeþ at þan ende.   (1121–32)

[If you are struck or shot,
then you might first be useful.
For they hang you on a stick,
and with your foul bag (body)
and your fearsome neck,
you protect men's corn from animals.
Neither is worth anything, your life or your blood:
but you are a very good scarecrow.
Where new seeds are sown,
sparrow, goldfinch, rook nor crow
dares never come near,
if your body hangs at the end.]

The Owl does not deny her foreknowledge of events, but her ability to foresee, she claims, is not witchcraft, since her foreknowledge—and here she again cites Christian doctrine—has nothing to do with the determination of events. Moreover, she puts her prophetic ability to good use in the service of man by warning him of impending disaster.[13] Again the Nightingale is upset by the cogency of her opponent's rebuttal: "& hohful was,

[13] John of Salisbury's discussion of "Omens in General" provides interesting background material for this phase of the debate. See *Frivolities of Courtiers and Footprints of Philosophers,* Being a Translation of the First, Second, and Third Books and Selections from the Seventh and Eighth Books of the *Policraticus* of John of Salisbury; trans. Joseph B. Pike (Minneapolis, 1938), pp. 48, 57–58. "Omens from the horned owl, the screech owl, and the night owl are always unfavorable. The night owl, however, for the reason that it is not blinded by the darkness of night, points to the watchfulness of a man of discretion. . . ." Though John of Salisbury asserts "that all omens are meaningless and [that] credence should not be given to augury," he does "not condemn those signs which have been conceded by divine ordinance for the guidance of man." For "in manifold ways indeed God instructs his creatures; now by the sound of the elements, now by signs of animate and inanimate nature he makes manifest what is to come in accord with what he knows to be expedient for the elect. . . . In this connection I think that birds have not been neglected by mother nature."
The Owl answers the Nightingale in related terms. Her ability to foresee is natural; it has been given her that she may guide man.

& ful wel miȝte" [and was anxious, and well might be] (1292). In fact, she thinks so much of the Owl's method that she attempts to exonerate herself from the charge that she is responsible for the fall of women by arguing in terms of the same distinction. Just as the Owl has admitted that she can prophesy misfortune but denies that she is responsible for it, so the Nightingale admits that she sings of love but denies that she is responsible for love misused. But the Nightingale's song remains a temptation to sin; the Owl's predictions consist of warnings against such temptations. Without concern for what has gone before, the Nightingale once more has fashioned an argument of expedience.

The discussion of women and sin introduced at this point by the Nightingale leads eventually to a defense of women by both debaters which has been convincingly described as reflecting the poet's sympathies in a contemporary controversy on "the abstract question of women in general."[14] The poet, however, does not allow his defense of women to supplant the main issue of service to mankind, though he may have allowed his sympathies temporarily to overshadow it. The Owl's part of the defense is consistent with the position she has so far maintained throughout the debate, even though she is often in agreement with her opponent and, as Kathryn Huganir notes, is "in reality going her one better" by defending wives as well as maidens.[15] She does not deny the Nightingale's opening arguments that desire in itself is not evil, that love stolen contradicts the laws of nature, and that sins of the spirit are of graver consequence than those of the flesh.[16] But she denies that carnal transgressions of maidens are more easily forgiven than those of wives; and if sin is to be considered essentially in terms of intention and determining circumstance (as it was by Abelard) her supporting argument is more telling than her opponent's.[17] The Nightingale, on the other hand,

[14] Huganir, *op.* cit., p. 133.

[15] Huganir, *op. cit.,* p. 136.

[16] The Owl thought the Nightingale had "wel speke atte frume" [spoken well at the beginning] (1513).

[17] Gilson, *The Spirit of Medieval Philosophy,* pp. 348–54.

involves herself in contradictions and seemingly concedes by default two of her opponent's earlier charges. She has given up the attempt to prove that her song of love is a reminder of heavenly joy and admitted that it may be put to improper uses. She now claims that it may afford both solace and instruction to innocent maidens.

> Ich [t]eache heom bi mine songe
> þat swucch luue ne lest noȝt longe:
> for mi song lutle hwile ilest,
> an luue ne deþ noȝt bute rest
> on swuch childre, & sone ageþ,
> an falþ adun þe hote breþ.
> . . . .
> Þat child bi me hit understond,
> an his unred to red[e] wend,
> an iseȝþ wel, bi mine songe,
> þat dusi luue ne last noȝt longe.   (1449–66)

> [I teach them by my song
> that such love does not last long:
> for my song lasts a little while,
> and love only rests
> on such girls and soon passes,
> and the hot passion subsides. . . .
> The girl understands it through me,
> and her ignorance is turned to wisdom,
> for she sees from my song
> that foolish love does not last long.]

In her haste to escape moral incrimination, she denies that she sings in the breeding season, although she had previously boasted of the fact: "ich ne singe nawt hwan ich teme" [I sing not when I breed] (1470). And she admits the Owl's earlier charges that her song is short-lived and of carnal love, by asserting now that it is analogous to love, the brief excitement "þat sone kumeþ, & sone geþ" [that quickly comes, and quickly goes]. The responsible judge must consider with respect to argumentative consistency whether the Nightingale has by default conceded the truth of the Owl's two earlier charges, just as he must consider with respect to service to man whether the Nightingale's song, by its very nature, though not evil in itself, is a temptation rather than a deterrent to carnal sin.

The debate is all but over. Simultaneously, the Owl answers an earlier charge, makes a new charge of her own, and claims she is of service even after death:

> Þu seist þat ich am manne [loð],
> . . . .
> Þah hit beo soþ, ich do heom god,
> an for heom ich [s]chadde mi blod:
> ich do heom god mid mine deaþe,
> waruore þe is wel unneaþe.
> For þah þu ligge dead & clinge,
> þi deþ nis nawt to none þinge;
> ich not neauer to hwan þu miȝt,
> for þu nart bute a wrecche wiȝt.
> . . . .
> ich not to hwan þu bre[d]ist þi brod,
> liues ne deaþes ne deþ hit god.   (1607–34)

> You say that I am hateful to men. . . .
> Though it be true, I do them good,
> and for them I shed my blood:
> I do them good with my death,
> which for you is hardly possible.
> For though you lie dead and shriveling,
> your death comes to nothing;
> I know not to whom you might be useful,
> for you are only a wretched creature. . . .
> I know not why you raise your brood,
> alive or dead they do no good.]

The debate proper has ended. The Owl's final argument is conclusively stated in terms of the very issue which the Nightingale, when attempting to prove her opponent a monster, had been the first to introduce, and which constitutes, as is apparent throughout the debate, the issue mutually accepted by both contestants as fundamental and decisive—which of the two birds by virtue of her respective character and song is of greater service to mankind. The Nightingale refuses to argue further and claims victory on a legal technicality. The other birds presently appear and celebrate the Nightingale's assumed victory over their common and natural enemy. But it cannot be said that the Nightingale displays great confidence in her claim of victory by default. Though professing herself willing, because of her law-abiding nature, to bring the case before Nicholas, whom she had originally suggested as a suitable judge, she now confesses that she knows not where he can be found. The Owl seems unmoved by the possibility that the judge will decide in favor of the Nightingale on the grounds of a legal technicality and demands that the controversy be decided by lawful judgment. Moreover, when the Nightingale expresses doubt as to whether anyone can recall in exact detail the debate as it has been argued, it is the Owl who confidently asserts:

> . . . for al, ende of orde,
> telle ich con, word after worde:
> an ȝef þe þincþ þat ich misrempe,
> þu stond aȝein & do me crempe.   (1785–88)

> [for all to the end
> I can tell, word for word:
> and if you think I go too far,
> oppose me and pull me up.]

The debate, then, is something more than "a story told for its own sake." Superficially, it is a bird fable in which each bird strives in terms of service to man to establish her own position in the divinely created hierarchy of being as higher than her opponent's. Pedagogically, it is a dialectical exercise in which two irreconcilable attitudes toward human experience—the one, essentially traditional and Christian, and the other, sensual and heretical—are represented respectively by a logician in quest of truth and a rhetorician in quest of sophistical victory. By exercising the qualities ascribed by the poet to Nicholas, by heeding the poet's observations on the progress of the debate, and by putting the arguments advanced by the debaters to the test of Christian dialectics, the reader as judge is expected to arrive at the final verdict intended by the poet. Such an interpretation does not exclude the possibility that the poem was written to present Nicholas of Guilford for preferment or that Nicholas, in fact, is the author of the poem. Rather, the theory of preferment strengthens the interpretation offered in this paper. If Nicholas is being presented for preferment to his ecclesiastical superiors, either by a friend or by himself, certainly he has not been placed in the rôle of judge to decide against the logician and defender of The Faith in favor of the sophistical rhetorician who involves herself in open contradiction and who identifies eternal happiness with physical pleasure.

THE PREDICAMENT OF GAWAIN

George J. Engelhardt

THERE IS A KIND OF PREDICAMENT SO EXCLUSIVE IN ITS CONDI-tions that ordinary men never find themselves in its toils. Such was the predicament that befell Gawain in the adventure that ended at the Green Chapel. It was a predicament not made for petty knights uninitiated in the mysteries of consummate chival-ric virtue; they could elude or ignore the dilemmas that it posed, just as the lesser knights in Arthur's hall shrank from the chal-lenge of the "aghlich mayster" [terrible master]. But for Gawain it was pat. By universal repute he was the perfect knight (lines 676, 914).[1] The pentangle or "endeles knot" [endless knot] em-blazoned on his shield was the symbol of his reputation. Like the tracery of that star, his virtue was reputed to be whole, without gap or inconsistency. This reputation was now to be put to the test. It was to be assayed in a predicament singularly adapted to the *eques pentagonalis* [knight of the pentangle]. From this pre-dicament was to emerge not only the moral of the poem but its suspense, its humor, its irony—its delight. This delight has been too often disregarded, just as the moral has long been obscured

Reprinted, by permission of author and editor, from *Modern Language Quarterly*, XVI (1955), 218–25.

[1] The text cited is the EETS, os, No. 210, edited by Sir Israel Gollancz, with introductory essays by M. Day and M. S. Serjeantson (London, 1940).

by extrinsic debate.[2] Because in this poem the two functions of "prodesse aut delectare" [to profit or to amuse] are integrally related, neither can be understood unless both are understood.

Because, furthermore, the symbol of the pentangle is so indispensable to the understanding of the poem, the poet devoted to an expatiation on its symbolism no less than forty-three lines (623–65). This symbolism is both graphic and numeric, but it is the graphic symbolism especially that serves determinatively in understanding the poem. As the pentangle may be drawn in one continuous movement, so it becomes the symbol of the complete man, whose integrity admits no imperfection; and it is this integrity in Gawain which the poem will show to be more apparent than real. The numeric symbolism, originating in the fivefold angularity of the pentangle, is secondary. It serves to reinforce the import of the graphic symbolism rather than to suggest itself the development of the poem. The fivefold schematization of the numeric symbolism is not structurally constitutive in this poem as it might well be in the rigorous structure, say, of an Alanus de Insulis. The poet did not, for example, provide five episodes intended to illustrate respectively his interpretations of the five angles; nor did he present five episodes corresponding to the five virtues that he assigned to the fifth angle.

Yet this expatiation upon the numeric symbolism is not to be regarded as artistically otiose. Rather it exemplifies that practice in medieval poetics which contemporary theorists called *dilatatio* [enlargement]. The very word *tary* which the poet uses in reference to his procedure recalls the Latin verb *morari* [to lin-

---

[2] The lack of "literary-critical attention" to *Sir Gawain and the Green Knight* has recently been signalized by John Speirs, "Sir Gawain and the Green Knight," *Scrutiny*, XVI (1949), 274 ff. Mr. Speirs's method is anthropological. In interpreting the predicament of Gawain, I have attempted to associate with the symbols of the poem not their hypothetical ultimate or near ultimate mythic import, but rather the meaning present to the consciousness of the poet and his contemporaries. I am persuaded that the latter method is less likely to detract from the integrity of this poem than a method which assumes that the poem is merely "near the surface, a Christian poem" (Speirs, p. 279).

ger], which from the time of Priscian's *Praeexercitamina* had been used to designate this practice. *Dilatatio* may well have had an effect upon medieval readers and auditors like that of *largo* in music; and in *Sir Gawain and the Green Knight* the importance of the symbolic pentangle was fixed in their minds by the prolonged elaboration of forty-three lines. Since, however, the five virtues assigned to Gawain in that *dilatatio* are not determinative or even quite discriminable, it has seemed more apt in this analysis to consider his predicament rather in terms of the three virtues that would govern the three domains of activity, the military, the religious, and the courtly, in which the complete knight, the veritable man, might demonstrate his perfection, or, as the poet has named it, his *trawþe* [truth]. These virtues shall be called valor, piety, and courtesy.[3]

The society in which Gawain lived was a valorous society. It stemmed from a race of bold men that loved strife (21). Its eponymous hero was "Brutus, þe bolde burne" [Brutus, the bold warrior], its sovereign the magnificent Arthur, whom youth and pride had addicted to hazardous quests. From its members it exacted both in peace and war the unremitting exercise of valor. Their lives were jeopardized even for diversion, as when they jousted in the lists or chased the boar. For their prowess the vassals of Arthur were world-renowned, but it was Gawain who especially excelled in valor. He was the nonpareil, the "prynce withouten pere / In felde þer felle men foȝt" [prince without peer in the field where fierce men fought] (873–74).

This superlative valor was nourished in Gawain by an equally great piety. Yet among his fellow knights Gawain was surely not

[3] On the symbolism of the pentangle see E. du Bruyne, *Etudes d'esthétique médiévale* (Brugge, 1946), II, 349 ff. The comprehensive symbolism of the pentangle, it should be noted, precludes the exclusive identification of Gawain with any single virtue such as chastity. For an application of *dilatatio*, i.e., augmentation and diminution, characteristic features of the *ars nova* of medieval poetics, to the *ars nova* of medieval music, see G. Reese, *Music in the Middle Ages* (New York, 1940), pp. 345–46. For a brief account of *dilatatio* see my "Mediaeval Vestiges in the Rhetoric of Erasmus," *PMLA*, LXIII (1948), 739–44.

unique in bearing upon his shield the picture of the Virgin Mary, nor in drawing strength from her image during the crises of battle. These knights were pious men, who faithfully attended mass, matins, and evensong, observed the law of fast, and said their prayers, *pater* and *ave, credo* and *mea culpa.* In the most desolate wastes they were never alone, never suffered the loneliness of the heathen *anhaga* [solitary one], because they could always speak with God and make their complaints to Mary. Even the Green Knight, that creature of Druidic lore and antique "fayryӡe" [fairy] (cf. line 240), had long since changed masters: he now swore "bi gog" [by Gog], and his station, the mound that once may have been a fairy *síd* [a fairy mound], was now called a chapel, a name symbolically apposite to the place where Gawain would make at the last his true confession.

The preëminence of Gawain did not end with valor and piety. The perfect knight was esteemed also for his superlative courtesy. Beyond Camelot and Logres, even beyond the Wirral, he was recognized by all who knew courtesy as the paragon not only of "alle prys & prowes" [all praise and prowess] but of "pured þewes" [refined manners] as well (912). "Gawan þe hende" [Gawain the courteous] was the exemplar of such refinement to a society that cherished courtesy. The members of this society were not, like a Beowulf, engrossed in virile exploits. "Justed ful jolile þise gentyle kniӡtes, / Syþen kayred to þe court, caroles to make" [These gentle knights jousted very gallantly, then rode to the court to sing carols] (42–43). It was the "lel layk of luf" [loyal sport of love] that inspired their feats and instructed their arms (1512–19). No doubt a Beowulf had as keen an appreciation of ceremony, as perceptive a sense of decorum, as the brethren of the Table Round or the gracious household of Bertilak; the guard of Hrothgar, for example, was no less civil than the "porter pure plesaunt" [faultlessly pleasant porter] of the castle beyond the Wirral. But "sleӡteӡ of þeweӡ / & þe teccheles termes of talkyng noble" [practiced manners and the spotless expressions of noble conversation] (916–17) were not all that the discreet retainers of Bertilak expected to behold in the exemplar Gawain. Last but not least, each man said softly to his companion, "I hope þat may hym here / Schal lerne of luf-talkyng" [I hope whoever may hear him shall learn the art of love-talk] (926–27).

If it was a sense of what is "semly" [fitting] (348) that led Gawain to intercept the challenge of the Green Knight, it was the ineluctable demands of valor that obliged him to persevere faithfully in their covenant. The renown of his valor would be forever marred by the blot of recreancy if after the twelvemonth Gawain did not come at the appointed hour and place to expose his neck to the blow from which there seemed to be no recourse. So hard was this fate that even the author intervenes to warn Gawain against dereliction:

> Now þenk wel, sir Gawan,
> For woþe þat þou ne wonde
> Þis auenture forto frayn,
> Þat þou hatȝ tan on honde.　　　　　(487–90)

> [Now think well, Sir Gawain,
> so that you may not neglect, because of danger,
> to try this adventure
> that you have taken in hand.]

Small wonder that Gawain's sleep was gloomy. It would be a noble stratagem if he could escape unslain, provided that his honor might also emerge unscathed. This was the first dilemma that Gawain faced in his predicament.

The very joy of living that made the prospect of death repugnant further complicated his predicament when Sir Gawain, in the prime of life (cf. line 54), met the fairest of chatelaines. Her beauty transcended the superlative; she was lovelier than the loveliest Guinevere (81–84, 945) and as forthputting as she was beautiful. Three times she proffered herself to him. Since it was a discreet household over which she was mistress—"Vche mon tented hys, / & þay two tented þayres" [Each one attended to his own, and they two attended to theirs] (1018–19)—the only restraints that might curb the "wallande joye" [willing joy] of Gawain were to be put there by himself. But he was not unmindful of his devotion to Mary (1768–69), not unmindful, too, of the hereafter awaiting the man that dies in mortal sin (1283–87, 1774–75).[4] Such then was the second dilemma of Gawain.

This gift of her body which the lady pressed upon Gawain was one that he could hardly reveal to her lord, much less return to him by the terms of their bargain. Not to exchange such a gift, moreover, would constitute a patent breach of the rules prescribed by courtesy (and valor and piety) for the conduct of man with man. But courtesy had prescribed rules, too, for the conduct of man with woman; and now Gawain was beset by a woman who never ceased to remind him of his reputation in this regard:

> Your honour, your hendelayk is hendely praysed
> With lordeȝ, wyth ladyes, with alle þat lyf bere.
> & now ȝe ar here, iwysse, & we bot oure one.　　(1228–30)

[Your honor, your courteousness are graciously praised among lords, ladies, and all that live.
And now you are here, indeed, and we by ourselves.]

The deft humor of this situation may be lost on many a modern commentator, but it was most surely present to the mind of the reader or listener in the fourteenth century.

[4] Cf. the twelfth-century Andreas Capellanus, *De amore,* ed. E. Trojel (Havniae, 1892), p. 160: "Quamvis igitur amor cogat omnes curiales exsistere et a qualibet homines rusticitate constituat alienos, tamen propter magna, quae sequuntur, inconvenientia et poenas gravissimas imminentes res timenda videtur et a nullis optanda sapientibus et praecipue odio habenda militibus. Nam quibus ex fortuitu proeliorum eventu mortis quotidie videntur instare pericula, maximo debent studio praecavere, ne talia committant, propter quae supernae patriae regi iudicantur offensi" [However, although love impels all men to become courteous and makes them strangers to whatever is crude, nevertheless, because of the great inconveniences that follow and the threat of very grave suffering, it seems a thing to be feared, to be chosen by no wise man, and especially to be hated by soldiers. For those who seem to be in danger of death daily from chance events in battle ought to take the utmost care to do nothing that might be judged offensive by the King of the Heavenly Land].

The importunacy of the chatelaine was regressive; she was the wooer—not the wooed—like her Celtic forebears or like Belyssant, the enterprising heroine of the epic *Amis et Amile*.[5] Like the love-longing sung in the old *chanson de toile* [spinning song], the passion the chatelaine affected would have reduced her to the "seruaunt" of the man (line 1240). Thus, in her way of love she seemed more primitive than the inaccessible *domna* [lady] or the *demoiselle difficile* [aloof lady] of courtly love.[6] The courtesy of Gawain, on the contrary, had progressed beyond those principles of courtly service recorded in the twelfth century by Andreas Capellanus and exemplified in the humiliation of the *Chevalier à la charrette*. The brutal lust which even in the eleventh century the Welsh imagination could link with the person of Arthur[7] was as alien to Gawain's code as to the *amour courtois* [courtly love],[8] but the service he offered the importunate chatelaine was not the *service d'amour* (1278, 1548, 1845). His code made him reject as sinful the love of another man's wife (1549—

[5] Cf. G. Cohen, *Chrétien de Troyes et son œuvre* (Paris, 1931), pp. 33–34.

[6] The tradition of courtly love preserved by Andreas Capellanus permitted the woman to take the initiative, provided that the lover had been proved worthy, yet was constrained from avowing the love he had otherwise evinced. Thus Andreas (ed. Trojel, pp. 199–200): "Sed nec illud nostris potest sermonibus obviare, quod dicitis, mulieris pudori obsistere, si ipsa suum offerat non petitum amorem; mulieribus enim nullo reperitur iure negatum suum sponte cuilibet probo largiri amorem. Potest ergo mulier, si ab aliquo provocetur amare, eum ad suum pulchre et curialiter invitare amorem, si cognoverit virum illud ob aliquam non exprimere causam" [But what we said cannot be contradicted by your remark, that it is contrary to a woman's modesty if she offers herself when no love is asked; for no rule exists to prevent women from giving their love freely to whom they please. Therefore a woman can, if she is inspired to love by someone, invite him graciously and courteously to love her, if she knows that something prevents the man from speaking of it].

[7] Cf. E. Faral, *La Légende Arthurienne* (Paris, 1929), I, 236 ff.

[8] The tradition of Andreas, which reserves courtly love to the middle and upper classes, expressly recommends the coercing of lower-class women (ed. Trojel, p. 236): "Si vero et illarum [*scil.* rusticarum] te feminarum amor forte attraxerit, eas pluribus laudibus efferre memento, et, si locum inveneris opportunum, non differas assumere, quod petebas et violento potiri amplexu. Vix enim ipsarum in tantum exterius poteris

53, 1774–75);[9] yet he must manage this rejection with humility and forbearance, with tact and a light touch. Least of all must he evince an unmanly irresponsiveness. The knight whom all the world honored for his courtesy must not prove a caitiff in the bower (1773). This was the third dilemma posed by Gawain's predicament.

In this supreme predicament, Gawain put his faith in a talisman. With this band of green silk, he thought to mitigate his predicament. Ironically, this self-delusion only made his predicament worse. It is true that the talisman was reputed to protect the wearer from death and that this power claimed for the talisman was not later disproved. It is likewise true that by accepting the

---

mitigare rigorem, quod quietos fateantur se tibi concessuras amplexus vel optata patiantur te habere solatia, nisi modicae saltem coactionis medela praecedat ipsarum opportuna pudoris" [If love for their (the peasants') women strongly incites you, remember to flatter them with lavish praise, and, if you come upon a convenient place, do not hesitate to take what you seek, and you can embrace them by force. For you can hardly soften their exterior stiffness so much that they will quietly grant you their embraces, or allow you to have the solaces you desire, unless you first apply some degree of force as a convenient cure for their modesty]. Cf. the *pastourelle*. There is reason to believe that Gawain disapproved even of such coercion. In verses 1495–97, the chatelaine seems to be arguing as follows. Major: a woman belonging to the villein class is a proper object of compulsion. Minor: a woman who denies her love to Gawain is behaving like a woman of the villein class (cf. "vilanous," line 1497). Therefore, a woman who denies her love to Gawain is a proper object of compulsion. If Gawain had taken the trouble to reject the minor premise alone, it might be inferred that he assented to the major. Since, however, in his retort he did nothing but reject the idea of compulsion itself, it may be inferred that he did not assent to the major premise.

[9] Cf. Andreas in his heavy-handed "rejection of love" (ed. Trojel, p. 314) : "Odit namque Deus et utroque iussit testamento puniri, quos extra nuptiales actus agnoscit Veneris operibus obligari vel quocunque voluptatis genere detineri" [For God hates those—and in both testaments punishment is demanded—whom he discerns are joined in the acts of Venus outside the marriage bonds or are engaged in any kind of voluptuous enjoyment]. Otherwise in a judgment ascribed by Andreas to the Countess of Champagne (ed. Trojel, p. 154) : "nulla etiam coniugata regis poterit amoris praemio coronari, nisi extra coniugii foedera ipsius amoris militiae cernatur adiuncta" [for no married woman can be crowned with the reward of the King of Love unless outside the bonds of marriage she is enlisted in the service of Love himself].

talisman from the chatelaine, Gawain was enabled to appease her and thus conveniently to preserve his reputation for courtesy toward women. But in that very act he proved ungenerous, and therefore discourteous, to her husband; he sinned against piety and derogated from his valor. When Gawain accepted this talisman from the lady, he agreed to conceal this gift from her husband; yet Gawain and the lord already had sworn to exchange whatever each might acquire. Thus Gawain had willfully placed himself in a new dilemma; he could not fulfill one compact without breaking the other. This, however, was a dilemma that Gawain chose not to face; he repressed it. Despite this full intention of committing sin, Gawain went to confession and sought absolution. He endeavored to safeguard his body by magic and his soul by a false confession. Thus, incongruously, the exemplar of piety took refuge in superstition and a false conscience.

The irony implicit in this compromise with virtue was augmented by the poet as he proceeded to the next episode in the testing of Gawain. Having just conspired in one act of deception, Gawain was now to be exposed again to this sin. While being conducted from the castle toward the chapel, he was accosted by his guide, who urged him to flee. But the guide did not rest there. He offered to swear a solemn oath of secrecy, averring that he would never reveal Gawain's defection. Gawain rejected this proffer brusquely; but the self-righteousness of his annoyance serves less to obscure than to heighten the ironic analogy between this oath proffered by the guide and an earlier promise of secrecy —that tendered by a more compliant Gawain to the more persuasive chatelaine.

This irony, like the action itself, is consummated in the scene at the Green Chapel, the fifth and last test of the pentagonal Gawain.[10] The scene begins with Gawain's disillusionment at the grass-grown chapel:

---

[10] I.e., the first three tests were staged by the chatelaine, the fourth by the guide. The initial challenge of the Green Knight, which stands apart from this fivefold cluster of tests, is not so much a test as the mode of access to the tests.

> "We, lorde," quoþ þe gentyle knyȝt,
> "Wheþer þis be þe grene chapelle?
> He[re] myȝt aboute myd-nyȝt
> Þe dele his matynnes telle."　　　　　(2185–88)

> ["Alas, Lord," said the gentle knight,
> "is this the green chapel?
> Here about midnight
> the devil might say his matins."]

With an ironic deflection, it proceeds to Gawain's self-disillusion-ment, when the black magic proves to be white,[11] and eventuates in his diatribe against women—a discordant diatribe for Gawain the courteous. Courtesy toward women was one virtue he had preserved. His valor and his piety had suffered some impairment, but for these defections he had already made amends, though in an order the reverse of the usual, by suffering penance for them under the axe of the Green Knight and then avowing them in a true confession. It is all the more ironic that the one virtue which had remained conspicuously intact should now undergo a conspicuous evaporation, that the exemplar of courtesy should rail like the misogynists, should echo the plea they had inherited from Adam: "Domine, erat femina" [Lord, it was a woman]. Unlike Adam, Gawain asked to be forgiven: "Þaȝ I be now bigyled, / Me þink me burde be excused" [Though I am now deceived, it seems to me I ought to be excused] (2427–28). Like Adam, he was forgiven, not because the poet disliked women, however, rather because he understood men.

There was no malice in the irony of this poet. It sprang from justice; it ended in mercy. This poet knew the frailty of human flesh and the self-complacency of the human spirit. The moral of his poem is not merely that man should curb his fear or rein his lust or keep his word; it is deeper and simpler. It is the moral of

---

[11] The upsurge of Gawain's mood after the grazing blow of the Green Knight is likened by Mr. Speirs (p. 298) to a "rebirth." I should prefer to construe it—less anthropologically and perhaps more literarily—as a step in the ironic progression of the episode; it prepares by way of contrast for the abashment of Gawain that immediately ensues.

a poet who has become long familiar with the very heart of life. It is the vanity of human pride—the pride of magnificent kings, of gray-eyed queens, of perfect knights whose perfection is illusory. That such pride should be chastened is just, and justice cannot seem otherwise than grim. Like the hard actualities, like winter storm and strife, justice is hard. Its instruments are not pleasant to look at, like the miscolored knight to whom Gawain made his true confession and Morgan la Fay, from whose body all loveliness had long since inexorably passed.[12] The arduous way that leads through self-knowledge to humility is harsh, like the journey of Gawain from Logres to the Wirral and beyond. Yet in the midst of the cold wilderness, Gawain found the castle, mercifully warm; and the grim monster proved to be one with the ever merry host. If the glow of life within the gracious castle made temptation the more insidious, this was but a reminder that man must not presume upon divine mercy, that his experience of mercy must not relax his vigilance any more than the apparent severity of justice must occasion despair. If the "game" the Green Knight played with Gawain was gruesome, the cut of his blade was slight, and his reproof was even gentler:

> As perle bi þe quite pese is of prys more,
> So is Gawayn, in god fayth, bi oþer gay knyȝteȝ.
> Bot here yow lakked a lyttel, sir, & lewte yow wonted,
> Bot þat watȝ for no wylyde werke, ne wowyng nauþer;
> Bot for ȝe lufed your lyf, þe lasse I yow blame.   (2364–68)

> [As a pearl beside the white pea is more praiseworthy,
> so Gawain is, in good faith, beside the other gay knights.
> But here you fell short a little, Sir, and in loyalty you were wanting,
> but that was for no intrigue, nor wooing either;
> but because you loved your life, I blame you the less.]

[12] The common assumption that Morgan la Fay is motivated in *Sir Gawain and the Green Knight* by envy of Guinevere is gratuitous: it receives no support from the text itself. The poet explicitly states that the joint (and it should be noted, the successful) purpose of Bertilak and Morgan was by means of extreme horror to test and tame the pride ("hawtesse," "surquidre") of the Round Table and Guinevere (2444–63). The reference to death in line 2460 is nothing more than an instance of hyperbole.

Thus mercy blends with justice in a poet for whom, as for numberless other poets, time fleets through the round of seasons, but for whom, unlike them, this elegiac round begins and ends in the joy of Christmastide.[13] This poet was not a rigorist.[14] He did not moralize on Gawain's false confession. He did not inveigh against Gawain's secularism. Gawain had resisted the flesh, he

---

[13] Cf. also the historical alternation expressed in verses 18–19.

[14] In a recent attempt to achieve an intrinsically valid interpretation (D. E. Baughan, "The Role of Morgan Le Fay in *Sir Gawain and the Green Knight*," *ELH*, XVII [1950], 241 ff.), the poem has been explained as "an apotheosization of chastity." This conception is based ultimately upon an interpretation of lines 330–37 that appears questionable for the following reasons:

(1) This interpretation construes Arthur's brandishing not as a limbering up, but as an actual attempt by Arthur to strike the Green Knight. This interpretation seems implausible, for the poet states that while Arthur is thus brandishing the axe, the Green Knight strokes his beard detachedly and then draws down his garment to expose his neck. Thus both men are engaged only in preparation for the blow—the Green Knight baring his neck to give his opponent clear access, as he will later do for Gawain, Arthur limbering his arm and adjusting it to the unusually large axe, which he must employ effectively on the first blow since there will be no second. The expression "mayn dinteȝ" [great blows] (336) is merely a stylistic variation or, as a contemporary rhetorician would have termed it, a *dilatatio* of "sturnely stureȝ" [brandishes grimly] (331).

(2) In support of this interpretation, it is asserted further that Arthur is prevented from striking the Green Knight because Arthur is unchaste. This, like the prescience imputed to Morgan under this hypothesis, is a quite extrinsic assumption. The fault of Arthur signalized in this poem is pride and not at all unchastity. What impels Arthur to take upon his royal person the challenge of the adventurer is affronted pride. What precludes the king's execution of the challenge is royal decorum; cf. lines 348 ff.

It is mistaking the spirit of this poem to term it an "apotheosization" of anything whatsoever. Actually it is a humane and sympathetic presentation designed to reveal how human and imperfect is even a supposedly perfect knight such as the pentagonal Gawain.

Furthermore, sexual purity as it figures in this poem is operative only in a limited sense. It refers not to abstention from extramarital sexual activity, but simply and solely to abstention from infringement upon the marital bond. Even Morgan, who under this hypothesis is assumed by her magic to be contriving an apotheosis of chastity, has not herself been chaste; she had, as the poet states, long practiced "drwry" [love] with

had defied the devil, he had succumbed to the world, and he had come to know himself. His humility, which in the beginning had savored somewhat of polite self-deprecation (354–57), had now become pure and genuine. The endless knot had been superseded by the knot of green silk (2487). This was enough.

Merlin, from whom she had learned this very magic. Nor is Gawain chaste per se, as would be expected if the poem were actually an apotheosis of chastity; his chastity is prudential. *Sir Gawain and the Green Knight* should not be confused with *Cleanness*. Neither should it be forgotten that to the medieval mind the spiritual sin pride, not the corporal sin lust, was the greatest of the deadly sins.

4

GAWAIN'S SHIELD AND THE
QUEST FOR PERFECTION

Richard Hamilton Green

1

Sir Gawain and the Green Knight IS AN ARISTOCRATIC romance which embodies the chivalric ideals of the English ruling class in the mid-fourteenth century. It is a highly stylized projection of the image of that class, a marvelous world where the virtuous hero represents the noble ideal and his antagonists the forces which threaten its ascendancy. Social historians have shown that the chivalric tradition, in its outward forms and theoretical formulations at least, persisted long after its institutional vitality had been sapped by economic, political and social change. It remained a characteristic attitude of the upper classes toward public and private secular affairs, partly out of nostalgia for the supposed glory of an earlier age, partly as a means of protection against the threats to vested interests implicit in change, partly as the familiar embodiment of ethical ideals rooted in a more stable religious tradition. One of the most obvious and attractive features of our poem is the clarity with which elegance of courtly manners, magnificence of costume and entertainment, the professional skill of noble pursuits are presented. These are attractive in themselves, and they provided the appropriate literary environment in which the noble virtues which pertained to this conspicuously noble life could be examined and tested.

Reprinted, by permission of The Johns Hopkins Press, from *ELH*, XXIX (1962), 121–39.

These virtues of the secular estate: valor and fidelity in the service of one's temporal lord, justice in dealing with the strong and the weak, sobriety and courtesy in the conduct of personal life, piety in the service of God, belonged to, and derived their value and ultimate sanctions from, the medieval doctrine of Christian perfection both institutional and individual. The chivalric ideal, however modified and tarnished by practice and human imperfection, was the imitation of Christ, the effort to realize in the individual and in society the perfection to which human nature aided by grace could aspire. The dominant image which bound the ideals of chivalric and Christian perfection was the image of the Christian knight, champion of the Church militant on earth, committed to the pursuit of personal virtue and the preservation of the divinely sanctioned social order. Add to this the image of life in the world as a *passage moralisé* [moral journey] in which perfection is an ideal to be sought, but achieved only in another world beyond challenge and frustration, and we have the moral world of the poem.

In this general way, *Sir Gawain and the Green Knight* is a romance which fits our customary expectations: an ideal society in a marvelous world where the virtuous hero represents the temporal and spiritual ideal, flattering and encouraging those whose model he is meant to be. That the English upper classes should feel themselves involved in Gawain's character and fortunes was a consequence of the medieval view of history. He was Arthur's knight, and Arthur was England's greatest king. The writer of romance, like the writer of chronicle, recorded the legendary events of a past which was seen as a continuing process of fulfillment; both poet and historian dealt imaginatively with tradition because both were primarily concerned with instruction, with providentially given models to be emulated or shunned. But romance is a complex genre and the *Gawain* poem is no run-of-the-mill example of its kind. It is the most skillfully made of the English romances, and the most complex in intention, exhibiting a subtlety of presentation and density of implication which we have only begun to appreciate.[1] It is also late in the history of the genre, and, since it is alive and original in ways that most of its contemporary pieces are not, we should not be surprised if it shows some of the stresses of the period in which it was made.

Because Arthur and Gawain are figures of England's destiny, and provided patterns of individual conduct and its consequences, the aims of the poet are essentially serious; but I find that the poem reveals a sense of humor which mitigates the seriousness of its themes and adjusts the magnitude of its exemplary hero to the temper of an age which produced the satires of Chaucer and Langland. The burden of my essay will be to examine some of the implications of the poem's comic tone for its central concern with the ideal of secular perfection. This poet is more than propagandist and entertainer; he is the amiably ironic teacher and conscience of the court. His poem manifests approval of the noble life and a lively enjoyment of its elegance. But beneath the brilliant surfaces he finds a dark world of potential failure, and subtly, sometimes comically, he warns of powers of evil which may corrupt even the most virtuous men and institu-

---

[1] For a full account of the present state of *Gawain* studies, including a judicious evaluation of current interpretations, see Morton W. Bloomfield, *"Sir Gawain and the Green Knight:* An Appraisal," *PMLA,* LXXVI (1961), 7–19. Since Bloomfield's appraisal will undoubtedly be the point of departure for future studies of the *Gawain* poem, a clear statement of the main difference between his approach to the poem and mine may be helpful at the outset. Bloomfield agrees with George Kane (*Middle English Literature* [London, 1951], pp. 73–76) that the conduct of the hero is not the main concern of the poem: "What is the poet's first intention? Although I do not agree with Kane that it is the decorative and visual which the poet wishes to elevate I think he is making an important point—that the ethical side can be overvalued. I do not believe the poem was written fundamentally to present us with a good man who emerges somewhat stained or humbled from his encounter with the world of evil or of the supernatural. The humor, suspense, and tone of the poem belie the centrality of this interpretation" (p. 17). My own view is that these are precisely the qualities of the poem which modify, embody, and shape the poem's central moral concern.

tions. He presents Gawain as the norm against which his audience is asked to measure its own achievement, and he warns against the folly by which even the most exemplary can be corrupted; but his presentation is sympathetic, graceful, informed with a humor that turns in upon itself, because the poet belongs to the society he pictures and has his own stake in the doubtful possibilities of its continued success.

At the very beginning of the poem we encounter the frame of time within which England saw the greatness of its origins and destiny; but the greatness of the past is marred by reminders of failure. Britain's ancient glory is marked by its beginnings in Troy, by the heroic figure of Aeneas, and Brutus the founder of Britain; but Troy was burned to ashes, Aeneas the atheling, the truest on earth, was tainted with treason, and the history of Britain to the time of Arthur has been a succession of war and woe, of bliss and blunder. Arthur is presented as the noblest of British kings, ruling his fair folk in their first age, the most fortunate under heaven, possessing all the weal of the world. Everything is superlative, suggesting at once England's pride in its hero-king and the poet's awareness of an excessive self-confidence deflated by events in the popular history he knew and believed, a confidence that will or ought to be shaken by events within the narrower dimensions of his tale. In Arthur's court are gathered the most famous knights, the loveliest ladies, and in their midst was Guenivere, the *comlokest* [fairest] that man ever saw. Into this description of lively, beautiful and accomplished people, gathered at Christmas, the time of the First Coming, at the New Year, in their first age, the poet introduces a discordant note, not obtrusive but sufficient to remind his hearers of what they already knew about the legendary Arthur, his beautiful but vulnerable queen, and his Round Table. The great king is "sumquat childgered" [somewhat childish-mannered] and restless, stirred by his young blood and wild brain.[2]

[2] What ensues is no "chyldys game." See William Matthews, *The Tragedy of Arthur* (Berkeley and Los Angeles, 1960), pp. 161–63.

In the midst of the feast there occurs the ominous intrusion of a figure from another world who cannot be ignored, however much he offends against the social proprieties of the occasion. The Green Knight comes to test the great fame of the court and its knights, the "wisest and worthiest of the world's kind." He is as gracious as he is terrifying; his urbane self-confidence is in telling contrast to the nervous silence of the court. Arthur rises to the occasion, and so, of course, does Gawain; but even the king seems somewhat petulant, and his ungracious challenge to a fight earns the Green Knight's scorn for these beardless childer. As his figure suggests, and as events prove, the Green Knight is no adversary to be overcome by physical prowess. He belongs to the world of mystery, a mixture of benevolence and malevolence, an ambiguous figure of forces beyond man's full understanding and control—as ambiguous as all the agents of divine trial. He has come to test their reputation for wisdom and fortitude of a different sort, the natural and supernatural virtues of the Christian Knight.

The Green Man wants a Christmas game, a test of mortality, but when he describes its rules he is met again by silence and fear. Arthur had wanted a marvel before dinner, but he wanted a marvelous story or some hand-to-hand combat with predictable consequences however painful. He had asked for nothing so mysterious, so fatal as this. The Green Knight breaks the shocked silence with contempt: is this the famous court of Arthur? can the Round Table be overwhelmed by one man's words? He laughs in their faces. With a humility which, as events prove, reflects more social grace than any profounder kind, Gawain volunteers. With this action we move from the wider sphere of institutional virtue to the test of the individual knight, the representative of Arthur's court, of English chivalry and Christian soldiership.

With masterful economy the poet marks the passage of the ecclesiastical and solar year, a figure some critics have used to support ecclectic readings which make the poem somehow an

75

account of a vegetation myth.[3] But this procession of seasons, within the Christian context explicitly and pervasively established by the poet, much more clearly indicates the passage of time from the First Coming to the Second, from man's undertaking the journey of life to the judgment which is its inevitable conclusion. The arming of the knight about to undertake his quest occurs on the morning following the celebration of All Saints Day on November first, the last great feast of the liturgical year when the medieval church celebrated the final victory of all those who had achieved the perfection which the Church Militant on earth still sought. When the ceremonial arming is completed, Gawain attends Mass and offers his homage at the high altar. He then returns to the court, takes leave of the king and the lords and ladies who kiss him and commend him to Christ. He mounts, takes his helmet, and—climactically—is presented with his shield. With the poet I intend to pause over the shield and its pentangle, though "tary hit us schulde" [it should delay us], because, as the identification of the hero, it is of the utmost importance for an understanding of Gawain's character and actions.

The shield is literally a means of physical protection, its heraldic device a conventional means of identification. But both are symbols, and since the poet leaves no doubt of the importance of their figurative meanings, we may with profit explore both the commonplace associations he could take for granted and the particular meanings he takes pains to specify. This shield and

[3] The most influential reading based on vestiges of pagan myth and ritual is found in John Spiers, *"Sir Gawain and the Green Knight," Scrutiny,* XVI (1949), 270–300. Bloomfield puts succinctly the most serious objection to such criticism as it has so far been applied to this poem: *"Sir Gawain* is one of the few undoubtedly aristocratic poems of the English Middle Ages extant. It would be surprising if in this courtly and Christian atmosphere of a poem perhaps written entirely or partly in high style, we could find alive mythic and ritualistic elements" (p. 14). This does not, of course, suggest that Christian myth and ritual are not immediately and pervasively *alive* in the poem. Many details of the poet's figurative representation of Christian ideas need further historical and critical investigation.

its device constitute an iconographical instance of extraordinary importance in the late Middle Ages, unique in its combination of rarity, elaboration, and focal position in the work as a whole.

For the Middle Ages, the basic figurative meanings of armor, and especially helmet and shield, were found in Ephesians, chapter 6, a passage so fully glossed in St. Paul's text and so widely used in medieval literature that to pursue it beyond its specific reminders for the action here would be pointless. "Be strengthened in the Lord, in the might of his power. Put you on the armor of God, that you may be able to stand against the deceits of the devil." That is, put on the virtues of Christian soldiership to stand against the adversaries of the spirit: "for our wrestling is not against flesh and blood; but against the rulers of this world of darkness. Therefore take unto you the armor of God, that you may be able to resist in the evil day, and to stand in all things perfect. In all things take the shield of faith, wherewith you may be able to extinguish all the fiery darts of the most wicked one." An English contemporary, or near contemporary, of the Gawain poet, Robert Holkot, writes in his commentary on Wisdom:

"Our shield is our faith. In all dangers take up the shield of faith by which you can extinguish all the fiery weapons of the most evil one. In the history of Britain it is written that King Arthur had a picture of the glorious Virgin painted on the inside of his shield, and that whenever he was weary in battle he looked at it and recovered his hope and strength. So, too, if we wish to triumph in the warfare of this present life, we should bear on the shield of our faith the image of the Virgin with her Son; we should look at her and be confident in her, because from her we derive virtue and strength."[4]

The heraldic charge which appears on the outside of the shield literally identifies the knight who bears it, but it is also, as the poet elaborately makes clear, the symbolic means of identi-

[4] *M. Roberti Holkoth in librum Sapientiae praelectiones CCXIII* (Basel, 1586), lect. 36, p. 127. The "History of Britain" referred to by Holkot is probably that of pseudo-Nennius. This text was called to my attention by Professor R. E. Kaske whose generous learning is felt elsewhere in this essay.

fying his characteristic virtues and aspirations. And since nearly everything that happens in the poem is governed by the behavior of the hero, the device which defines his character is likely to be of pervasive significance for the entire action. The poet himself stresses the importance of the pentangle's symbolism when he explains its meaning and why it "apendeȝ to þat prynce noble" [belongs to that noble prince]. It is, he says, a sign that Solomon set in betokening of truth, by the symbolism that it has.

> Hit is a syngne þat Salamon set sumquyle (625)
> In bytoknyng of trawþe, bit tytle þat hit habbeȝ,
> For hit is a figure þat haldeȝ fyue poynteȝ,
> And vche lyne vmbelappeȝ and loukeȝ in oþer,
> And ayquere hit is endeleȝ; and Englych hit callen
> Oueral, as I here, þe endeles knot.
> Forþy hit acordeȝ to þis knyȝt and to his cler armeȝ,
> For ay faythful in fyue and sere fyue syþeȝ
> Gawan watȝ for gode knawen, and as golde pured,
> Voyded of vche vylany, wyth vertueȝ ennourned
>   in mote; (635)
>   Forþy þe pentangel nwe
>   He ber in schelde and cote,
>   As tulk of tale most trwe
>   And gentylest knyȝt of lote.

[It is a sign that Solomon set as a symbol
of truth once, by the description it has,
for it is a figure that holds five points,
and each line overlaps and locks in another,
and it is everywhere endless; and the English all over,
as I hear, call it the endless knot.
Therefore it befits this knight and his bright arms,
for ever faithful in five and in each five ways
was Gawain, known for goodness and pure as gold,
free of every villany, graced with virtues in castle;
      therefore the new pentangle
      he bore on shield and coat armour,
      as man of word most true
      and knight most gentle of speech.]

> Fryst he watȝ funden fautleȝ in his fyue wytteȝ, (640)
> And efte fayled neuer þe freke in his fyue fyngres,

And alle his afyaunce vpon folde watȝ in þe fyue woundeȝ
Þat Cryst kaȝt on þe croys, as þe crede telleȝ;
And quere-so-euer þys mon in melly watȝ stad,
His þro þoȝt watȝ in þat, þurȝ alle oþer þyngeȝ,
Þat alle his fersnes he feng at þe fyue joyeȝ
Þat þe hende heuen quene had of hir chylde;
At þis cause þe knyȝt comlyche hade
In þe more half of his schelde hir ymage depaynted,
Þat quen he blusched þerto his belde neuer payred.   (650)
Þe fyft fyue þat I finde þat þe frek vsed
Watȝ fraunchyse and felaȝschyp forbe al þyng,
His clannes and his cortaysye croked were neuer,
And pité, þat passeȝ alle poynteȝ, þyse pure fyue
Were harder happed on þat haþel þen on any oþer.[5]

[First he was found faultless in his five wits,
and secondly the man never failed in his five fingers,
and all his trust on earth was in the five wounds
that Christ received on the cross, as the Creed tells;
and wheresoever this man was in the midst of battle,
his steadfast thought was in this, beyond all other things,
that all his strength he derived from the five joys
that the gracious queen of heaven had of her child;
for this reason the knight had fittingly
on the larger half of his shield her image depicted,
so that when he glanced at it his courage never failed.
The fifth five that I find the man practiced
were generosity and fellow-love before all things,
his purity and courtesy never failed,
and compassion, that surpassed all points; these pure five
were fixed more firmly in that knight than in any other.]

Gawain was endowed with all the five fives in the perfect unity
of the endless figure by which they were represented—a wholly
virtuous knight, the best that his society had to offer. The poet's
exegesis is sufficiently enigmatic in itself, but in its narrative
context (apart from an undercurrent of suspicion which I shall
take up in a moment) it supports the idea that Sir Gawain is the
exemplar of Arthur's court, and so of all England; he is, or ought

---

[5] The text cited is that of J. R. R. Tolkien and E. V. Gordon (Oxford, 1925).

to be, the model of the secular, militant estate, the ideal of the ruling class, presented for the admiration and emulation of the contemporary audience.

The hero's claim to the perfection indicated by his charge can only be confirmed by the success of the quest which he is about to undertake. But Sir Gawain's most notable action in the course of his trial, the one which breaks the pattern of our easiest expectations, is a failure; the exemplar of chivalric virtue is false, treacherous, cowardly, recreant in that "lewté þat longeȝ to knyȝteȝ" [loyalty proper to knights] (2373–84). At this moment near the end of the poem, we should recall those earlier ominous signs of youthful pride which suggest, in however low a key, that Arthur's court and its hero are somewhat less perfect than the ideal to which they aspire. If we have not noticed them, it may be that we have found attractive those relatively minor signs of human weakness which establish the congenial brotherhood of the imperfect. As one recent critic has put it, speaking for many: Gawain is a likeable man, all the more human for his slight fault, a model for the very best human conduct in spite of that "slightest compromise," the deceit of accepting the magic girdle.[6] But our poet is not so complacent, and neither is his hero; the ideals of fourteenth-century England were neither as flexible nor as earth-bound as that. A feeling of

[6] Alan M. Markman, "The Meaning of *Sir Gawain and the Green Knight, PMLA,* LXXII (1957), 574–86. Markman's thesis is bluntly stated: "To come at it directly, I suggest that the primary purpose of the poem is to show what a splendid man Gawain is" (p. 575). Markman properly finds that ". . . human conduct is the heart of the poem . . ." and that Gawain represents ". . . the ideal feudal Christian knight . . ." (p. 576), but his reading of the poem is quite literal and his notions of the ideals of human conduct are much more modern than medieval. George J. Engelhardt, in "The Predicament of Gawain," *MLQ,* XVI (1955), 218–25, establishes the moral issue which is central to the poem's action and characterization by showing that, in spite of reputation and real virtue, the hero does succumb to the world's imperfection. My own interpretation may be regarded as an elaboration of Engelhardt's assessment of the poem's subject, and a substantial modification of his treatment of the poet's tone and historical meaning.

sympathy, like the note of subdued amusement, is in the poem, but neither indicates a lack of commitment to the heroic ideals which Gawain represents and to which noble men must aspire. To recognize the inevitability of partial failure, and to weigh it ironically against reputation and pretentions, is not to transform vice into virtue for the sake of the general comfort. It remained for later ages to reduce human aspirations to human size, and to exorcize guilt with the reassurances of statistical togetherness. We can only recover the moral world of a poem devoted to chivalric perfection by recalling what was meant *then* by perfection. The key to the evidence in the poem is found in the device inscribed on the shield of the hero.

2

Little that has so far been written of Gawain's pentangle has been shown to belong to the age in which the poem was made or to bear directly on the poet's use of the device.[7] The pentangle is as old as history and as ubiquitous as the gammadion, a situation which has given readers a false sense of confidence while obscuring the fact that the device is very rare in the Middle

---

[7] In addition to the brief and general notes supplied by editors and translators of the poem, see V. S. Hopper's discussion in connection with his general treatment of the number five. *Medieval Number Symbolism* (New York, 1938), pp. 123–25. Among those who have interpreted the pentangle in the terms established by the poem, Engelhardt comes nearest the poet's interpretation, but he finds it to be simply "the symbol of the complete man, whose integrity admits no imperfection" (pp. 218–19). His only documentation of the concept of the *eques pentagonalis* [knight of the pentangle] is a reference to Edgar de Bruyne on this variation of the medieval *homo quadratus* [morally complete man] in *Études d'esthétique médiévale*, II (Bruges, 1946), pp. 348–50; but de Bruyne finds no pentangles from Vitruvius to Leonardo da Vinci. We might call attention to the pentangles, used as aids to drawing in the tradition which extends from Vitruvius to the late Renaissance, found in the sketchbook of Villard de Honnecourt (1225–50). See Theodore Bowie, *The Sketchbook of Villard de Honnecourt* (Bloomington, 1959), plates 35, 36, 37, 39. However, Erwin Panofsky observes that, in spite of medieval concern for "the God-ordained correspondence between the universe and man," medieval theories of proportions had degenerated into a code of practical

Ages. We have been told that it has been found scratched on Babylonian pottery, that it is a sign of the Pythagoreans' perfect number, that it is an alternate to one of the suits in the Tarot pack, that it is used in Freemasonry and in Jewish iconography on account of its associations with Solomon, and we are reminded that as the *drudenfusz* [pentagram] it appears in *Faust* and elsewhere in German. But all this is early and late, or almost wholly undocumented, and while some of it may have a remote, or psychologically profound, bearing on our poem, I should like to explore some possibilities which are nearer the explicit and implicit interests of a skillful and well-informed court poet of the second half of the fourteenth century.

First, the pentangle, or pentalpha, or pentagram, is called a sign set by Solomon as a token of truth. The poet could hardly have chosen a more ambiguous patron for Gawain's virtue. For Solomon is a figure of perfection; there was no man like him and his reputation reached the corners of the world (III Kings 4:29–34). He was for the Middle Ages a figure of Christ, the exemplar of wisdom and kingship, of power over demons. But in the Bible, and everywhere in the exegetical tradition, he is a gravely flawed figure, remarkably wise, but in the end guilty of follies that cost him his kingdom; and though he had power over demons, he was ultimately their victim, for his weakness for women turned him away from God and he built temples to the

---

rules which had lost all connection with harmonistic cosmology. "The History of the Theory of Human Proportions as a Reflection of the History of Styles," *Meaning in the Visual Arts* (Garden City, N.Y., 1955), pp. 83–91. In my opinion, philosophical uses of the analogies between geometrical figures and natural relations (e.g. Dante's comparison of the pentagon and the soul: see below, pp. 84–85) are related more closely to the *Gawain* poet's use of the pentangle.

Robert Ackerman, in a recent article on Gawain's shield (*Anglia*, LXXVI [1958], 254–65), attempts to associate Gawain's five fives with the sacrament of Penance and the vernacular penitential literature of medieval England. He fully documents the conventional use of the sins of the five senses as categories for the examination of conscience, but his efforts to show a similar connection for the other pentads are unconvincing.

powers of darkness (III Kings 11:1–9). In the late Middle Ages theologians debated whether or not he was saved.[8] Gawain himself, late in the poem after he has acknowledged his failure, associates himself with Solomon's weakness when he comforts himself that others had been driven to folly and sorrow by the wiles of women: Adam, Sampson, David, and Solomon (2414–28).[9]

If Solomon is a dubious figure, so is his pentangle. It is not found in the Bible, not even in the elaborate decoration of his temple, though we do find there significant fives and even a pentagon. Nor is it associated with him in medieval art and literature apart from this poem, with a single exception. It is found in the books of magic associated with his name which were known and occasionally described as idolatrous books of necromancy.[10] Hugh of Saint Cher and others do comment favorably

[8] Henri de Lubac, *Exégèse médiévale*, I (1959), pp. 285–90.

[9] Chaucer's Parson attests the conventionality of this ancient pattern of human imperfection: "Ful ofte tyme I rede that no man truste in his owene perfeccioun, but he be stronger than Sampsoun, and hoolier than David, and wiser than Salomon," *The Parson's Tale*, I. 955. The Venerable Bede, in his commentary on Proverbs 7.26, has much the same catalogue of strong men who were deceived by women: *Et fortissimi quique interfecti sunt ab ea.* Ut ipse Salomon sapientissimus virorum, ut Sampson fortissimus, ut David mansuetissimus a mulierum decipula, ut Origenes ab haeretica doctrina, quem post apostolos Ecclesiae magistrum fuisse, quandiu recte sapuit, qui negaverit, errat [*And many of the strongest were slain by her.* Such as Solomon, himself, the wisest of men, and Sampson the strongest, and David the mildest, all went astray through the snares of women, just as Origen went wrong by heretical teaching, who, though it has been denied, was the teacher of the Church, next to the Apostles, as long as he knew rightly], *Super Parabolas Salamonis Allegorica Expositio*, I, vii (PL 91, col. 964).

[10] Lynn Thorndike gives abundant evidence for the association of Solomon and magic in the late Middle Ages. Among writers of the thirteenth century, he cites William of Auvergne, bishop of Paris, who declares that there is no divinity in the angles of Solomon's pentagon, and that the rings and seals of Solomon are a form of idolatry and involve execrable consecrations and detestable invocations and images. *De legibus*, ch. 27. Albertus Magnus (in *Speculum astronomiae*, ch. 2) lists five treatises current under the name of Solomon as evil books of necromantic images. *A History of Magic and Experimental Science*, II (New York, 1923), esp. p. 280. C. C. McCown, in his edition of the Greek text of *The Testament of Solomon* (Leipzig, 1922), says that

on certain figures of Solomon, inscribed on gems, which had the power of casting out demons, but I have not found these specified as pentangles.[11] The crucial fact is, however, that in the poem the pentangle is not a magic charm with inherent power; it is a sign or token of inner virtue. The test is of virtue, not of magical power; in this romance enchantment belongs to the poet's finely controlled mode, not his subject. Here, with exquisite irony that serves his thematic purposes, the poet transforms a suspect magical sign into an emblem of perfection to achieve the simultaneous suggestion of greatness and potential failure. These suggestions are strengthened if we turn to the significance of five, and the pentagon, as figures of human perfection.

The pentagon appears in Dante's discussion of human excellence in the *Convivio*, where he uses the pentagon to illustrate

---

books of magic attributed to Solomon flourished in the Middle Ages, and that the most popular was the *Clavicula Salomonis,* in which there are many "pentacles," or magical drawings (p. 100). Against these books, he cites a steady line of condemnation. The only text of the *Clavicula* I have been able to see (S. L. MacGregor Mathers, *The Key of Solomon the King* [London, 1889], in the Houdini Collection of the Library of Congress) is edited from seven MSS, the oldest being no earlier than the end of the sixteenth century. McCown's edition of the Greek *Testament* is based on Harleian MS 5596, among others, written in the fifteenth century. In a late recension of the *Testament* the seal engraved on Solomon's ring is a pentagram, a type identified by McCown as belonging to the western tradition of the ring (p. 86). In summary, such evidence as I have seen indicates that, in the late Middle Ages in the West, the pentangle was associated with Solomon, and both with magic, in a popular tradition which was condemned by the Church. The *Gawain* poet's adaptation of the pentangle seems to be wholly original.

[11] "Excogitavit etiam characteres quosdam, qui inscribebantur gemmis, quae antepositae maribus arrepitii cum radice quadam Salomoni monstrata, statim illum a daemonibus liberabant. Haec scientia plurimum valuit antiquitus in gente Hebraeorum; ante adventum Christi saepius homines a daemonibus vexabantur" [For he devised certain characters which, set before possessed men with a certain root shown to Solomon, immediately freed them from demons. In antiquity this knowledge was of great importance to the Hebrews; before the coming of Christ men were often vexed by demons], Hugo de Sancto Charo, *Opera* (Venice, 1703), ad II Regum iv. f. 266r. Note Hugh's caution with respect to this "scientia."

man's natural perfection.[12] Just as the pentagon is one, but includes potentially the figures which are contained in it, so the human soul, which is one and rational, includes potentially the four lower kinds of vital activity which belong to lesser living things. If the fifth, specifying power of the rational soul be removed or subdued by the lower power of the sensual appetites, we are left with a brute animal, a dead man. Dante takes his doctrine, and his figures, from Aristotle's *De anima*, and he finds his specifically medieval elaborations of it in the scholastic commentators, notably St. Thomas.[13] But note that the pentagon symbolizes *natural* perfection as the philosopher knew it, not supernatural perfection to which man, by reason of the fall and the grace of redemption, was called. A pentagon in the Biblical tradition associated with Solomon has a similar significance. The doors to the Holy of Holies, the doors to eternal life, are hinged on pentagonal posts five cubits high (III Kings 6:31–32). Bede's comment, repeated in the *Glossa Ordinaria* and therefore standard throughout the late Middle Ages, explains that the pentagonal posts signify the body with its five senses which is destined to be admitted to heaven, and the five cubits signify that this destiny can be achieved only by those who serve God with the five senses of the body and the five senses of the heart.[14]

The number five as symbol is limited in the same way as the

---

[12] *Il Convivio*, ed. G. Busnelli and G. Vandelli, 2nd ed. (Florence, 1954), IV, vii, vol. II, pp. 79–80. Cf. Enrico Proto, *L'Apocalissi nella Divina Commedia* (Naples, 1915), pp. 186–87.

[13] Aristotle, *De anima*, II, iii, 279–98 (414ᵃ 28—414ᵇ 31); and St. Thomas, *Comm. in Aristotelis lib. de anima*, Lect. 5, 279–98. *Aristotle's De Anima in the Version of William of Moerbeke and the Commentary of St. Thomas Aquinas,* trans. Kenelm Foster, O. P., and Silvester Humphries, O. P. (New Haven, 1951), pp. 196–203.

[14] *De Templo Salomonis* Lib. XV (PL 91, col. 770). Of the five senses of the body and those of the heart Bede writes: "corporis videlicet cum per eosdem sensus aliquid pro illo [Domino] agunt; cordis vero, cum sobrie, et iuste, et pie cogitant de iis quae per ipsos corporis sensus agere decernunt" [Of the body, since through those same senses they do something for God; of the heart, since soberly, justly, and piously they think about that which they decide to do through the senses of the body].

pentagon.[15] In Macrobius and Martianus Capella, and generally in the Fathers and later commentators, pentads of almost any sort stand for the senses, and, by extension, for the body and the sensual appetites. The five senses are limited inasmuch as they need the government of reason, just as the pentagonal soul is limited by its dependence on grace. In Durandus' great work on the liturgy, ritual fives are also found to signify the five wounds of Christ, the five kinds of mercy necessary for salvation, and perhaps most significantly, the secular estate as opposed to the spiritual estate whose number is four.[16]

These traditional views fit well enough the poet's enigmatic explanation of Gawain's five fives. To be found faultless in his five wits is to have achieved, at least by reputation and aspiration, natural control over the senses, interior as well as exterior. Not to fail in his five fingers is a darker, but nonetheless conventional attribute which, so far as I know, has not so far been

[15] For general discussions of the number five, see Hopper, *Medieval Number Symbolism*, pp. 120 ff., Proto, *L'Apocalissi*, pp. 181–89, and R. E. Kaske, "Dante's 'DXV' and 'Veltro,' " *Traditio*, 1961, pp. 197–98.

[16] *Rationale divinorum officiorum* (Lyons, 1568). For ritual fives signifying the senses and the five wounds of Christ see I, vii, 35r, and other "cruces quinque" in index; for his elaborate explanation of the number five as the number of the secular estate as opposed to four, the number of the spiritual estate, based on the historic difference in the number of weeks of Advent, see VI, ii, 255: "Seculares, qui rebus transitoriis student, quae quinque corporis sensibus administrantur, per quinque hebdomadas intelliguntur, iuxta illud Evangelii Joani: *Erant viri quasi quinque millia.* Siquidem quinque millia viri, Deum secuti, designant eos, qui in seculari adhuc habitu positi, exterioribus, quae posident, bene uti noverant: ipsi namque saturantur quinque panibus, quia legalia instituta eis proponenda sunt, qui per quinarium numerum propter quinque libros Mosi intelliguntur" [Men of the world, concerned with transitory things which are managed by the five senses of the body, are meant by the five weeks, according to the gospel of John: *There were almost five thousand men.* For the five thousand men who followed God designate those who, while still in this worldly condition, knew how to use well the exterior things they possess: they are abundantly filled with five loaves of bread because legal institutions must be established for those who, on account of the five books of Moses, are meant by the number five].

satisfactorily explained.[17] Perfection in the five fingers was, in the Middle Ages, a conventional figure for the five virtues which, in the words of John of San Geminiano, "are necessary for man in order that his works should be perfect." The thumb stands for justice because—as Aristotle and Avicenna had said—justice works with the other virtues and is equal to them in strength, just as the thumb works with, and is equal to, the other fingers. The index finger signifies prudence, the third finger temperance, the ring finger fortitude, and the *digitus auricularis* figures obedience with respect to the divine will, to human authority, and to one's own reason.[18] This interpretation points to the natural virtues, and therefore to natural perfection, and thus it fits the pattern of the number five, the figure of the pentagon, and the domain of the five senses. With the five wounds of Christ and the five joys of Mary we move from the signs of natural perfection to figures of the theological virtues of faith and hope.

For the five wounds there is a pentangle in the Renaissance which was probably known in the fourteenth century. In Valer-

---

[17] Ackerman finds Gawain's integrity in his five fingers a natural development of his lack of fault in his five wits; the poet "resorted to the established tradition of allegorizing the five fingers, just as did Chaucer and Langland" ("Penitential Doctrine," p. 263). Earlier, Ackerman had argued that Chaucer's Parson "twice develops allegories on the five fingers . . ." (p. 261). In the passages in question, the five kinds of gluttony are said to be the fingers of the devil's hand by which he draws folk to sin (825–30), and the five steps of luxury are the devil's other hand (850–55); neither figure strikes me as being close to this sign of Gawain's perfection. The Langland figure (C. XX, 109–167) is even more remote: in it the Trinity is elaborately compared to the unity and interdependence of fist, palm and fingers in the human hand.

[18] Joannes de Sancto Geminiano, *Summa de exemplis et rerum similitudinibus* (Antwerp, 1630), VI, xlviii, 326–27: "Est enim manus quinque digitis munita in quibus quinque virtutes designantur, quae necessariae sunt homini ut opera eius sint perfecta" [For the hand is furnished with five fingers in which are designated the five virtues necessary to man in order that his works may be perfect]. In addition to assigning a major virtue to each of the five fingers, Joannes goes on to elucidate three aspects of each virtue as represented by the three bones of each finger. Cf. *De bestiis et aliis rebus*, III, lx (PL 177, col. 124–25), formerly attributed to Hugh of Saint Victor.

iano, Carteri, a Lapide and others the pentangle appears as a symbol of ὑγιεία, or *salus* [health], in ancient times a charm against illness or bodily injury, but in Christian times a figure of salvation because it is a figure of the five wounds of Christ.[19] Valeriano illustrates the figure with a nude Christ, arms and legs moderately extended with the wounds in hands, feet and breast connected by lines to make a pentangle. Says Cornelius a Lapide: "this pentalpha is God, who is alpha and omega; and Christus Salvator; whence Valeriano justly adapts the figure to the five wounds of Christ." And Valeriano: "But since these stories of the preternatural power and symbolic meaning of the pentagram in antiquity may not seem sufficiently agreeable, I have decided to pass over many stories of this sort, especially since it ill becomes men given to serious things to occupy themselves with such worthless legends. But I certainly cannot pass over the fact that we can accept as signifying true "salvation" (*verae salutis*) the five wounds of Christ . . . which appropriately constitute a pentalpha."[20]

3

In summary, then, the device on Sir Gawain's shield indicates the moral perfection to which the knight as *miles Christi* [soldier of Christ] aspires. The heraldic charge signifies the character of the hero about to undertake the "anious viage" [noxious journey] which will test his right to the device as it will test the right of the court he represents to its reputation for perfection. But, as we have seen, the sign that Solomon set as a token of truth is fraught with suggestions of human weakness in the face of the powers of darkness; the hero will do well to keep his gaze fixed on the image of spiritual perfection, the "hende heuen quene" [gracious queen of heaven], painted on the inside of his shield.

[19] Piero Valeriano, *Hieroglyphica* (Basel, 1556), pp. 351–52; V. Cartari, *Le Imagini dei Dei de gli Antichi* (Venice, 1587), p. 69; Cornelius a Lapide, *Commentarius in Apoc.* (Lyons, 1732), ad I. 8, p. 18.
[20] *Hieroglyph.*, p. 351.

Alone, with no companion but God, he undertakes his journey. He is an alien, far from friends, and surrounded by enemies. Against such obvious adversaries as dragons and trolls his valor and piety are sufficient. The real test comes in the familiar social environment of Bercilak's castle where, divested of armor and shield, warm and well fed and admired, he must struggle against the dark powers within himself, aroused and concealed by the softening influences of society. On the final day of his journey, Gawain is keenly aware of the liturgical season. It is the solemn vigil of Christmas, a day of penance and expectation. Still wandering in the wilderness he prays to the Virgin to hear Mass on the great feast, and he cries for his sins.

But after a gracious and admiring welcome at the castle, when he is comfortably settled before the fire in the great hall, Gawain forgets both the perils of the journey and the implications of the season—not to speak of the doom he must face on the octave day. The vigil of Christmas was a day of fast and abstinence, but Gawain is served a fish dinner fit for a gourmet with an insatiable medieval appetite. With amused irony the poet records Gawain's graceful compliments on the feast, and the protests of the waiters: this is a penitential dinner; wait until you see what we have tomorrow. The poet also notes that the hero seemed to have a better and better time as the wine went to his head. After dinner, the lord of the castle, his ladies, and his honored guest go to the chapel for solemn Vespers, and, while I should not want to take too solemn a view of this episode, what goes on in the chapel between the well-fed hero and his host's beautiful wife suggests devotion to something other than the liturgy. Under other circumstances, the lady's bare breast and bright throat might claim even the perfect knight's attentive concern— but not in the chapel. There is laughter in the poet's voice as he contrasts the broad buttocks of the ugly older matron with the beauty of the young wife: she was a "more likkerwys on to lyk" [sweeter one to like] (966–69).

The courteous flirtation continues next day, the day, as the poet remarks, that "dryȝtyn for oure destyné to deȝe watȝ borne" [God for our destiny was born to die]. The tone of the poem at this point surely does not suggest the stern moralist's condemnation, but neither is it a simple celebration of noble manners. It is designed to suggest some softening in the moral fiber of a hero distracted from a quest which will try his virtue to the utmost. It would be gauche of the poet, and so of the critic, to spoil this party, but in the context of the total action it is not amiss to remind ourselves that Gawain is falling somewhat short of the perfection of his five wits and fingers, not to speak of the five wounds, especially since it is just such genteel compromises with heroic and single-minded virtue which will result in his fall within the week.

Nor is the virtue displayed by Gawain in the bedroom as impressive as it has been taken to be by most modern readers. These scenes are high-style parody of a discredited literary convention in striking contrast to the simplicity and coarseness of the analogous scenes in *The Carl of Carlyle*. Here again the note of amusement invests the action and dialogue. Everything is excessive and mildly ridiculous: the great Gawain lies in bed far into the morning while his host is out in the forest engaged in the chivalric exercise of hunting. His wife, a gentle lady, is engaged in a hunt of her own, and with all the *courtesie* of a sophisticated trollop. "Here you are . . . and we are alone," she says, as she sits on his bed. "My husband and his men have gone for the day . . . the door is locked. Since I have in my house the man whom the whole world praises, I shall spend my time well, while it lasts. You are welcome to my body, to use it for your pleasure." If this falls somewhat short of *gentilesse* [high breeding] Gawain's reply is mildly ridiculous enough to complete the parody of *amour courtois* [courtly love]: "In faith, that would indeed be a favor, but I am unworthy to reach for such reverence as you suggest" (1230–44). To read these scenes as though they were a solemn exercise of Gawain's chastity, or a demonstration of his skill as a courtier who will not, whatever the provocation, offend a lady, is to mistake game for earnest. This is a gentle mockery of manners mistaken for morals, and further evidence that Gawain is in fact more vulnerable than he knows.

The poet's handling of Gawain's religious conscience is more subtle, and equally amusing. When, after the third grueling morning of temptation in the bedroom, he accepts the magic girdle because he thinks it can preserve him from death, he breaks his faith as a knight to his host, to his fearful antagonist, and most of all to himself. The pentangle is shattered and in its place taken by a new sign, now indeed a magic charm—or so he hopes—which he will later call "a token of untruth," the analogue of the foul skin of the fox in the parallel symbolism of the hunt. At once the hero wants to go to confession, and in the scene which follows the poet adds to his pervasive comic irony an extraordinary revelation of medieval psychology. This is no ordinary confession; it is the last chance for a doomed man. Gawain confesses "the more and the mynne," his great and small sins, and he is said to be shriven so clean that Judgement Day should come in the morning—as, of course, it will. But he has repressed the only serious sin of which we can imagine him guilty; and, if it does not seem serious to us, it will to him when he has to face it at the Green Chapel, and that is sufficient to make it so. But face to face with his confessor in the castle he cannot acknowledge it, even to himself, for to do so would be to lose the protection he thinks it offers. To suppose, as a recent interpreter of the confessional scenes does, that Gawain makes an invalid confession, and faces the perilous confrontation at the Green Chapel in bad conscience, is to think worse of the hero than the poem as a whole permits.[21] There are moral issues which the rational mind will not face, or face dispassionately, when survival seems to be at stake and when so many mitigating circumstances can be invoked to cloud the issue.

The irony of muddled conscience is sustained through the New Year's journey to the green mound and to the end of the quest. When his guide suggests flight, Gawain gallantly refuses, because, he says, "Ful wel con dryȝtyn schape / His seruanteȝ

[21] John Burrow, "The Two Confessional Scenes in *Sir Gawain and the Green Knight*," MP, LVII (1959–60), 73–79.

for to saue" [God can very well contrive to save his servants] (2138–39). And later, "To Goddeʒ wylle I am ful bayn. And to hym I haf me tone" [To God's will I am fully obedient, and to him I have committed myself] (2158–59). Does his hand stray unconsciously to the supposedly magic girdle; and do we, who know of its existence, smile sympathetically at this exemplary Christian knight who hedges his bets against impending doom? Only when he is confronted directly with the evidence of his *untruth* does Gawain acknowledge the flaw in his virtue. And, as essentially good men will, especially those who tend to over-confidence in virtue, he is overwhelmed by shame and greatly exaggerates the degree of his failure. He accuses himself of cowardice, treachery, and untruth—and, significantly, of disgrace to his class, recreancy in the "larges and lewte that longeʒ to knyʒtes" [generosity and loyalty proper to knights] (2374–88).

But the Green Knight will not condemn him, nor will the poet, nor will the reader. Sir Gawain is one of the best who ever walked, but here he lacked a little in fidelity to that perfection to which he aspired, and for which he stood. In this self-discovery the hero made a beginning in the necessary virtue of humility. Will Arthur's court profit by the lesson? The poem suggests that it probably will not. The knight who went out to vindicate the honor of the court bore on his shield the sign that Solomon set as a token of truth; he returned with new knowledge of his limitations, carrying the girdle about his neck as a token of untruth. But the lords and ladies of the court, still somewhat *childgered* [childish-mannered] and given to pride, laughed loudly and decided amiably that the knights of the Round Table would wear the green lace in honor of Gawain. Will the four-teenth-century courtiers profit by the lesson? They will at least have been reminded of the ideal to which they were called, and of the weakness which afflicts even the best. But the poem has not demanded tears or terror. Amid the relieved laughter of the knights and ladies one sees the wry smile of the amiable poet: it is enough if some of the laughter is directed at themselves.

THE IMAGERY AND DICTION OF *THE PEARL:* TOWARD AN INTERPRETATION

Wendell Stacy Johnson

1

SINCE ITS FIRST PUBLICATION IN 1864 THE FOURTEENTH-CEN-tury poem *The Pearl* has been the subject of considerable research, theorizing, and dispute: problems of textual emendation, of origin, sources, and above all of symbolic interpretation have engaged and sometimes vexed scholars for these many years, not always with clearly positive results. A record of such engagements and vexations is given by René Wellek in his study of the poem, and Professor Wellek concludes:

All these debates, we feel, about dialect, authorship, elegy versus allegory, theology, symbolism, etc., though they have been almost the only occupation of scholarship, say very little about the Pearl as a work of art. We may grant that a rigid conception of the poem has cleared the way for an artistic appreciation, but the actual study of the artistic value of the poem is still in its beginnings.[1]

The difficulty of this, we are tempted to reply, is that there is in fact no "rigid conception" yet, as Professor Wellek's own survey of scholarship indicates. But the intention of these remarks is certainly a good one, and it may be that they do point in the

Reprinted, by permission of The Johns Hopkins Press, from *ELH,* XX (1953), 161–80.

[1] "The Pearl: An Interpretation of the Middle English Poem," in *Studies in English* (Prague, Charles University, 1933), IV, 28.

right direction. For it proves almost impossible to investigate the artistic value of the poem without turning back to the subject of meaning. What, after all, is the poetic art other than meaning— pure sound or visual "decoration" or an inconceivable manner without matter? And the very investigation of what might be called "artistic" elements in the poem leads, perhaps on a new and better path, to the central problem of symbolism and sense, the problem of interpretation.

Interpretations previously made can be summed up briefly. Such early scholars as Sir Israel Gollancz, Carleton Brown and C. G. Osgood agree in seeing the poem as primarily, if not entirely, elegiac, but this idea is attacked by W. H. Schofield, who, in two articles, insists upon its allegorical nature.[2] The Schofield position is maintained by most subsequent writers on the subject, and the fantastic and wholly unwarranted biographies of the poet built up by Gollancz and others to explain his relationship with the Pearl-maiden are repudiated at the same time that new and sometimes equally unwarranted readings of the allegory are evolved and published. W. H. Garrett takes the poem to be an allegorical representation of the Eucharist;[3] Jefferson B. Fletcher sees the pearl as a symbol of innocence and of the Virgin Mary, but considers it possible for the poem to be at once an allegory and an elegy;[4] and according to Sister Mary Madeleva the pearl is the poet's own soul, and the poet is a mystic writing his own spiritual autobiography.[5] There are other points of view: W. K. Greene believes that the parable of the vineyard workers represents the poet's major theme and that the pearl-maiden is simply a poetic device.[6] René Wellek suggests

[2] See I. Gollancz. ed. (London, 1891); Carleton Brown, "The Author of the Pearl . . . ," *PMLA,* XIX (1904), 115–53; C. G. Osgood ed. (Boston, 1906); and W. H. Schofield, "The Nature and Fabric of the Pearl, " *PMLA,* XIX (1904), 154–215.

[3] *The Pearl: An Interpretation,* University of Washington Publications in English, IV, 1 (Seattle, 1918).

[4] *JEGP,* XX (1921), 1–21.

[5] *Pearl: A Study in Spiritual Dryness* (New York, Appleton, 1925).

[6] "The Pearl: A New Interpretation," *PMLA,* XL (1925), 814–27.

that the poem's symbolism is subtle and shifting, the pearl coming to represent not only a single pure maiden but the whole realm of heaven.[7] Not inconsistent with this, there is the moderate view expressed by J. P. Oakden, who holds that the poem is about a real child who gains heaven "by innocence through the rite of baptism," and that this innocence is the pearl of great price which she advises the poet to buy: as *Purity*, probably by the same author, has it, "through shrift and penance [the sinner] may become a pearl, [that is, he may] regain his former innocence."[8] Finally, a recent note by D. W. Robertson, Jr. discusses the symbolism of the pearl on four levels, taking it to represent both innocence and the kingdom of heaven.[9] These last three views seem most reasonable, if only on the grounds of the close reading of text which Professor Wellek urges.

This paper, while largely in agreement with the expressed views of Professors Wellek, Oakden, and Robertson, attempts to go further in the examination of specific details than their remarks do, and at the same time to avoid forcing the details into a too esoteric allegory. The result is an emphasis upon a ubiquitous sense of contrast between the nature of heaven and the nature of earth, the revelation of which seems, for our present reading, to be the poem's main purpose. This new emphasis— not a complete interpretation, but the basis for one—depends primarily upon internal evidence, upon a significant imagery and a closely related form and plot.

2

The plot situation of *The Pearl* is a perfectly familiar one, for the poem is basically a dream or vision allegory in the popular medieval tradition. We are introduced to our poet's subject in the

[7] In *Studies in English*, IV, 17–28.

[8] *Alliterative Poetry in Middle English: A Survey of the Traditions* (Manchester, Manchester University Press, 1935), p. 75.

[9] "The 'Heresy' of *The Pearl*," *MLN*, LXV (1950), 152–54. Robertson points out that the parable of the vineyard is not heretically misinterpreted; he defends the *Pearl* poet's consistent orthodoxy.

opening stanza, an apostrophe to the pearl which he has lost "in an *erbere*," in a garden;[10] and the next two stanzas elaborate on this obviously symbolic gem's virtues, as well as the poet's pain in his loss. Then the story begins: on a certain festal day in August, on the very spot where the pearl was lost, our narrator falls into a sleep as he is complaining of his bereavement. Quickly his spirit "sprang in space" (IV): and so we enter the second and central part of the poem. The poet wanders in a paradise of crystal and jewels, refreshed by the beauty of this magical realm in which he finds himself, until he comes to a stream, its banks paved with precious stones. It appears that even in paradise there is discontent, for the dreamer longs to cross over to the other side of the water, where the land is even more bright and fair. At this point his desire is only increased by the discovery of a maiden standing on the other side, a pure maiden all in white, crowned and decked with pearls, whom he identifies as his real pearl, the very subject of his plaint. Now at least one level of allegory is clarified, whether the pearly maiden is only a literal person or another symbol. The pearl recognizes the poet (as her "jeweler"), but she chides him for his sorrow: if he loved her, he would rejoice in her present state, although they are parted. She counsels him, if he wishes to join her in that place across the river, to wait patiently, with faith—which he avows, faith in Christ, Mary and John, now, rather than in the maiden, as "grounde of alle my blysse." The maiden expounds the blissfulness of her present state, calling herself bride of the Lamb, and Queen. At this the dreamer is surprised. Is not Mary the Queen of Heaven? Yes, replies the maiden, she is Queen of Courtesy; but there are many Queens here where all are noble. And if this seems strange, it is because the standards of eternity are not those of the temporal world: there is no quarrel between more or less in heaven. St. Matthew's story of the workmen in the vineyard illustrates this contrast between

[10] The text used is that of C. G. Osgood. Quotations from it are identified simply by line numbers in parentheses.

the judgments of heaven and those of earth, the difference between God's grace (manifest in the sacrifice of Christ) and man's justice. Jesus called the children, the pure and spotless, to him; and so this child-like maiden is one of his band of brides in the New Jerusalem. The new city is itself a pure and divinely perfect structure, and it contrasts with the old Jerusalem as God's eternal grace does with man's temporal standards, and as the pearl in her present state does with the mortal "rose" which she was (on earth). The dreamer is fascinated by all that he is told, and particularly by the idea of the new city, the abode of the Lamb, which he longs to see. He is allowed to gaze upon it briefly, then, from across the river; and he describes this Jerusalem in the imagery of St. John's Apocalypse, as a city of precious jewels, with a throng of virgins proceeding toward the throne of the Lamb Himself, the throne surrounded by Angels and Elders singing His praises. This ecstatic and genuinely moving descriptive passage, the climax of the vision, is broken off as the poet returns to the mound where he has fallen asleep. Then, still under the effect of his experience, he declares his fealty to the God "Þat, in þe forme of bred & wyn, / Þe preste vus scheweȝ vch a daye" [that, in the form of bread and wine, the priest shows us each day] (1209–10).

This synopsis suggests the three-fold division of the poem into a very brief introduction, in the garden (five stanzas); a major section, the vision (some eighteen times as long); and a (five stanza) conclusion. The consistent use of the same word to end five (in one case six) consecutive stanzas, along with the linking device of *concatenatio*, or the repetition, in each stanza's first line, of this last word from the preceding stanza, provides a tightly constructed form of twenty five-stanza groups.[11] The stanzas are unified, as well as distinguished, by this form, which is complementary to a three-fold division of the matter. In discussing the imagery and diction of *The Pearl* it will often be necessary to allude to both the work's formal structure and its

---

[11] See Osgood on stanza construction, in the introduction to his edition.

thematic structure, in an effort to show how all these elements unite to make a whole. For this is a poem whose nature is at least largely revealed by itself: it is not so much a *secret* allegory as a work of art in which art and meaning are one.

As the following paragraphs are intended to show, the imagery of the poem can in the main be divided into two groups: on the one hand, images out of the world of growing things, images of the garden and the vineyard which are associated with the dust of the earth; on the other, images of light and of brilliant, light-reflecting, gems, free of any spot (dust) and associated with whiteness and with emblems of royalty. These two groups are directly and explicitly opposed to each other, sometimes in the manner of an obvious symbolism and sometimes only in implied contrasts. In either case the opposition is significant both for the sake of meaning and for its aesthetic effect, which contributes to the meaning.

The first five stanzas, which constitute the first stanza group and the first "plot" division, in the *erbere,* deserves a good deal of attention because they introduce the work's basic imagery and because they offer certain significant verbal problems. We begin with the description of the pearl "plesaunte to prynces paye" [pleasant to a prince's pleasure] (this phrase will be echoed and will take on great importance at the end): it is small, round, smooth, and *reken*, noble or radiant. Here, as throughout the poem, there is conscious ambiguity, for ideas of both radiance and nobility are to be attached to the gem. The first eight lines of this opening stanza, describing the unique and precious object, are in dramatic contrast with the final four lines (the final four lines are indented, as in all stanzas, by Gollancz), which tell of the pearl's falling into the common earth. The speaker pines for the loss of "þat pryuy perle wythouten spot" [that dear pearl without spot]; and the idea of purity ("wythouten spot" = without blemish) is strikingly opposed to that of the pearl's being now in the (pearl-blemishing) ground. The possibility of an ambiguous reading, again, associates the gem's disappearance with its purity: "wythouten spot" could also mean without location or place. *Spot* in the rest of this stanza group has only this meaning. The phrase is an important one, since *spot* is the key word for this first part of the poem, occurring in the first and last line of the next four stanzas; further, it represents the major and recurrent theme of unearthly purity and brilliance. But it gives some difficulty: the poet, in III, speaks of *þat spot* where the gem was lost, where spices and brilliant flowers must bloom, "Þer such rycheȝ to rot is runne" [where such riches to rot has run] (26); and if one accepts the reading "wythouten spot" = without place, then it is paradoxical that the pearl's decay should enrich *this spot*. However, the paradox becomes a quite meaningful one for us if we consider that the poet's phrase is intended to signify what the poet *as a dramatic figure* could not know before the vision, and that the very opposition of these two ideas, the expressed one of the pearl's decay in the earth and the implied one of its being without worldly location, is a first aspect of the contrast upon which the poem's construction and meaning depend.

To elaborate upon the imagery of the first several stanzas: we have first the clear contrast of a perfect gem with the ground of a garden, the unique and individual with the common, the pure and shining with the literally earthly. The pearl's "color" is "clad in clot" [clad in clay]: "O moul, þou marreȝ a myry iuele" [Oh mould, you mar a fair jewel] (22–23); and so mould and clay stain the jewel's bright beauty. The products of this earth are, themselves, beautiful: in this harvest season ("Quen corne is coruen wyth crokeȝ kene" [When corn is cut with sharp sickles]—(40) the garden spot is covered with lovely flowers giving off a fair fragrance. Yet, even in the midst of this beauty, the poet is not comforted, but longs for the precious jewel he has lost. Earth at its best—an earth which that jewel's decay must, as the bereft man supposes, enrich—offers no loveliness to take the place of the pearl. The images of vegetable life—flowers and fruits and herbs, all growing things—pale beside the image of perfectly pure and simple sphere, the gem *wythouten spot*. For the symbols of life are also those of death: the garden mound is like a grave, the pearl's grave. "Vch gresse mot grow of grayneȝ dede" [Each plant of grass must grow from dead seeds] (31). And the minor fact that this is harvest season adds to a sense of the life-death cycle in this place.

So, using these images of unearthly purity and of earthly nature, the poet must imagine that his spotless gem is mortal, that it returns to the common earth, and he grieves for its destruction in spite of Christian teaching, "þaȝ kynde of Kryst me comfort kenned" [though *kynde* of Christ gave me comfort] (another ambiguity: *kynde* = both nature and kindness, or mercy). While faith points beyond, the poet's understanding, in this first part, is limited to the spot, to earth which is a grave. The rest of the poem is an extending of this vision (through *a* vision) toward its outer limits, to include and reconcile this world and another world.

Falling into a deep slumber, the poet remains on the flower-covered grave, but his spirit springs forth *from the spot* into space. The region where, by God's grace, he finds himself—"I ne wyste *in þis worlde* quere þat hit wace" I knew not *in this world* where it was]—is fantastically bright and gorgeous, a wonderland which is much more intriguing to all the senses than the beautiful *erbere* where he has been. The key word in the second stanza-group is *dubbement, splendor*, with the participial form meaning *arrayed*, and the imagery presents transfigured phenomena, the world arrayed in a strange glory: all is shining, shimmering, gleaming, glowing, flaming, bright; the colors have an incredible brilliance; and the very gravel on the ground is pearl. The effect which the poet describes is that of supremely intense light cast upon all natural objects, the basic image being one of *reflected* brilliance. The dreamer sees the *array*, the clothing of that very world he has left, the world of "Þe playn, þe plontteȝ, þe spyse, þe pereȝ / & raweȝ & randeȝ" [the field, the plants, the spices, the pear-trees, and hedgerows and banks]

(104–5), by supernal light. Compared with this, natural light is dim: "Þe sunnebemeȝ bot blo & blynde / In respecte of þat adubbement" [the sunbeams are dark and dim compared to that splendor] (84). At last, when the wandering dreamer approaches a river, the passage reaches a climax: "I wan to a water by schore þat schereȝ; / Lorde, dere watȝ hit adubbement!" [I made my way to a stream that divides two shores; Lord, rare was its splendor] (107–8). Certainly the river is extraordinary enough. It flows with a kind of music, and it is paved with glowing jewels. According to Howard Rollin Patch, this "river barrier suggests something of the Latin visions [of the other world], and the jewels in the stream and the fragrant fruit remind one of the Garden of Eden. . . ."[12] The land on this side of the river, that is, bears a considerable resemblance to the Earthly Paradise of the medieval accounts. And the stream as a barrier *and* a way to heaven is a familiar means of separating the Earthly and the Celestial lands. But, as both C. G. Osgood and Professor Patch point out, the *Pearl* poet's treatment of these motifs is not entirely a stock treatment; it is original in several details as well as in omissions of traditional accessories to the vision of paradise.[13] Water could properly be associated with the natural world, with its fertility and its cyclical nature; but this river, shining bright and paved with gems, is obviously allied, too, with the other images, those of spotless brilliance. The river of gems is a common part of the literary vision, but it fits significantly into the scheme of this uncommonly subtle poem.

On this side of the stream is a natural land of fruits and plants and hedgerows, of wonderful birds: a land in which nature is transformed by light, but in which the source of light does not appear. On the other side is the even more wonderful realm of light itself. The more he follows the stream, the more is the

[12] *The Other World* (Cambridge, Harvard University Press, 1950), p. 190.
[13] See Patch's chapter on Allegory, pp. 175–229.

dreamer's joy, and yet the more he longs to pass over to the other side. *More* is repeated until the word has an almost hypnotic effect in establishing the intensity of the desire. To live on this side of the water is to experience this ever-increasing desire to cross into greater beauty, greater brightness: the feeling is, in fact, the mystic's wish for union with the perfect, the desire to attain to a state of perfection. That highest state is conceived of aesthetically as pure light; psychologically as *royal*:

> I seȝ byȝonde þat myry mere
> A crystal clyffe ful relusaunt;
> Mony ryal ray con fro hit rere.   (158–60)

> [I saw beyond that beautiful stream
> a crystal cliff all gleaming;
> many royal rays did from it rise.]

In these, the grandest terms he can command, the poet describes the apparently perfect place.

Beneath these "royal rays" sits a bright maiden, like ivory and dressed in pure white, glowing as a light, and "as glysnande golde" [as glistening gold]. This maiden, whom the dreamer quickly recognizes, is explicitly identified as his pearl, and she is appropriately adorned with pearls. In the section which describes her, the fourth, *pyȝt* (adorned) is the key word; and the adornment is plainly significant. The ideas of whiteness, purity, and light are associated with her nature, as with the pearls. Now *perle* has taken on several senses: the appropriate decoration, the person, and the "wonder perle wythouten wemme / In myddeȝ her breste" [the wondrous pearl without flaw in the middle of her breast] (221–22), obviously a symbol, to be associated with all the lesser pearls and with the pearl-maiden. The poem has passed from the vision of nature arrayed in (reflecting) light to one of a land and a person set in gems and adorned by an "inner" brightness, of which gem and crown are radiant symbols.

When he speaks to her, the bereaved man repeats the theme of his opening lines: he has lost this very pearl, and is now a "joyle₃ juelere" [joyless jeweler]. The maiden replies that he is mistaken, and she proceeds to explain why. Here, in her contrast between the earth-flower and vision-jewel sets of images, we come to a crucial point in the poem's symbolism. The pearl calls this *cofer*, in which she now dwells, a "gardyn gracios gaye" [lovely, joyous garden] (260); and the symbolic contrast between earthly garden and (heavenly) jewel seems to break down with this fusion. But the similarity between *erbere* and *gardyn* is consciously utilized here. The emphasis is to be put upon *this* garden (as opposed to the first one in the poem) which is a *coffer*, and hardly garden-like in any literal sense: not an earthly flower—or fruit—garden but a place of gems (*cofer* = jewel case or strongbox) quite unlike the normal kind. It may seem to be forcing a point to declare for a mild irony in the word, but the descriptions of the land across the river, as well as the conjunction of *cofer* and *gardyn*, indicate at least that there is an important distinction to be made between the garden of flowers and the garden of jewels. The maiden's declaration that she was on earth *not* a pearl, but a perishable flower, only strengthens and clarifies the distinction. It is through the poet's imagination that the mortal maiden has seemed to be a gem: the true pearl could not, did not, decay; but the rose, part of the garden-grave world, did. What the poet commenced by imagining—the perfection of his loved one—comes, in the vision, to be true. And so we see that the *erbere* world is one where perfection is an appearance only, while this vision-land, according to the maiden, is the perfect gem's rightful home.

If the earth-heaven contrast is imagined here in the images of the flower and the pearl, it is also implied in the closely associated imagery of natural or reflected light and the brilliance of this land. Only through the nature of that *kyste* or coffer did the rose become more than a reflection of light—become a part of the realm of light, a pearl. Earth's flowering, through *kynde* (both the heavenly *nature* and *kindness*), is proved ("put in pref") a "perle of prys" [precious pearl] (272). (Again in the same stanza, *kynde* is used to mean both *grateful* or *loving* and *natural*: if you complain about your own pearl's being proved truly a pearl, says the maiden, then "Þou art no kynde jueler" [you are no *kynde* jeweler].) Thus the distinction between the *erbere* and the land of light and of brilliant gems is made explicit, with some implied transition from one to the other. Plainly, the antithesis is one between mundane and spiritual realms. The spiritual is infinitely brighter and better. And the jeweler who can rightly judge the nature and the value of a gem (as the poet has failed to do) will see this, not literally but by faith.

Further carrying out the contrast, the poem now makes clear a difference between the earthly body and the soul in that realm across the river:

> Þou wylneʒ ouer þys water to weue;
> Er moste þou ceuer to oþer counsayl;
> Þy corse in clot mot calder keue;
> For hit watʒ forgarte at paradys greue. (318–21)

> [You wish to come over this water;
> first you must attain another purpose;
> your body must sink colder in clay;
> for it was made corruptible in the garden of paradise.]

The significance of "this water" is intensified by its association with the water imagery of later sections. Now, however, the emphasis is upon the two lands, and the idea is extended in the seventh stanza grouping, where the key word is *blysse*, and the repeated phrase (in the last line of each stanza) *grounde of alle my blysse*. The earthly maiden (the pearl or rose) has been the ground of the poet's bliss; now her heavenly estate is this *ground*. So, as they can help him to be with her in this estate, are the mercy of Christ, of the Virgin, and of St. John. And, on a higher plane, she espouses "My Lorde þe [the] Lamb" as the unearthly "rote [root] & grounde of alle my blysse" (420). *Blysse* here suggests not only joy but also blessedness. The mortal and divine *grounds* represent the two realms, the one of *stok* and *ston* [stock and stone] in which man is "bot mol," only dust (and where joy's grounds are mortal), and the one in which the (transfigured) maiden, whose blessedness is grounded in Christ, can be made the Bride of the Lamb and be crowned a queen.

The pearl can be crowned because of divine *cortayse*, graciousness (or simply grace, theologically speaking), of which quality the blessed Virgin is the epitome. This is appropriate, this and the association of *cortayse* with the crown and symbols of royalty pertaining to the pearl, in view of the word's origin and connotation: it describes the virtue of the court, of royalty (here, in conferring royalty). And so the images of this (eighth) part are those of nobility and rank; an importance of all the body's parts in the unity of the body (Christ) makes each part noble. The psychological effect of the idea of royalty must be a great one for the mediaeval poet. Royalty is consistently associated with his images of light and jewelry, and we recall the natural association in the opening phrase "Perle plesaunte to Prynces paye" [Pearl pleasant to a Prince's pleasure], as we come to think of Christ as a Prince.

The image-structure thus far represents a progression toward the fuller understanding of this symbolic picture: the contrasting impressions of earth and of another place associated with jewelry, brightness, royalty. Now a new aspect of the contrast between these image groups is introduced with Matthew's parable of the vineyard workers. In this, the ninth group of stanzas, bodily labor is opposed to royal reward, and earthly time to divine timelessness. *Date* is used in the senses of *position, limit* ("Þer is no date of hys goodnesse" [there is no *date* of his goodness]—493), *season, goal, time*. In God's mercy there is no limit, time, or season (the rich ambiguity of the word here is exploited by the whole passage), while human judgment is based upon these earthly limits. In the vineyard, a place of vegetation comparable with the garden-grave, the sense of *more* is possible (the desire for more reward or for more bliss and beauty, as in the land just this side of the river), but in the divine sense the *more* is freely given: not limited by the standard of time, but demanded by the quality of mercy, which is infinite. So

> Queþersoeuer he dele nesch oþer harde,
> He laueȝ hys gyfteȝ as water of dyche,
> Oþer goteȝ of golf þat neuer charde.   (606–8)

> [Whether he metes out what is soft or hard,
> he pours his gifts as water from a dike,
> or streams from a source that never ceases to flow.]

God's mercy must always be enough.

Innoghe is the key word in the eleventh stanza-group. The water imagery, picturing divine grace as a never-exhausted fountain, is reinforced with the traditional symbols of the water and the blood: grace given in the form of baptism and of the saving sacrifice. Through baptism the maiden has attained grace:

> Innoghe of grace hatȝ innocent;
> As sone as þay arn borne, by lyne
> In þe water of baptem þay dyssente;
> Þen arne þay boroȝt into þe vyne.   (625–28)

> [Sufficient grace has the innocent;
> as soon as they are born, in a line
> they descend into the water of baptism;
> then they are brought into the vineyard.]

For

> Innoghe þer wax out of þat welle,
> Blod & water of brode wounde:
> Þe blod vus boȝt fro bale of helle,
> & delyuered vus of þe deth secounde;
> Þe water is baptem, þe soþe to telle,
> Þat folȝed þe glayue so grymly grounde,
> Þat wascheȝ away þe gylteȝ felle
> Þat Adam wyth inne deth vus drounde.   (649–56)

> [There flows enough from that well,
> blood and water from broad wounds:

the blood bought us from the torment of hell,
and delivered us from the second death;
the water is baptism, to tell the truth,
that followed the spear so cruelly ground,
that washes away the many guilts
with which Adam drowned us in death.]

When we consider the emphasis upon baptism in this passage, a possible symbolic importance of the water flowing before the crystal cliff comes to mind; the river may be associated with the baptismal water, and thus not only mark the boundary between the land of *reflected* light (the Earthly Paradise) and heaven, but also represent, in a sense, the means of passing even into the realm of light. This river, we see later, is apparently identified with the river of the water of life which flows from the Lamb's throne. And of course the water of life is represented by the water of baptism. Further, there is some precedent for this interpretation. While the river barrier between earth and heaven is a familiar motif in mediaeval and classical lore, the application of Hebrew symbolism to the Styx is neither rare nor surprising: for one example, in the *Pelerinage de Vie Humaine*, Guillaume de Guileville, using the dream framework, sees the very heavenly Jerusalem which our dreamer is to see, and on his way toward it he must be plunged into the "River of Baptism." [14] Finally, the water as a symbol for baptism is perfectly consistent with later details and with the whole sense of the poem, and, according to this reading, would be the appropriate passage from an earthly to a heavenly state.

By the means of grace—Christ's sacrifice and the subsequent salvation of the baptized—all is made right, and men are justi- fied. *Ryȝt* is used in both the sense of *privilege* and *justice* in the twelfth group: compare "þe innosent is ay saue by ryȝte" [the innocent is always saved by *ryȝt*] and "by innocens & not by ryȝt" [by innocence and not by *ryȝt*]. The state of perfection symbolized by the pearl of great price could be attained either

[14] Patch, p. 188.

by simple baptism of the child or by the virtue of the man who is faithful in confession and in receiving communion. The water and blood are closely associated, then, with baptism and eucharist. But *perfection* is a loose term as used here. Professor Oakden speaks of a sinner's regaining *innocence* when he calls attention to the significant first and second stanzas of the thirteenth group, where the maiden first says that no one can come to Christ who is not as morally spotless as a child, and then identifies her own child-like spotlessness—or innocence—as the biblical pearl of great price.[15] But neither word is entirely satisfactory, due to a shift in the symbolism in these stanzas. Because of this shift and because these are crucial lines for interpretation, the only lines which specifically provide meaning for the symbol of the pearl, we may as well look at them a little more carefully. The maiden reminds us that Jesus would have us child-like, "Harmleȝ, trwe, & vndefylde, / Wythouten mote oþer mascle of sulpande synne" [Harmless, true, and undefiled, without stain or spot of polluting sin] (724–25). To the person with these qualities (or negatives!) the gate of heaven is unbarred; and there, in heaven, is the *blys* [bliss] which the biblical jeweler sought when he sold all his goods to purchase a spotless pearl: for heaven is like that pearl,

> Wemleȝ, clene, & clere
> & endeleȝ rounde, & blyþe of mode,
> & commune to alle þat ryȝtwys were.   (737–39)

> [Flawless, clean, clear,
> endlessly round, serene of temper,
> and belonging equally to all who were righteous.]

And, the maiden continues, the Lamb set it, this pearl, in her breast. Depending on whether the antecedent of *hit* [it] (in lines 737, 740, and 742) is the symbolic pearl of great price or literally the realm of heaven—and it could be either—the large pearl is symbolically or actually heaven itself. So, when she bids

---

[15] Oakden, *Alliterative Poetry . . .* , p. 75.

the "jewler" to "porchase þy perle maskelles" [purchase your matchless pearl], the pearl maiden is telling him to buy heaven, the pearl of great price. If she has heaven set in her own breast, it is because a part of heaven is *heavenliness*.[16] Obviously, this purity, perfection, innocence, whatever else the quality can be called, is available to a grown man as well as to the baptized innocent, although it is equated, since the pearl herself seems to be a child, with the spotlessness of childhood. It is common to all who are *ryʒtwys*, righteous, or set right, including both the innocent, who are baptized, and shriven sinners. The pearl means, then, both heaven and the personal freedom from sin which is salvation and heaven within and which reflects the heavenly nature. Both child and adults are saved by *ryʒt,* one by *privilege* and the other by *righteousness*; and the two senses are included in *ryʒtwys,* so that the pearl of heavenliness belongs to both.

The objection that, from an earthly point of view, there must be only one bride and queen, brings about a final and climactic reiteration of the earth-heaven contrast. When the poet calls her *makeleʒ* as well as *maskelleʒ,* the maiden takes the word to mean *mateless* rather than *matchless,* and she replies that she is not without mate: she is one of the brides of the Lamb, described by St. John's Apocalypse, in the New Jerusalem. Then she speaks of the crucifixion of her Lamb in the language of courtly romance ("in Jerusalem watʒ my Lemman slayn" [in Jerusalem was my lover slain]), describing Him "as trwe as ston" [as true as stone], a phrase which recalls the symbolic overtones of jewel-stone imagery in the poem. And she compares this old Jerusalem, in which the most exalted was humbled, to the new Jerusalem, where all, like the Lamb, are spotless white, where there can be no such thing as negative, and no strife, all being "In honour more & neuer þe lesse" [in honor more

---

[16] According to Robertson ("The Pearl As A Symbol," *MLN,* LXV [1950], 155–61), the pearl may represent both the soul that attains innocence, or the freedom from sin, and life in the Celestial City.

and never less] (852). In the new city of God there is no sense of lesser degree, and this is emphasized by the repetition of the word *less* (in stanza-group XV).

> "Lasse of blysse may non vus bryng
> Þat beren þys perle vpon oure bereste,
> For þay of mote couþe neuer mynge,
> Of spotless perleȝ þat beren þe creste." (853–56)[17]

> [Less in bliss may none bring us
> who bear this pearl upon our breast,
> for they could never think of dispute,
> who bear the crest of spotless pearls.]

The city, of course, is the heaven we have been told about before, the city symbolized by the pearl. In it everyone has the qualities of the gem: all the maidens in the train of the Lamb are like him in hue (white), are individual pearls (as contrasted with the clay of their earthly corpses), and "Vchoneȝ blysse is breme and beste, / & neuer oneȝ honour ȝet neuer þe les" [the bliss of each is full and best, and one's honor is yet never less] (863–64). In a psychological sense, theirs is a new world. So, externally, the flawless Jerusalem is not a physical city like the old one.

The dreamer can hardly understand what is meant by Jerusalem, and, still confused, asks about the difference between this abode of the Lamb and the old Jerusalem of the Jews. "I am bot mokke & mul among, / & þou so ryche a reken rose" [I am only among muck and dust, and you so rich and radiant a rose]. The distinction between his own earthbound nature and her *reken* one is the reason for his obtuseness, for it is hardly easy to ascend at once from an earthly to a clearer understanding. Although he calls her *rose* here, he refers to all the brides in this place a few lines later as "So cumly a pakke of joly juele" [so beautiful a company of shining jewels] (929) who must have a wonderful dwelling. And this dwelling, fit for such jewels, the maiden des-

---

[17] Note that Osgood believes this passage to be an interpolation. See his edition, p. xlvi.

cribes: it is a *mote* (city on a hill) both without *mote* (blemish) and without *moote* (moat) (948), a city unlike the earthly place symbolized by old Jerusalem; and the contrast between the two is expressed in imagery throughout this passage. The antithesis is between crowned and pearl-decked maidens and earth-stained bodies; the radiant gems and "mokke and mul," white shining objects and dirt. The heavenly city, according to St. John, is a place of ineffable brilliance. Going toward the water's source, the poet sees this city, across the river from him: it is described as being constructed of gems; the supreme source of light is here; and all details bear out the idea of whiteness and brilliance. From the eighty-third through the eighty-seventh stanzas there is a parable devoted to the ennumeration and description of the precious stones of which the city is built, all suggested by the Apocalypse. Section eighteen, repeating the comparison of divine with natural light, shows the moon itself as *spotty* [spotted] and *grym* [ugly] beside the stream flowing from God's throne, presumably the stream which the poet has followed.[18] All beneath the moon is blemished; all in Jerusalem is pure. The climax of this, and of the poem, is the ecstatically described procession of virgins, headed by the Lamb himself, the divine Person, described as a *Lantern*, the source of light. This emotional climax is epitomized in the repeated word *delyt*. And in delight the vision ends.

3

The contrast between heaven and earth is made explicitly, as well as through the sets of images which can be traced through

---

[18] Stanza XC describes the twelve trees which bear the fruit of life, or time, growing "aboute þat water" (1077). These trees are to be associated with the earthly and mortal world of the garden rather than with the city of gems, and they might seem to be out of place here. But "aboute þat water" is a vague phrase, and the trees probably are intended to stand on the stream's edge but not in the heavenly city. The idea that the life of earth proceeds from this stream is perfectly fitting, particularly if one remembers the association of baptismal water with fertility myth.

the poem, for it is not only a physical and symbolical one. The repetition of the words *more* and *less*, for instance, and the maiden's insistence that earthly ideas of degree are not valid for heaven, all point to this distinction. In fact, the concepts of degree and judgment are the specific ones in which the poem's intellectual content centers. The idea that there is degree in heaven only in that there is *greater* blessedness is of course illogical: the maiden seems to be saying that the least one in this realm has enough grace that there *may* be superiority but *can* be no inferiority; that perfection, heavenliness, admits of increase and yet that no one can have *less* of it than another. This appears to be perfectly meaningless unless we suppose that the maiden is representing the feelings and attitudes of the blessed, the pearl-like: unlike the person who is aware of inferiority in earthly society, the pearl could have no sense that another's blessedness detracts from her own. In any case, this heavenly negation of negation is difficult if not impossible to understand, and the poet is quite conscious of presenting a paradox when he makes the divine ideas of degree only positive; the paradox is beyond our limited and human understanding.

In the same way divine and human judgment differ. In the beginning of the sixth stanza the maiden condemns, as false and blind, the man who believes only what he sees: God's word, she says, conveys a larger and truer vision than what man's unaided sense reveals. The idea of a vision beyond earth is emphasized in these lines, contrasting the good judgment of an ordinary man with the judgment of God and of the true jeweler. Man judges only on the basis of his erroneous impressions, but God judges men perfectly, with complete knowledge. Thus the two senses of *deme* are played upon, *to deem* and *to judge* or *doom*.

So, in symbol and also in stated contrasts, the natures of the heavenly and the earthly are probed. If we consider the poet's probable intention, to justify a position of blessedness for a person whose loss grieves him, for a soul departed from earth before it could labor long in the vineyard, we find the poem's development perfectly natural. The vineyard is the earth (as the mound or grave is); and according to the understanding of men who remain at work in it, remain on earth, the innocent infant could hardly deserve a place with saints and martyrs or even with those who lived and suffered long: her position must be inferior. But the biblical parable of the vineyard itself refutes this belief, and the poet turns to that parable to justify his faith that heaven does not discriminate against the infant. And how can the idea of what heaven *is* like for the innocent maiden be communicated graphically, poetically? The vineyard parable presents no actual vision of reward, but only the application of divine judgment to earth and to men. Because he needs a positive means of symbolizing the celestial life, the poet uses the most vivid one accessible, the one found in the Apocalypse. And from these two biblical passages—the parable of the vineyard and the Apocalyptic description of the heavenly city—the poem draws its imagery and substance.

Thus the basic image-scheme of *The Pearl*: the vineyard with its vegetation, its cyclical nature, its beauty and fertility purchased only by toil and by death, symbolizes the earthly nature; the city, with its jewels, its perfect hardness and constancy, its brilliance and purity—the very opposite of dust—all associated with royalty and with light, symbolizes the heavenly. But there is a third set of images which becomes increasingly important near the end of the poem: that which includes water and blood. In the water and blood, liturgical symbols which are, again, drawn from the Bible, the poet imagines the connection between heaven and earth. The link is the saving blood of Christ symbolized in the water of baptism and the wine of Eucharist.[19] It was

[19] Garrett suggests that the Eucharist is the basis for the allegory of the poem, but a more convincing starting point for its symbolism, and one which has never been much emphasized, is the rite of baptism. Whiteness and purity have always been associated with this rite; and the poem's specific concern with the fate of a baptized child, as well as its specific mention of the baptismal water which flows from the dying Christ, are tied up with these ideas. The poet's use of both white and shining gar-

the baptismal water which brought the maiden to salvation, and
this water is shown as the boundary between earthly and heavenly realms; it is the blood of Christ which saves all men, and
which, in the form of wine, must be accepted by them as a way
to heaven: and so, appropriately, the poem ends with an allusion
to the Lord "Þat, in þe forme of bred & wyn, / þe prests vus
scheweȝ vch a daye" [that, in the form of bread and wine, the
priest shows us each day] (1209–10).

The central symbol in the poem, the pearl itself, can best be
understood as a part of this whole scheme. It may stand for a
righteous person, for the perfect or *potentially* perfect soul (the
poet pledges his own pearl to the Lord), or, in its largest sense,

---

ments and light for symbols of purity could be derived in part from the
use of both symbols in the ancient Catholic rite: the baptizing priest
gives the infant a veil, saying "Receive this white garment, which mayest
thou carry without stain before the judgment seat of Our Lord Jesus
Christ, that thou mayest have eternal life"; and a candle, saying "Receive
this burning light, and keep thy baptism so as to be without blame." See
"Baptism," in *The Catholic Encyclopedia* (New York, 1907), II, 273.
Furthermore, the pearl's allusion to Christ's words, "Of such is the kingdom of heaven," is appropriate to the baptism service; the passage
quoted from Mark (10: 13–16) is used in the Anglican baptism, and
may well have been so used in the fourteenth century. Finally, the poet's
naming of John (along with Christ and Mary) as ground of his future
bliss might intend John the Baptist rather than Saint John the Divine (in
spite of his use of the latter's Apocalyptic City): in a very early sixteenth
century *Ritus Baptizandi,* part of the York manual, the passage John 1:
1–14, is prominent, and this passage is full of light imagery connected
with John and with the idea of baptism: "And the light shineth in darkness; and the darkness comprehend it not. There was a man sent from
God, whose name was John. The same came for a witness, to bear
witness of the Light, that all men through him might believe" (1611
version). See *Manuale et Processionale ad Usum Insignis Ecclesiae
Eboracensis,* in the Publications of the Surtees Society, LXIII (Durham,
1875). The use of these verses might well extend back to the fourteenth
century in various parts of England. In any case, all these associations
make plausible the notion of the poet's starting to justify the salvation
and high estate of a child saved by baptism with the use of imagery
suggested by this rite: the water of life, the brilliant Light as divine
symbol, and so on. Then he may have been led naturally into the
parabolic and Apocalyptic use of appropriate and allied imagery.

for the kingdom of heaven. Further scholarship in the background for this symbolism may augment these levels of meaning and supply a full interpretation—answering the problems of the pearl's possible use to represent the poet's own soul, or the Virgin Mary, or particular qualities—but it must take into account the complete scope of the imagery, of gem, earth, and water images, which makes *The Pearl* a picture of two worlds and the means of transition between them, a vision embracing heaven and earth.

6

THE MEANING OF THE
MIDDLE ENGLISH *PEARL*

Marie Padgett Hamilton

A SOLUTION TO THE MYSTERY OF *Pearl* MUST MEET CERTAIN tests if it is to answer the questions: What is typified by the jewel and the jewel-maiden, and how are they related? What is the symbolic import of the story? Specifically, as J. P. Oakden has indicated, the gem must stand for something which the poet could represent as a pearl and at the same time as a maiden who had died in infancy and had been redeemed by Christ. Further, says Oakden, it must signify something that the poet (or his protagonist speaking in the first person) "lost, mourned, and could recover through the grace of God, strengthened by partaking of the Blessed Sacrament."[1]

What is more, the pearl found by the dreamer in his vision must be the same as the one he had grieved for, except that it

Reprinted, by permission of the Modern Language Association, from *PMLA*, LXX (1955), 805–24. See also Professor Hamilton's "Notes on Pearl," *JEGP*, LVII (1958), 177–91. Some other recent articles of interest are John Conley, *"Pearl* and a Lost Tradition," *JEGP*, LIV (1955), 332–47; Charles Moorman, "The Role of the Narrator in *Pearl," Modern Philology*, LIII (1955), 73–81; Stanton de Voren Hoffman, "The *Pearl:* Notes for an Interpretation," *Modern Philology*, LVIII (1960), 73–80; A. C. Spearing, "Symbolic and Dramatic Development in *Pearl," Modern Philology*, LX (1962), 1–12; Robert W. Ackerman, "The Pearl Maiden and the Penny," *Romance Philology*, XVII (1964), 615–23.

[1] *Alliterative Poetry in Middle English,* II, 70.

has been transformed by divine grace. The identity of the two jewels, notwithstanding the fact that it has been denied by more than one interpreter,[2] is everywhere implicit in the poem and is twice affirmed. The dreamer in the beginning of his dialogue with Pearl supposes her to be the gem that he had mourned for, and she confirms the assumption by rebuking him for having concluded that his pearl was "al awaye" [all away], when in reality it is now secure, as in a treasure-chest, in the gracious garden where he sees her (241–64). He then rejoices at finding the jewel that he had believed to be "don out of dawes" [done out of days], and is chided, not for identifying Pearl lost and Pearl found, but for trusting the testimony of his fallible senses that she is bodily present in the pleasant vale where he beholds her, and for his naive assumption that he may dwell with her there forthwith, without begging leave (277–300).

For clues to the nature of the treasure lost, then, we must look to the treasure found. It is twofold. Besides the maiden in her pearl-embroidered vesture and crown of orient pearl, there is the wondrous jewel at her breast, which she clearly identifies with the Pearl of Great Price and interprets as eternal felicity, "the blys that con not blynne" [the bliss that can not cease].[3] This gem, which like the kingdom of God is common to all the righteous, was bestowed upon her, she says, as an earnest of the Atonement ("in token of pes" [peace]) by the Lamb "that schede hys blode" [that shed his blood] (732–43). Clearly Pearl herself, as the "jeweler" (one "seeking goodly pearls") finds her in the enchanting garden, is a regenerate soul, restored by the sanctifying grace of baptism to the state of innocence

---

[2] Sr. Madeleva, *Pearl: A Study in Spiritual Dryness,* pp. 192–93; and Sr. Mary Vincent Hillman, "Some Debatable Words in *Pearl* and Its Theme," *MLN,* LX, 243.

[3] St. 61, especially lines 729–32: "Þer is þe blys þat con not blynne / Þat þe jueler soȝte þurȝ perré pres, / And solde alle hys goud, boþe wolen and lynne, / To bye hym a perle watȝ mascelleȝ" [There is the bliss that cannot cease that the jeweler sought through precious jewels and sold all his goods, both woolen and linen, to buy for himself a pearl that was matchless]. Cf. D. W. Robertson, *MLN,* LXV, 159.

and favor with God which mankind enjoyed before the Fall. No mere personification of purity, innocence, or any other abstract quality, she typifies the soul made pure by sacramental grace through the merit of Christ,[4] and as such speaks with authority for the entire company of the blessed, whether living or dead, for God's kingdom, "Godes ryche." There is justice in Sister Mary V. Hillman's conception of her as "the Soul."[5]

Here, then, is the double treasure found in the vision. First there is Pearl, the maiden soul, who through baptismal regeneration and incorporation into the Mystical Body of Christ, the Church, has become "a perle of prys" [a precious pearl] (257–76). Secondly, there is the *pretiosa margarita* [pearl of great price] of Matthew 13: 45–46, the gem of eternal life and beatitude, which is the maiden's distinctive endowment and adornment as a bride of Christ, a soul in grace.

Both jewels, I take it, were lost in the primal bereavement announced in the first ringing stanza of the poem:

> Perle, plesaunte to prynces paye
> To clanly clos in golde so clere,
> Oute of oryent, I hardyly saye,
> Ne proued I neuer her precios pere.
> So rounde, so reken in vche araye,
> So smal, so smoþe her sydeʒ were,
> Quere-so-euer I jugged gemmeʒ gaye,
> I sette hyr sengeley in synglere.
> Allas! I leste hyr in on erbere;
> Þurʒ gresse to grounde hit fro me yot.
> I dewyne, fordolked of luf-daungere
> Of þat pryuy perle wythouten spot.[6]

> [Pearl, pleasant to a prince's pleasure
> to fairly enclose in clear gold,
> greater than the orient, I boldly say,

---

[4] Note her account of Christ's cleansing her garments before crowning her "in virginity" (766–68).

[5] Cf. Sr. Madeleva's views, *op. cit.* My debt to Sr. Madeleva is considerable and hereby is gratefully acknowledged. My theory was full grown before Sr. Mary Hillman's interpretation was published.

[6] *Pearl*, ed. E. V. Gordon (Oxford, 1953), 1–12.

nor found I ever her precious peer.
So round, so beautiful in every setting,
so small, so smooth were her sides,
wherever I judged beautiful gems,
I set her apart as unique.
Alas! I lost her in a garden;
through grass to earth it went from me.
I languish, wounded by the power of love,
for that dear pearl without spot.]

"Alas! I lost her in a garden." If the Anglo-French (*h*)*erbere*
here had been accurately rendered in modern English versions,
the theme of the poem might have been sooner understood.[7]
Competent fourteenth-century readers must have recognized the
erber(*e*) as the Garden of Eden, where the maiden soul of man
fell to earth and was lost, with her potential endowment of
everlasting life and blessedness.

Not without reason Pearl's possessor had cherished her as
unique among gems, "sette hyr sengeley in synglere." (St. Gregory Nazianzen, in a poem addressed to his soul, calls her "Of all
bright things prized highest / Beneath the rolling sun.")[8] Appropriately, too, the man bereft of Pearl speaks of her as meet for a
prince, for his pleasure, "to enclose in clear gold," gold being a
symbol of the divine kingdom,[9] to which man was to have been
transferred in time had he not sinned in Eden.[10] William Drummond of Hawthornden in *The Cypress Grove* employs the same

[7] S. P. Chase, *The Pearl . . . in Modern Verse*, translates *erbere* as
"garden plot." Gollancz in his ed. of 1921, *Pearl, An English Poem of
the XIVth Century, Edited with Modern Rendering*, translates it "garden"
and insists upon this meaning, but obscures it by adding, "The poet is
thinking of the graveyard as a garden." Gordon glosses *erber*(*e*) as "a
grassy place, a garden, often among trees."

[8] *Songs and Hymns of the Earliest Greek Christian Poets*, tr. Allen W.
Chatfield, p. 106.

[9] Emile Mâle, *Religious Art in France in the Thirteenth Century*, tr.
Dora Nussey, p. 214.

[10] A commonplace. See. e.g., Aquinas, *Summa Theologica*, "Treatise on
Man," Q. 102, Art. 4: St. Athanasius, *The Incarnation of the Word of
God*, newly translated into English by a religious of C.S.M.V. (1947),
pp. 28–29.

metaphor in an address to his soul: "Think then . . . that thou art a pearl, raised from thy mother, to be enchased in gold, and that the death-day of thy body is thy birthday to eternity."[11]

With equal propriety the disconsolate man speaks in the second stanza of *Pearl* of his distress at the thought of his once spotless gem, now fallen and marred by earth, her delicate hues shrouded in clay:

> To þenke hir color so clad in clot.
> O moul, þou marreȝ a myry iuele,
> My priuy perle wythouten spotte. (22–24)

> [To think of her color so clad in clay.
> Oh earth, you mar a fair jewel,
> my dear pearl without spot.]

Thus in a single metaphor the poet alludes to the bodily death entailed in the decree "Unto dust shalt thou return," and to the spiritual death and defilement by original sin which the soul incurred in the Fall. The ancient figure of the clay-pent soul appears in similar idiom in Giles Fletcher's "Christs Victorie in Heaven" (st. 17), wherein "wretched man" is described as "Proude of the mire in which his soule is pend, / Clodded in lumps of clay, his wearie life to end."[12] (Compare Honorius of Autun, *Elucidarium,* Lib. III: "Cum homo peccat, anima moritur; quia a vita Deo deseritur, et in corpore quasi in sepulchro sepelitur" [When man sins, the soul dies; because it is severed from life by God, and buried in the body as in a sepulcher].)[13]

In like manner throughout *Pearl* the fitness of the metaphors and allusions when applied to the soul is apparent. By a studied ambiguity the poet carries out his design, with the result that the reader, while responding to the moving story of a man's desolation at the death of a rare maiden, who was the wellspring of his

[11] Ed. Samuel Clegg, 1919, p. 57.
[12] *Giles and Phineas Fletcher's Poetical Works,* ed. F. S. Boas, Vol. I, p. 21. Cf. Donne, "The Harbinger to the Progress," in *The Progress of the Soul,* lines 9–11.
[13] Migne, *Patrologia Latina,* CLXXIII, 164.

happiness, is at the same time made aware of the allegorical and mystical intent of the poem by the vagueness and strangeness of the references to the girl's death and by the concurrent motive of the jewel, fallen, sullied by earth, lost.

This contrapuntal technique also underscores the fact that two gems were forfeited in the garden, both the soul and her patrimony of sanctifying grace, which included the gifts of blessedness and eternal life. The poet had the authority of tradition for making the pearl an emblem for each of these. The Fathers often construe the parabolic Pearl of Price as everlasting life or beatitude; only the equation of the gem with Christ rivaled this interpretation in popularity.[14] The undefiled human soul, or the soul redeemed in baptism, also was typified by the pearl, and sometimes was identified with the *pretiosa margarita*,[15] as apparently it is in *Pearl* 272. There the maiden explains that the jewel which the dreamer had regarded as lost has become "a perle of prys" by virtue of the chest that now encloses it.

The poet also had ample precedent for making the two treasures and what they stand for appear at times as a single pearl, involved in a single tragic loss. Compare the gem lamented by Macbeth (*Macb.* III, i, 69–70) as "mine eternal jewel, / Given to the common enemy of man," sometimes construed as "his eternal salvation," but more often as "his immortal soul." The

[14] For the *Pretiosa margarita* of the parable as eternal life or blessedness see Gregory the Great (*PL*, LXXVI, 1115); Bede (*PL*, XCII, 69); Rabanus Maurus (*PL*, CXII, 996); Walufridus Strabo (*PL*, CXIV, 133); Bruno Astensis (*PL*, CLXV, 192); Hugh of St. Victor (*PL*, CLXXV, 794); and at least five other writers in *PL*. Cf. D. W. Robertson, *MLN*, LXV, 160.

[15] Noted by Gollancz, 1921 ed., pp. xxvii–xxciii; Sr. Madeleva, *op. cit.*, p. 95; Sr. M. V. Hillman, *op. cit.*, p. 243; D. W. Robertson, *op. cit.*, p. 160. Richard Delbrueck in *The Art Bulletin*, XXXII (June 1952), 142, discusses the pearl as an early Christian symbol of "the soul redeemed, the Christian purified through baptism." For Patristic and medieval testimony see Cornelius á Lapide's celebrated digest, *Commentaria in Scripturas Sacras*, XV, 334; *The Book of the Knight of La Tour Landry*, ed. T. Wright (*EETS*, o.s. 33), p. 158; Sermon 84 in *Select English Works of John Wyclif*, ed. T. Arnold, I, 286–87.

distinction, though convenient and even indispensable in ordinary parlance, is theologically more apparent than real. The soul, St. Thomas Aquinas affirms, was the force which preserved the human body from corruption: hence the loss of it and the forfeiture of bodily immortality were one and the same.[16] The soul in one sense was regarded not merely as man's hope of eternal life; it *was* that life. As *anima* signifies both "soul" and "life," so also in Early English "life" is often synonymous with "soul"; thus it appears in the Wycliffite Bible and in *Pearl* 305 and 687. (In line 687 "lyf" translates the Vulgate *animam* of Psalm 23:4, rendered "soul" in the Douay and King James Bibles, as in some Middle English versions.) In medieval allegory, therefore, the Lady Anima may appear as Dame Life, as she does in the Middle English poem "Life and Death," or as the Soul, "a lovelie lemmon lyk to [God] him-self" [a lovely lover similar to (God) himself], as she is called in *Piers Plowman*; and the identity between "life" and "soul" gave rise to finespun speculation and analysis.[17] In the language of the theologians, what was lost in the Garden of Eden was the supernatural life of man, or sanctifying grace, and that included the gift of life eternal or beatitude.[18]

Pearl is following this tradition when she castigates the dreamer for assuming that his jewel was "al awaye" (258), or

[16] *Sum. Theol.*, "Treatise on Man," Q. 102, Art. 2.

[17] Here, e.g., are excerpts from St. Bernard's Sermon 81, *Cantica Canticorum*, ed. Samuel Eales, pp. 495–96: "Life is indeed the soul which is living, but it lives not other whence than from itself, and on this account we speak of it with propriety, not so much as living, as being itself life. . . . The soul of man alone can reach the higher life, in as much as it is seen to have been constituted as life by Him who is Life. . . . God is Life; the soul also is Life; it is then like unto God, but it is not equal to Him."

[18] *Catholic Encyclopaedic Dictionary*, articles on "Original Sin" and "Grace"; *Dictionnaire de Théologie Catholique*, article on "Innocence." Edwin Wintermute's statement, *MLN*, LXIV (Feb. 1949), 83–84, is right as far as it goes: "The pearl means sanctifying grace, the possession of which is essential to the enjoyment of the Kingdom of Heaven." Cf. W. K. Greene, *PMLA*, XL, 814–27: *Pearl* "as a whole was designed to illustrate the doctrine of Divine Grace."

"don out of dawes" (282), and thereby imputing a lie to God, who had "loyally promised" to raise his "life," though fortune in punishment of Adam's sin had caused his flesh to die:

> I halde þat iueler lyttle to prayse
> Þat loueʒ wel þat he seʒ wyth yʒe,[19]
> And much to blame and vncortayse
> Þat leueʒ oure Lorde wolde make a lyʒe,
> Þat lelly hyʒte your lyf to rayse,
> Þaʒ fortune dyd your flesch to dyʒe.   (301–306)

> [I hold that jeweler little to be praised
> who loves well what he sees with eye,
> much to be blamed and discourteous
> who believes our Lord would lie,
> that loyally promised to raise your life,
> though fortune caused your flesh to die.]

(Cf. Heb. 10:23, Titus 3:7–8, and more especially, Titus 1:2: "In hope of eternal life, which God, that cannot lie, promised before the world began.")

The soul, poetically conceived as feminine, time out of mind, was represented in medieval art as a child,[20] and the figure of the maiden soul of man, raised from her fallen state and espoused by Christ, is a commonplace of medieval mystical treatises, religious lyrics, and allegorical narratives, where not infrequently the legend is recast in terms of chivalric romance.[21] In

---

[19] In this line (302) I reject the Oxford *leueʒ*, "believes," in favor of *loueʒ* (MS, Osgood) "praises" or "loves."

[20] Louisa Twining, *Symbols and Emblems of Early and Mediaeval Christian Art*, pp. 141, 142–46; F. R. Webber, *Church Symbolism*, 2nd ed. rev., p. 362. Cf. Mâle, p. 250, on miniatures of the Assumption depicting the soul of the Virgin as a child borne in Christ's arms. In El Greco's *Burial of the Count of Orgaz* the departing soul is a babe carried heavenward by an angel. Cf. the souls in Abraham's bosom.

[21] For a general treatment of the motive see Mary A. Ewer, *A Survey of Mystical Symbolism*, and W. R. Inge, *Christian Mysticism*, 5th ed., Appendix D. The Atonement as a divine romance is well handled by R. W. Battenhouse, *PMLA*, LXI, 1049–51. For the Redemption in terms of chivalric romance see Sr. Marie de Lourdes le May, *The Allegory of the Christ Knight in English Literature*, Catholic Univ. (1932); and W. R. Gaffney, *PMLA*, XLVI, 155–68.

one variation the allegory becomes a murder story. *The Goodman of Paris* describes the soul as the daughter of God, given
to each of us "without stain or blemish," but poisoned by
"draughts of mortal sin"; God will hold us accountable for her
death.[22] The Pearl-poet's double metaphor for the soul as both
jewel and bride of Christ appears also in a lyrical poem by St.
Peter Damian: Christ addresses the regenerate soul as "soror,
conjux, gemma splendissima" [sister, consort, most brilliant
jewel.][23] Traditionally, too, the soul as spouse (i.e., the soul in
a state of grace) was depicted as adorned, like Pearl, with precious stones, sometimes specified as pearls, betokening virtues
bestowed upon her by the Celestial Bridegroom.[24]

So much for one of the questions with which this essay began:
What is typified by the jewel and the jewel-maiden, and how are
they related? The foregoing reply goes far toward answering the
related question, What is the import of the story? Pearl, at the
centre of her defense of her rank as a queen in God's kingdom,
gives a résumé of the Fall and the Redemption (637–60): Mankind, created for perfect happiness, forfeited it through Adam,
and so was condemned to death and the pain of Hell; but there
came a remedy. Water and noble blood flowed on the Rood. The
blood delivered us from Hell and "the second death"; the water
is baptism, "that washes away the fell guilt in which Adam
drowned us." Consequently no barrier remains between us and
bliss, and bliss itself is restored "in sely stounde" [in a blessed
time].

---

[22] *The Goodman of Paris,* tr. Eileen Power, p. 60. Cf. Chaucer's
"Melibee" and its source. Melibeus' daughter Sophie, wounded by his
three enemies (the world, the flesh, the devil), is equated with his own
soul.

[23] P. S. Allen, *Medieval Latin Lyrics,* p. 223.

[24] St. Bernard, *Sermons on the Canticles,* tr. by a Priest of Melleray,
I, 306, in a glowing account of the soul in her jeweled nuptial garments,
specifies that her gems are pearls symbolizing virtues. For other refer-
ences to the jewels of the soul as virtues, see Hugh of St. Victor, *The
Soul's Betrothal Gift,* tr. F. Sherwood Taylor (1945), pp. 22–23; Albertus
Magnus, *De Laudibus B. Mariae Virginis,* lib. XII, 4.9.7., as cited by
Fletcher, *JEGP,* XX, 11: Honorius of Autun, *PL,* CLXXII, 859–60, 966.

The whole of *Pearl* is a finely wrought elaboration of this theme, the Biblical epic of the soul in delicate miniature, seen in the epitome of one man's passionate experience. The hero is not literally the poet, but "a type of the whole race of fallen man, called to salvation," like Dante, the pilgrim of the *Commedia*, though less learned than Dante. What Francis Fergusson says of the relationship between Dante as author of the *Commedia* and Dante as pilgrim might apply as well to the Pearl-poet and the "I" of his narrative. "The distinction between Dante speaking as author, and Dante the Pilgrim, is fundamental to the whole structure," Mr. Fergusson reminds us. "The author knows the whole story in advance, the Pilgrim meets everything freshly for the first time. The two perspectives together produce a sort of stereoptical effect, that of an objective and partially mysterious reality. . . . The Pilgrim's awareness is always moving towards the author's."[25] In the English poem the dreamer's awareness is constantly moving towards Pearl's, as hers approaches the author's. Indeed, the dreamer is presented as one conveniently naive in theology, so as to call forth the inspired maiden's account of the plan of salvation, the plenitude of the divine grace, and the blessedness of souls wedded to Christ; for the poet's design, identical again with Dante's, is "to remove those living in this life from a state of wretchedness and lead them to the state of blessedness."

The Pearl-maiden, though typifying the soul of man, lost through "the fell guilt in which Adam drowned us," is the individual soul of the man who tells the story, his own "privy perle" [dear pearl] (24).[26] The universal historical bereavement was at the same time his immediate personal tragedy, shared by the reader, too, who also is expected to participate in the happy ending of the poem by heeding its lessons. The conception of an individual person or soul as epitomizing all persons or souls in

[25] *Dante's Drama of the Mind*, pp. 9–10.
[26] Cf. Sr. Madeleva, p. 132: The maiden of the vision "is the personification of his [the poet's] own soul in the state of such potential perfection . . . as is congruous to it at this time of his life."

like condition is too basic to medieval patterns of thought to need comment. It is implicit in the doctrine of the solidarity of the human race as springing from Adam, and of the corporate nature of the Church as the Mystical Body. "We are bidden everyone to the spiritual marriage at which the Bridegroom is Christ our Lord," writes St. Bernard. "Spouse indeed we are to him, if this seem not to you incredible; both all together one spouse, and every soul by itself a spouse singly."[27] As C. S. Baldwin, after quoting Bernard's words, warned, "Neglect of this mediaeval habit has hindered the interpretation of *Pearl*."[28]

Certainly the poet assumed his readers' acceptance of the doctrine set forth in Rom. 5:12–19, that the will of all mankind rebelled in Adam when by disobedience he forfeited the gift of supernatural life. St. Augustine's "All men were that one man Adam,"[29] restated by Aquinas,[30] had found popular expression in the Middle English version of *The Castle of Love*: "Þorw Adam we sungedon furst uchon / And eeten þe appel wiþ him anon" [Through Adam we sinned first each one and ate the apple with him then] (1381–82). The consequence of universal man's complicity in original sin is elsewhere stated in this rhymed allegory: "Alle heo beoþ I-brought to grounde / þat of his of-spring beoþ I-founde" [All of them are brought to earth who are accounted among his offspring] (111–12).[31] The protagonist in *Pearl* apparently assumes responsibility for the loss of supernatural life when his soul was "brought to ground." He speaks in the first person: "I leste hyr in on erbere; / Þurȝ

---

[27] *PL*, CLXXXIII, 158, quoted by C. S. Baldwin, *Medieval Rhetoric and Poetic*, p. 174.

[28] *Three Medieval Centuries in England (1100–1400)*, p. 275, n. 21. Cf. *ibid.*, pp. 174, 272, 275.

[29] "Quia omnes homines fuerunt ille unus homo, scilicet Adam" [Because all men are that one man, namely Adam] (*De Peccatorum Meritis*, Cap. 10, as quoted by Lapide, XVIII, 99).

[30] *Sum. Theol.*, II (2nd number), Q. 81 (tr. by the Fathers of the English Dominican Province), p. 401.

[31] "A Sawley Monk's Version of Grosteste's 'Castle of Love'," in *Minor Poems of the Vernon MS. (EETS, O. S. 98)*, Part I, ed. C. Horstmann.

gresse to grounde hit fro me yot" [I lost her in a garden; through grass to earth it went from me] (9–10). "Wilt thou," Donne asks in *A Hymme to God the Father*, "forgive that sinne where I begunne, / Which is my sin, though it were done before?"

As a type of the fallen race of man the dreamer in *Pearl* waited in longing[32] for that weal which had elevated his lot and his well-being (16); and in a peaceful season was heartened by "never so sweet a song" (st. 2), heralding a brilliant harvest from his lost riches in decay. Spice-bearing plants, he is promised, will burgeon from that seed, the pearl without spot:

> Þat spot of spyseʒ mot nedeʒ sprede,
> Þer such rycheʒ to rot is runne;
> Blomeʒ blayke and blwe and rede
> Þer schyneʒ ful schyr agayn þe sunne.
> Flor and fryte may not be fede
> Þer hit doun drof in moldeʒ dunne;
> *For vch gresse mot grow of grayneʒ dede;*
> *No whete were elleʒ to woneʒ wonne.*
> Of goud vche goude is ay bygonne;
> So semly a sede moʒt fayly not,
> Þat spryngande spyceʒ vp ne sponne
> Of þat precios perle wythouten spotte.   (st. 3)

[That spot must needs be spread with spices,
where such riches to rot has run;
blooms yellow and blue and red
shine there very bright against the sun.
Flower and fruit may not be withered
where it sank into dark earth;
for each plant of grass must grow from dead seeds;
no wheat would otherwise come to be in barns.
From good each good is always begun;
so beautiful a seed must not fail,
that flourishing spices might not spring up
from that precious pearl without spot.]

These lines (the substance of the song heard by the hero), phrased in the mystical language of spiritual renewal and fruition, echo Christ's pregnant metaphor for his own approaching

---

[32] There is no textual warrant for the statement in modern renderings that the dreamer waited *on the spot* where the pearl fell to earth.

death and resurrection, his allusion to the grain that must fall to earth and die ere it bring forth wheat (John 12:24; cf. I Cor. 15:36–38). An utterance linking this allusion to the promise of a spice-garden of flowers and fruit that may not be "fede," "withered," together with a mention of the "precious pearl" (reminiscent of the *pretiosa margarita* of Matt. 13:46), can hardly be anything short of a reference to the Incarnation and the Resurrection. The Biblical corn of wheat was so habitually associated with the Word made flesh, the Last Supper, and the Resurrection that only wheat flour might be used for the Eucharistic bread;[33] and the grainfield had become a familiar symbol of the Church. "The multitude of grain," Wyclif calls it, sprung from "Christ, the first corn," and deriving its virtue from the divine seed.[34]

Appropriately, it was "when corn is cut by sickles keen" that the protagonist of *Pearl* entered the garden on the occasion of his vision. "In August in a high season," it probably was at the Feast of Our Lady in Harvest (the Assumption), a proper time for religious revelations[35] and particularly for this one, for the festival commemorates the restoration through Mary of what mankind forfeited through Eve. Lessons for the feast from Ecclesiasticus 24 tell of flowers and fruits redolent of sweet odors, chosen as fitting metaphors for Mary, who in her Assumption was sometimes likened to a restored Eden,[36] and who in her

[33] Aquinas, *Sum. Theol.*, III (3rd number), Q. 74, Art. 3.

[34] Sermon 59 in *Select English Works*, I, 179. This figure appears in beauty in Masefield, *The Everlasting Mercy*, and in recent poems by Thomas Merton; it is a commonplace with the Latin Fathers: *PL*, XXXVII, 1279, 1730; LI, 314; LXXV, 1150; CXII, 926, 1440; CXC, 256, e.g., cf. Piers Plowman's acre.

[35] Edmund Gardner (*Dante and the Mystics*, p. 284) reports that high festivals were regarded as specially propitious for revelations and spiritual consolation. Adam Davy in his series of visions about Edward II dreamed by the ecclesiastical calendar (O. F. Emerson, *A Middle English Reader* (1948), pp. 227–32).

[36] *St. John Damascene on Holy Images*, tr. Mary Allies, pp. 160–61, apostrophizing Mary in her Assumption: "Thou art a spiritual Eden, holier and diviner than Eden of Old, The heavenly Bread of Life . . . took flesh of thee." Again St. John of Damascus describes her in the Assumption as "the living garden of delight, wherein the condemnation

virginity was typified by a garden, in allusion to the *hortus conclusus* [closed garden] of Canticles 4:12.[37] The familiar symbol had a special relevance when, as is the case in *Pearl,* the garden grew medicinal herbs, regarded as a token of the Virgin's healing powers.[38]

Nevertheless, the medicine is Christ, the *flos campi* [flower of the field] of Canticles 2:1,[39] still heralded in Advent Masses through Isaiah's prayer: "Let the earth be opened up and bud forth a Saviour." The garden as a type of Mary was but a natural corollary of the ancient metaphor of the garden of Canticles as prefiguring Christ's human nature,[40] into which He descended, as the bridegroom descended into his garden; or as shadowing forth the Incarnation.[41] The garden also was said to signify Christ's Resurrection[42] and, above all, His spiritual body, the Church. In the 1914 issue of the Douay Bible the notes on the Canticles interpret the spice-garden as the Church, in keeping with a tradition at least as old as Origen, who regarded the Garden of Eden itself as an allegorical adumbration of the future Church.[43] The plants of the Terrestrial Paradise were sometimes

---

was annulled and the Tree of Life planted" (quoted by Gardner, *op. cit.,* pp. 212–13).

[37] See, e.g., Yrjö Hirn, *The Sacred Shrine,* pp. 438, 446–48; Lapide, VIII, 76, 81, 142, 240; St. Peter Damian, *PL,* CXLV, 938; St. Bernard, *Sermons on the Cantica Canticorum,* ed. Eales, pp. 259–70; Alanus de Insulis, *PL,* CCX, 95, 109.

[38] Cf. Carleton Brown, *Religious Lyrics of the Fourteenth Century,* p. 12.

[39] Alanus, *PL,* CCX, 64–65: 'Campus dicitur humana Christi natura. . . . Hujus campi flos fuit Christus' [The field means the human nature of Christ. . . . The flower of that field was Christ] ("Elucidatio in Cantica Canticorum").

[40] *Ibid.,* col. 91. Cf. n. 37 above.

[41] Lapide, VIII, 90.

[42] St. Bernard, *PL,* CLXXXIII, 1059–60 (quoted by Erich Auerbach, *Speculum,* XXI, 479–80, who also attributes the figure of the garden as the Resurrection to Gregory the Great and Richard of St. Victor).

[43] Origen, *PG,* XI, 99, 375, as cited by Mâle, p. 134. H. R. Patch, *The Other World,* pp. 136, 143, 145–47, 153, cites Cyprian, Isidore of Seville, Bede, Rabanus Maurus, and St. Bonaventura as treating the Terrestrial Paradise as a type of the Church.

described as medicinal,[44] and Honorius of Autun, identifying the garden of Canticles with the Church, notes that the Church likewise yields curative herbs for the wounds of sin.[45] The garden-symbol for the Church was, indeed, so generally a favorite with the Fathers and other theological writers[46] that it is not surprising to find the metaphor appearing and reappearing in Dante's *Commedia*[47] and occurring in the reported visions of other medieval mystics.[48]

The idea gained in sanction from the important rôle of gardens in the life of Jesus, as theologians with tireless ingenuity sought parallels between these and the garden of Eden or the *hortus conclusus* of the Song of Songs, in their search for analogies between the Old and the New Adam, the Fall and the Atonement. Lapide in his celebrated digest of Patristic and medieval exegesis, *Commentaria in Scripturas Sacras,* repeats the familiar idea that the sepulchre of Christ was in a garden because Adam sinned and incurred the sentence of death in the garden of Paradise. The Passion, he declares, also began in the garden on Mt. Olivet, in order that Christ "might suffer and expiate that sentence, and plant and institute that most delightful garden (*hortum amoenissimum*), burgeoning with the flowers and fruits of every virtue, namely the Church."[49]

---

[44] Patch, *op. cit.,* pp. 139, 153. Bernard of Silvester, *De Mundi Universitate* (ed. Carl S. Barach and Johann Wrobel, 1876), Lib. I, Part III, 1. 3., devotes ll. 360–414 to the medicinal plants in the Earthly Paradise.

[45] *PL,* CLXXII, 423, 425.

[46] Cassiodorus (*PL,* LXX, 1078, 1105), Augustine (*PL,* XLIII, 153–55, 227–28), Gregory (*PL,* LXXV, 799; LXXIX, 513), Alcuin (*PL,* c, 653), Rabanus (*PL,* CXI, 530), Hugh of St. Victor (*PL,* CLXXV, 275), *St. Ambrose 'On the Mysteries,'* tr. T. Thompson (ed. J. H. Srawley, pp. 71–72); Lapide, VIII, 73–74, 77–78, 87–88, 238–40, 641.

[47] *Paradiso,* XII, 70, 104; XXVI, 64; XXXI, 97; XXXII, 39; cf. XXIII, 71–72. The Church Militant fittingly appears in the *Commedia* in the hilltop setting of the restored Earthly Paradise (*Purgatorio,* XXIX, XXX, XXXII).

[48] Gardner, *op. cit.,* p. 290; Ewer, *op. cit.,* p. 61.

[49] Lapide, VIII, 641. Cf. XV, 566; XVI, 606, and Giles Fletcher, "Christ's Triumph and Death." For the Garden of Gethsemane as the Church, see also *PL,* VIII, 59.

Such, I take it, is the "erber grene" where the dreamer of *Pearl* falls asleep, an aromatic garden of healing spices, including tropical ginger, which was alien to English gardens and the graves of English babes:

> On huyle þer perle hit trendeled doun
> Schadowed þis worteȝ ful schyre and schene,
> Gilofre, gyngure and gromylyoun,
> And pyonys powdered ay bytwene.
> Ȝif hit watȝ semly on to sene,
> A fayr reflayr ȝet fro hit flot.
> Þer wonys þat worþyly, I wot and wene,
> My precious perle wythouten spot. (41–48)

> [On the hill where the pearl rolled down
> were shadows of these bright and glittering plants,
> gillyflower, ginger, and gromwell,
> and peonies scattered everywhere between.
> If it was beautiful to look upon,
> so also a fair fragrance floated from it.
> There dwells that glorious one, I know and believe,
> my precious pearl without spot.]

Note that the plants are said to give forth shade *on* the hill where the pearl had fallen. The illustration in the manuscript of *Pearl* clearly pictures the dreamer asleep on the sloping crest of a hill that is shadowed by trees and flowers,[50] and not as lying on or beside a grave or clump of plants, as has been suggested. Thrice in the poem "hill" (*huyle,* 41; *hylle,* 1172; *hyul* or *hyiil,* 1205) designates the place where the pearl fell to earth. In the five other occurrences in *Pearl* the word invariably renders or refers to *mons* [mountain] in the Vulgate, and twice (976, 979) it stands for the *montem magnum et altum* [great and lofty mountain] of Apocalypse 21:10—evidence hard to reconcile with Gollancz's contention that the "hill" of the lost pearl and the sleeping dreamer is an infant's grave or a clump of plants.[51]

---

[50] *Pearl, Cleanness, Patience and Sir Gawain,* reproduced in facsimile from the unique MS. Cotton Nero A. X. in the British Museum, introd. Sir I. Gollancz, *EETS.*

[51] In his 1921 edition of *Pearl,* pp. xviii, 119, n. 41.

Hills and mountains, perennial types of contemplation and spiritual enlightenment, are frequently the scenes of religious visions.[52] In *Pearl*, however, a more precise meaning may be intended. The Terrestrial Paradise, where the pearl had "trendeled doun," was traditionally placed on a hill or mountain. Consequently it would seem logical to a medieval man for the restored Eden of the Church to have the same setting, and the more so since hill and mountain were recognized symbols of Christ and the Church,[53] and the metaphor of the Church as situated on a hill was also familiar.[54] Lapide suggests the idea in a commentary already cited above,[55] in speaking of the ecclesiastical garden planted by Christ in the Passion, which began in the Garden of Gethsemane on the Mount of Olives. The holy hill or sacred mountain of the Jews was interpreted in the light of the hill-settings of events in the drama of Redemption. Lapide, for example, identifies the mountain of myrrh in Canticles 4:6 with Mount Calvary, and the hill of frankincense in the same passage with "the lofty garden" (*hortus altus*) of Christ's entombment and resurrection.[56]

The habit of mind which linked the garden and hill settings of the Fall with those of the Redemption also associated the Cross with the Tree of Life, and sometimes with the Forbidden Tree, as every student of the Middle Ages knows. The convention is echoed in a proper Preface in the Ordinary of the Mass:

[52] Among ME vision poems, hill-settings are found also in *Piers Plowman, Winner and Waster, The Vision of Life and Death, The Shepherd on a Hill He Sat,* and *Quia Amore Langueo.*

[53] The incomplete subject-indices of Migne's *PL* yield some dozen references to *mons* as *Ecclesia* and numerous references to *mons* as *Christus.* In *Pearl* 678–79, the rendering of Ps. 24: 3–4 ("Lorde, quo schal klymbe thy hygh hylle" [Lord, who shall climb thy high hill], etc.), 'hygh hylle' translates the Vulgate *montem Domini,* which is glossed as *Ecclesia* in the twelfth-century *Allegoriae in Sacram Scripturam (PL,* CXII, 1000–1002), formerly attributed to Rabanus Maurus.

[54] See D. W. Robertson and Bernard F. Huppé, *Piers Plowman and Scriptural Tradition,* pp. 35–37.

[55] See note 49, above.

[56] Lapide, VIII, 55–57.

"Who has appointed that the salvation of mankind should be wrought on the wood of the Cross: that whence death arose, thence life might rise again." The Latin Fathers generally credit the legend that Adam (or Adam's skull) was buried on Mount Calvary, in anticipation of his resurrection there through the life-giving blood destined to flow at the Crucifixion.[57]

The same tradition apparently is reflected in St. Ambrose's statement that the Crucifixion took place on Mount Calvary because "it was fitting that the first fruits of our life should be situated where death had its beginnings."[58] However, a legend that the Earthly Paradise was actually in Jerusalem gained enough currency to evoke denials from St. Athanasius and from Epiphanius,[59] and whatever its medieval fortunes were, a similar idea reappears in Donne's "Hymn to God my God in My Sicknesse" (21–23):

> We thinke that Paradise and Calvarie,
> Christs Crosse and Adams tree, stood in one place.
> Look Lord and find both Adams met in me.

Donne may refer to the legend that the Cross was made of wood from the tree of the knowledge of good and evil.[60] He probably did not expect his bold juxtaposition of the scenes of Paradise lost and Paradise regained to be taken literally, any more than the ancient metaphor of the Adams meeting in him, or the identity of "West and East in all flat maps" (14). He trusted the

[57] Lapide, XV, 615 (cf. I, 26, 84; VIII, 499), attributes this opinion to Origen, Tertullian, Athanasius, Epiphanius, Ambrose, Augustine, Cyril, "and others of the Fathers, Jerome excepted." Cf. representations of the Crucifixion in medieval and Renaissance art with Adam's skull beneath the Cross.

[58] Lapide, XV, 615: "Unde St. Ambrosius, in Cap. xxxiii Lucae, docet Christum [fuisse] in Golgotha crucifixum quia congruebat, inquit, ut ibi vitae nostrae primitiae locarentur ubi fuerant mortis exordia" [Hence St. Ambrose, in Luke 33, teaches that Christ was crucified on Golgotha because it was fitting, he said, that the beginning of our life should be placed where the beginning of death had been].

[59] Patch, op. cit., p. 135 and n. 6.

[60] See, e.g., H. Oelsner's note to Dante's Purgatorio, XXXII, in the Modern Library ed. of the Divine Comedy, p. 388.

reader to recognize all three as arresting images of the paradoxical truth at the heart of his poem. *Pearl's* author, nurtured in the same religious tradition as Donne, also could count on his enlightened, and probably highly selected, readers to recognize the meeting place of the two Adams in the spot where the dreamer slept, as he could depend on them not to interpret the poem literally when it identifies the setting of the hilltop garden where the treasure was lost with that of the Church, where the reclaimed jewel has become a pearl of price.

The fragrance of the herb-garden also is noteworthy. The dreamer says that it produced the "sleeping-death" or trance whereby he was granted the vision:

> I felle vpon þat floury flaȝt,
> Suche odour to my herneȝ schot;
> I slode vpon a slepyng-slaȝte
> On þat precios perle wythouten spot.　　　(57–60)

> [I fell upon that flowery turf,
> such odor rose to my brains;
> I slipped into a sleeping-death
> on that precious pearl without spot.]

A perfume with special properties is a recurrent feature of saints' lives and visions, Grail legends, and accounts of mystical gardens, including the Earthly Paradise.[61] Sometimes the fragrance typifies the merit of Christ ("in whom the sweet odor of virtue dwells in its fullness and . . . flows out to others")[62] or of his saints; again it signifies divine grace, the infusion of the Holy Spirit.[63]

---

[61] For Grail legends see D. Kempe, *The Legend of the Holy Grail, EETS,* 95, pp. xxvi–xxxvii. For religious visions and the Terrestrial Paradise see Patch, pp. 26, 88, 96, 97, 100, 103, 105, 111, 113, 115, 132, 137, and Arnold Van Os, *Religious Visions,* pp. 30, 31–32, 36, 64, 67, 72, 80, 162, 166, 171, 253. For fragrance in symbolic gardens see n. 63 below.

[62] *The Catholic Missal,* arranged for daily use by Rev. Chas. J. Callan and Rev. John A. McHugh (1934), Introd., p. 31.

[63] Aquinas, *Sum. Theol.,* III (3rd no.), Q. 83, Art. 5; Lapide, VIII, 77–78, 85, 90; *Select Metrical Hymns and Homilies of Ephraem Syrus,* pp. 116–17; *St. John Damascene on Holy Images,* p. 197, Cassian, "Conferences," quoted by Ewer, p. 51.

Either or both of these allied meanings would be appropriate to the "fayr reflayr" [fair fragrance] described by the dreamer (46, 58), but the fact that it induces the salutary trance leading to his vision suggests the operation of the Holy Ghost, for it is "in Godes grace" that the man's spirit is rapt in ecstasy (63–64).

After a somewhat detailed attention to the garden because of its importance in understanding the nature of *Pearl*, we may well review the evidence for its symbolic character. 1. The burgeoning of the garden is heralded by a song alluding to the Biblical corn of wheat, commonly identified with the incarnate and risen Christ, whence sprang the harvest of the Church. 2. As yielding spice plants, it is reminiscent of the garden of Canticles, traditionally interpreted as the Virgin, the Incarnation, the Church; so that a garden became a frequent emblem for each of these. 3. All of the plants of the garden that are named in *Pearl* are medicinal, in keeping with the healing function of the Church. 4. The flowers and fruit may not grow dull or wither ('be fede,' 29). 5. Their remarkable fragrance, characteristic of mystical gardens, becomes a trance-inducing redolence, leading to a religious vision and a conversion. 6. The vision fittingly occurs during a high festival of the Church. 7. Like the Earthly Paradise, the garden is on a hill, symbol of contemplation and an appropriate setting for the garden of the Church, conceived as the recovered Eden. 8. In soil enriched by the decay of a unique pearl the garden has grown up from "that seemly seed," and now is the dwelling place of "that glorious one," the precious pearl without blemish.[64]

That the man who tells the story has become associated with the ecclesiastical garden, with access to its healing graces, is apparent from his presence there, especially at an important Church festival, "a high season," when concerned for the fate of

[64] The immaculate gem mentioned at the close of stanzas 3, 4 and 5 may be Christ Himself as the Pearl of Great Price in the setting of His Church, the Second Adam having replaced the first. Yet it may well be the dreamer's soul restored to innocence and thus identified with the ecclesiastical garden.

his lost jewel, the soul, and apparently in an attitude of prayer (49), he is granted the mystical slumber, which is both the sign and the herald of spiritual illumination. Already, he tells us, he had found consolation in the nature of Christ ("kynde of Kryst me comfort kenned" [the nature of Christ gave me comfort], (55),[65] and Reason would have brought peace to his warring members (52) had not his "wretched will" caused him to prolong his lament for the lost pearl (st. 5). Assailed by doubt and a perilous despondency, he needs direct and unmistakable testimony that his soul has indeed shared in the Atonement and the restored Paradise. This need is met in what Sister Madeleva aptly calls "his supernatural intercourse with his own soul."[66]

Their conversation is no medieval debate between Body and Soul. The man's body remains on the crest of the blossoming hill while his rapt "spyryt" [spirit] soars past riven cliffs to the wondrous garden where the maiden Pearl upbraids and consoles him. It may be sheer coincidence that the compiler of the twelfth-century *Allegoriae in Sacram Scripturam*, under the caption "Anima," specifies contemplation as the proper function of *spiritus*, one among nine faculties of the soul in the broader sense.[67] However, some division of the non-material element in man into higher and lower faculties was assumed by every medieval thinker; and, strictly speaking, only the superior or rational soul was regarded as the image of God.[68] Contemplation as the Mid-

---

[65] Christ's dual nature? His human nature, sometimes symbolized by field or garden (n. 37 above)? Wyclif said in a sermon (*Select English Works*, I, 286): "The manheed of Crist is o margerite that worshipith his Chirche and confortith mennis hertis" [The manhood of Christ is one pearl that ennobles his Church and comforts men's hearts].

[66] Sr. Madeleva, *op. cit.*, p. 132.

[67] *PL*, CXII, 852.

[68] Thomas Merton, "Poetry and the Contemplative Life," *Figures for an Apocalypse* (1947), pp. 95–111. This exposition, based on the Augustinian psychology, "the traditional substratum of Christian mystical theology" (p. 103), also looks back to the testimony of Gregory the Great, Aquinas, John of the Cross, Teresa of Avila, Ruysbroeck, Bonaventura, and Bernard, and agrees with the views of Bonaventura and the Victorines (Hugh and Richard), which I quote below. See especially Merton, pp. 103–4, 108.

dle Ages understood it normally began in converse with one's own higher soul, reformed by grace to the divine likeness. "The soul," says Peter Lombard, "is a mirror in which in some way we know God."[69] St. Bonaventura teaches that "the spirit of man beholds itself immediately, and in this vision comes to a cognitive union with God."[70] The eye of contemplation was given us "to see God within ourselves," declares Hugh of St. Victor. "The way to ascend to God is to descend into oneself."[71] Richard of St. Victor, agreeing that "the ascent is through self above self," warns: "Let him who thirsts for God clean his mirror; let him make his own spirit bright."[72]

There is, then, nothing alien to Catholic mystical tradition in the situation of the dreamer's rapt spirit in communion with his superior soul, reformed to God's image, endowed with His life, and inspired by the spirit of wisdom and understanding, gifts of the Holy Ghost. Striking analogues to the interview appear in Hugh of St. Victor's colloquy of a man with his soul, entitled *The Soul's Betrothal Gift* (*de Arrha Animae*),[73] except that here it is the man who rebukes his soul for her want of humility and gratitude for the transcendent beauty, splendor of jeweled attirings, and royal state bestowed upon her unworthy self in her betrothal to Christ. The contrasting abasement of our dreamer in the presence of Pearl, his "lyttel quene" [little queen] (e.g., in 905–6), is matched by St. Gregory Nazianzen's humility in addressing his soul; for all her divine aspiration, he tells her, she while yoked to him is "as queen in butcher's clutches."[74] The tradition was still eloquently alive in seventeenth-century Protestant England; witness Willam Drummond's apostrophe to his

---

[69] *PL*, CXCI, 1662, as quoted by Sr. Rita Mary Bradley, "Backgrounds of the Title *Speculum* in Mediaeval Literature," *Speculum*, XXIX (Jan. 1954), 111–12; cf. 106–8.

[70] R. E. Brennan, O.P., *A History of Psychology from the Standpoint of a Thomist*, p. 58.

[71] W. R. Inge, *Christian Mysticism*, p. 141 and n. 2.

[72] *Ibid.;* cf. Sr. Rita Mary Bradley, *op. cit.,* p. 108, quoting St. Basil.

[73] See n. 24 above.

[74] See n. 8 above.

soul in *The Cypress Grove*, [75] as he reminds her of her superlative beauty, wisdom, and power as a microcosmic Trinity, an image of God.

The colloquy with Pearl reveals her true state, as I hope to demonstrate in a later publication. Here a bare outline may suffice to indicate the relevance of the interview to the poet's central argument. The conversation falls into three parts. The maiden's teaching (241–360) is at first rather sternly disciplinary, as she corrects the dreamer's misconceptions regarding her and chides him for the pride and blindness of heart which have prolonged his grief and led him to set more store by his own opinion and the testimony of his senses than by God's faithful promise "to raise" his "life," though fortune (through Adam's fall) had caused his flesh to die (301–6). The humbled and submissive dreamer now expresses his longing for the unity with Pearl that he had once enjoyed, and courteously implores her to tell him of her life in her present high estate, which he declares to be the highway of his own felicity (385–96).

Pearl's reply to this request constitutes the second phase of the colloquy (397–768). First she describes her union with Christ (409–20), of whose Mystical Body each Christian soul is a member, "a longande lym" [a belonging limb] (457–68). Then she explains how she was raised to that eminence and citing the Parable of the Laborers in the Vineyard (493–564), gives an orthodox defense of her rank, as justified by the innocence that was hers through the grace of God and the merits of Christ, which were bestowed upon her in baptism. Thus was she "brought into the Vineyard" (cf. 628) and "made queen on the first day," even though she at that time "had not lived two years in our country" and knew neither Creed nor Paternoster (483–86).

Her plea for her right to be paid her wage in this manner, though she was but a newcomer to God's kingdom, is in its wider implications the Pauline argument for the New Law of grace ver-

[75] *The Cypress Grove*, pp. 52–58.

sus the Old Law of justification by works, the Law being upheld by the dreamer until Pearl convinces him of his error. In its immediate purpose, however, the debate is a defense of infant baptism, with the skeptical dreamer supplying the usual arguments of its opponents, in order that his inspired soul, bearing the image of the Divine Wisdom, may refute his reasoning and thereby quiet his doubts concerning the efficacy of his christening in infancy. This accomplished, the child of grace, as though to clinch her argument, speaks of "the matchless pearl" of everlasting bliss which "stode" (shone forth?) on her breast when Christ placed it there "in token of peace"; and straightway counsels the dreamer to "forsake the mad world" and purchase his "pearl without blemish" (729–44).

The converted man, profoundly grateful, no longer argues, but asks eager questions, as the girl proceeds to the third division of her discourse (745–960). A rhapsody on the Lamb, as conceived in turn by Isaiah, John the Baptist, and St. John the Divine in the Apocalypse, here leads naturally to an account in Apocalyptic imagery of the jocund company to which Pearl belongs, the Lamb's own retinue, and thence to a description of their city, the New Jerusalem.

The revelation, its expository phase now complete, moves on to its climax in a visual demonstration of what Pearl has said about her place among the redeemed, when the dreamer is conducted (as St. John was) to a hill, and thence beholds the New Jerusalem and the maiden hosts of the Lamb in procession, the radiant Pearl amongst them (960–1150). The ecstatic man's awakening, after his impulsive attempt to join the throng by crossing the stream that separates him from his "little queen" (1151–73), is moving close to the adventure in contemplation, which had already reached its apex and served its purpose by convincing the dreamer that the Redemption had indeed taken place and that his soul has shared in it.

Early in his vision of Pearl, we may recall, he expressed delight at learning of her exalted rank and declared it to be the highway of his own joy:

For I am ful fayn þat your astate
Is worþen to worschyp and wele, iwysse;
Of alle my joy þe hyȝe gate
Hit is, in grounde of alle my blysse.   (393–96)

[For I am very glad that your condition
has come to honor and happiness, certainly;
of all my joy it is the highway,
the foundation of all my bliss.]

On awaking from his trance he acknowledges the same relationship between Pearl's fortunes and his own by concluding that all is well with him in "this dungeon of grief" if she does indeed go adorned with a "gay garland" (the crown of pearl) and is pleasing to the Prince:

"O perle," quod I, "of rych renoun,
So watȝ hit me dere þat þou con deme
In þis veray avysyoun!
If hit be ueray and soth sermoun
Þat þou so stykeȝ in garlande gay.
So wel is me in þys doel-doungoun
Þat ȝou art to þat Prynseȝ paye."   (1182–88)

["Oh, Pearl," said I, "of rich glory,
so was it dear to me what you did speak
in this true vision!
If it be a true account
that you are set so in a gay garland,
then all is well with me in this dungeon of grief,
that you are a pleasure to that Prince."]

The earthly prison-house has been transformed for him by his insight into the potential welfare of his soul, the avenue to his own blessedness. It remains, nevertheless, for the awakened dreamer to heed the girl's admonition to purchase his jewel: "I rede þe forsake þe worlde wode / And porchace þy perle maskelles" [I counsel you to forsake the mad world and purchase your faultless pearl] (743–44). At his baptism in infancy his soul had been endowed with the pearl of eternal life solely on the faith of the Church, after sponsors on his behalf had made the essential professions of faith and for him had renounced the prince of the power of this world and "all his works and all his pomps."[76] Now, as a responsible adult, the man must redeem his right to the jewel by an active personal faith and by renouncing worldly desires of his own volition.[77] To do so is to redeem the soul as well as the pearl of felicity. St. Augustine declares that we are not free to earn the "one precious margarite," for which the price is ourselves, until we have first liberated ourselves by despising the temporal possessions that have shackled us. To purchase the margarite, he explains, we must first reclaim and possess ourselves.[78] Further, if the dreamer is not in a state of grace, he must restore the innocence that was his after the guilt of original sin had been remitted in baptism; Pearl had specified that he must purchase his "pearl without blemish" ("maskelles"). For one already baptized "who sins anew," she had explained, the cleansing must be effected through the sacrament of penance (649–72). A sinful man may "shine" through shrift, we read in the companion-piece *Cleanness*; through penance he may "become a pearl," an undefiled soul.[79]

At all events we find the hero at the triumphant close of the story in a state of grace and friendship with God, as he quietly purchases the pearl, first of all by giving it up. Having learned, with St. Paul and Dante, that "His will is our peace" (1153–1200), the awakened dreamer commits his soul to God in terms

[76] The medieval baptismal services in England are described by H. B. Swete, *Church Services and Service Books before the Reformation*, pp. 138–43; Wm. Maskell, *Monumente Ritualia Ecclesiae Anglicanae* (2nd ed., 1882), I, 3–43.

[77] "The solemn renewal of this promise [the renunciation of Satan and his works and pomps] is a favourite exercise of piety, often undertaken in common at the end of a mission or retreat" (*Catholic Encyclopaedia*, article on "Baptismal Vows").

[78] *PL*, XXXV, 1571. Cf. D. W. Robertson, *MLN*, LXV, 158, who defines "world" in this utterance of Pearl's as "cupidity for temporalia."

[79] Lines 1113–16: "Þaȝ þou be men fenny / And al to-marred in myre, whyl þou on molde lyves, / Þou may schyne þurȝ schryft þaȝ þou half schome served, / And pure þe wiþ penaunce tyl þou a perle worþe" [Though you are a soiled man and all marred in mire, while you live on earth, you may shine through confession though you have served shame, and purify yourself with penance until you become a pearl].

of the Psalmist's prayer (Ps. 31:5), repeated by our Lord on the Cross ("In manus tuas commendo spiritum meum" [Into your hands I commit my spirit]):

> Ouer þis hyul þis lote I laȝte,
> For pyty of my perle enclyin,
> And syþen to God I hit bytaȝte.　　　　(1205–07)

> [Upon this hill I received this lot,
> prostrate out of sorrow for my pearl,
> and then I committed it to God.]

Recited in the Daily Office, this prayer of Christ and David was also used commonly in the vernacular devotions of the laity, with *commendo* usually rendered by "bytake" or "byteche," and *spiritum* by "soule," "soule and lyf(f)," or "soule or lyf(f)."[80]

The passage in which the verses just quoted appear, the final stanza of *Pearl,* announces the triumphant culmination to which the poem has tended from its opening line ("Perle, plesaunte to pryces paye" [Pearl, pleasant to a prince's pleasure]):

> To pay þe Prince oþer sete saȝte
> Hit is ful eþe to þe god Krystyin;
> For I haf founden hym, boþe day and naȝte,
> A God, a Lorde, a frende ful fyin.
> Ouer þis huyl þis lote I laȝte,
> For pyty of my perle enclyin,
> And syþen to God I hit bytaȝte.
> In Krysteȝ dere blessyng and myn,
> Þat in þe forme of bred and wyn
> Þe preste vus scheweȝ vch a daye,
> He gef vus to be his homly hyne
> Ande precious perleȝ vnto his pay.　　　　(1201–12)
> 　　　　Amen.　　　　Amen.

> [To please the Prince or bring about peace
> is very easy to the good Christian;
> for I have found him, both day and night,

---

[80] See *OED* under *betake* and cf. F. A. Patterson, *The Medieval Penitential Lyric,* pp. 87, 120; C. Horstmann, *Yorkshire Writers,* I, 236; *Minor Poems of the Vernon MS.,* I, 231, lines 363–66; *The Wycliffite New Testament,* ed. Henry H. Baber, Luke 23:46.

> a God, a Lord, a most noble friend.
> (1201–04; see below for remainder.)]

The lines may be taken in more than one sense. According to the traditional reading the speaker commended his jewel to God in the Blessed Sacrament, and the last two verses constitute a prayer that we may be servants in God's household and pearls of price according to His pleasure. As I have punctuated the stanza here, however, the last five lines simply affirm the privilege offered to mankind in the Eucharist, wherein the friendship with God, just mentioned, finds its supreme sacramental expression. Thus construed, the final passage (1205–12), an epitome of the story and its message, would read as follows: "This lot befell me on this hill, bowed in sorrow for my pearl, and afterwards I intrusted it to God. In the dear blessing and memorial of Christ, whom the priest shows us daily in the form of bread and wine, He granted us to be servants of His household and pearls of price for His delight." The appended "Amen, Amen" then becomes the usual closing prayer, a corroborating petition, "So be it."

Fortunately, though, minor differences of interpretation cannot obscure the central import of the closing stanza. A Catholic Paradise Lost and Regained, beginning with the death of the soul and occupied at its center with the Atonement and the grace of baptism, by which the soul is reborn to supernatural life, would hardly close without some recognition of the prime sacrament by which that life is sustained. "Baptism is the beginning of the spiritual life," writes St. Thomas, "and the door of all the sacraments; whereas the Eucharist is, as it were, the consummation of the spiritual life, and the end of all the sacraments. . . . Baptism is the sacrament of Christ's death and Passion, according as a man is born anew in Christ in virtue of his Passion; but the Eucharist is the sacrament of Christ's Passion, according as a man is made perfect in union with Christ who suffered."[81]

The dreamer's friendship with God is the continuation of his

---

[81] *Sum. Theol.*, III, Q. 73, Art. 3.

144

infant soul's espousal to Christ,[82] described and confirmed in his dream, a union which is both symbolized and actualized in the Eucharist. His part in the sacrament as a member of the Mystical Body also epitomizes his fellowship with Pearl's companions of the vision, the host of redeemed souls among the living and the dead, "the blessed company of all faithful people." Thus within the limits of daily mundane life he sustains the relationships which in his trance were revealed ideally, under the aspect of eternity.

The tests for a consistent reading of the allegory which were specified at the outset of this essay have been met in the interpretation it proposes. The soul is something which the poet, with ample warrant, could represent as a pearl and at the same time as a maiden who had "died" in infancy and had been redeemed by Christ. The jewel of immortal life, with which the soul was identified and endowed, is something that the poet, and his hero, "lost, mourned, and could recover through the grace of God, strengthened by partaking of the Blessed Sacrament."

[82] "Grace" (*Catholic Encyc.*): "The Friendship with God is one of the most excellent effects of grace. . . . According to the Scriptural concept (Wisdom, 7: 14; John 15: 51) this friendship resembles a mystical matrimonial union between the soul and its Divine Spouse"(Matt. 9: 15; Apoc. 19: 7).

7

THE CONSTRUCTION OF
PIERS PLOWMAN

Henry W. Wells

MANY STRIKINGLY DIVERGENT VIEWS HAVE BEEN ADVANCED AS
to the structural integrity or looseness of *Piers Plowman*. Its
early critics, to be sure, had little to say upon the subject but
there seemed to be general agreement in the view that the work
is loosely put together. The long summaries by Morley and
others, for example, give small evidence that the critics had detected any strong organizing elements in the design. With the
strenuous attack by Professor Manly, a new epoch in the criticism of the work began. Scholars who favored multiple authorship naturally agreed that the poem lacks a well-defined plan,
and even advanced the view that we have in fact not only from
two to five authors but from two to five poems, all upon themes
in important respects dissimilar and more or less loosely constructed. While Professor Manly tore Piers' seamless coat

Reprinted, by permission of the Modern Language Association, from
PMLA, XLIV (1929), 123–40. For further developments of the view
expressed here, see Neville Coghill, "The Character of Piers Plowman
Considered from the B-Text," *Medium Aevum*, II (1933), 108–35;
Henry W. Wells, "The Philosophy of *Piers Plowman*," *PMLA*, LIII
(1938), 339–49; R. W. Chambers, *Man's Unconquerable Mind* (London,
1939), pp. 88–171. For dissenting views, see S. S. Hussey, "Langland,
Hilton, and the Three Lives," *Review of English Studies*, N.S., VII
(1956), 132–51; R. W. Frank, Jr., *Piers Plowman and the Scheme of
Salvation* (Yale University Press, 1957), pp. 29–33.

asunder, the advocates of a single authorship—somewhat less emphatically, to be sure—found relative coherence in the poem as a whole and discounted the view that the style is excessively digressive. Throughout the controversy the critics dealt largely with textual problems, only occasionally turning to consider the primary subject-matter of the work. The articles of Mensendieck furnished the most important contributions to an interpretation of an underlying plan, especially in regard to the most difficult section, the *Vita de Do-Well*. His chief concern, however, was with a few theses relating to special passages, so that his studies hardly deal with the larger problem of the enveloping thoughts of the poem, if indeed such thoughts exist. Thus far investigation has resulted in many contradictory views but in no detailed statement upon the cardinal problem in the interpretation of *Piers Plowman*.

The problem of the authorship of the poem actually bears only indirectly on that of the poem's organization. It should not be forgotten that some of the most loosely constructed of Elizabethan plays, as *Old Fortunatus*, are apparently the work of one poet, while some of the best unified, as *The Maid's Tragedy*, and *Eastward Ho!*, are known to have been written by two or more poets. I cannot regard the assumption of divided authorship as decisive one way or another in determining the philosophical or æsthetic coherence of the medieval poem. Certain of the conclusions reached in the present investigation seem favorable to divided authorship, while rather more of them favor single authorship. But I do not wish the present article to be viewed as a contribution to the controversy in any but a distinctly secondary degree.

Undoubtedly the author or authors enjoyed the effect of violent transitions and surprises and definitely sought this effect in the poem. This is merely to recognize it as a dream poem, composed in the same spirit that dominates gothic architecture. The poem undoubtedly has a rough surface. To read it is like riding over a bad road; we are jerked and bounced and tossed. But so we may be at the hands of the most rigorous logician. That the poem has a rough surface should by no means prejudice us as to its fundamental coherence or incoherence. Thus, although Dean Swift's sermons are as smooth as polished marble and Donne's as rough as a thistle, the latter are quite as likely to be fundamentally coherent as those by the Dean of Saint Patrick's. That a poem is of the gothic spirit really tells us nothing of its essential organization or disorganization. The latter qualities cannot be felt by mere surface touch, such as we employ for style. An alligator's skin may be rougher than the surface of a pile of sand, but one covers an exquisite organism and the other is merely a confused heap. We cannot "sense" the answer to our problem; we must analyze the poem.

In this discussion I shall distinguish the two chief parts of the poem by the names generally employed in the colophons themselves. The first part of the work, which concludes with the story of Piers' pardon and the poet's reflections thereon, I shall call the *Visio*, and the remainder of the poem, the Vita, which is itself divided into three parts, the *Vita de Do-Well, Do-Bet* and *Do-Best*. I shall examine first the *Visio* and the *Vita*, secondly the relations to each other of the subsections of the *Visio* and finally the relations of the subsections in the *Vita*.

1

The relation of the *Visio* and the *Vita* has never been carefully stated and often has been, at least from my own point of view, ill understood. The *Visio* is a study of the life of the laity both as it is and as it should be. We have in this part of the poem that which the common communicant ought to know, and nothing more. We have no abstruse theological or philosophical problems, no allegory of learning, no account of the saintly life and no thorough and detailed analysis of the functioning of the Church as the coördinating principle in society. On the other hand, we have such social satire and such an account of man's religious duties as the humblest medieval reader might be expected to understand. If he follows the road here traced by the poet, he is considered to be sure of salvation. With the *Vita* the theme is changed. We have an account of the world as seen by the thinker who has passed through the medieval disciplines of learning, asceticism and priestly responsibility. He has known the intellectual life, the mystic and the active life, and so fulfilled the more arduous duties which heaven imposes upon its specially chosen warriors. In this part of the poem the satire falls not upon delinquencies in secular duties, but upon faults peculiar to persons dedicated to the life of scholarship and religious practice: upon those who, like the gluttonous Doctor, the feigning Hermit and the over-indulgent Confessor, betray learning, devotion and the institution of the Church. This part of the poem deals with ideals superfluous to and improper in a layman, but to which God's select soldiers must conform if they are to remain loyal and in turn win their salvation.

To a certain point the two Lives agree. This is why the author of the so-called A-text continued his poem beyond the *Visio*. The *Vita* begins humbly. It gives an account of the life of man from his birth to his intellectual and spiritual maturity. It contains passages dealing successively with the creation of the world, the birth and care of children, marriage and the preliminary disciplines of study. The chief figures encountered in the allegory are Will, the name symbolically given to the Christian Pilgrim at birth, Thought, who meets him in his earliest years, Wit, his first teacher, and Study, who gives him elementary training and who introduces him to Scripture and to Clergy, who is with Scripture. But in the A-text the pilgrim learns little from Scripture and nothing from Clergy, who will have nothing to do with him. The word Clergy the poet here uses, of course, as virtually synonymous with learning. In short, the A-text breaks off just where the education of the more enterprising layman would be expected to conclude. Born with will, early endowed with thought and wit, acquainted with elementary learning, he represents the foundation upon which, after all, even the greatest seer and the deepest thinker of the Church must build.

We may now see why the A-text was circulated so widely. It contained what the common man needed to know and no more. If the A-text had ended with the *Visio*, it would have instructed the layman in all his primary duties to God and man, but it would not have shown him concretely his place in society and his relation to the Clergy and the Religious. Thus the section of the *Vita* included in the A-text formed a part of that Manuscript Version as circulated among the people. I have no opinion as to whether the author soon after writing the A-text died, or continued his poem and encouraged reproductions of the A-text even after the B-text had been finished. I observe, however, that the A-text ends at a point which, if unsatisfactory from an æsthetic standpoint, is entirely satisfactory from a doctrinal standpoint. The *Vita* repeats certain elements of the *Visio*. The man of religion must be born, possess will, thought and wit, and know his ABC's just as a common communicant. His salvation comes from the same source. Piers the Plowman saves one no less than the other. Each must to some degree Do Well. Each must know and seriously consider the Creed and Paternoster and follow the road of the Ten Commandments. Each requires the same sacraments. Thus in each section we have allusions to baptism and burial and elaborate passages dealing with penance and the Mass. These repetitions may or may not, I take it, be viewed as inartistic, but are clearly necessary to the subject in hand. The poem in its design may be thought of as one of those great canvasses which Veronese and Tintoretto delighted to paint in which a pillar divides the picture into two finely balanced scenes of approximately equal magnitude, although one is slightly more significant than the other.

My view is confirmed by colophons in the B-text Manuscripts which describe the part of the poem that the *Vita de Do-Well* and the A-text have in common as both a part of the *Visio* and of the *Vita*. The foregoing conclusions may be expressed in tabular form as given [below].

While the *Vita* is clearly stated to be divided into three parts, it is commonly observed that the *Visio* is also divided into three parts. Closely following upon the first vision of the Field of Folk and of Holy Church, which is clearly introductory, we have the Story of Lady Meed, the Confession and Absolution of the Sins at Church, and the two concluding Passus dealing with Piers and his servants and concluding with the story of the Pardon. I

The *Visio*	The *Vita* (A-Text)	Remaining Section of the *Vita*
The life of the common communicant: the demands of nature; plowmen, artisans, knights, ladies, merchants and lawyers: *Conscience;* the Ten Commandments; the elements of the faith; sacramental needs	Common attributes of laity and clergy: the demands of nature; *Anima, Inwit, Will, Thought, (elementary) Study; Conscience;* the Ten Commandments; the elements of the faith; sacramental needs	The higher order of perfection required of the Priesthood, or *Clergy*

shall later examine the character of the transitions in greater detail. For the present, however, I am concerned only with observing those parallels which I believe to be deliberate between the three parts of the *Visio* and the three parts of the *Vita*. A tabular scheme may here prove useful [see page 153].

The first main part of the *Visio*, namely the Story of Lady Meed, deals with the problem of secular government and nearly at its conclusion introduces us to a figure named Reason, who decides for the king the quarrel between Meed and Conscience. Reason thus becomes the central figure in this section of the poem. The first part of the *Vita,* or the *Vita de Do-Well*, deals with problems of theology. Again Reason proves the culminating figure, since all the preceding allegorical types in the *Vita de Do-Well* lead up to it, and after its appearance we enter the long

	Visio	*Vita*
	Story of Lady Meed	*Vita de Do-Well*
Part I	Problems of economic and secular government; temporal welfare; *Reason;* the Active Life	Problems of theology and Church government; eternal salvation; *Reason;* the Active Life (Part I): *Activa Vita*
	The Sins	*Vita de Do-Bet*
Part II	Inner life of the ordinary Christian; preparation for the Mass	The Contemplative or Religious Life: solitude and faithful hermits; preparation for the Mass
	The Plowman's Pardon	*Vita de Do-Best*
Part III	The plow of the honest laborer; hope for salvation of the individual; satire on indulgences; the Active Life	The mystic plow with which Christ cultivates souls; despair for the spiritual welfare of Christian Society (*Unitas*); satire on indulgences; the Active Life (Part II): Christ as Preacher; the cure of souls

transition to the *Vita de Do-Bet*. The chief problem in the Story of Lady Meed is man's well-being in this world. The chief problem debated in the *Vita de Do-Well* is man's eternal well-being. One section deals with the active life of secular affairs, the other, with the active life of industrious theological study. The Story of the Confession and Absolution of the Sins deals obviously with the more personal, intimate and inner life. It concludes with an allegory of the Mass, the sacrament which restores man to the Grace of his Creator. The *Vita de Do-Bet* deals with the life of solitude and contemplation (of this I shall have more to say later), and concludes with the bells that ring in Easter and which summon the dreamer to the sacrament. The Story of Piers in the *Visio* deals with the theme of honest work and its reward, which is pardon and salvation. Here for the first time we meet the image of the plow, in this case simply the plow of the farmer. In outward appearance at least even Piers himself is no more than an overseer or even a participant in these physical labors. He exacts honest labor and receives no easy indulgences in his pardon. In the *Vita de Do-Best* we have an allegory of the entire community envisaged as *Unitas* laboring at its myriad tasks under the guidance of the Church. Here Piers and his plow once more appear, but Piers is now indubitably Christ, his plow the word of God, man the harvest and the barn the heaven of divine rest. This imagery has, to be sure, been hinted in the *Vita de Do-Bet*, but here is first objectified. Piers' wicked servants, the unscrupulous priests and friars, grant easy indulgences. In the *Visio* we have seen the promise of salvation for the honest worker. The individual may be saved. In the *Vita* we have the picture of society retrogressing rather than progressing. Individuals, as notably an honest priest, may still be saved. But the community goes from bad to worse. We should, I think, regard as deliberate both these comparisons and these contrasts between the six major sections of the poem. In each case the lines seem to me to have been too sharply drawn to be accidental. I believe that the author or authors deliberately repeated the major elements in the design.

2

The *Vita* is obviously the more complex part of the poem, as it is also the longer part. It has, however, been the less discussed. I shall glance comparatively briefly at the outstanding features in the construction of the *Visio*. I consider that they show a point of view by no means haphazard or confused. For each of the major images presented there can, I think, be given convincing reasons as to why it is pertinent to the theme of the poem as a whole and as to why it occupies the position which it actually holds in the work.

We are introduced to the Field of Folk because the poet begins his teaching not with revelation nor with religion but with nature. So he begins later in his *Vita de Do-Well* and at the conclusion of that section of the poem assures us that even Saracens in substance know the first Person of the Trinity. Moreover *Piers Plowman*, unlike the poems by Dante and Milton, contains no scene in heaven. Once only and for the space of but three hundred lines the scene sinks to the deep dungeon and dark from which Christ rescues our forefathers in darkness. With the exception of the Harrowing of Hell the poet avoids all scenes that belong to another life than that of this world. In short, the scene of *Piers Plowman* is precisely the opposite of that of Dante's poem. The Italian poet deals only with life beyond the grave, the English poet only with life upon this side of the grave. The whole poem deals in this sense with the Field of Folk. Its author or authors contrived most vividly and forcefully to state an initial proposition. The work remains in this respect at least remarkably true to its premises. Even from an aesthetic standpoint it holds faithful to this field and to this earth. Its varied imagery always breathes earth-odors.

Holy Church, the figure who next appears, begins her instructions with homely and materialistic observations. She too acknowledges first of all the animal nature of man. Three things she tells the dreamer are necessary, food, drink, and clothing. From this characteristic teaching she elevates her discussion till at the last she states the doctrine of the Redemption and its moral of charity. But she always fulfills the function of a Prologue. She never tells the dreamer more than any child might be expected to know. She reads him, as it were, his catechism, stating simply those ideas upon which the whole of the Christian System rests: the doctrine of free will, of the depravity of the body, of obedience to God, of charity and of grace.

In her last words Holy Church warns the pilgrim of evil and bids him be wary of distributing blame. She disappears, after serving not only as a Prologue but as a link to the first part of the story proper, the allegory of Lady Meed. The Greek mind would of course have left the problem of the state to the last, as the highest and most important of all problems. The medieval poet, however, true to premises already contained in his poem, regards religion and the Church as the supreme guide in life, and treats the state as an initial problem to be faced before proceeding to far graver problems. Thus the political life vividly introduces us to sin. Man's error lies not in false political theory but in his personal weakness. Sin becomes the vital issue. Thus we are logically led to the second chief division of the *Visio*, the Story of the Confession and Absolution of the Sins.

If it should be urged against my view of the distinct functions of the *Visio* and the *Vita* that of the six or seven characters representing the sins (for the number differs in the different texts) one of the characters is a priest, I should reply that in embodying sloth in human form the poet followed a well-tried tradition in making Sloth a priest. It should be noted that the faults ascribed to this idler include many omissions and commissions not in the least peculiar to his profession. He is the eternal truant from duty. His truancy, not his duty, concerns the poet here. Sloth cannot be said to represent the short-comings of the Clergy as such. A further objection might be raised in that the C-text of the *Visio* and this only contains a passage of some length on the sins of monks and friars. The lines occur in the sermon of Reason, which introduces the Story of the Sins and links it with the preceding Story of Lady Meed, wherein Reason is also a character. Reason's sermon is obviously intended to enumerate the outstanding sins of all orders of society. That in two texts the clergy and the religious receive slight notice and in the third no more than a moderate proportion of attention, seems to me on the whole to support rather than to damage my position. The clergy appear almost forgotten in many long passages. In the lines dealing with Hunger we hear of the friars only as laborers in the common fields, driven by famine to desert their normal course of life. We should of course remember that the *Visio* reflects life as the layman sees it, not merely as he lives it. Although not a participant in their peculiar problems, he both observes the clergy and the learned and recognizes the great influence which they exercise upon him.

The confession of the Sinners is followed by their absolution and by the quest of society for a better life. This leads us to the third section of the *Visio*. The extremely popular appeal of the *Visio* as a whole is powerfully enhanced by the allegory in the Passus dealing with Famine. Although in this section of the poem the activities of the higher orders of society are noted, as that of knights and ladies, we hear most of the common laborers and especially of their unwillingness to do honest work in the plowfields. The opening of the last Passus of the *Visio* gives a list of all classes, in which the clergy are but hastily mentioned, while detailed attention is accorded to merchants, lawyers and, once more, to laborers. Laymen pretending to be priests are condemned.

We should observe caution in our interpretation of Piers' pardon. It states that all who do well shall be saved and that all who do evil shall be damned. Later the author gives his own view as somewhat more moderate, for he grants that the Pope and the prayers of the Church have some power to save souls, although to trust in such aids is not so safe as to do well. Piers' pardon is simply *Do-Well* as applied in particular to the laity. The clergy and the religious must also *Do-Well*, and in a more exacting degree. By "doing" and by "working" medieval authors do not of course mean merely temporal actions. Thus Hilton's treatise *On Daily Work* deals in large part with prayer and meditation. Piers never of course fancied that a Christian could forsake faith, devotion and the sacraments and by mere bodily works go to heaven. He meant that a man must be saved primarily upon his own merits and by God's grace, and not by the aid of indulgences. It is not from the nature of this pardon but from the character of the *Visio* as a whole that we may safely regard the *Visio* as addressed primarily to the laity. Piers' pardon, even in the *Visio*, applies to all mankind. That a priest scorns it, however, helps us to perceive its applicability to the people. The

Visio ends with the pardon because with the need for a pardon it begins. Man is shown in a transient state. He may, on dying, go either to the deep dungeon or to the fair tower. The first prayer which the pilgrim passionately addresses to Holy Church consists in the one vital question for every devout medieval man. The question is simply, how may I save my soul? We may conclude then that so far as the larger contours of form are concerned the *Visio* is a well-arranged poem. Like the typical dream allegory, it appears even wildly discordant upon the surface. But when the meanings of the symbols are considered, we become aware of the presence of no inconsiderable design.

3

The *Visio* introduces us not only to the name of *Do-Well* but to the need for the *Vita* as a whole. In his last speeches Piers in the *Visio* states that he will change his course of life: instead of being so busy about his physical welfare, he will do as the apostles did and turn chiefly to the cultivation of his soul. This forewarns us of the change which we are about to encounter in the Second Part of the poem. And here we are faced with our gravest problems, to which, however, answers may be given I think with

Do-Well	Do-Bet	Do-Best
The Active Life of intellectual studies and priestly duties; *Activa Vita;*	The Contemplative Life; discussion of faithful hermits;	The Active Life expressed in the corporate Church, or *Unitas;* especially the rule of the Bishop;
self-rule; the Ten Commandments and the Seven Sins; allegorical figures and contemporary allusions; the protection of the Father	self-obliteration; the three Contemplative or Christian Virtues; many scriptural figures; the protection of the Son	the cure of souls; the four Active or Moral Virtues; allegorical figures and contemporary allusions again; the protection of the Holy Spirit

even more assurance than in the case of the *Visio*. Again I have ventured to clarify my views by the use of a tabular scheme.

Let us review a few of the outstanding features of the *Vita de Do-Well, Do-Bet* and *Do-Best*. This part of the poem represents the search of an imaginary pilgrim for three "lives" or "virtues" or, as we should be more likely to say in the language of present-day psychology, three states. The pilgrim meets many characters, the chief of whom are in the order in which he meets them, Thought, Wit, Study, Scripture, Clergy, Nature, Patience, Hawkin the Active Man and Piers Plowman. From most of these characters the pilgrim inquires who are Do-Well, Do-Bet and Do-Best, and from no two of them does he receive quite the same answer. Had they agreed, he might possibly have given up the quest. Wit tells him that Do-Well is to labor honestly, while Clergy tells him that Do-Well is principally to be loyal to the Faith. Clearly each character has something to contribute to the pilgrim's growing knowledge of his life's journey. Each represents a progressive stage in his education. The different answers show not that the poet himself is confused (the poet knew, I think, his answer from the beginning) but that his pilgrim is groping his way, as do all men toward a solution of life's difficulties. He quarrels with all his teachers, makes mistakes, falls by the way, because of his peculiar temperament profits more from some teachers than from others and ultimately reaches the knowledge which he desires, only to find that in forgetting himself and taking upon him the burden of society he has borne Christ's cross. For the individual Christian may be saved, but society as a whole is not destined to achieve harmony on earth. The kingdom of Piers the Plowman is not of this world.

The three stages of life are always described as three grades of holiness. About the last grade we have from the first the greatest agreement. Again and again it is allegorized in the image of the bishop who guards his flock. To rule others is to Do Best. To rule one's self is to Do Well. Do-Bet is described as an advanced state of charity and humility. But the states are clearly and consistently presented in themselves, that is, in the three several parts of the poem; and we need not be over-puzzled by what the first persons whom the pilgrim meets say about them. We may I think say confidently on the basis of the entire character of the Passus dealing with Do-Well that this state is one of self-culture through knowledge. All the chief figures whom the pilgrim meets until very near the end of this section of the poem are evidently stages in his scholastic training. If he lapses for a time to follow Desire of the Eyes and Lust of the Flesh, he in time returns. Even his detour with Nature is at least a part of his academic life. The Life of Do-Bet begins with a long passage in praise of faithful hermits and in behalf of a true priesthood, introducing us to the three Christian or contemplative virtues—faith, hope and charity—here named Abraham, Spes and Piers Plowman. This part of the poem is centered in the biblical narrative. Its chief images are not, as elsewhere, of the poet's own invention, but are drawn from the synoptic Gospels and from the Apocrypha. The *Vita de Do-Best* narrates the history of the Church from its beginning in the Resurrection, through the period of its primitive purity to its present state of degeneration. The story is told primarily not from the individual but from the social point of view. It is the story of *Unitas*, of Piers' family. It deals in particular with the government, or misgovernment, of this family, and hence with the responsibility of those who rule the Church, the confessors and prelates. It tells of the Christian Society that, although protected by the Holy Spirit and sustained by the bread of the sacrament, is subject to ceaseless incursions from its enemies, led by Satan. The four active or cardinal virtues—justice, prudence, fortitude and temperance—are discussed at considerable length. Allusions of a clearly secondary importance, however, are still made to the pilgrim, who is now old and hoar, but has not as yet attained true happiness on earth. The Field of Folk cannot give such happiness. Salvation is not of this world. Here the poem ends.

Once in the course of his journey the Pilgrim expresses surprise to learn that there are three states of life instead of two. He had always supposed that the two stages were the active life and the contemplative life. But he finds himself unmistakably in a world ordered in patterns of three. His teacher at this point gives just such an ambiguous answer as a good teacher always gives when he knows that it is best for his pupil to find the answer in his own experience. Yet the doctrine upon which the triple division of the poem has been made was really a familiar one in medieval thought. Saint Thomas expresses it as follows:

Vita contemplativa simpliciter est melior quam activa quae occupatur circa corporales actus: sed vita activa, secundum quam aliquis praedicando et docendo contemplata aliis tradit, est perfectior quam vita quae solum est contemplativa: quia talis vita praesupponit abundantiam contemplationis. Et ideo Christus talem vitam elegit (*S.T.*, Part III, Quæst. XL, A. 1).

[The contemplative life simply taken is better than the active life that is occupied with corporeal acts: but the active life that involves transmitting to others by preaching and teaching what has been contemplated is more perfect than the life which is contemplative alone: because a life of this kind presupposes an abundance of contemplation. Such a life, therefore, was chosen by Christ.]

A summary of Bernard's view may be found in a work very popular in England in the fourteenth century, the *Meditationes Vitae Christi*. As the reader will at once observe, this passage agrees with the poem in some interesting points of detail.

Est igitur vita actiua, quae designatur per Martham. Sed actiuae vitae, sicut ex dictis Bernardi colligere possum, duae sunt partes. Prima pars, qua quis se exercet ad suam principaliter vtilitatem corrigendo se, emendando a vitiis, & informando virtutibus. Et idem secundario sit ad vtilitatem etiam proximi per opera iustitiae, & obsequia pietatis, & charitatis. Secunda pars eius est, quo modo quis principaliter suum exercitium confert in vtilitatem proximi, quamvis ad suum etiam maius meritum, vt alios regendo, docendo, & adiuuando in animarum salutem, vt faciunt Praelati, & Praedicatores, & huiusmodi. & inter has duas partes vitae actiuae, est vita contemplatiua, vt iste sit ordo, quod primo quis se exerceat, & laboret in oratione, & sacrarum studio literarum, & aliis operibus bonis, & obsequiis in conuersatione, quasi corrigendo se a vitiis,

& acquirendo virtutes. Secundo quiescat in contemplatione, solitudinem mentis quaerens, & soli Deo vacans toto posse. Tertio per praedicta duo exercitia, virtutibus, & vera sapientia imbutus & illuminatus, & feruidus effectus, ad aliorum salutem intendat. Primo, igitur, vt tetigi, oportet, quod in prima actiua parte, mens expurgetur, depuretur, & roboretur per exercitia virtutum: deinde in contemplatiua informetur, illuminetur, & instruatur: postea confidenter potest ad aliorum profectus exire, vt eos possit adiuuare.

[There is, therefore, the active life, which is designated by Martha. But of the active life, as I can gather from the remarks of Bernard, there are two parts. The first part is that whereby one strives principally toward his own advantage by improving himself, by freeing himself from vices and informing himself with virtues. Let him be the same, furthermore, with respect to his neighbor's advantage, through works of justice and the pursuit of holiness and charity. Its second part is in the way one devotes his efforts principally to his neighbor's advantage, even though to his own greater merit as well, such as by ruling, teaching, and helping others to the salvation of their souls, as do Prelates, Preachers, and the like. And between these two parts of the active life is the contemplative, and this is the order, that first one exerts himself and labors in prayer, in the study of sacred literature, and in other good works, and by compliance in his manner of living, just as by correcting his own vices and acquiring virtues. Second, let him repose in contemplation, seeking solitude of mind, and thus undistracted he can do all things for God alone. Third, through the aforesaid exercises having been imbued and illuminated with virtues and true wisdom, and then rendered fervent, he may exert himself for the salvation of others. First, therefore, as I have mentioned, it is necessary that in the first active part the mind be purged, cleansed, and strengthened by the exercise of virtue: then in the contemplative part let it be moulded, illuminated, and instructed: afterward one is able confidently to go out to the service of others, so that he is able to help them.]

Here we have the chief elements comprising the three "lives" in *Piers Plowman*. Walter Hilton in the fourteenth and Thomas Pecock in the fifteenth century also evince the popular interest in the problem of the three states. The *Meditationes*, which was commonly ascribed to St. Bonaventura, was translated into English during the later century by Nicholas Love.

There is still a further organizing factor to be noted in the instance of the poem. St. Augustine had advanced what has come to be known as the "psychological trinity." *Piers Plowman* does not follow Augustine's thought but presents a somewhat similar conception. The poet several times quotes the familiar text which declares man to be fashioned in God's image. He evidently considered that, since God is a Trinity, man must in some sense also be a trinity. Each of the three Parts of the *Vita* begins with allusions to the interrelation of the three parts of the Trinity and each is clearly dedicated to a special Person of the Trinity. At the conclusion of the *Vita de Do-Well* we are told that even the Saracens believe in God the Father. It is this Person of the Trinity who clearly presides over the Life of Do-Well. Christ as Piers the Plowman is the central theme of the *Vita de Do-Bet*. In this part of the poem the life of Christ, his crucifixion and the harrowing of hell supply the chief narrative elements. The *Vita de Do-Best* is no less clearly dedicated to the Holy Spirit, since it narrates at considerable length the descent of the Spirit at Pentecost, the Gifts of the Spirit and the rule of the Spirit within the Church, protecting it from even greater inroads than have as yet been made by the armies of Anti-Christ. Such is the spiritual trinity of man according to *Piers Plowman*, a thought of no inconsiderable importance in the organization of the work.

It would be manifestly impossible in the brief space of this paper to discuss any large number of details in the *Vita* which indicate the organizing genius of its author or authors. I should prefer to allow my statements relative to the major plan of the poem to stand out for the time being conspicuously, rather than to run the risk of smothering these primary outlines under a mass of detail, however interesting that detail might be to careful students of the poem. A few observations of lesser importance may however detain us.

In the first place it will not of course be assumed that because the Life of Do-Best is dedicated to God the Holy Spirit and the Life of Do-Well to God the Father that the poet had fallen into the heresy of holding the Third greater than the First Person of the Trinity. The poem and the states are of course cumulative. The poet learns early in his career that the Life of Do-Best for example presumes that of Do-Bet. And it not only presumes this preceding life, but includes it. This the imagery of the poem makes clear. Piers the Plowman is still active in the Life of Do-Best. But to know Piers the Plowman it becomes necessary to meet him in the Life of Do-Bet. Man never loses his need for learning or contemplation. He does not outgrow these powers but by them and by their constant use attains a third power, namely, the ability and the right to rule other men. It is better to know two persons of the Trinity than to know one, and better to know three Persons than to know two. Indeed none can truly be known without a knowledge of all.

The first third of the *Vita de Do-Well,* that is, the part contained in the A-text, is naturally the easiest and most straightforward. We should never here be seriously in doubt of the reasonable sequence of the thought. As first episode we have the meeting of the pilgrim with the two friars. The friars give him no satisfactory answer to his questions. The poet probably means to satirize the friars, who in reply to a serious question give merely an entertaining story. In any event, the incident teaches the pilgrim the need of searching for Truth deeply and the vanity of relying upon persons. He learns at once that no glib phrases can solve his problem. He must labor himself. He cannot as the illiterate poor, merely believe what he hears without long pondering upon it. He must use his own wit and go through the arduous disciplines of thought, study, learning, reason, humility and contemplation.

Having brushed specious explanations aside, the pilgrim is prepared to begin his quest in earnest, and to consider man from the cradle to beyond the grave. He first hears from Wit, who is of course Mother Wit or the primitive natural reason, of the creation of the world and of the soul, of the vital principle, or *anima,* and of the rational nature of man, or Inwit. This Inwit, we are told, is the greatest of gifts after the grace of God. By an exercise of Inwit the pilgrim is of course to advance on the road to knowledge. But Inwit does not exist in drunkards, imbeciles and children. Therefore men should avoid excessive drink and care for helpless children and imbeciles. The theme of child-care leads naturally to the subject of marriage. The pilgrim has now reached a stage in his progress when a new teacher is required. He goes therefore to Dame Study, who begins with a long satirical address against the abuse of study and learning by the unfit. Study says that she has taught Scripture the rudiments of learning, and in due time turns over the youthful adventurer to his new master. He has now passed through trivium and quadrivium and may commence his theological studies. These studies however begin badly. The pilgrim is recalcitrant, and quotes Augustine to the effect that many a poor man enters the palace of heaven with no other help than good works and a paternoster. Naturally Scripture and Clergy (learning) will have nothing to do with such a perverse pupil. Here the A-text ends.

The B- and C-texts relate how the pilgrim, after trying the joys of a worldly life, returns at length to his old teachers, Scripture and Clergy. But he returns by no means wholly cured of his bad manners, and shortly after some reckless words (in the C-text they are assigned to Recklessness, but this is merely a name which the pilgrim assumes during a reckless stage in his career) he goes off with Nature. This teacher however can give him no knowledge which aids the solution of the supreme problem, that of salvation. He now meets one Imaginatif who recalls to him all the points in the previous debates, and carefully sets him right as to the advantage of learning, the necessity of a priesthood, the danger of overemphasizing the virtues of poverty and the vanity of merely natural reason. Much rectified in heart, he now enters the house of Theological Reason, accompanied by Patience and by Conscience. Conscience is of course also a character in the *Visio*.

Here occurs some fine satire on false Doctors of Divinity, with their gross habits and really superficial learning. The pilgrim sees however that the best learning has its limitations. Learning is not enough. It is necessary also to lead the life of penance, devotion and contemplation. The figure of Activa Vita appears and confesses himself unworthy and a sinner. He must purge himself by meditation. The poet passes therefore to an account of the contemplative life, which begins in the despising of earthly goods and in the love of meekness and poverty. His new teacher informs him both wherein the true life of devotion consists and how basely the clergy and the religious have in the fourteenth century betrayed their duty towards that life. Thus we are introduced to the *Vita de Do-Bet*.

The Life of Do-Well is in fact the only part of the second half of the poem difficult to follow. This is because throughout his Life the pilgrim engages in many arguments with his teachers, showing all the restlessness of a disputatious nature. We easily infer from it how lively and contentious medieval schools of philosophy and theology as a rule became. The scholar's obstinacy accounts for the vitality of this section of the poem and totally precludes the insipidity into which an allegory of the life of learning is only too likely to fall. The relatively straightforward arguments of the *Vita de Do-Bet,* depicting the Christian or Contemplative Virtues, and of the *Vita de Do-Best*, depicting the reception which the four Active or Moral Virtues meet with at the hands of the Christian world, scarcely need further comment than that which they have already received in preceding paragraphs.

4

I have now stated as briefly as possible what I consider to be the chief organizing elements in the thought of *Piers Plowman*. But I do not wish to have it appear that I consider the poet or poets incapable at times of virtual irrelevancies, of digressions and repetitions. Certain of the repetitions, as already pointed out, arise from reduplications necessitated by the two-fold division of the poem. The author evidently realized his embarrassment, for he, or his collaborators, not infrequently shifted passages about, especially in the C-text, where many passages formally in the *Vita* have been brought forward to the *Visio*. This, however, is much more confusing to the eye of the reader of Skeat's edition than to the content of the poem. It is not by these transpositions that the essential organization is bettered or defaced. The poet, however, shows throughout a fondness for certain topics that push themselves unceremoniously to the fore and break the flow of the argument. First of all we have the author's singular affection for the theme of poverty. In the *Visio* he again and again digresses from what seems his main line of argument to urge patient, honest work. In the *Vita* he may at any moment break out into the praise of poverty. This thought clearly belongs to the Prologue of the *Vita de Do-Bet,* which is the life of contemplation. It is not so clear that it becomes other parts of the work. In both *Vita* and *Visio* he may at any time incite his reader to pity the sufferings of the poor. Two long passages added in the C-text, one in the *Vita* and one in the *Visio,* deal with this theme. The very pervasiveness of these digressions makes them, to be sure, in a sense less digressive. Like a recurrent theme in music, they give a unity of tone to the work as a whole. Yet, to repeat, they do interfere with the argument of the poem, and must in that respect be considered a defect.

Another characteristic of the poet is his fondness for satire, especially against the clergy. Most of this satire occurs in the *Vita*, where it has the better right to be. Yet it does not always seem logically introduced. We feel it often as an artistic fault. The poet of B.xi pleasantly confesses at least one of his sins as follows:

This lokynge on lewed prestes hath don me lepe fram pouerte,
The whiche I preyse there pacyence is more parfyt than richesse.

[This looking at ignorant priests has made me leap from poverty, which I praise where patience is more perfect than riches.]

Another prejudice which the poet reveals in his somewhat iras-cible poem is disgust at lawyers. A more orderly author would presumably have found one Passus in which the law might prop-erly have been discussed, said therein all that he had to say on the subject, and from thenceforth held his peace. Not so, how-ever, the author or authors of *Piers Plowman*. This is something more than a merely stylistic feature. With problems of style I am, of course, not concerned in the present paper. In so far as the intrusion of passages on poverty, ecclesiastical satire and satire upon the lawyers breaks the argument of the poem as a whole, we might conceivably deduce evidence in favor of divided authorship. Such intrusions are often artistic faults. On the other hand, the pervasive nature of these intrusions, noticeable not only in the C-text, and by no means in one section of the poem more than in another, suggests a single authorship, and certainly gives unity of tone to the work when viewed in its entirety.

I have attempted in this paper to show the poem to be a really finely built structure, the nave for the people, the choir for the clergy, yet, like many a church in the Middle Ages, so crowded with tombs, rood-screens, chantries and side altars, that the total effect is a most curious blending of order and confusion. On the whole I am chiefly impressed by the order of the work, and this has I feel certain been the aspect of the poem the more slighted by its critics. However, I should not wish to deny that *Piers Plow-man* is rough in certain elements of construction as well as in language. Nor do I regard the departures from logical precision to be invariably artistic defects.

8

THE PARDON SCENE IN

PIERS PLOWMAN

Robert Worth Frank, Jr.

THE PARDON SCENE IN *Piers Plowman* IS PERHAPS THE MOST critical passage in Langland's great work, for it is the climax of the first main division of the poem, the so-called *Visio*, and at the same time it is the gateway to the second section, the visions of *Dowel, Dobet,* and *Dobest.* If we misread the Pardon Scene, we may misread what has gone before, and we shall probably misread what follows. The purpose of this article is to point out the principal misconceptions about this scene, to lay bare its fundamental meaning, and to clear the way for a more correct understanding of the poem, particularly the *Dowel, Dobet,* and *Dobest* sections. I shall concentrate largely on the B-text, but I shall refer to relevant material in the A-text and C-text, and what I say about B will apply to A and C also.[1]

Reprinted, by permission, from *Speculum,* XXVI (1951), 317–31, published by the Mediaeval Academy of America. Professor Frank's interpretation of the poem as a whole is developed in his *Piers Plowman and the Scheme of Salvation* (Yale University Press, 1957).

[1] The texts of *Piers Plowman* referred to in this article are those edited by W. W. Skeat for the Early English Text Society: *Piers Plowman, "A-Text"* (O.S. 28, London, 1867); *"B-Text"* (O.S. 38, London, 1869); and *"C-Text"* (O.S. 54, London, 1873). I do not raise the question of single or multiple authorship in this article. Although I believe that Langland wrote all three versions, I assume here only that, since the authors of A, B, and C were contemporaries, the author of C may well have understood A and B, and the author of B may well have understood A.

The main lines of Langland's thought in the first two visions lead directly to the Pardon Scene. These two visions dramatize the way to salvation and the way to damnation. The two themes are introduced figuratively in the field of folk and explicitly in the speech of Holy Church. The field full of folk midway between the tower and the dungeon are the people of this world, Holy Church explains, their lives bounded by heaven and hell. The way to salvation, she reveals, is to follow Truth, that is, to love God and man; the way to damnation is to follow Wrong or False: specifically, to follow Lady Mede, to love worldly reward above all else (B.I.1–II.50). In the narrative of Lady Mede, Langland dramatizes this pernicious and pervasive desire for worldly reward. The sole way by which society can control this desire and check the drift toward damnation is to follow the dictates of conscience and reason. Above all, the machinery of justice and the king himself must be ruled by these faculties (B.II.51–IV.195).

In the second vision Langland shows how the field of folk can begin to follow Truth and move toward salvation. First there must be repentance, the necessary prologue to all good action (B.V.61–516). Repentance comes in response to the voice of reason, which exhorts man to mend his ways, perform dutifully the tasks to which God has called him in this world, and follow Truth (B.V.10–60). What is the way to Truth? Piers Plowman, the faithful laborer, knows: meekness, obedience to conscience, and good deeds, especially the observance of the ten commandments, lead to Truth's castle; grace enables one to enter; and if grace be lacking, it may be secured through the mercy of Christ and Mary (B.V.570–647). But before man can begin his journey toward Truth he must do his feudal duties in this world (B.VI.3–116). Even this rule, however, is not always obeyed. Although hunger will drive the lazy and rebellious to labor, it vanishes with the harvest and they return to idleness (B.VI.117–319).

It is at this point that the Pardon Scene occurs. To Piers and to all those who do perform their duties, Truth grants a pardon, *a pena & a culpa* [from punishment and guilt] (B.vii.1–105), which reads,

> Et qui bona egerunt, ibunt in vitam eternam;
> Qui vero mala, in ignem eternum.
>
> [And those who have done good shall go to eternal life;
> who have done evil, to eternal fire.]

"This is no pardon!" declares a priest, translating, and Piers, for "pure tene" [pure vexation], tears up the pardon and says, " 'Si ambulauero in medio vmbre mortis, non timebo mala; quoniam tu mecum es' [If I walk in the midst of the shadow of death, I shall fear no evil; for thou art with me]. I shall not work so hard, nor shall I be so busy about my belly-joy anymore. Henceforth my plow shall be prayers and penance. The Psalter and the Evangels counsel this way of life" (B.vii.106–29). The priest sneers at Piers' learning, they quarrel, and the Dreamer wakens to ponder on what he has witnessed. Pardons from popes may be of some help, he concludes, but Dowel is a more certain aid to salvation (B.vii.130–200).

1

There has been considerable discussion as to the exact significance of these events which conclude the second vision. The principal difficulty, of course, is Piers' tearing of the pardon. Is he rejecting the pardon or the priest's judgment? Henry W. Wells says that Piers accepted the pardon, but Wells limits its value. Since his main thesis is that the *Visio* contains religious teaching for the laity and that *Dowel, Dobet,* and *Dobest* contain religious teaching for "persons dedicated to the life of scholarship and religious practice,"[2] he believes that the pardon is

---

[2] "The Construction of *Piers Plowman*," *PMLA*, XLIV (1929), 124–25.

addressed primarily to the laity and that the priest's objections indicate it is not primarily for those in the church.[3]

R. W. Chambers, on the other hand, says that Piers rejects the pardon: ". . . the voice of authority seems to be on the side of the priest. So Piers abandons his charter. It is disputed: so be it: he will trust no longer to parchment, to bulls with seals, but to the Psalmist's assurance that death can have no terrors for the just man."[4] Moreover, according to Chambers, in this scene Piers decides to abandon the Active Life for the Contemplative: "It is clear that his vexation is really directed against himself. Piers has suddenly realized that *Do-well,* the life of honest labour, which has hitherto been his earnest aim, is not enough. Implicit in the passage is the higher ideal which the poet was to depict later under the name of *Do-Better.*"[5]

Until recently Nevill Coghill also shared this view that Piers is obedient to the Church, believes the priest, commits himself to "the pure assurance of his Faith rather than to a piece of parchment," is mortified because he feels that perhaps the simple life of action was of insufficient merit in spite of his fifty years of following Truth, and so decides to lead the Contemplative Life of prayers and penance.[6] Recently Coghill has changed his opinion in part. Since he now agrees that the pardon was given by Truth rather than by the Pope, he accepts it as efficacious and

---

[3] *Ibid.,* p. 131.

[4] *Man's Unconquerable Mind* (London and Toronto, 1939), p. 119.

[5] *Ibid.,* p. 121.

[6] "The Character of Piers Plowman Considered from the B Text," *Medium Aevum,* II (1933), 117–18. In this same vein is George Winchester Stone's analysis of the pardon in the A-text: The pardon commands Piers to continue working, but Piers "thought in his old age to supplant fifteen years of active service to Truth with a period of contemplation of Truth." Piers quotes verses from Scripture that recommend, not labor, but a more contemplative life. The priest tells Piers to continue his labor. "But the contemplative life seems the easier and the reward the same; so Piers persists in his change of attitude." (In other words, Piers rejects the pardon and turns to the Contemplative Life.) "An Interpretation of the A-Text of *Piers Plowman,*" *PMLA,* LIII (1938), 666.

rejects the priest.[7] Yet he quotes with approval the first passage from Chambers cited above, refers to the Dreamer's remark *in the next vision* that the just man sins seven times in a day, and says the question is, Who is just? "If none can do well, if all are goats, what is the force of a Pardon for sheep?"[8] This comment really denies the pardon any general validity. Coghill also believes that the pardon was enigmatic, even to Langland, when he first wrote the scene (in the A version), and that the A-text *Vita de Dowel, Dobet, et Dobest* is an unsuccessful effort to explain it. The B-text *Dowel, Dobet,* and *Dobest* represents a second, successful effort.[9] In other words, the Pardon Scene is not complete and clear in itself.

Francis A. R. Carnegy also limits the validity of the pardon. He argues that since it is given conditionally to all men except Piers (B.VII.1–105), and since the Prologue and the failure of the search for Truth have shown that no group meets those conditions, "the Pardon is of little or no value in the attainment of that goal which the dreamer is striving to reach, viz. the salvation of mankind."[10] "Small wonder then, that Piers tears it in two, for he sees in it little or no help to mankind for the solution of the problems so important to them."[11] ". . . Therefore a solution of the problem is sought elsewhere, viz. in the search for Dowel."[12]

Bernard Huppé believes that Piers accepts the pardon,[13] but,

[7] *The Pardon of Piers Plowman* (Sir Israel Gollancz Memorial Lecture, British Academy, 1945) in *Proceedings of the British Academy,* XXXI, pp. 17–19.

[8] *Ibid.,* p. 20.

[9] *Ibid.,* pp. 9, 37–38.

[10] "The Relations between the Social and Divine Order in William Langland's 'Vision of William concerning Piers the Plowman'" (*Sprache und Kultur der germanischen und romanischen Völker,* A, Anglistische Reihe, XII [1934]), p. 17. But the search for Truth does not fail. Salvation is not actually secured until after death.

[11] *Ibid.,* pp. 17–18.

[12] *Ibid.,* p. 44.

[13] "The Authorship of the A and B Texts of *Piers Plowman,*" *Speculum,* XXII (1947), 601.

like Coghill and Carnegy, he thinks it is no pardon for mankind in general: the pilgrims, he says, are unable to deal with the simple truth, embodied by Piers, that without Dowel (Good Works) no one may come to Truth: "Piers understands the pessimistic import of Truth's message: that he cannot save his fellow-men in spite of themselves. They are, for the most part, slaves of rapacity and indolence, and without Dowel no spiritual progress is possible."[14] Like Chambers, Huppé believes that in the Pardon Scene Piers decides to lead a more contemplative life.[15]

Finally, E. Talbot Donaldson suggests that Piers is disappointed in both the priest and the pardon: in the priest as "a disagreeable, probably sophistical, man of education and authority"; in the pardon because he "apparently expected some larger, less commonplace sanction for his manner of life [than the Athanasian Creed]."[16] Donaldson also believes that Piers in this scene in A and B turns from the Active Life to the Contemplative.[17]

Taken together, these critics make three points. First, they attack the validity of the pardon. Second, they say that, since the pardon is no pardon, the *Visio* ends inconclusively and the visions which follow continue the lines of thought of the *Visio* instead of developing new though related ideas (Carnegy, Coghill, Huppé, and, to a degree, Wells). Third, they argue that

[14] *Ibid.,* p. 600, n. 41. Huppé's argument, even more than Carnegy's, depends on our carrying over the issue of the ploughing scene into the Pardon Scene, i.e., the problem of the idlers in society. But that issue was treated in the ploughing scene and then dropped. The opening of passus VII proves that. The question in the Pardon Scene is, which gives greater promise of salvation, doing well or indulgences? This is a new problem.

[15] *Ibid.,* pp. 601–2. One point in his argument requires comment here. He says Holy Church taught the Dreamer at A.II.29–30 that it is better to be contemplative than active. This is incorrect. Holy Church advises him to have nothing to do with Mede and her crew, another matter entirely.

[16] *Piers Plowman: The C-Text and Its Poet* (New Haven: Yale University Press, 1949), pp. 162–63, n. 3 and n. 8, and 166. I see no weight in the suggestion that the Athanasian Creed would be a disappointing authority. On the Creed see below, esp. n. 25.

[17] *Ibid.,* pp. 158–61, 162, n. 8; on the changes in C bearing on this point, see pp. 163–68.

the scene contains a rejection of the Active Life and a recommendation of the Contemplative Life (Chambers, Coghill, Stone, Huppé, and Donaldson). All these points, I believe, are incorrect.

2

All of these comments reveal a skepticism about the value of the pardon. This skepticism assumes two forms. Some say that the pardon has no real validity, for Piers rejects it (Chambers, Stone, Coghill at one time, and Donaldson). Others say that the pardon is of only limited value. Piers accepts it, but it is valid only for him, not for the rest of mankind, and it was salvation for mankind that Langland was seeking (Coghill recently, Carnegy, and Huppé); or it is valid only for the laity (Wells). But the poem, when read carefully, refutes both these views. Langland presents the pardon in circumstances which prove it is valid for all. And Piers' words and actions in the scene mean he accepts it.

Putting aside for a moment the question of Piers' reactions, the most dramatic moment in the passus but also the most obscure, let us see what light the text throws on the validity of the pardon for mankind in general. If the pardon is not valid, Langland has been laying an elaborate false trail throughout the *Visio.* Holy Church advised man to lead a good life, and her lines are almost a translation of the Latin of the pardon:

> And alle þat worche with wronge . wenden hij shulle
> After her deth day . and dwelle wiþ þat shrewe [Lucifer].
> Ac þo þat worche wel . as holiwritt telleth,
> And enden as I ere seide . in treuthe, þat is þe best,
> Mowe be siker þat her soule . shal wende to heuene. . . .[18]

> [And all who work with wrong shall go
> after their day of death and dwell with that shrew (Lucifer).
> But those who work well, as holy scripture tells,

[18] B.I.126–30. Cf. also A.I.117–22 and C.II.130–34.

> and end, as I said before, in truth, which is the best,
> may be sure that their souls shall go to heaven.]

Elsewhere in her speech she had advised kings, knights, rich men, and clergy to conduct themselves properly if they would follow Truth (B.i.94–101; 173–201). Reason's sermon, which opens the second vision, gives similar advice to priests, religious, kings, popes, and lawyers (B.v.42–60) and, less directly, to the common people (B.v.24–41). Implicit in the confessions of the sinners is the necessity of reforming and leading good lives. The ploughing of the half acre dramatizes the importance of fulfilling one's worldly duties. Since those to whom the pardon is given are those who conduct themselves in the fashion which the whole vision has been advising, those who do well, it must be valid or the whole vision has been a tasteless practical joke.[19]

But the skeptics say that, although the *Visio* teaches that doing good merits salvation, it also teaches that mankind cannot do good. But does it? Langland concentrates on the sins of man, it is true, but we must not let the moralist's inevitable preoccupation with the one lost sheep mislead us into thinking that the ninety-nine who are safe are lost also. There are good men in the field of folk (B.Pr.20–22, 25–29, 33–34); the scene in the half acre shows many performing their duties (B.vi. 107–13, 161–68, and cf. the implications of vi.7–75); and the advice to the various groups in society in the first hundred lines of passus VII implies Langland's belief that many men can meet the conditions of the pardon. All men did not meet them, but this fact does not invalidate the pardon. The Gospels did not teach, the Church did not preach, and Langland would not expect that *all* men would be saved.

The Dreamer's complete acceptance of the pardon is further proof that it is valid for all mankind. The Dreamer, who was seeking the way to salvation (B.i.83–84), concludes after the

---

[19] Cf. Father Dunning's comment that the pardon epitomizes the teaching of the first six passus: *Piers Plowman: An Interpretation of the A-Text* (London, New York, Toronto, 1937), p. 148.

vision that men should obey the message of the pardon and "do well." Coghill's suggestion that the Dreamer is puzzled by the pardon is completely without foundation. The story of Piers, he says, ends in paradox, "leaving the poet to supply what explanation he could."

> All this maketh me . to muse on dreams
> Many a time at midnight . when men should sleep,
> And on Piers the plowman . and what a pardon he had.
> (A.VIII.152–54.)

And he roamed about, looking for an explanation, "All a Summer season. For to seek Do-well" (A.IX.2.).[20] But this citation of evidence involves a more mighty leap over embarrassing verses than that of Langland's Learned Doctor himself! After A.VIII. 154 (B.VII.167; C.X.317) and before A.IX.2 (B.VIII.2; C.XI.2) there is a great deal that is important. It becomes clear that the Dreamer's doubts are the conventional doubts about the trustworthiness of dreams and doubts concerning the relative value of papal indulgences and doing well. He decides that dreams can reveal the truth and that doing well is superior to indulgences. This last he asserts fortissimo as the passus ends. He concedes some value to pardons from Rome,

> Ac to trust to þise triennales . trewly me þinketh,
> Is nouȝt so syker for þe soule . certis, as is dowel.
> . . . .
> For-þi I conseille alle cristene . to crye god mercy,
> And Marie his moder . be owre mene bitwene,
> Þat god gyue vs grace here . ar we gone hennes,
> Suche werkes to werche . while we ben here,
> Þat after owre deth-day . dowel reherce,
> At þe day of dome . we dede as he hiȝte.[21]

[But to trust in these triennials, truly it seems to me,
is not so sure for the soul, certainly, as is Do-well.
. . . Therefore I counsel all Christians to cry God's mercy,
and Mary his mother to be our intermediary,

[20] *The Pardon of Piers Plowman*, p. 20.
[21] B.VII.179–80, 195–200. Cf. A.VIII.166–67, 182–87; C.X.330–31, 346–51.

> that God give us grace here before we go hence,
> such works to work while we are here
> that after our death-day Do-well may testify,
> at the day of judgment, that we did as he commanded.]

A more complete acceptance of the message of the pardon would be difficult to imagine. He appears to have no doubt of its meaning, and he believes it applies to mankind in general: it is, he says, a pardon "alle þe peple to conforte" [to comfort all the people].[22]

The final evidence in the text proving the general validity of the pardon is the authority which supports it. The mediaeval regard for authority is well-known. And the particular authority supporting the pardon was familiar to Langland's readers. Langland himself says the pardon was given by Truth,[23] and by Truth he means God. Though his readers would know this, Holy Church's speech about Truth makes the fact absolutely clear (B.I.85–207). Moreover, the lines of the pardon have an authority not of Langland's giving, for they come from the well-known Athanasian Creed.[24] The Creed was popular in the Middle Ages because of the succinctness with which it stated the essential beliefs of the Church.[25] No doubt this quality appealed to Langland. The Creed answers in forthright fashion the question that interested him above all others: What shall a man do

[22] B.VII.146. Not in A. In C.x.300 it is "þe puple to gladen" [to gladden the people].

[23] A careless phrase in A.VIII.8 might suggest for a moment that the pardon was from the Pope rather than from Truth, but other lines in A (VIII.1–3 and 95) clearly show that Truth grants the pardon. Coghill's discussion of the problem in A neglects the evidence of A.VIII.95: *The Pardon of Piers Plowman*, pp. 17–19. The careless phrase is removed in B and C. See also E. T. Donaldson, *op. cit.*, p. 161, n. 1.

[24] First noted by Konrad Burdach, *Vom Mittelalter zur Reformation* (Berlin, 1926–32), III², 267, n. 1. Cf. also Greta Hort, *Piers Plowman and Contemporary Religious Thought* (London, 1937?), p. 167. Coghill mentions that the pardon comes from the Athanasian Creed but fails to draw the proper conclusions: *The Pardon of Piers Plowman*, pp. 19–20, and p. 19, n. 2.

[25] J. Tixeront, "Athanase (Symbole de Saint)," *Dictionnaire de Théologie Catholique* (Paris, 1931), I², 2186–87.

to be saved? For it opens and closes by asserting that its tenets are essential to salvation. Indeed, its opening words, "Quicumque vult salvus esse" [Whoever wishes to be saved], state the very theme of *Piers Plowman*. And immediately following the article which Langland quotes, the thirty-ninth, the Creed closes by warning men to respect its authority: "Haec est fides catholica: quam nisi quisque fideliter firmiterque crediderit: salvus esse non poterit" [This is the catholic faith: unless one shall have believed it trustingly and firmly, he shall not be able to be saved].[26]

Langland did not tell his readers that the pardon came from the Athanasian Creed, but there can be little doubt that he knew the source and that his audience did too. The Creed was particularly important in the Church, for it was not only a creed but a part of the liturgy and was actually considered a psalm,[27] known familiarly as the "Quicumque vult." A commentary on the "Quicumque vult" in a contemporary Commentary on the Canticles (apparently a Lollard work in this portion) shows us the position of the Athanasian Creed in Langland's day:

It is seid commounli þat þere ben þre credis. Þe first is Apostlis, þat men knowen comounly. Þat oþere is crede of þe Chirche þat declariþ þe former crede. Þis þridde crede is of þe Trynyte, þe whiche is sungun as a salme, and was made in Greek speche of oon þat is clepid Athanasie, and was aftir turnyd to Latyn, and sum deel amendid, and ordeyned to be seid at þe first hour. Þis Salme telliþ myche of þe Trynyte. . . .[28]

---

[26] For the Latin text of the Creed see Philip Schaff, *Creeds of Christendom* (New York, 1877), II, 66–70.

[27] "L'autorité qu'on lui attribue est évidemment celle qui s'attache à l'écrit d'un grand évêque comme Athanase, sanctionné et adopté par l'Église: c'est à la fois celle d'un chant, d'une oeuvre liturgique devenue officielle, et d'un symbole proprement dit" [The authority attributed to it is evidently that which attaches to the writing of a great bishop like Athanasius, sanctioned and adopted by the Church: it is simultaneously that of a song, of a liturgical work become official, and of a symbol properly so-called]. J. Tixeront, *op. cit.*, col. 2186.

[28] *Select English Works of John Wyclif* (ed. Thomas Arnold, Oxford, 1869–71), III, 71–72.

[It is commonly said that there are three creeds. The first is the Apostle's, which men know commonly. The other is the creed of the Church that declares the former creed. The third creed is of the Trinity, the which is sung as a psalm, and was made in the Greek tongue of one that is called Athanasius, and was afterward turned into Latin, and somewhat amended, and ordained to be said at the first hour. This Psalm tells much of the Trinity.]

Langland and his audience must have been familiar with the Creed, then, just as they were with the Psalms, and they often heard it recited as part of the service at Prime.[29]

The Creed was also circulated outside the liturgy of the Church, for there was a Middle English translation.[30] And there is some evidence that the particular lines Langland quoted may have had, as Coghill suggests, "some vogue as a catch-phrase about salvation towards the end of the fourteenth century and a little later. . . ."[31] He points out that they are used at the climax of the last scene of the *Castle of Perseverance*.[32] The use of the lines in a fourteenth century Middle English sermon also suggests that they were popular.[33]

[29] The frequency with which it was recited at Prime varied according to custom. The Symbolum Athanasium is used at Prime on Sundays in the Roman Rite, daily at Prime in many Roman derivatives (e.g., the Sarum) and in the Ambrosian Rite: Henry Jenner, "Creed, Liturgical Use of," *The Catholic Encyclopedia* (New York, 1913), IV, 479. According to the Sarum Breviary it was recited daily except from Maundy Thursday to the end of Easter Week: William Chatterley Bishop, "A Plain Introduction to the Structure and Arrangement of the Salisbury Breviary," *Breviarium ad Usum Insignis Ecclesiae Sarum* (Cambridge, England, 1882–86), III, p. xxxi. In the Psalterium of the York Breviary the Creed is prefaced with these instructions: ". . . dicitur de feria: vel ferialiter de dominica" [said for ferial days: or ferially for Sunday], *Breviarium ad Usum Insignis Ecclesie Eboracensis* (Durham, 1880), I, 882 (Publications of the Surtees Society, LXXI).

[30] See George Hickes, *Linguarum Vett. Septentrionalium Thesaurus* . . . (Oxford, 1703–05), I, 233–35; and W. Heuser, "Eine Vergessene Handschrift des Surteespsalters und die dort eingeschalteten Mittelenglischen Gedichte," *Anglia*, XXIX (1906), 385–412.

[31] *The Pardon of Piers Plowman*, p. 19, n. 2.

[32] *The Macro Plays*, ed. F. J. Furnivall and A. W. Pollard, EETS, Extra Series 91 (London, 1904), p. 186.

[33] *Middle English Sermons*, ed. Woodburn O. Ross, EETS, O.S. 209 (London, 1940), p. 29.

The exact parallel between the message of the pardon and the ethical teaching of the rest of the *Visio*, the Dreamer's complete acceptance of the pardon, and its great authority are proof that Langland offered it as valid for all mankind.

If Piers' reactions in the scene appear to contradict the evidence we have just been considering, we must nevertheless interpret the scene on the basis of this evidence rather than Piers' words and actions. His reactions are dramatic; they are not essential to the primary meaning of the scene. Otherwise, how could they be omitted completely from the C-text? Immediately after the priest says the pardon is no pardon, Piers and the priest jangle "of the pardon" and the Dreamer awakes (C.x.288–93). A dramatic passage was removed because it was confusing; it could be dropped completely only because the essential meaning of the scene is communicated without it, i.e., in the other passages which we have been examining.[34] Moreover, the Dreamer, on awakening, comments only on the pardon and the priest's impugning of it, not at all on Piers' reaction (B.vii.145–47), which suggests that it does not contain the principal message of

---

[34] Long ago Jusserand called the passage in A and B "a serious blemish" and said the suppression of the passage in C was "to the immense advantage of the scene." (*"Piers Plowman,* The Work of One or Five," *Modern Philology,* VII [1909–1910], 321.) In the C-text the earlier part of the passus is expanded considerably with remarks about what kinds of people and actions do and do not merit Truth's pardon, but nothing is added between the priest's request to see the pardon and the end of the passus. In other words, the revisor felt free to add to the passus, but felt the conclusion of the vision was clear without the action and speech of Piers and without the addition of anything to the conclusion. Piers' speech, of course, states an important doctrine—the doctrine of patient poverty. Langland is describing Dowel and preparing for the scene where patient poverty is recommended to the Active Man (B.xiv. 28–332). But the doctrine is not essential to the Pardon Scene. All that is essential is that Dowel, the good life, should be thrown into sharp antithesis with indulgences, to the disadvantage of the latter. Langland apparently came to see that the passage was confusing and so omitted it. His views about indulgences are clearly conveyed to the reader by the Dreamer after he wakens. (E. T. Donaldson, p. 163, suggests the passage was cut because it might be misconstrued by the ignorant and offend the learned.)

the scene. The only issue for the Dreamer is the one raised by the priest's rejection of the pardon: which gives greater promise of salvation, the good life or papal indulgences?

Nevertheless, since Piers' reaction is part of the scene in A and B, we must ask, What does it mean? If it means that Piers rejects the pardon, the rejection does not invalidate it, for, as we have seen, Langland has presented it as good for all mankind. The rejection can only be Langland's way of showing how the Church's practice of selling indulgences leads men astray, which is one point Langland wants to make.[35] There is, however, a great difficulty with the view that Piers rejects the pardon: it contradicts Langland's main purpose in the scene and the symbolic value he has already given Piers. As the Dreamer's comments reveal, Langland's main purpose is to attack papal indulgences. The priest apparently supports them. To give the priest a convert weakens Langland's position. And to make the convert Piers, the symbol of right conduct, the follower of Truth (B.v. 544–56), confuses his message and destroys the value of Piers as a symbol. Also, this view puts Piers at one moment on the priest's side, but a moment later at loggerheads with him (B.vii.136–38). And in the C-text Piers opposes the priest and so supports the pardon. The view that Piers rejects the pardon creates too many difficulties to be tenable. But can Piers' tearing of the pardon, his quotation from the Psalter, and his anger signify acceptance? A careful analysis reveals that they do.

The act of tearing implies rejection only if we disregard the special character of the pardon. When Coghill and Chambers say that Piers decides not to put his trust in a piece of parchment, to bulls with seals, they overlook something. Just as Piers' Testament (B.vi.88–106) is not really a will but a device for

[35] Cf. R. W. Chambers, "Long Will, Dante, and the Righteous Heathen," *Essays and Studies by Members of the English Association,* IX (Oxford, 1924), 53: "When the priest, representing current ideas, refuses to accept it [the pardon], the poet is brought up against the contrast which he feels so bitterly, between his own sense of justice, and that which seems to him to prevail in the current practice of the Church."

communicating an ethical message dramatically because of the contrast between the conventional form and its novel content,[36] so too the pardon is not really a pardon but a device for stating an ethical principle dramatically. The clash between form and content is even sharper here, for this pardon contains a message which is by implication an attack on pardons and which does in fact lead to such an attack by the Dreamer. How, then, can we speak of it as we would of a conventional pardon, as a piece of parchment, a bull with seals? That is exactly what it is not. In trusting its message, Piers is *rejecting* bulls with seals. In tearing the parchment, Piers is symbolically tearing paper pardons from Rome. One had to possess such pardons to receive their supposed benefits. But this pardon, once its message has been read and taken to heart, has served its purpose and is only a worthless piece of paper. (And so, the implication may be, are all pardons.) Piers has lost nothing by tearing it. The act, then, because of the special character of the pardon, was intended by Langland as a sign that Piers has rejected indulgences and accepted the command to do well. Unfortunately, it was a very confusing sign.[37]

---

[36] The fact that the Last Will and Testament was a kind of literary convention does not affect the point. It exploited the contrast with the legal form. On the genre see Eber Carle Perrow, "The Last Will and Testament as a Form of Literature," *Transactions of the Wisconsin Academy of Sciences, Arts, and Letters,* xvii (1913), I, 682–753.

[37] Another interpretation of the tearing of the pardon which, like the one I give, makes it an act of affirmation, is that of H. H. Glunz, *Die Literarästhetik des europäischen Mittelalters* (Bochum-Langendreer, 1937), p. 529 (Vol. II of *Das Abendland: Forschungen zur Geschichte europäischen Geisteslebens,* edited by Herbert Schöffler). Glunz asserts that in the structure of the poem the letter of indulgence serves a double function. It confirms, for the various classes in the ploughing scene, the fact that they are on the right road, in which each serves the community. Piers symbolizes the perfect man, who satisfies the common weal as well as the individual good. But at the same moment that this first goal is reached, Piers tears the letter. One direction to do good he has fulfilled, to do good for the community. Now he hears the call of another do good: as an individual to prove his worth in personal righteousness. The tearing of the pardon signifies the end of one condition and the beginning

Piers' quotation from the Psalter, " 'si ambulauero in medio vmbre mortis, non timebo mala; quoniam tu mecum es' " (Psalm XXII in the Vulgate) is also a sign that he accepts the pardon. The line is interpreted by several mediaeval glosses as an affirmation of faith, and Langland knew a gloss on the line, for, as Chambers has pointed out,[38] Langland quotes the same verse at B.XII. 289 and adds, " 'Þe glose graunteth vpon þat vers a gret mede to treuthe . . .' " [The gloss grants upon that verse a great reward to truth]. Though there are several glosses on the verse, we can be reasonably sure that Langland was referring to one found in both the *Glossa Ordinaria*[39] and Peter Lombard's *Commentarius in Psalmos Davidos,*[40] which interprets "mecum es" as meaning (following Augustine), "In corde per fidem, ut post umbram mortis ego tecum sim" [In the heart through faith, in order that after the shadow of death I may be with you]. Langland clearly associates the verse with the idea of reward to the faithful man, for when he quotes it at B.XII.289, it comes after a discussion of men who believe steadfastly; and immediately preceding the verse is another Latin line: "Deus dicitur quasi dans vitam eternam suis, hoc est, fidelibus" [He is called God as it were giving eternal life to his own, that is, to the faithful].[41] If the line, then, is an expression of Piers' faith, what is Piers resolved to have faith in? If the line has any relevance to the dramatic situa-

---

of a new condition for the Ploughman.

Though Glunz is instructive, there are two main objections to this analysis. First, the issue in the second vision is the salvation of mankind. The economic good of the community is only secondary. Second, it is dangerous to read so much into the simple act of tearing the pardon, especially when the action is omitted in C. The action can hardly express more than acceptance of the pardon, rejection, or anger at the priest.

[38] "Incoherencies in the A- and B-texts of 'Piers Plowman' and their Bearing on the Authorship," *London Mediaeval Studies,* I (1937), 34.

[39] J. P. Migne, *Patrologiae Latinae Cursus completus* . . . (Paris, 1844–64), CXIII, p. 876. (The *Patrologiae Latinae* will be referred to hereafter as Migne, *PL.*) Chambers, in the passage referred to above, believes Langland used the *Glossa Ordinaria.*

[40] Migne, *PL,* CXCI, 243.

[41] The Latin is evidently an acrostic, for the initial letters of 'dans vitam eternam suis' spell 'deus'—'dves' as the phrase appears in Langland.

tion in which it occurs, it must mean either that Piers will have faith in the priest or that he will have faith in the pardon. Langland would not have Piers quote the Psalter to support papal indulgences. There is no difficulty if he quotes it in support of the Athanasian Creed. He is resolved to have faith in the pardon, in spite of the priest's objection. Moreover, faith for Langland corresponded in meaning with the message of the pardon and meant moral action, doing well. He believed faith without works was dead. (He quotes James 2:20 at B.I.185.) The faithful man is, for Langland, the man of good works. So he has Piers announce at once that he will do prayers and penance. These would be considered good works[42] and imply a rejection of indulgences.

As for Piers' "tene," it may be directed against himself, as Chambers suggests; he may be vexed to discover that he has wasted precious time being busy about his belly-joy. But it is more logical to assume that it is directed against the priest. He is angry with him a few lines later. And Langland is angry with him, the supporter of papal indulgences, the misleader of souls. The priest is the one logical object in the scene for Piers' anger.

3

If our critics are unjustified in their attacks on the pardon, they can hardly be correct about the relationship between the *Visio* and the visions of *Dowel, Dobet,* and *Dobest.* If the pardon is really a pardon, the *Visio* is complete in its thought, not incomplete as they suggest, and the visions of *Dowel, Dobet,* and *Dobest* develop new though related themes, and are not a second attack on the problems posed in the *Visio.* Of course, Langland has not said everything there is to say about doing good or about salvation. But the fact that the Dreamer asks questions about Dowel in the succeeding visions does not mean that Langland

[42] So says Father Dunning, *Piers Plowman,* p. 147. He cites *St. Bernard's Sermons* (Dublin, 1921), II, p. 274.

has not finished with his theme here. The Dreamer had asked about the way that leads to the Dungeon of Care and the way that leads to the Tower of Truth, and he has been shown both ways. Hereafter we hear no more of either the Dungeon or the Tower. Whatever the search is for in *Dowel*, it is not for the way to Truth. We must assume that this quest has ended in success. Langland has shown the principle of action which will lead to damnation—the desire for mede, for riches—and the principle of action which will lead to salvation—honest work and doing well. He has made his point decisively and dramatically.[43] In *Dowel, Dobet,* and *Dobest* he will show in detail what man must do in order to be saved. But this is a new problem, not a second try. The problem of the *Visio* has been answered.

There are, moreover, details in the first two visions which show that Langland thought of them as an artistic whole. They have unity of place. The Dreamer falls asleep in the Malvern Hills for the first vision and awakens there when the second vision is ended.[44] The Malvern Hills do not figure in the later visions. Moreover, the field of folk is the scene on which the curtain rises for both visions;[45] we never see the field in *Dowel, Dobet,* or *Dobest.* The *Visio* also has unity of time. The Dreamer falls asleep on a May morning, with the sun in the east, and dreams his first dream; he wakens for a brief period, dreams again, and wakens from the second dream in the late afternoon, with the sun setting in the west.[46]

[43] Huppé (*op. cit.*, p. 600) says that if Langland's main interest in the *Visio* is simply to picture the good and evil in the world, the ending seems lame and inconclusive. But is it? The final passus of the *Visio* arouses intense interest in the pardon; the doctrine of doing good is announced in a highly dramatic scene; and Langland has the Dreamer repeat it when he wakens. Both Piers in the vision and the Dreamer after the vision have definite opinions about doing good. What point is made if not that doing good is the way to salvation? And how could an ending be more dramatic and more conclusive?

[44] See A.Pr.5, viii.130; B.Pr.5, vii.141; C.i.6, x.295.

[45] A.Pr.17, i.2, v.10; B.Pr.17, i.2, v.10; C.i.19, ii.2, vi.111.

[46] This is the time scheme in A and B: Cf. A.Pr.5, 13; v.5–8; viii.129. B.Pr.5, 13; v.5–8; vii.140. The unity of time is destroyed in C by the

4

The third point made about the Pardon Scene is that it shows Piers turning from the Active to the Contemplative Life. So say Chambers, Coghill, Stone, and Huppé. Although this view depends in part on the belief that there is a rejection of some kind in the Pardon Scene, it must be answered by a careful examination of Piers' speech after he tears the pardon.

The view is based first of all on the assumption that Dowel is the kind of bodily labor we have seen in the ploughing of the half-acre. Since Piers says he will not do so much bodily labor hereafter, he must be rejecting Dowel and moving on to Dobet. But the assumption is without foundation. Langland never calls bodily labor "Dowel." He uses the phrase for the first time when the priest translates the pardon and when the Dreamer comments on the message of the pardon. So Dowel must be something more than bodily labor. (We should also note in passing the unreasonableness of the assumption that Langland makes Piers move on to something better than Dowel at the very moment when we first hear about Dowel.)

The assumption that Piers is abandoning bodily labor *completely* is also not supported by the text. As Father Dunning reminds us, Piers "does not say that he will work no more: he merely says he will not work *so hard,* nor be *so busy* about providing himself with means of sustenance. . . . Piers merely declares that he will give the interests of his soul a decided preference over the interests of the body."[47]

Furthermore, the prayers and penance that Piers says he will perform do not prove that he is taking up the Contemplative

---

long interlude between the first and second visions: C.vi.1–108. But as in A and B the Dreamer falls asleep for the first time in the morning (C.i.6, 14) and awakens after the Pardon Scene in the late afternoon (C.x.294).

[47] *Piers Plowman,* p. 149. Father Dunning's analysis of the Pardon Scene (*op. cit.,* pp. 145–52) is essentially sound, except that he argues that the priest does not attack the pardon (p. 148).

Life. Prayers and penance are not confined to contemplatives, nor do they distinguish the Contemplative Life from the Active. In Walter Hilton's *Epistle on Mixed Life,* "bodely werkes" [bodily works], the appropriate religious activities of those leading the Active Life ("worldly men & wymen the whiche lefully vsen worldly goodes, & wylfully vsen worldly besynes" [worldly men and women who lawfully use worldly goods, and purposely use worldly business]) are contrasted with the activities of contemplatives. These "bodely werkes" include "al maner of god werkis þat thy soule doth by þe wyttes & þe membris of thy body" [all manner of good works that your soul does by the senses and the members of your body], such as fasting, waking, restraining of fleshly lusts by doing penance, doing deeds of bodily or spiritual mercy to one's fellow Christians, and suffering bodily harm for the love of righteousness.[48] The program for those in the Active Life recommended in Hilton's piece *On Daily Work* is even more rigorous.[49]

If we want to understand what was meant by the Active Life and the Contemplative Life in the mediaeval period, we shall do best to go to Gregory the Great, who provided the descriptions of these ways of life from which most writers borrowed. He characterizes them as follows:

Activa enim vita est, panem esurienti tribuere, verbum sapientiae nescientem docere, errantem corrigere, ad humilitatis viam superbientem proximum revocare, infirmantis curam gerere, quae singulis quibusque expediant dispensare, et commissis nobis qualiter subsistere valeant providere. Contemplativa vero vita est charitatem quidem Dei [et] proximi tota mente retinere, sed ab exteriore actione quiescere, soli desiderio conditoris inhaerere, ut nil jam agere libeat, sed, calcatis curis omnibus, ad videndam faciem sui Creatoris animus inardescat; ita ut jam noverit carnis corruptibilis pondus cum moerore portare, totisque

---

[48] *Yorkshire Writers: Richard Rolle of Hampole . . . and his Followers,* ed. C. Horstman (London, 1895–96), I, 264–66. The passage I refer to occurs in a piece affixed to some of the "younger MSS." of the *Epistle.* Father Dunning has (pp. 146–47) material showing that the command to do good refers to "the good works of a virtuous life."

[49] *Yorkshire Writers,* I, 137–56.

desideriis appetere illis hymnidicis angelorum choris interesse, admisceri coelestibus civibus, de aeterna in conspectu Dei incorruptione gaudere.[50]

[For the active life is, to give bread to the hungry, to teach the word of wisdom to the ignorant, to correct the erring, to recall the proud neighbor to the way of humility, to bring care to the sick, all of which it is suitable to dispense to each and everyone, and, having thus committed ourselves, to see that these things continue. The contemplative life, however, is to maintain with the whole mind love indeed of God and neighbor, but to refrain from exterior action, to cling solely to the desire for the maker, so that one no longer is pleased to be busy, but, with all cares trampled down, the soul burns to see the face of its Creator; so that now it knows how to carry the burden of corruptible flesh with sorrow, and with all desires to seek to participate in that chorus of angels singing hymns, to be among the heavenly citizens, to rejoice in everlasting incorruption in the sight of God.]

Gregory's definitions were circulated in the *Glossa Ordinaria*[51] and so were generally known. We get the same characterization of the two lives in St. Thomas Aquinas' "Treatise on the Active and Contemplative Life" in the *Summa Theologica*,[52] in Walter Hilton's *Epistle on Mixed Life,* in the *Book of Vices and Virtues*,[53] and in the *Meditationes Vitae Christi* once attributed to St. Bonaventura. This last describes the Active Life as

that manere of lyuynge by the whiche a mannis besynesse stant principally in that exercise that longeth to his owne goostly profiȝt / that is to seie in amendynge of him selfe / as withdrawynge fro vices and profityng in vertues; firste as to profite of hym self / and afterwarde as to his neiȝebore by werkes of riȝtwisnes and pitee / and dedes of mercye and charite. . . .

[that manner of living by which a man's business stands principally in that exercise that tends to his own spiritual profit, that is to say in amend-

---

[50] Gregory discusses the two lives in *Moralium Libri Job,* VI, 37 (Migne, *PL,* LXXV, 760–66), and in *Homiliarum in Ezechielem Prophetam Libri Duo,* II, 2 (Migne, *PL,* LXXVI, 948–58), from which the above passage is taken (col. 953).

[51] Migne, *PL,* CXIV, 287, the gloss on Luke 10:38.

[52] Pars II-II, qq. 179–82.

[53] A Fourteenth Century English Translation of the *Somme le Roi* of Lorens d'Orléans, ed. W. Nelson Francis, EETS, O.S. 217 (London, 1942), pp. 220–21.

ing himself as by withdrawing from vices and profiting in virtues; first to the profit of himself and afterward to that of his neighbor by works of righteousness and piety and deeds of mercy and charity.]

In the Active Life "a man trauaille and ȝeue hym to good exercise in prayere / and in studie of holy scriptures / and othere gode worchynges in comoun conuersacioun . . ." [a man travails and gives himself to good exercise in prayer and in the study of holy scripture and other good works in the common manner of living]. The Contemplative Life is described as "restynge in contemplacioun / that is to saye in solitude at the leste of herte / forsakynge all worldes besynesse / with all his myȝte be aboute contynuelly to thenke on god and heuenly thinges / onely tentinge to plese god" [resting in contemplation, that is to say in solitude at least of heart, forsaking all business of the world, with all his might being concerned continually to think of God and heavenly things, trying only to please God].[54]

The Active Life, then, is not physical labor, but just the kind of activity that Piers pledges himself to: prayers and care for his spiritual profit. The Contemplative Life necessitated withdrawal from the world; it was to be quiet from all outward action; its goal was to see the face of God. There is no hint of this in Piers' speech.

Piers' determination not to worry about food any longer is, says Chambers, "the Contemplative Life as Walter Hilton defines it: when men forsake 'all business, charges, and government of worldly goods, and make themselves poor and naked to the bare need of the bodily kind. . . .' "[55] But the Gospel passages which Piers quotes[56] were not interpreted in Langland's day as recom-

---

[54] *The Mirrour of the Blessed Lyf of Jesu Christ,* a translation of the Latin work entitled *Meditationes Vitae Christi* attributed to Cardinal Bonaventura, made before the year 1410 by Nicholas Love, Prior to the Carthusian Monastery of Mount Grace; ed. Lawrence F. Powell (Oxford, 1908), p. 159.

[55] *Man's Unconquerable Mind,* p. 124.

[56] Matthew 6:25; Luke 12:22 ff. Patience preaches the same doctrine and quotes the same verse from Matthew ("ne solliciti sitis") to Haukyn the Active Man (B.xiv.28–33); Haukyn accepts the doctrine (B.xiv.320–

mendations to the Contemplative Life. According to the *Glossa Ordinaria,* the verses say, not that man shall not labor, but that he shall not be *too solicitous* about his food: ". . . non prohibet providentiam, per quam in sudore vultus panis, praeparatur, sed vetat sollicitudinem quae mentem perturbat et ab aeternis revocat" [it does not prohibit the foresight by which bread is prepared for by the sweat of one's brow, but it forbids the solicitude which disturbs the mind and calls it from eternal matters].[57] God will provide for the righteous man, even as he has provided for the fowls of the air: "Qui dedit majora, id est vitam et corpus, dabit et minora, id est victum et vestes. In his promissis veritatis nemo dubitet: sit homo quod esse debet, mox adduntur ei omnia propter quem sunt facta" [He who has given the greater things, that is life and body, will also give the lesser, that is food and clothing. In these promises of truth let no one doubt: let man be what he ought to be, thereupon are added to him all things made for him].[58] The *Catena Aurea* expresses concisely the meaning of the quotations for Piers and Langland: "Be not withdrawn by temporal cares from things eternal."[59]

As the commentaries show, the quotations have nothing to do with the Contemplative Life. They express Langland's solution of a fundamental problem: how to provide for the body without destroying the soul.[60] Langland's answer, here and elsewhere, is this: Care for the soul, and God will help you care for the body.

---

31), though he remains in the Active Life (cf. B.xiv.1–2). All this would imply that the doctrine is for those in the Active Life. But since Chambers says the Contemplative Life is being urged on Haukyn by Patience and Haukyn rejects it (*Man's Unconquerable Mind,* p. 154), I cannot cite the passage without discussing its real meaning in detail, and that is a separate problem.

[57] *Glossa Ordinaria* on Luke 12:22: Migne, *PL,* CXIV, 296.

[58] *Ibid.,* cols. 105–106 (on Matthew 6:25).

[59] *Catena Aurea, Commentary on the Four Gospels collected out of the Works of the Fathers,* by St. Thomas Aquinas (New edition, Oxford and London, 1870), I, 251. See also Father Dunning on this point: *Piers Plowman,* pp. 148–51.

[60] He treats this problem at length in the scene with Haukyn: B.xiii. 220–xiv.332.

He had already given this advice to beggars earlier in the passus (B.VII.84–88). It is the advice Patience gives to Haukyn the Active Man (B.XIV.28–33). It is the answer which Nature gives the Dreamer himself in the last passus of the poem as death draws nigh: Love, Nature has told him, is the best craft to learn. What of the needs of the body, the Dreamer asks:

> "How shal I come to catel so . to clothe me and to fede?"
> "And þow loue lelly," quod he . "lakke shall þe neure
> Mete ne wor[l]dly wede . whil þi lyf lasteth."[61]

> ["How shall I come to goods in order to clothe and feed myself?"
> "If you love loyally," said she, "you shall never lack
> meat nor worldly clothing while your life lasts."]

Finally, Konrad Burdach's investigation of the doctrine of "ne solliciti sitis" [be not concerned] in the Old and New Testament and in Augustine and other mediaeval writers demonstrates that in using this text Langland was urging a doctrine that had been preached by many before him and that would have a familiar ring for many of his readers.[62] Burdach shows that in the mediaeval period the doctrine of "ne solliciti sitis," together with the doctrine of poverty that Langland preaches more explicitly in *Dowel*, was associated with the *idealization of labor*,[63] the very antithesis of the Contemplative Life. Therefore, we do not have in the quotations or in Piers' other remarks any indication that he is about to adopt the Contemplative Life.

5

The Pardon Scene, therefore, is in fact what it ought to be, the climax of the second vision and of the *Visio*, not a miserable anticlimax. The pardon offered is valid for all mankind, and

[61] B.XX.208–10.
[62] *Vom Mittelalter zur Reformation*, III², 268, 269–83, 308–10, 310, n. 2, 351–58. See also the quotation from Wyclif, 306, n. 1.
[63] *Ibid.*, 294 (point three, on the cult of poverty and Wyclif's poor priests), 294–96 (point six, on the moral duty of active work), 295–96, n. 1 (the quotation from Wyclif), 351–54.

Piers Plowman accepts its message. The pardon states the basic rule that man must follow if he would be saved. This rule is, simply, that he must do well. The rule is stated in a form (the unorthodox "pardon") calculated to show the falseness of the contrary view, that man can purchase salvation. This attack in the Pardon Scene on the philosophy of money applied to the scheme of salvation is paralleled and to some extent prepared for by the attack on the philosophy of money applied to the social order in the Lady Mede episode. Similarly, the support (in the ploughing scene) of the philsophy of work applied to the social order parallels and prepares for the support of the philosophy of work applied here to the scheme of salvation. For the pardon says man must "work" (do well) to be saved, and it is offered to, and accepted by, the personification of the good workman, Piers Plowman. Just what man must do in order to do good and how he is able to do good Langland will explain in the rest of his poem. The titles of the visions that follow—*Do Wel, Do Bet*, and *Do Best*—indicate that they will be an elaboration on the principle stated in the pardon—do well. Since the Dreamer (i.e., the poet himself) is satisfied with the message of the pardon, Langland can hardly have thought of the scene as abortive or obscure and as necessitating a second attack on the same problem in later visions. If there is, moreover, any recommendation of the Contemplative Life in *Dowel, Dobet,* and *Dobest* (I am certain there is not), it does not have its roots in the Pardon Scene, for the issue is never raised there. It can be found in the scene only by misreading Piers' words and misunderstanding the nature of the Contemplative Life. The scene simply tells man that he cannot buy salvation, he must do good to attain it. Langland had been saying this one way or another throughout the *Visio.* Here he said it by means of the pardon, its authority, Piers' acceptance of it, and the Dreamer's satisfaction and his comments. Having presented his message in these several ways, Langland brought the *Visio* to a close. The simple, emphatic message is still there, in his text, for all who will read it carefully.

9

PIERS PLOWMAN AND THE
PILGRIMAGE TO TRUTH

Elizabeth Zeeman

"THE SENCE IS SOMEWHAT DARCKE, BUT NOT SO HARDE, BUT that it may be understonde of suche as will not sticke to breake the shell of the nutte for the kernelles sake." In spite of these confident words with which Robert Crowley prefaced his mid-sixteenth century edition of *Piers Plowman*, the effort to reach the kernel of its meaning continues. While critics agree basically on the fact that the poem must be given a number of interpreta-tions—the deepest of which is of a most subtle spirituality—we are still far from a complete understanding of Langland's intent and procedure.

That the orthodox contemplative writings of the medieval church may resolve some problems is already recognized. Walter Hilton's definitions of the various kinds of Christian life have

Reprinted, by permission of the author (Elizabeth Salter) and The English Association, from *Essays and Studies*, N.S., XI (1958), 1–16. For a fuller development of views expressed here, as well as discussions of other aspects of the poem, see Elizabeth Salter's *Piers Plowman: An Introduction* (Oxford: Basil Blackwell, 1962). Some other recent studies are David C. Fowler, *Piers the Plowman: Literary Relations of the A and B Texts* (Univ. of Washington Press, 1961); Morton W. Bloomfield, *Piers Plowman as a Fourteenth-Century Apocalypse* (Rutgers University Press, 1962); John Lawlor, *Piers Plowman: An Essay in Criticism* (New York, 1962); A. C. Spearing, "The Art of Preaching and *Piers Plow-man*," *Criticism and Medieval Poetry* (New York, 1964), pp. 68–95; Ed-ward Vasta, "Truth, the Best Treasure, in *Piers Plowman*," *Philological Quarterly*, XLIV (1965), 17–29.

been used to clarify certain terms used in the poem[1] and a recent study of the C version discusses Langland's basic theme in the specific context of Bernardian mysticism.[2] The general line of inquiry is rewarding if pursued with care. There are strong connexions between the development of the allegory in *Piers Plowman* and mystical processes, but it is a mistake to insist on close equations with any particular doctrine.[3] Working as a poet, with the greatest freedom and imaginative range, Langland is not to be circumscribed in this way; we must be prepared for comparisons to reveal divergence of outlook and method as often as agreement. With these reservations, the treatises of the English mystics, Langland's contemporaries, do throw light on some of his most vital concepts and aims. Especially important, they show us how much emphasis should be placed on certain parts of the allegory if our reading is to be soundly based and comprehensive—confirming, for instance, how necessary it is, if we are to have a proper grasp of the enigmatic character of Piers Plowman himself, to take seriously the directions he gives, early on in the poem, for the momentous Pilgrimage to St. Truth:

> Ac if ȝe wilneth to wende wel . this is the weye thider,
> That I shal say to yow . and sette yow in the sothe.
>
> (B.V. 568–69)[4]

> [But if you wish to go well, this is the way thither,
> that I shall say to you and set you in the truth.]

[1] R. W. Chambers, *Man's Unconquerable Mind* (London, 1939), pp. 104–6.

[2] E. T. Donaldson, *Piers Plowman: The C Text and its Poet* (New Haven, 1949), Chapter VI.

[3] Warnings of this are given by T. P. Dunning, "The Structure of the B Text of *Piers Plowman*," *R.E.S.*, N.S. vii (1956), 225, and by J. Lawlor, "The Imaginative Unity of *Piers Plowman*," *R.E.S.*, N.S. viii (1957), 113–14 etc. Donaldson, *op. cit.*, who wishes to find in the poem three stages corresponding to St. Bernard's humility, charity and unity, has to admit "this progress seems to have stopped short of its goal" (p. 197).

[4] The text of the poem used throughout is that of W. W. Skeat, *The Vision of William concerning Piers the Plowman in Three Parallel Texts* (Oxford, 1886).

This Pilgrimage to Truth is undertaken by reader and poet-dreamer no less than by Piers and his crowd of penitent, stumbling pilgrims, and the going is sometimes rough. As always with Langland, however, the difficulties lie in the details of the route, not in the statement and achievement of main objectives. For the broad features of his spiritual geography are well-marked. In the "toure on a toft" [tower on a hill] lives Truth, who is God, as Holy Church points out to the inquiring dreamer:

> "The toure vp the toft," quod she . "treuthe is there-inne,
> . . . he is fader of feith . fourmed ʒow alle . . ."
>
> (B. I. 12, 14)

> ["The tower upon the hill," said she, "truth is therein,
> . . . he is the father of faith, formed you all.]

The need to seek Truth is the first clear theme which emerges from the poem; when the dreamer asks how he may save his soul, Holy Church replies:

> Whan alle tresores are tried . . . trewthe is the best.
>
> (*Ibid.*, 85)

> [When all treasures are tried . . . truth is the best.]

She says, further, that the way to Truth is love:

> Loue is leche of lyf . and nexte owre lorde selue,
> And also the graith gate . that goth in-to heuene . . .
>
> (*Ibid.*, 202–3)

> [Love is the healer of life, and next to our Lord himself,
> and also the direct road that goes into heaven.]

Nothing in *Piers Plowman* ever contradicts these words; in a very real sense they are final. And they are richly associative; the approach to God through love, recommended here so decisively as the only possible direction of activity, is not only recommended but experienced and analysed by men and women such as Richard Rolle, Dame Julian of Norwich, or the author of *The Cloud of Unknowing*. The words of Holy Church are echoed in

> By loue may he be getyn & holden; bot bi þou3t neiþer.
> (The Cloud of Unknowing, 26/4–5)[5]

[By love he may be received and held; but by thought never.]

and in

> . . . the soul that of his special grace seyth so forforth of the hey mervelous godenes of God, and that we arn endlesly onyd to hym in love . . .
> (Julian Of Norwich, Revelations of Divine Love, f. 60)[6]

[. . . the soul that from his special grace sees so far into the high marvelous goodness of God, and that we are endlessly united to him in love . . .]

But this is a general correspondence only; it is particularized when, after the examination and confession of the Seven Deadly Sins, the search for Truth takes full allegorical shape as a pilgrimage:

> A thousand of men tho . thrungen togyderes;
> Criede vpward to Cryst . and to his clene moder
> To haue grace to go with hem . Treuthe to seke.
> (B.V. 517–19)

> [A thousand men then thronged together;
> cried upward to Christ and to his pure Mother
> to have Grace to go with them to seek Truth.]

For this large, miscellaneous body of pilgrims the way to Truth must be defined exactly. And Piers, making his dramatic entry into the poem as guide for the journey, gives detailed instructions which, though they may be grounded in ordinary homiletic teaching on the good Christian life, reach out to spiritual matters within the compass of the mystic alone.

At this stage a similar allegorical pilgrimage in Walter Hilton's manual for the contemplative life, the Scale of Perfection,[7] becomes relevant. The pilgrim in Hilton's book is anxious to set

---

[5] ed. P. Hodgson, EETS, O.S. 218 (1944).

[6] Since no good edition is yet accessible, the text of the Revelations has been taken from British Museum MS., Sloane 2499.

[7] The text of the Scale of Perfection used in this article is that contained in Corpus Christi College, Cambridge, MS. 268.

out for Jerusalem which "be tokenyth contemplacyoun in par-
fyte loue of God . . . a syght of ihesu . . ." [signifies contemplation in perfect love of God . . . a beholding of Jesus]. And like
Langland's pilgrims, he looks for a guide:

> Ther was a man þat wold gon to Ierusalem| And for he knew nout the
> weye . he cam to an othir man that he hopid knew þe weye thedyr| And
> he askyd hym if he myth comyn to that cyte| (f. 119b)

[There was a man who would go to Jerusalem. And because he knew not
the way, he went to another man who he hoped knew the way there. And
he asked him how he might go to that city.]

His guide speaks of the route with assurance and authority,
claiming:

> And if þu wylt holdyn this weye and don as I haue seyd . I undirtake
> thyn lyf . that þu shalt nout be slayn . but wol comyn to þat . that þu
> coveytyst.   (f. 120a)

[And if you will keep to this way and do as I have said, I assure you on
your life that you shall not be slain, but will come to that which you
desire.]

So, too, in *Piers Plowman*, when the ordinary plowman addresses the hopeful crowd of travellers, his words are by no
means ordinary. He shows a far deeper knowledge of religious
mysteries than we might expect from even the best of the obedient sons of Holy Church; the springs of growth and change are
already in Piers when we first meet him. The way to St. Truth,
as he describes it, lies first through meekness and conscience
and the commandments; man begins to travel to God through
belief and obedience. The verse in which Langland sets these
directions is hardly beautiful, but it is clear. The allegory is kept
simple; it is a map such as a child could understand, and this
in itself is a virtue, for the pilgrims who wait, listening to Piers,
have become "as a little child" in order that they may be
received into the kingdom of Heaven:

> ȝe mote go thourgh Mekenesse . bothe men and wyues,
> Til ȝe come in-to Conscience . that Cryst wite the sothe,

That ȝe louen owre lorde god . levest of all thinges,
And thanne ȝowre neighbores nexte . in none wise apeyre,
Otherwyse than thow woldest . he wrouȝte to thi-selue.
And so boweth forth bi a broke . Beth-buxom-of-speche,
Tyle ȝe fynden a forth . ȝowre-fadres-honoureth, *Honora patrem
et matrem, etc.*
Wadeth in that water . and wascheth ȝow wel there,
And ȝe shul lepe the liȝtloker . al ȝowre lyf-tyme.
And so shaltow se Swere-nouȝte- . but-if-it-be-for-nede-
And-namelich-an-ydel . the-name-of-god-almyȝti.
Thanne shaltow come by a crofte . but come thow nouȝte there-inne;
That crofte hat Coveyte-nouȝte- . mennes-catel-ne-her-wyves
Ne-none-of-her-serauntes- . that-noyen-hem-myȝte;
Loke ȝe breke no bowes there . but if it be ȝowre owne.
    Two stokkes there stondeth . ac stynte ȝe nouȝte there,
They hatte Stele-nouȝte, Ne-slee-nouȝte . stryke forth by bothe;
And leue hem on thi left halfe . and loke nouȝte there-after;
And holde wel thyne haliday . heighe til euen.
    Thanne shaltow blenche at a berghe . Bere-no-false-witnesse,
He is frithed in with floreines . and other fees many;
Loke thow plukke no plante there . for peril of thi soule.
    Thanne shal ȝe se Sey-soth . so-it-be-to-done-
In-no-manere-ellis-nauȝte- . for-no-mannes-biddynge.
                                                    (B.V. 570–93)

[You must go through Meekness, both men and wives,
until you come to Conscience, which Christ knows truly,
that you love our Lord God dearest of all things,
and then your neighbors next harm in no way,
otherwise than you desire that they do to you.
And so turn by a brook, Be-Mild-Of-Speech,
until you find a ford, Honor-Your-Father, *Honor father and
mother, etc.*
Wade into that water and wash yourself well,
and you shall run the more lightly all your life.
And so you shall come to Swear-Not-Unless-Necessary-
And-Especially-in-Idleness-The-Name-Of-God-Almighty.
Then you shall come to a field, but do not go in;
that field is called Covet-Not-Men's-Goods-Nor-Their-Wives-
Nor-Any-Of-Their-Servants-That-Might-Injure-Them;
see that you break no boughs there, unless it be your own.
Two stakes stand there, but do not stop,
they are called Steal-Not, Nor-Slay-Not, pass forth by both;

and leave them on your left side, and look not back at them;
and keep well your holy day right up until evening.
Then you shall turn aside at a hill, Bear-No-False-Witness,
it is enclosed with florins and many other fees;
see that you pluck no plant there for fear of your soul.
Then shall you see Speak-Truth-As-It-Should-Be-And-
In-No-Other-Manner-At-No-Man's-Bidding.]

If this were all, then there would be reason to agree that Piers'
description of the highway to Truth "has been little more than
an outline of the virtuous active life."[8] But he continues with
more significant material. By now the pilgrims are within sight
of "a courte as clere as the sonne" [a court as bright as the sun];
it is the dwelling of Truth, the "toure on a toft" seen so sharply
in the opening panorama of the vision. Piers then completes his
account of the approach to God in plain, reduced poetry, which
echoes most strongly the spiritual directions given to Hilton's
aspiring contemplative. For Piers sends the travellers across the
moat of mercy, by means of a bridge of prayer; the walls of the
court which faces them are of wit, buttressed by belief and christendom. The entrance has pillars of penance, and the gates hang
on hinges of alms-deeds. The whole court is roofed with love:

> Thanne shaltow come to a courte . as clere as the sonne,
> The mote is of Mercy . the manere aboute,
> And alle the wallis ben of Witte . to holden Wille oute;
> And kerneled with Crystendome . man -kynde to saue,
> Boterased with Bieleue-so . or-thow-beest-nouȝte-ysaued.
> And alle the houses ben hiled . halles and chambres,
> With no lede, but with Loue . and Lowe-speche-as-bretheren
> The brugge is of Bidde-wel- . the-bette-may-thow-spede;
> Eche piler is of Penaunce . of preyeres to seyntes,
> Of Almes-dedes ar the hokes . that the gates hangen on.
>
> (B.V. 594–603)

[Then you shall come to a court as bright as the sun,
the moat is of Mercy around the manor,

---

[8] Donaldson, *op. cit.*, p. 168. Lawlor, *op. cit.*, p. 112, also sees Piers'
account of the route as inadequate—"stiff, signpost-like allegory"—and
thinks that he later rejects it.

and all the walls are of Wit to hold Will out;
and crenellated with Christendom to save mankind,
buttressed with Believe-So-Or-You-Are-Not-Saved.
And all the houses are covered, halls and chambers,
with no lead, but with Love and Humble-Speech-As-Brethren.
The bridge is of Bid-Well-The-Better-May-You-Speed;
each pillar is of Penance of Prayers to saints,
of Almsdeeds are the hinges that the gates hang on.]

Hilton's guide has also stressed obedience, meekness, prayer, repentance:

The begynnyng of þe heigh weye in which þu shalt gon . is reformyng
in feyth grounded mekly in the feyth . and in þe lawys of holy cherche.

(f. 120a)

[The beginning of the highway on which you shall go is the reforming in
faith, grounded humbly in the faith and in the laws of Holy Church.]

. . . a soule be first smet doun fro the heite of þe self by drede and
meknesse and be wel examynid and brent in the fyer of desyer and as it
were puryfied from alle gostly fylthe by long tyme in deuout preyerys
and othir gostly exercise.   (f. 129a)

[. . . a soul is first struck down from the height of the self by fear and
humility, and is well examined and burned in the fire of desire, and as
it were purified from all spiritual filth by long periods in devout prayers
and other spiritual exercise.]

And love must work with meekness:

Thanne yf þu wylt spedyn in thyn goyng . and makyn goode iornys . þe
behouith to holdyn these to thyngis oftyn in thyn mende meknesse and
loue.   (f. 120b)

[Then if you desire to speed in your travel, and make good journeys, it
behooves you to hold these two things often in mind: meekness and love.]

Piers brings his pilgrims up to the gates of the court, and, as
the climax draws near, the poetry noticeably warms and relaxes.
Grace is the porter—"a gode man for sothe" [a good man in
truth]—and his servant is Amende-ȝow:

Biddeth Amende-ȝow meke him . til his maistre ones,
To wayue vp the wiket . that the womman shette,
Tho Adam and Eue . eten apples vnrosted . . .

And if Grace graunte the . to go in in this wise,
Thow shalt see in thi-selue . Treuthe sitte in thine herte,
In a cheyne of charyte . as thow a childe were.

(B.V. 610–12, 613–16)

[Bid Amend-You to humble himself once to his master,
to waive up the wicket-gate that the woman shut,
when Adam and Eve ate unroasted apples . . .
And if Grace grants you to go in in this way,
you shall see in yourself Truth sitting in your heart,
in a chain of charity, as if you were a child.]

These last lines give bold and eliptical expression to a profound spiritual concept, familiar in mystical writings—man's discovery, by divine grace and through divine love, of the divine within himself. Hilton speaks of it frequently:

the trewe lith is the perfite loue of Jesus felt thurgh grace in a manys
soule.

(f. 124b)

[the true help is the perfect love of Jesus felt through grace in a man's soul.]

His pilgrim is told of the "indwelling" of Christ in the soul—Christ who is the real source and centre of energy for the search at the same time as he is the goal, Jerusalem, to be striven after:

Coveite þu this ʒifte of loue principaly as I haue seid ffor if he wil of his grace ʒevyn it on that maner wyse . it shal opynyn the reson of thyn soule for to seen sothefastnesse that is Jesus . and gostly thyngys. . . .

[Covet this gift of love principally, as I have said, for if he wishes of his grace to give it in that manner, it shall open the reason of your soul in order to see truth, that is Jesus, and spiritual things.]

And it shal werkyn in thyn soule only as he wold and þu shalt holdyn hym reuerently with sothfastnesse of loue and sen how he doth. Thus biddith he be his prophete that we shuld don . seying thus. . . .
Behold ʒe me ffor I do al. I am loue and for I loue . I do al þat I do and ʒe don nout. And that this ys soth . I shall wel shewyn ʒow ffor ther is no good dede don in ʒow . no good thout felt in ʒow . but if it be don thurgh me that is thurgh myth wisdam and loue. I only do all ʒoure good dedys . and ʒoure goode thowtis . and goode louis in ʒow . and ʒe don ryth nout.

(f. 148a)

203

[And it shall work in your soul only as he wishes, and you shall hold to him reverently with steadfastness of love and see how he does. Thus he bids by his prophet what we should do, saying thusly. . . .
Behold you me, for I do all. I am love, and for love I do all that I do, and you do nothing. That this is true I shall show you, for there is no good deed done in you, no good thought felt in you, unless it is done through me, that is, through strength, wisdom, and love. I alone do all your good deeds and your good thoughts and the good desires in you, and you do nothing at all.]

Where Hilton is writing directly towards those in the religious life, Langland has in mind a more varied public; his pilgrimage must attract all classes of men—the finding of Truth must be possible on many levels of experience. But the lines

> Thow shalt see in thi-selue . Treuthe sitte in thine herte
> In a cheyne of charyte . . .

coming as they do after the painful stress on penance, amendment, prayer, have greatest power of meaning as the climax of a process akin, if not identical to that described by Hilton. Piers sees the pilgrimage to Truth in a far wider context than that of "obedience to the tables of the law."[9] The poem has multiple allegorical sense, and the discovery of long-sought Truth, bound by love, in the pilgrim's own heart, asks for various interpretations. On the plane of ordinary Christian morals, it may be understood as the achievement of a life controlled and shaped from the inside by God's truth and love. On a rare spiritual plane, however—that of Hilton's pilgrimage to Jerusalem—it speaks most coherently of the mystic's apprehension of God in himself, the mapping of the divine into the human, brought about by grace.

If, however, this passage is to justify itself completely, it must not only gather up and re-express with greater precision what has been said earlier in the poem about the "way to Truth." The lines of action it prescribes must be traceable, somehow, over the rest of the allegory. And here we begin to deal in complexi-

[9] Donaldson, *loc. cit.*

ties, for from this point onwards Langland turns his full creative powers to the exploration of the search for Truth. The allegory becomes increasingly complicated; there appear, at times, to be not one but a score of themes and sub-themes. As far as we know, these particular pilgrims, instructed by Piers, never embark upon their journey. Yet the pilgrimage to Truth, once announced, is never abandoned. It is the great imaginative motif of the whole work; the activity of travel, whether material or spiritual, involves the major characters of the allegory—Piers and the dreamer, no less than minor figures such as Conscience and Patience[10] and Hawkin,[11] the unreformed man of active life. The successive searches for the three lives or states, Dowel, Dobet and Dobest, are only subdivisions of the large search for Truth. Struggle towards illumination, on every level—moral, theological, mystical—is a constant element in the shifting dream-world to which Langland admits us. And the main pattern of this journeying is forecast by Piers, as he describes in the simplest terms what he knows of the approach to and the dwelling-place of God.

So, in a general sense, the dreamer and many of those connected with him are taught the difficult lessons of obedience, humility, repentance as they make their way towards Truth. At the Feast of Learned Doctors (cooked by Contrition) the dreamer is given the sour bread of penitence to stomach;

> He sette a soure lof to-for us . and seyde *"agite penitenciam."*
>
> (B. XIII. 48)

> [He set a sour loaf before us and said, *"do penance."*]

Hawkin's sinful cloak is cleansed by Conscience, and he takes humbly "fiat voluntas tua" [thy will be done] to sustain him ever after.[12] The dreamer is persuaded, gradually, that "Truth

---

[10] B. XIII. 215. "Conscience tho with Pacience passed . pilgrymes as it were" [Conscience then passed with Patience, pilgrims as it were].

[11] Hawkin moves towards good, with the help of Patience; see B. XIII. 220 onwards.

[12] B. XIV. 36 onwards.

dwells in him, in love," for his inmost comprehension of divine matters is only achieved through love. The passage in which one of his many anxious inquiries about the meaning of Dowel, Dobet and Dobest is met by Clergye with the simple reply "Piers and his doctrine of love"[13] tells us of the transformation of Piers, but also of the growth of understanding in the dreamer himself. His journey to Truth, on its own limited but sound level, is being fulfilled in the name of love; and the power to love, as he was first informed by Holy Church, is created in man's heart by God:

> And in the herte, there is the heuede . and the heiȝ welle;
> . . . And that falleth to the fader . that formed vs alle,
> Loked on us with loue . and let his sone deye
> Mekely for owre mysdedes . to amende vs alle.
>
> (B. I. 162, 164–6)

> [And in the heart, where the source is, and the high fount;
> . . . And that falls to the Father who formed us all,
> looked on us with love and let his son die
> meekly for our misdeeds to amend us all.]

As confirmation of what he is learning about divine love and truth, he is allowed to witness the Crucifixion and the Harrowing of Hell; the gates are indeed opened to him, by grace, as he *sees* Truth bound by charity, Christ willingly sacrificed in love, so that he may gain entry to man's heart. Piers' words:

> And if Grace graunte the . to go in in this wise,
> Thow shalt see in thi-selue . Treuthe sitte in thine herte,
> In a cheyne of charyte . . .

> [And if Grace grants you to go in in this way,
> you shall see in yourself Truth sitting in your heart,
> in a chain of charity . . .]

prophesy the dreamer's experience in no uncertain manner.

But there is another way in which the pilgrimage to Truth takes place over the rest of the poem. This way is mystical in

---

[13] See below, p. 208.

concept, although its literary form could only have been devised by an essentially poetic imagination. For Langland has his plowman-guide, Piers, suffer in person and on the most exalted level, all he dictates to others about the search for and the finding of Truth; he enlarges the significance of Piers until he becomes a symbol of the operation of the divine upon the human—God's relationship with man through Christ. At his most powerful, he is neither wholly man nor God; he represents much more the state of grace in which both are united. Piers, in the highest spiritual sense, discovers (both to himself and to us)

> Treuthe sitte in thine herte,
> In a cheyne of charyte . . .

He not only gains but *is* the apprehension of God within, worked by love. What we watch, in Piers, is

þe eendles merueilous miracle of loue, þe whiche schal neuer take
eende . . .   (*The Cloud,* 19/10–11)

[the endless marvelous miracle of love, which shall never end . . .]

by which

oure soulè, bi vertewe of þis reformyng grace, is mad sufficient at þe
fulle to comprehende al him by loue . . .   (ibid., 18/17–18)

[our soul, by virtue of this reforming grace, is made fully sufficient to comprehend all of him by love.]

Now especially, in this process of spiritual alchemy, the writings of men such as Hilton or the *Cloud* author confirm and clarify. We see Piers, who has already shown, by his knowledge of the route to St. Truth, some acquaintance with mysteries, beginning his long transformation in Passus VII. And he dedicates himself to a life of prayer and penance. He is no longer using the metaphor of the pilgrimage in such detail as before, but his opening quotation:

si ambulauero in medio umbre mortis, non timebo mala, quoniam tu
mecum es.

[if I walk in the midst of the shadow of death, I shall fear no evil, for thou art with me.]

reaffirms the idea of travelling. In fact, although his experiences take place in a finer context, he will, as he advised others, seek his God, St. Truth, across the bridge of prayer and come face to face with the pillars of penance:

> Of preyers and of penaunce . my plow shal ben herafter,
> And wepen whan I shulde slepe . though whete-bred me
>   faille.
> The prophete his payn ete . in penaunce and in sorwe
> . . . *Fuerunt michi lacrime mee panes die ac nocte.*
> (B. VII. 119–21, 123)

> [Of prayers and penance shall my plow be hereafter,
> and weep when I should sleep, though I lack wheat-bread.
> The prophet ate his bread in penance and in sorrow . . .
> *My tears were for me my bread day and night.*]

His absence in the next section of the poem (Passus VIII–XV)[14] does not remove him from the consciousness of either dreamer or reader. He is kept in mind by skilfully placed references which seem to indicate that he is in some kind of activity, and certainly increasing in power and significance. By Passus XIII he has progressed far enough through and beyond prayer and penance to represent the doctrine of love itself:

> For one Pieres the Ploughman . hath impugned vs alle,
> And set alle sciences at a soppe . saue loue one,
> And no tixte ne taketh . to meyntene his cause,
> But *dilige deum.* . . .   (B. XIII. 123–26)

> [For one Piers the Plowman has impugned us all,
> and set all sciences at small value, except love alone,
> and he takes no text to maintain his cause,
> except *love God.* . . .]

Far from deserting the dreamer, he is still acting as guide; those

---

[14] In the C text he makes one brief appearance (C. XVI. 138–50) which does not contribute much to the main development of the narrative.

taking part in the narrative of events reach out to him as to the resolution of all problems:

> Thanne passe we ouer til Piers come . and preue this in dede. . . .
> (B. XIII. 132)

[Then pass we over until Piers comes and proves this by deeds. . . .

And this intangible leadership is most strongly reminiscent of the part played by Christ in Hilton's Pilgrimage to Jerusalem; with these words indeed, Hilton might be describing the function of Piers in this part of the poem:

> behold hym wel . he goth beforn the nout in bodily lyknesse . but unseably bi[15] priue presens of his gostly myth. Therefore se hym gostly if þu may and ellys trowe hym and folwe hym whydir so he goth ffor he shal ledyn the in the ryth weye to jerusalem. (f. 124b)

[behold him well, he goes before you not in bodily likeness, but invisibly by the secret presence of his spiritual power. Therefore see him spiritually if you may, or else believe him and follow him wherever he goes, for he shall lead you in the right way to Jerusalem.]

It is no surprise when, in the next Passus, Reason says of charity:

> With-outen helpe of Piers Plowman . . . his persone seestow neuere.
> (B. XV. 190)

[Without the help of Piers Plowman . . . his person you shall never see.]

and neither dreamer nor reader can be entirely unprepared for the positive words which follow:

> There-fore by coloure ne by clergye . knowe shaltow hym neuere,
> Noyther thorw wordes ne werkes . but thorw wille one.
> And that knoweth no clerke . ne creature in erthe,
> But Piers the Plowman . *Petrus, id est, Christus.* (B. XV. 203–6)

[Therefore by appearance or by learning you shall never know him, neither through words nor works, but only through the will.

[15] The Corpus Christi College MS. reading here is "onsaciably priuy" [unsociably secret]; the emendation has been made from Trinity College, Cambridge, MS. B. 15. 18.

> And that is known by no cleric nor creature on earth,
> except Piers the Plowman, *Peter, that is, Christ.*]

It is not, I think, in mistaken enthusiasm that Langland gradually persuades us to think of Piers in terms of love and Christ.[16] He is dealing with ideas very close to those of Hilton when he says to his pilgrim:

If þu wost wetyn thanne what this desier is . sothly it is Jesus for he makith this desier in the and he it is that is desyryd and desiryth . he is al and he makith al. If þu mytist sen hym þu dost nout . but sufferyst hym werkyn in thyn soule . assentyst to hym with gret gladnesse of herte . that he wold vouchsaf for to don so in the . þu art nout ellys but a resonable instrument . wherinne that he werkyth.   (f. 124a)

[If you wish to know what this desire is, truly it is Jesus, for he makes this desire in you and it is he that is desired and desires, he is all and he makes all. If you strive to see him you do nothing but allow him to work in your soul, assent to him with great gladness of heart, that he would vouchsafe so to work in you that you are nothing else but a rational instrument through which he works.]

Piers is by now a large symbol of spiritual activity. He is the "Christ element" in man which aspires, searches, goes on pilgrimage—"he it is that . . . desiryth." So Piers pledges himself to pilgrimage twice over—first when he offers to travel with the confused penitents on their lowly way to St. Truth:

> "And I shal apparaille me," quod Perkyn . "in pilgrimes wise,
> And wende with ȝow I wil . til we fynde Treuthe."
> (B. VI. 59–60)

[“And I shall dress me,” said Perkyn, “in the manner of a pilgrim, and I will go with you until we find Truth.”]

and then at a high point of devotion, setting out on the hard contemplative path to God: *"si ambulavero in medio umbre*

---

[16] Donaldson, *op. cit.,* p. 195: "emphatic, and misleading, couplings of Piers with Christ which culminate in the phrase *Petrus, id est, Christus."* It is true, as he says, that this phrase disappears in the C text but Langland's alterations at that stage were as often prompted by extreme caution as by a radical change of attitude. The B text stands consistent, although audacious, in its main approach.

mortis. . . ." He is the Christ-guide who leads and moreover *is* the way—"he goth beforn the . . . unseably bi priue presens of his gostly myth"—and he is even Christ the object of the search —"he it is that is desyryd. . . ." So Piers directs to St. Truth, and, almost imperceptibly, *becomes* the "way" which Holy Church first sketched in outline, and he completed; he draws all with him, for he becomes love, "the graith gate. that goth into heuene. . . ." And at the very end of the poem he is to be sought for as urgently as St. Truth was at the beginning.

But now, after the decisive statement, *"Petrus, id est, Christus,"* the re-entry of Piers into the poem is awaited. The dreamer, beginning to grasp something of what Piers symbolizes, reaches a crescendo of excitement as the moment comes near. The question is "What charite is to mene" [What charity means] (B. XVI. 3), and Piers is mentioned:

> "Piers the Plowman!" quod I tho . and al for pure ioye
> That I herde nempne his name . anone I swouned after.
> (ibid., 18–19)

> ["Piers the Plowman!" I said then, and out of pure joy
> that I heard his name called, I swooned immediately after.]

It can be objected that when the moment does arrive, in Passus XVI, Piers, although in a position of great authority,[17] is not able to take such an ambitious interpretation as that suggested above. Moreover, the figure who

> Barfote on an asse bakke . botelees cam prykye
> (B. XVIII. 11)

> [Barefoot on an ass's back bootless came riding]

is firmly defined by Langland as Christ, and not Piers. Christ simply assumes the human nature of Piers for the "jousting in Jerusalem":

---

[17] He has the Tree of Charity under his care (B. XVI. 15–16) and the fruit of mankind which is to be wrested from the Devil is "Pieres fruit."

> This Iesus of his gentrice . wole Iuste in Piers armes,
> In his helme and in his haberioun . *humana natura.*
>
> (B. XVIII. 22–23)

[This Jesus of his noble birth will joust in Pier's arms,
in his helmet and in his coat of mail, *human nature.*]

The Piers symbol, built up accumulatively over the poem, now seems to be weakened.

Here the differences between Langland, the poet-allegorist, and Hilton, the prose-writer, become clear. Langland's allegory cannot long remain purely didactic; its natural movement is towards drama. He has, therefore, a far more difficult problem of communication to meet and overcome. The vital comment on the nature of Christ, made so succinctly by Hilton (see page 210 above) must, if rendered as a play of personages, appear full of paradox, and, if then judged by either realistic or symbolic standards, full of complexity. In fact, there is a paradox at the root of the matter: the co-existence of human and divine in the being of Christ, and, through grace, in the nature of man. Such a subject needs delicate handling; neither Hilton nor Langland could have wished to say without reservation that the pilgrim travelling to Truth by way of love is identical with Truth and love, that Piers and Christ are exactly the same person, and that man can become divine by his own efforts. The dangers of heresy would have been sufficiently clear to any Christian of the later fourteenth century. Yet they do wish to say that through the sacrifice of Christ and the grace obtained for man thereby, a divine element exists potentially in even the simplest of creatures. The prose writer is able to make the distinction brief and clear:

he is al and he makith al . if þu mytist sen hym þu dost nout . but sufferyst hym werkyn in thyn soule . . . þu art nout ellys but a resonable instrument . wherinne that he werkyth.

Hilton's words are paralleled in other contemplative texts; the author of *The Cloud of Unknowing* expresses himself with economy:

only bi his mercy wiþ-outen þi desert arte maad a God in grace, onyd
wiþ him in spirit wiþ-outen departyng, boþe here & in blis of heuen wiþ-
outen any eende. So þat, þouȝ þou be al one wiþ hym in grace, ȝit þou
arte ful fer bineþe hym in kynde.   (120/16–20)

[only by his mercy without your merit are you made a God in grace,
united with him in spirit without separating, both here and in the bliss
of heaven without end. So that, though you are completely one with him
in grace, yet you are very far beneath him in nature.]

Dame Julian of Norwich with meticulous care:

And I saw no difference atwix God and our substance but as it were al
God, and yet myn understondyng toke that our substance is in God, that
is to say that God is God, and our substance is a creature in God.
                                                    (f. 74)

[and I saw no difference between God and our substance, but, as it were,
all God, and yet my understanding took it that our substance is in God,
that is to say that God is God, and our substance is a creature in God.]

Langland has a more daring plan; he sets out to show us, in
full imaginative and dramatic form, how this "working in the
soul" takes place. We are allowed to understand how the devout
human being, Piers, changes in significance from plowman to
the principle of divine love in man: Christ works so perfectly in
his soul that indeed in this sense "*Petrus, id est, Christus,*" Piers
is "maad a God in grace." But although we can be told of this in
his absence, we cannot be allowed to see Piers displayed before
us as the total sum of divine love. The living and speaking Piers
must remain separate from the divine force which operates mys-
teriously and triumphantly in him. Man's aspiration and God's
condescension meet in the soul—but they are not the same
thing: "our substance is a creature in God."

Consequently, the Crucifixion and the Harrowing of Hell, in
Passus XVI-XVIII, are experienced by Christ, not by Piers the
Plowman. And in the last few Passus of the poem, Piers is intimately connected with the Holy Spirit, but is not identical with
it. He has discovered God's Truth within—Truth "sits in his
heart"—but he is not to be mistaken for its divine essence, St.
Truth himself.

The deepest theme of *Piers Plowman* might, then, be viewed as an exploration of the journey to God through Christ—the reaching of the "treasure of Truth" along the highroad of Love: a study of the way in which Christ, with his doctrine of love, enables the pilgrim to Truth and his goal, Truth, to become one:

> "I am *via et veritas*," seith Cryst. "I may auaunce alle."
>
> (B. IX. 159)

["I am *the way and the truth*," says Christ, "I may advance all."]

The powerful welding of the two concepts of the going out towards God, and the ultimate finding of God within, is not unique to Langland; it can be found in both Hilton and Dame Julian:

> . . . he shewid him in erth thus as it wer in pilgrimage that is to say he is here with us bidand[18] us and shul bin till whan he hath browte us all to his bliss in hevyn . he shewid him dyvers tymes regnand as it is aforn seyd but principally in mannys soule he hath taken there his risting place and his worshipful cyte out of which worshipfull see he shall never risen nor removen without end.　　　　(f. 106)

[Thus he showed himself on earth, as it were on pilgrimage, that is to say, he is here with us, calling us, and shall be until he has brought us all to his bliss in heaven. Divers times he showed himself reigning, as has been said before, but principally in man's soul he has taken his resting place and his glorious city, out of which glorious see he shall never rise nor take leave without end.]

Langland, however, *is* unique in that he not only tries to express but also to personify it through the Piers-Christ figure— a powerful, composite symbol which he manipulates freely and sensitively, so that it commands moral, mystical and poetic significance.

In some ways, the fact that Langland always needed to turn to the drama of flesh and blood was a serious limitation; the difficulty of animating subtle spiritual truths is formidable, and there are minor failures and inconsistencies in *Piers Plowman*.

---

[18] This should probably read "ledand" [leading].

But in other ways his instinct for drama was sure and triumphant. However rarified the doctrine he presents to us, we never lose touch for long with the warm humanity of the plowman who first "put forth his head" and offered to lead us to St. Truth. Even if we are not destined to know the fulness of God's love in contemplative rapture, we can all travel with Piers the Plowman, who, "wiþ þe drawȝt of þis loue & voise of þis cleping" [with the attraction of this love and the voice of this calling][19] leads us irresistibly through an experience as rich as it is sometimes perplexing and challenging.

[19] *The Cloud,* 14/19.

10

JOHN GOWER IN HIS MOST
SIGNIFICANT ROLE

George R. Coffman

NO MAJOR FIGURE IN THE RANGE OF ENGLISH LITERARY HISTORY
has suffered more from the "slings and arrows of outrageous fortune" than John Gower. Thanks in no small part to Lowell and
Jusserand, during the past century he became almost a popular
legend as a "monument of dulness and pedantry."[1] Adjudged a
great medieval encyclopedist, he has been held superficial and
unspeculative in the fields of scientific and philosophic thought.[2]
During the eighteenth and nineteenth centuries especially, he
came to be widely regarded as an "ingrate and a sychophant" in

---

Reprinted, by permission of the University of Colorado Press, from
Elizabethan Studies and other Essays in Honor of George F. Reynolds,
University of Colorado Studies, Series B, II (1945), 52–61. For a recent
biographical and critical study of Gower, see John H. Fisher, *John
Gower: Moral Philosopher and Friend of Chaucer* (New York University
Press, 1964).

[1] *E.g.,* James Russell Lowell, "Chaucer," in *My Study Windows* (Boston, 1871), pp. 258–60, and J. J. Jusserand, *A Literary History of the
English People* (London, 1925), I, pp. 264–72. The unwritten chapters on
Gower's literary reputation would include a long roll of those who have
been uncritical in both their praise and their depreciation of him. That
chapter is no part of this brief paper, which constitutes prolegomena to a
larger and more comprehensive study.

[2] *E.g.,* George H. Fox, *The Mediaeval Sciences in the Work of John
Gower* (Princeton, 1931), Princeton University Studies in English, No.
6 *passim.*

his personal and political relationships.[3] It is not the purpose of this paper to attempt an assessment of these critical dicta and indictments. It is rather to suggest that the social instead of the literary aspects of Gower's writings may form the basis for an interpretation of him in his most significant role.

The age in which he lived, frustrated in its onward march just a few years before his death, is a tremendously exciting one. And more than any other single writer he mirrors directly the whole social range of that cosmic and chaotic period—albeit with a somewhat myopic vision. In a large and significant sense it may be more important to study him as a recipient of the heritage of certain ideas which he adapts to a functional end than as a writer who assimilates his materials for the purposes of literary art. And possibly even his poetry may assume greater validity and vitality if we consider his work as a whole rather than as fragmentary bits. Two more statements must suffice before I turn directly to the subject of this paper. A survey of his writings, with the little that we know about his life, will, I believe, confirm in the reader's mind G. C. Macaulay's cautious judgment against charges of political timidity and obsequiousness on Gower's part. And a survey of his writings, with their clear and repeated personal references, gives one the opinion that through them he comes to know Gower's spiritual and social biography.

As I follow through Gower's French, Latin, and English works I find something akin to a guiding principle. This in total-

---

[3] All of this, again, is part of a long, involved, and incomplete chapter in Gower's biography. Obviously there is space here to give the curious and interested reader only a few notable references: e.g., John Urey, Works of Geoffrey Chaucer (London, 1721, Introduction, d, (4); Joseph Ritson, Bibliographica Poetica: A Catalogue of the English Poets of the Twelfth, Thirteenth, Fourteenth, Fifteenth, and Sixteenth Centurys (London, 1802), pp. 24–25; Karl Meyer, John Gower's Bezichungen zu Chaucer und König Richard II (Bonn, 1889), passim. William Godwin, Life of Geoffrey Chaucer (London, 1803), I, pp. 240–46, presents a spirited defense of Gower in his relations with Richard II. G. C. Macaulay, The Works of John Gower (Oxford, 1899–1902), I–IV, gives a brief, judicial review of the matter (II, xxi–xxvi). Incidentally, all quotations in this paper are from this, the standard edition of Gower's works.

ity indicates that he was rightly called the moral Gower. He is an advocate of a moral order. By this he means God's order for the universe and the established order for human society. This moral order is preserved by reason, a divine gift which is added to the four elements constituting man's physical being. In practical application a man of reason is characterized by wisdom and virtue. Since Gower's writings show that he has no faith in the common people, his social gospel presupposes no social equality but is limited to fostering honesty and integrity within established society by all members of it. This social aspect of Gower is stressed by G. R. Owst, *Literature and the Pulpit in Medieval England*, albeit he implies a more democratic spirit than Gower possesses.

In all the literature that has been published (in medieval England), it would be difficult to find a more perfect mirror of the social gospel as presented by the pulpit, in its artistry as well as its doctrine, within a single frame, than his *Mirour de l'Omme*, or *Speculum Meditantis*.[4]

His literary pattern for his social cause is the *Speculum* of the medieval encyclopedist or the *Manual* of the homilist; or it may be the direct verbal scourge or whiplash of the reformer. In the sweep of his materials Gower ranges over the whole world and includes all classes of society but always with particular reference to contemporary England. In sum, as represented by the *Mirour, Vox Clamantis,* and *Confessio Amantis,* and his lesser poems, he progresses with consistency and growing clarity toward his central thesis. The rule of reason, to repeat, is the basic element in his conception of an ordered universe. The use of this God-given intellectual power will, he is convinced, result in a world of peace and harmony, in proper human relations, in worthy rulers, and in a prosperous England.

But Gower makes clear that this program here outlined is man's responsibility. He maintains that God in endowing man with reason charged him, the microcosm, with complete control

[4] (Cambridge University Press, 1933), pp. 230–231.

of the material universe, the macrocosm. In fact, he made him through the elements so essentially a part of the universe that failure to act in accordance with wisdom and virtue adversely affects all nature. This is the place to call attention to a long passage in the *Mirour* (26605–27240), which lays the basis for his whole doctrine of individual responsibility.[5] All classes of society have become corrupted. The blame is laid on the age. After having questioned the elements, the planets, and the stars, the author returns and makes man the cause. The logic of the manner in which this reacts on nature follows. Gower accepts the authority of books as to the creation,[6] and as to the promises of God for the prosperity of the good. Furthermore, through the addition of evidence of plagues, pestilences, tempests, and other unfavorable manifestations of nature he accepts the word that God through creating man a microcosm and endowing him with the divine power of reason has established an unbreakable pantheistic and sympathetic relationship with the macrocosm. Through failure to observe the precepts of wisdom and virtue, the component elements of God-given reason, and through the consequent corruption of church and court, dishonesty in professional and business life, and discontent and rebellion among the farmers and artisans, the destructive forces of nature are unleashed against the human race. Here he goes a step beyond the preacher or homilist to make clear that this is not merely an immediate and possibly capricious act of an angry God to punish man. It is rather that the cosmic relationship of all created things with man, their ruler, inevitably makes this come to pass in the scheme of the universe. This idea is reflected

[5] This idea is repeated with variations or modifications in *Vox Clamantis* (VII, esp. vii), and in the Prologue to *Confessio Amantis* (ll. 905 ff.).

[6] Macaulay in his notes refers especially to Gregory's *Hom. in Evang.*, ii, 39: "omnis autem creaturae aliquid habet homo. Habet namque commune esse cum lapidibus, vivere cum arboribus, sentire com animalibus, intelligere cum angelis" [but man has something of all creatures. To be, he has in common with stones; to live, with trees; to feel, with animals; to understand, with angels].

Coffman: *John Gower*

through medieval theology in the immediate effect of Adam's sin on external nature. In other words, Gower believes the evidence of books and *thinks* that God's plan really works. The thing for man is not merely to do wishful thinking and feeling even through prayer, but to use his divine wisdom to study and reflect, and to develop proper human relations through a change of heart. Thus he would recreate a paradise on earth.[7]

[7] Two modern instances, *mutatis mutandis,* may not be impertinent here. The first is from R. E. Sherwood's preface to *There Shall Be No Night* (Scribner's, 1940). He is justifying the theme of this play—that man is insane—as a thesis which he has been developing through twenty years. The essence of this he expresses in the words of Squier, the representative of the modern human beast in *The Petrified Forest.* After having talked of the monstrosities of the perverted intellectual of today he asks Gabby, one of the other characters, if she knows what is causing the present world chaos. This is his answer to her negative reply: "It's nature hitting back. Not with the old weapons—floods, plagues, holocausts. We can neutralize them. She's fighting back with strange instruments called neuroses. She's deliberately inflicting mankind with the jitters. Nature is proving that she can't be beaten by the likes of us. She's taking the world away from the intellectuals and giving it back to the apes" (p. xxi). One will recall that Sherwood expressed this same idea through Dr. Valkonen in *There Shall Be No Night.* The second instance is from Arthur H. Compton's *Freedom of Man* (Yale University Press, 1935). He, too, is talking about man's relation to nature: " 'Is nature friendly to us?' Assuredly if we will learn her laws and adapt our lives accordingly. If we do not, she may become our merciless enemy. Such is the stern yet kindly dictum which science has to offer. . . . Two Old Testament statements embody the same idea in deistic terms: 'All things work together for him who serves the Lord,' is the exact parallel of nature's laws that are friendly to the well-adapted organism. On the other hand, nature's ruthless attitude toward the man who will not adapt himself is accurately caught in the proverb 'The wages of sin is death.' . . . Coming back then to the view that the laws of nature are the method in which our intelligent God works, we must believe that His attitude toward us is revealed by the way nature treats us. Is He friendly? Yes, if we obey His laws" (pp. 113–14).

It is pertinent also here by way of corrective to call attention to a failure to interpret this passage in the *Mirour,* in relation to its context [T. O. Wedel, *The Medieval Attitude Toward Astrology* (Yale, 1920), pp. 134–41]. Here quoting from *Mirour, Vox Clamantis,* and *Confessio Amantis,* Wedel concludes that "It is not so much the man of character as the man of prayer who rules the stars" (p. 141). In the implications of this statement Dr. Wedel ignores one aspect of Gower's most signifi-

221

In kinship with Thomas Aquinas before him and Milton afterwards Gower affirms that if reason be the guide for the human race all will go well. The difference is that Gower is not interested in the abstract theological, philosophic, or scientific aspects of this. He is concerned with its relation to man in contemporary society.

All this is the groundwork for convincing man of his freedom and fixing his responsibility. To this end he attacks the exponents of astrology and the supporters of a fatalistic attitude represented by the word *fortune* or *fate*. Since the wise man with God aiding will rule the stars,[8] man simply confesses his failure to use his reason if he blames astrological influences for his lot. Fortune also is the subject of repeated attacks by Gower.[9] The

---

cant role. God *will* aid man in answer to his prayers but only if his character and his actions accord with reason. George G. Fox, *op. cit.,* pp. 92–93, referring to the same passage says, "When Gower attempts to vindicate free will . . . he does it by arguments that are anti-astrological and non-scientific. That is, he insists on the purely obvious influence of celestial bodies, and tacitly denies the occult emanation upon which all astrology is based. He is more pious than the theologians." The cogent refutation of Fox is that Gower bases his statement on the logic of the argument that reason has power over the stars.

[8] See *Confessio Amantis,* VII, 633 ff., esp. pp. 651–54. The astronomer has just been quoted as saying that the stars rule man's destiny. Gower adds:

> But the divin seith otherwise,
> That if man weren goode and wise
> And plesant unto the godhede,
> Thei scholden noght the sterres drede.

> [But the divine says otherwise,
> that if men were good and wise
> and pleasing to God,
> they should not fear the stars.]

See also the Latin stanza preceding line 633, and *Vox Clamantis,* II, 239, which embodies the well-known proverb: In virtute dei sapiens dominabitur astra [In the power of God the wise man is ruled by the stars]. Cf. Wedel, *op. cit.,* pp. 134–35.

[9] One illustration must suffice here. In his review of man's attempt to shift the responsibility for his evil state to fortune and the stars (Prologue to *Confessio Amantis,* lines 529–47), Gower anticipated Shakespeare in

reason is that although it and fate were by his and Chaucer's day principally decorative literary terms, survivals of a functional element in an earlier civilization, they still remained symbols for an attitude which shifted the blame for one's own weakness.

Gower's ethical basis for an ordered universe through the responsibility imposed on the individual by the divine gift of reason finds expression in his reaction to Richard II and Henry IV. Specifically, it represents the application of his rationale to the practice of kingship. The ruler, whether by appointment or line of descent, is a responsible agent and is subject to indictment by his fellow countrymen. Space does not permit even the briefest survey of the heritage from Thomas Aquinas, Dante, Marsiglio of Padua, William of Ockham, and Wycliffe. It must suffice for the present to give an epitome of the system of Aquinas by a distinguished medievalist:[10]

The world of Thomas Aquinas was dominated by a few great simple universal ideas, of which the life of man, both individual and associated, was the reflex. At the heart of things was God, revealed in the uniformity and harmony of nature. The center and crown of creation was man, to whom was given the rule over the earth, which again was the center of the material universe, served by the obedient sun and accompanied by the planetary and starry host in tributary homage. Corresponding to this manifest order of nature, the associated life of man was also an image of ordered unity. It had, to be sure, its varieties of race, nation and social class, but these varieties were only the differentiations of an essentially unified system. The one and only God had made one sole and sufficient revelation of himself and his revelation had included a scheme of social order.

This I quote *in extenso* because it might well be an epitome of Gower's entire rationale. In Gower's indictment or approval of government he may seem to the casual reader to be choosing

his attribution to Edmund of a cynical negation of the power of fortune and the stars and his declaration of immediate parental responsibility for his present bastard state.

[10] Ephriam Emerton, "The Defensor Pacis of Marsiglio of Padua," *Harvard Theological Studies*, VIII (1920), p. 2.

from Aquinas, Dante, Marsiglio of Padua, William of Ockham, and Wycliffe in an eclectic manner. Actually he selects with discrimination those elements of government which seem best adapted to his general principles for responsible human beings and for an ordered universe. In brief, a king's acts should be dictated by reason, that is, wisdom and virtue.

Gower was the monitor for Richard II through *Vox Clamantis* and *Confessio Amantis*; and he made him the object of a moralist's denunciation in the *Cronica Tripertita*. And in the poem *To Henry IV in Praise of Peace* he was the herald of what he hoped would be a new day under Henry IV. Here the only important thing to stress is that his ambitions and his hopes were all a part of his ethical system. As is well known, in *Vox Clamantis*, he first defends the boy king because unwise councillors are responsible. Later he blames Richard himself as a heedless and undisciplined youth. Similarly in *Confessio Amantis,* written at the king's request and at first expressing confidence in him, he later deletes all favorable references to him, holds him primarily responsible for the evil state of affairs, affirms that the book was written for England's sake, and presents it to the future Henry IV. Even in the *Mirour*, citing Siriach (22801 ff.), he admonishes Edward III in his dotage and under the domination of Alice Perrers—a king ought to cherish truth and to obey in everything. After a reference to Edward III's weakness he prays God to bring discord to all laws when a woman reigns in the land and the king is subject to her. Entirely to the point for Gower's significant role is his indictment in *Vox Clamantis* (VII, xvii) of all individuals who are victims of their passions, which closes with the assertion that a king ruled by his vices rather than by reason is only a slave to his body. An indictment in the *Cronica Tripertita,* directly condemnatory, echoes Wycliffe's doctrine that no man in mortal sin can hold dominion or lordship.[11] The passage from the *Cronica Tripertita* reads:

[11] See especially *De Officio Regis* (Wyclif Society, London, 1887) (ed. by A. W. Pollard and Charles Sayle), *passim*. For concise summary, see editors' introduction, pp. xxvi ff.

Est qui peccator, non esse potest dominator
Ricardo teste, finis probat hoc manifeste.   (III, 486–87)

[Who is a sinner cannot be a conqueror.
Witness Richard, the end clearly proves this.]

Again in Book VII of *Confessio Amantis*, which is devoted entirely to instructing a king in proper conduct, Gower repeats this idea in phrasing which might well have come from English puritans when they indicted Charles I over two centuries later:

> For thing which is of kinges set,
> With kinges oghte it noght be let.
> What king of lawe takth no kepe,
> Be lawe he mai no regne kepe.
> Do lawe awey what is a king?
> Wher is the riht of eny thing,
> If that ther be no lawe in londe?
> This oghte a king wel understonde,
> As he which is to lawe swore,
> That if the lawe be forbore
> Withouten execucioun,
> It makth a lond torne up so doun,
> Which is unto the king a sclandre.   (3071–83)

> [For a thing that is appointed for kings,
> with kings ought not be omitted.
> The king who has no regard for law
> may preserve no realm by law.
> Do away with law and what is a king?
> Where is the right of anything
> if there is no law in the land?
> This a king ought to understand well,
> as one who is sworn to law,
> that if the law is left
> without execution,
> it turns a land up-side-down,
> which is a disgrace to the king.]

All this is of fundamental importance. A king who does not govern himself and does not use good judgment in ruling his people violates the law of reason and thus is in the category Gower established in the *Mirour*.

The constructive teaching of his ethical system is to be found in the poem entitled by Macaulay *To King Henry IV in Praise of Peace*. This eulogy is an epitome of the central theme of Marsiglio of Padua's *Defensor Pacis*: the end of government is peace. After justifying Henry IV's claim to his title, as does Chaucer, through line of descent and election by Parliament, he returns to his constant theme that reason (good judgment) above all things is to be praised in a king:

> Aboute a kyng good counseil is to preise
> Above alle othre thinges most vailable;
> Bot yit a kyng withinne himself shal peise,
> And se the thinges that ben reasonable,
> And ther uppon he shal his wittes stable
> Among the men to sette pes in evene,
> For love of him which is the kyng of hevene. (141–47)

> [Around a king good counsel is praiseworthy
> above all other things as most valuable;
> yet a king shall deliberate within himself,
> and see what things are of good judgment,
> and he shall fix his mind thereupon
> to set peace equally among men,
> for love of him who is the King of Heaven.]

Incidentally, his repeated concern for the welfare of England and his love for the home of his birth provide an immediate motive for illustrating through these English rulers the basis of his ethical standards. Its high point comes in a well-known lyric passage in Book VII of *Vox Clamantis*.

> Singula, que dominus statuit sibi regna per orbem,
> Que magis in Christi nomine signa gerunt,
> Diligo, set propriam super omnia diligo terram,
> In qua principium dixit origo meum.
> Quicquid agant alie terre, non subruor inde,
> Dum tamen ipse foris sisto remotus eis;
> Patria set iuvenem que me suscepit alumpnum,
> Partibus in cuius semper adhero manens,
> Hec si quid patitur, mea viscera compaciuntur,
> Nec sine me dampna ferre valebit ea:

Eius in aduersis do pondere sum quasi versus;
Si perstet, persto, si cadat illa, cado.[12]   (1289–1300)

(See footnote for translation.)

The climax in the last ringing line recalls the height of Churchill's great argument in England's darkest hour four years ago [1941]:

Si perstet, persto, si cadat illa, cado.

Another aspect of this whole matter of kingship sets Gower in artistic integrity over one hundred years beyond Boccaccio, Chaucer, and Lydgate, and allies him with the Elizabethan *Mirror for Magistrates* and Tudor tragedy. In the Latin summary of his three major works appearing at the close of *Confessio Amantis,* both the version concerning *Vox Clamantis* which fixes the responsibility on the nobles and the one which fixes it on the king, specifically place Richard's fate in the category of cause and effect and *not* as a result of capricious fortune. The earlier version, which absolves the boy king, states clearly (evidencius declarat) that such calamities (the peasants' rebellion) happened among men from certain causes and not from fortune:

Secundus enim liber, sermone latino versibus exametri et pentametri compositus, tractat super illo mirabili euentu qui in Anglia tempore domini Regis Ricardi secundi anno regni sui quarto contigit, quando seruiles rustici impetuose contra nobiles et ingenuos regni insurrexerunt. Innocenciam tamen dicti domini Regis tunc minoris etatis causa inde excusabilem pronuncians, culpas aliunde, ex quibus et non a fortuna talia inter homines contigunt enormia, euidencius declarat. . . .[13]

[For the second book, a discourse in Latin composed in hexameter and

[12] The following is an attempted paraphrase of this fine passage: I love the separate Christian kingdoms the Lord has established throughout the world; but above all I love the land in which I was born. Whatever other lands may do, I am not shaken if I am outside their portals. But if my native land, which bred and reared me, suffers injuries, I too must suffer. Without me she cannot be strong to bear these ills. I bend under the weight of her adversities. If she stands firm, I stand firm. If she falls, I fall.

[13] Macaulay, *op. cit.,* III, pp. 479–80, fn.

pentameter verses, treats of that marvelous event which happened in England in the time of the ruler, King Richard II, in the fourth year of his reign, when impulsively country serfs rose up against the nobles and the freeborn of the realm. Declaring, however, the innocence of the aforementioned ruler, excusable since the King at that time was a minor, it states clearly the faults of others, from which, and not from fortune, such enormities happen among men.]

The later version states that "the cruel king himself falling down from on high by his own evil doings, was at length hurled into the pit which he dug himself."

Secundus enim liber sermono latino metrice compositus tractat de variis infortuniis tempore Regis Ricardi Secundi in Anglia contingentibus. Unde non solum regni proceres et communes tormenta passi sunt, set et ipse crudelissimus rex suis ex demeritis ab alto corruens in foueam quam fecit finaliter proiectus est. Nomenque voluminis huius Vox Clamantis intitulatur.[14]   (See footnote for translation.)

In a word he accepts the essence of the definition of Chaucer's Monk preceding his tale but rejects pointedly any attribution to the Chaucerian "capricious fortune." He makes this a consistent example of man's responsibility, cause and effect, reason versus passion.

Here then is the word of a middle-class Englishman. He did not see the revolt as "a popular front." He saw it only as an uprising that was destroying the established order, the only one he could imagine. In this respect he was a spiritual brother of the author of *Piers Plowman*: both wanted merely spiritual conversion of individuals, with no social upheavals.

Gower's *Confessio Amantis* might well be called his *summa moralis*. In its totality it records this principle of man's responsibility resulting from the gift of reason. The author has suffered

---

[14] *Ibid.* See Macaulay's translation *CHEL* (Cambridge, 1908), II, pp. 158–59. "The second book, metrically composed in the Latin language, treats of the various misfortunes which happened in England in the time of king Richard II, whence not only the nobles and commons of the realm suffered great evils, but the cruel king himself, falling from on high by his own evil doings, was at length hurled into the pit which he dug himself. And the name of this volume is *Vox Clamantis.*"

from piecemeal interpretation of this work to a greater extent than any other writer to my knowledge. The work has a large integrity and unity based on a defense of his ethical scheme for the universe. Read in the light of his *moral system* it transcends any mechanical pattern. Gower tells in the Prologue exactly what he is going to do. He does it well. It is worth doing. And he recapitulates in the Epilogue. In a major respect, *Confessio Amantis* is a King's Courtesy Book. In his earlier version he states this specifically. Also he states definitely in the Prologue that he is going to write of love, which subdues many a wise man, and is going to consider those in high office with relation to the virtues and vices of their offices.

> Whan the prologe is so despended,
> This bok schal afterward ben ended
> Of love, which doth many a wonder
> And many a wys man hath put under.
> And in this wyse I thenke trete
> Towardes hem that now be grete,
> Betwen the vertu and the vice
> Which longeth unto this office. (73–80)

> [When the prologue is spent,
> the rest of this book shall afterward treat
> of love, which does many a wonder
> and has subdued many a wise man.
> And in this way I intend to treat
> of them that are now great,
> in relation to the virtue and the vice
> that belongs to this office.]

In the second place he treats of reason versus passion as relating to love between the sexes. In the third place he makes personal application of this to his own life—an old man in love with a young girl, with reason reasserting itself in the end. Furthermore, his approach and his return in the poem to England and its welfare are consistent with this dominant note in all three of his major works. Gower's complete works are as much a justification of the ways of God to man as are Milton's. His most significant role is his explanation and illustration of the ethical basis of God's universe for this little world of man.

This brings us to a brief comment on the question of courtly love, the theme of an able chapter by C. S. Lewis, in defense of Gower as a literary artist.[15] Gower recognizes in connection with love and reason that there is the law of kind. As far as possible within the established order he would have all relationships between sexes culminate in marriage. In the same mood that fortune and fate evoked his indictment, he has no time for courtly love because even though it may be no more than a literary convention or a decorative pattern for fiction, it is a symbol which might encourage those who wish through their passions to violate the laws of nature and of established society. His common-sense recognition of the "law of kind" and the self-willed corrupt nature of man justifies his writing of the perversities of sexual passion but does not permit him in his stories to sanction the vices as codified in the rules of Andreas Capellaneus. The important thing here is that this becomes a program for action as first based on his *apologia* for reason in the *Mirour*. His *Traitié* and his *Balades* represent again the constructive side of his theme. Both "are made especially for those who expect their love affairs to be perfected in marriage." The former sets forth also "the evils springing from adultery and incontinence." Lewis with all his excellent appreciation of the literary values in the stories told by the Confessor misses the largest informing element in failing to observe that the outer circle of the story carries his constant theme of England, that he makes clear his theme of reason versus passion in his love stories, and that the immediate pattern was in part at least a King's Courtesy Book. Lewis speaks of Book VII as a "general digression on education." It is not a "general digression." It is a body of specific instructions as to the education and behavior of a king. Lines 73–80 of the Prologue, quoted above, have prepared us for it.

[15] *The Allegory of Love: A Study in Medieval Tradition* (Oxford, 1936), pp. 198–222.

Space does not permit even reference to the detailed evidence which would prove to the hilt that *Confessio Amantis* is Gower's *summa* and can be justly interpreted only as such. The palinode beginning with Book VIII, line 2009, and closing with line 2970 stresses for Gower himself the place of reason in his life. The Confessor says (2023), renounce love unless you can keep the proper balance between love and reason; and Venus in her final words (2925–27) tells him, after Cupid has withdrawn the dart of love and restored his reason, to return where *moral virtue* dwells—that about which he has been writing through almost twenty years.

We shall have to wait until we come to Milton before we find another English writer who, to paraphrase Macaulay, treats "the whole field of man's religious and moral nature, . . . the purposes of Providence in dealing with him" and "the method which should be followed by man in order to reconcile himself to God." Like Milton also he seems to record his spiritual biography in his works. Gower did "bolt to the bran" [pierce to the muscle] for his contemporaries problems of man's responsibility, the place of a ruler in a kingdom, and the whole question of courtly love in literature and life. This is because he was interested, not in philosophic thought or an abstract philosophy of life, but in a philosophy of living. There is no reason to doubt that in the well-known phrase "the moral Gower" Chaucer meant to express high regard for his fellow poet. An attempt at a modern phrasing of his most significant role is that he is an exponent of the practice of wisdom and virtue and of the gospel of individual responsibility, both directed toward "a good life" for contemporary society and the welfare of England, his own dear land. A study to which this is not even an adequate introduction may reveal, I am convinced, that as a practical conservative-liberal he was one of "the most thoughtful and intelligent" men of his age.

11

"the hoole book"

D. S. Brewer

WHEN *The Works of Sir Thomas Malory* APPEARED, THE TITLE gave us both a sense of relief and an unpleasant shock. It was a relief to find how the concept of eight separate romances seemed to clarify what had before seemed muddled and inconsistent. It seemed to explain the apparent resurrections of once slaughtered knights, and the introduction of knights full-grown whose birth and upbringing are only recounted later. Even more, the nature of Malory's literary achievement, of the way he broke down the interwoven cyclic romances that were his sources, became clearer and more enjoyable. But it was also disagreeable to find that what we had been brought up on as one book, however muddled, was now supposed to be eight distinct books. Part of this response may have been no more than the natural reaction to the disturbance of set ideas. Nevertheless, even now, when we are used to the idea of there being eight entirely separate romances, when all the advantages of the theory have been considered, a careful examination of Malory's work makes one doubt it. Illuminated and indeed convinced as one is bound to be by Professor Vinaver's brilliant display of Malory's treatment of his sources, no one, surely, "uncorrupted with literary prejudices after all the refinements of subtilty and the dogmatism of learn-

Reprinted, by permission of the author and the Clarendon Press, from *Essays on Malory,* ed. J. A. W. Bennett (Oxford, 1963), pp. 41–63.

ing" can avoid an impression of *The Works* as one book—"the hoole book" as Caxton called it. It is not quite that one disagrees with the theory of the limited separateness of the tales, but that one is bound to reject what seem to be the implications of Professor Vinaver's thesis—that Malory's romances are as separate as the various novels of a modern author; that the romances may be taken in any or no particular order; and that they have no cumulative effect.

Our difficulty in discussing the form of the *Morte Darthur* is partly due to the lack of satisfactory descriptive and critical terms for the kind of literary experience that Malory gives us. It is natural for those who are dissatisfied with the idea of completely separate romances to assert some kind of unity for Malory's work. But obviously unity here cannot mean structural unity of a kind we expect from a modern novel, or that we find in an ancient epic; and the term unity (which I have used in the past) is probably misleading and should be abandoned. If we assert the connectedness of the constituent works we shall be on safer ground, but there are not specific connexions everywhere, and the term does not include those impressions of unity of atmosphere and of underlying concepts which Professor Vinaver himself has never denied, and which are an important part of the general literary effect. Perhaps the best term, of a useful elasticity, is *cohesion*.[1] The cohesion of Malory's *Works* is greater than that of the separate works of a modern novelist, though it is different from that Coleridgean concept of "organic unity" with which we now approach a work of art.

The emphasis must be on "the work of art." In the last resort, when all has been learnt that can be known of authorship and source, Malory's work must be judged, like any other, in and for itself alone. It is the more important to emphasize this in Malory's case because, as Professor Vinaver has shown us, Mal-

[1] Professor Vinaver has himself suggested the use of this term to me. I am grateful to him for this and for several other suggestions generously made to me on the subject of this essay.

234

ory had a peculiar relation to his sources. He has rehandled them, to be sure, in accordance with his own strong feeling for form and moral content, but he is also completely at their mercy. Unless they move him, he cannot move. The essence of the matter was put by a reviewer of Vinaver's edition in *The Times Literary Supplement* (7 June 1947): "we are not reading the work of an independent artist. . . . Whatever he does, Malory's personal contribution to the total effect cannot be very great, though it may be very good." When we look at Malory's work—or works —we are not looking at the work of one man, but perhaps of a dozen, far separated in time and space, occupation and outlook. Each writer built on what had been made before. The work of art is cumulative and transcends any one, or any group, of its makers. Malory's very dependence on his sources makes us insist, paradoxically, that in terms of art neither the sources nor Malory himself are of the least importance. Malory's personal contribution is less than the book as a whole, and the book may create effects of which Malory is little more than the scribe.

Here is perhaps the root of the differences, which, after all, are rather of emphasis and nomenclature than of principle, between Professor Vinaver and those who are reluctant to accept the complete divisions proposed in his great edition of 1947 and further emphasized in his edition of *The Death of King Arthur.* In his major edition Professor Vinaver was chiefly concerned to show the nature and as it were the machinery of Malory's personal contribution. That he has brilliantly succeeded, and in so doing has made an important contribution to our understanding of Malory's work, and of an important phase in literary history, is beyond dispute. But it may also be argued that in his perfectly proper and highly illuminating emphasis on Malory's personal contribution, and perhaps because of his own vast knowledge of the whole Arthurian *corpus,* he has taken for granted what needs equal emphasis in an aesthetic judgement: that is, the inherent tendencies to cohesion of that *corpus,* and Malory's reflection of that tendency to cohesion, even while he simplified its complexities. His simplification, indeed, inevitably made the cohesion more evident.

Yet I do not wish to underestimate Malory's personal contribution even to the sense of cohesion in the whole Arthurian *corpus*. At the very least he brought out what was only suggested, and the completed work shows that his whole attitude to the material differed from his predecessors'. Professor Vinaver's consciousness of Malory's dependence on, yet divergence from, his sources sometimes leads him to measure Malory against the French and find him wanting, where to the less learned reader it seems merely that Malory is attempting and achieving something different. A minor example of this is Malory's detail of the twenty thousand pounds it cost the Queen to find Lancelot (*W* 831), which Professor Vinaver once deplored and Professor Lewis defended. Granted the different premises, each critic is right. But if we judge Malory's work by the standards of its source, rather than by its effectiveness within its own context, we may miss, or misinterpret, the special quality of the work of art itself.

Thus for two opposite reasons, Malory's dependence on his sources, and Malory's differences from his sources, we must make a clear distinction between Malory's personal contribution and the actual book he left. Sometimes the effect of the book is due primarily to Malory's source, and sometimes it is due primarily to Malory's own personal contribution. Fascinating and important as it is to distinguish, guided by Professor Vinaver, between what is derived and what is personal[2], such a distinction cannot affect our final judgement on the total work of art, which must be judged in its own right, as a whole, obeying its own laws, holding and shaping the reader's imagination by its own power. (I do not deny the value of anything that will help us to a clearer understanding of the work of art, especially in places where it is obscure or to some extent unsuccessful; a

---

[2] The distinction is obviously artificial; in fact the two may merge indistinguishably. Nevertheless, the two elements exist separately.

knowledge of the sources is particularly relevant to understanding much of Malory, and the knowledge that Professor Vinaver has put at our disposal enormously increases our understanding and enjoyment of Malory's aims and achievements.)

When, therefore, we disregard the peculiar mixture of source and personal contribution in Malory's book, and look "at the thing in itself, as it really is," we shall be more than ever impressed by a sense of its cohesion. How far that impression is due to Malory's sources does not for the moment matter. It would not even matter if Malory's personal contribution had only been to attempt to break down that sense of cohesion; it is still there. And in fact the case is not so desperate. It is possible to show, thanks to Professor Vinaver's own edition, that there are bonds still left between the various tales, and that Malory also made a deliberate attempt to link the beginnings and ends of his tales together. It is also possible to show that the tales could not have been put together in any order other than the present one; that the succession of romances has a cumulative effect; and that there is a kind of shapeliness in the whole book, even though the shape is one that is difficult to describe.

We must first emphasize what is indeed indisputable, the unity of tone and atmosphere, the continual moral concern of a special kind. All the tales are concerned with the romance of knight-errantry, of strange adventures in which the wrongs of the oppressed are to be righted, and in which the High Order of Knighthood is justified and glorified. There is certainly a development in Malory's concept of true morality, and certainly the earlier books are fiercer, more primitive; but the same conception of the moral quality of knightliness, most movingly expressed in Ector's lament for Lancelot, underlies them all.

Then all the stories are concerned with the same kind of people, and all these people are associated with the same central group, the court of Arthur. Indeed, one of Malory's great achievements is his portrayal of this passionate, limited and aristocratic society, with its own standards of success and failure.

Next, within this society some half-dozen characters are dominant in most of the tales and continually recur. Of these Arthur and Lancelot are the most important. Now it is very noticeable that the tales, in the order that we have them, observe the proper sequence of events in the lives of Lancelot and Arthur. There is a biographical continuity observed throughout the tales which effectively links them together. This is worth exploring. Its existence reduces to minor proportions certain apparent inconsistencies in the treatment of minor characters. There are no inconsistencies (though perhaps some lack of realism) in the presentation, in due order, throughout all the tales, of the lives of the chief characters.

The passage of time, and the development of character and event are particularly strongly felt in the first two and last three tales. The first two tales show us the birth of Arthur, his first flowering as a knight, and his triumph as a great king over many lands—though with this essential theme there are, in Spenserian terms, "other adventures intermedled." The second tale, of Arthur's war against Rome, is especially interesting because in it the young Lancelot appears for the first time. He is rapidly brought forth as a hero subsidiary to Arthur alone; and Professor Vinaver shows that Malory invents almost everything that is said about Lancelot in this tale, while diminishing the roles that other knights have in his source. At the end of the second tale Arthur is triumphantly established as the greatest English king, ruling from Ireland to Rome, surrounded by his knights of the Round Table, devoted to the High Order of Knighthood. It seems to a reader natural and logical enough that the third tale should go on to establish in his own right the prowess of Malory's second hero, Sir Lancelot. Once Lancelot is established, the next tales reinforce the sense of continuity by going on to give the histories and to reveal the glorious deeds of other knights of the Round Table. These are the short tale of Sir Gareth and the inordinately long one of Sir Tristram. The reason why Malory leaves out the tragic end of the French tale of Sir Tristram, and leaves

Sir Tristram in cheerful domesticity, is surely because these central tales of Lancelot, Gareth, Tristram, and a number of minor characters, are all devoted to the glory and success of the knights of the Round Table. Arthur and Lancelot, once they have been established, recede somewhat into the background. But Arthur is the point of departure and return for all the knights, and their glory is his; while Sir Lancelot, even where he is not a central figure, is frequently mentioned as the type of ideal knight. The praise of Sir Tristram is that his fame at one time began to overshadow Sir Lancelot's, and there could be no higher praise. In these fourth and fifth books, therefore, if Arthur and Lancelot are less active it is not because they have been supplanted.

In all the French books, and in the English *Morte Arthure* which is the principal source of Malory's second tale, the story of the Roman campaign and triumph is followed forthwith by the story of Arthur's downfall. Malory places the story of Lancelot's adventures immediately after Arthur's return from Rome. Professor Vinaver argues from this that Malory was ignorant of the position of the *"Lancelot* proper" in the Arthurian cycle (*W* 1398). But Malory knew, if only from the English source of his second tale, that the death of Arthur followed the Roman campaign, and he probably knew this from French tales as well. The change he introduced was probably deliberate. He postponed the tragic end and turned his second tale into a tale of triumph, possibly in tribute, as Professor Vinaver suggests, to Henry V, but also in tribute to Arthur, and to all that Arthur stands for in his imagination. The triumphant second tale establishes the chief hierophant of the Order of Knighthood. Arthur has to be established in his own greatness before we feel the greatness of his court, his knights, and the ideals they express. On the other hand the crowning of Arthur is the climax of his personal triumph. Further adventures of his own could not effectively add to it. His glory is extended in the next three tales by the glorious deeds of his knights. These anglicized paladins, with their noble achievements, by acknowledging him as their lord add their renown to his. Certainly, Malory was not interested in subtle analysis of courtly feeling, but it is fruitless to blame him for this. We must take what we can get. What we are offered is essentially the story of the Golden Age of English history, and how it came to its tragic end. So it is fitting that the time of Arthur's triumph should be separated from the time of disaster. It makes Arthur's fame in later ages more comprehensible, it allows us to dwell somewhat on the English glory of the Round Table and of the Order of Knighthood. And as a literary result, it makes the final tragedy more moving by allowing to flourish somewhat the flower which is to be so cruelly lopped; for the final tragedy is not only one of persons but of "the flower of chivalry of the world"; of a whole noble way of life.

After the second book there are no precise notations of age, but it is nevertheless true that we have been introduced to the chief actors in their youth, and that we follow them through the glory of their maturity to their sad decline and exemplary deaths. Within this general biographical chronology, which is never violated, inconsistencies in the treatment of some minor characters are unimportant. Such as they are (and they have been over-emphasized) they tend to occur in the middle books, where the sense of the passage of time, though not neglected by Malory, is less important. Thus, taking the events in the lives of Arthur and Lancelot as our main guide, we can see a clearly perceptible progression throughout the first two books, which corresponds to the rise in Fortune's wheel; a less perceptible movement in the next three books, when Arthur's glory is at its height; and a further progressive movement in the last three books, gathering momentum especially in the last two, whose downward movement is the wheel's adverse turn. Whether or not Malory consciously intended this form is perhaps disputable. If he did not, he would not be the first or last author to have built better than he knew. In any event, Malory's conscious intentions are undiscoverable and unimportant, except in so far as they reveal themselves in the book. The test of the form I have suggested is whether it corresponds to the details of the book; whether it makes sense in itself; and whether equal sense could be made of a different arrangement of the books.

The form makes sense in itself because it describes a general chronological progression just like those in life, and also comprehensible to medieval views of life. Growth, flowering, and decay; rise, supremacy, and fall not only completely accord with normal experience, but can easily be imaged in such medieval terms as Fortune's wheel. If we disorder the tales, this general pattern which holds them together is lost. And to insist on the completely separate nature of the *Works* is inevitably to insist that there is no literary value in reading them in any specific order; to insist that there will be no loss if we read of Arthur's death, before we read of his triumph or birth. How can we insist on such a crippling procedure, once we have realized the chronological order of the tales in their present sequence?

In looking more closely at the details of arrangement we should bear in mind that for Malory the material he was arranging was historical material. For various reasons medieval writers make a different distinction from ours between *fabula* [fable] and *historia* [history]; or rather, the two kinds intermingled for them in a way that is strange to us. Chaucer's treatment of the story of Troilus and Criseyde is perhaps the most obvious example, but there are many others.[3] Furthermore, it is well known that from the late twelfth to the early seventeenth centuries practically all Englishmen thought that Arthur was a genuinely historical figure; and it is clear both from the general situation and from his own remarks (e.g., *W* 1229) that Malory shared this view. Caxton in his Preface to the *Morte Darthur* "coude not wel denye but that there was suche a noble kyng named Arthur." He refers to Malory's work as "a joyous history," even if "to gyve fayth and byleve that al is trewe that is conteyned herein, ye be at your liberte." Malory is not writing a work—or,

---

[3] Cf. my *Chaucer*, 3rd edition, 1961, pp. 95, 127, 148, 158, for examples from Chaucer.

not to beg the question, even works—of "pure" fiction; nor is he writing an historical novel. Yet he is not writing chronicle-history either. His relation to the historical "truth" may be compared to Shakespeare's. Shakespeare's handling of history is that of an artist: he feels free to embroider; but he does not go against the essential historical truth as it is known to him. Shakespeare, also, knew three types of history. First, relatively recent English history; second, Roman history (each of these being fairly realistically chronicled in their differing degrees); and third, legendary history, mostly English, though it included the story of Hamlet as well as that of Lear and Cymbeline. There is no reason to think that the third type seemed any less genuinely historical to the Elizabethans than the first two, but it was obviously much less authoritatively recorded, with less realistic detail, and consequently gave far greater freedom of interpretation and invention. We are greatly in Professor Vinaver's debt for his valuable account of the way in which medieval writers varied the interpretation of a given story; but it does not seem that the use of interpretation and invention destroyed the feeling of history, of basic historical fact, for Malory any more than for the authors of *Troilus and Criseyde, Paradise Lost*— or the gospel of St. John. For all his recasting, the effect of Malory's treatment of his subject was if anything to increase its historical nature. This is partly the result of a rather factual turn of imagination, as seen, for example, in the famous "twenty thousand pounds." It is also the result of his chronological treatment, through the series of tales in their order as we have them, of the birth, life, acts, and death of the greatest English king, who created, with his knights, the High Order of Knighthood. By and through the life and death of Arthur, Malory half created from the interwoven threads of his sources something quite different from what he found—a pattern of tragedy, and a tragedy in history.

It is this "historical" basis that does much to explain our sense of the cohesion of Malory's separate tales. It would be strange, however, if this cohesion rested only on general impressions, and the general course of the narrative. It does not. There is plenty of evidence in the actual conduct of the individual stories, in the actual words that Malory uses, which confirms our feeling, and which is indeed largely the basis of our feeling, that with whatever local failure to master the material, Malory is dealing with one tract of time, one general course of events, throughout the whole series of tales. This evidence is found in the numerous references back and forth which establish continuity and connexions throughout the various books; and in the deliberate links invented by Malory, which form bridges between the main tales, and which further confirm the need to read them in the order in which they have come down to us.

To take some of the references forward and back. In the first tale, at the end of its first section, there is a reference forward to Mordred coming to court "as hit rehersith aftirward and towarde the ende of the *Morte Arthure*" [as it is recounted afterward and toward the end of the *Morte Arthure*] (*W* 56). This comment is apparently not in the French original. It may refer either to the French *Mort Artu* or to Malory's own later version. If to the latter, Professor Vinaver suggests that the comment is a scribal insertion not due to Malory himself. But the comment appears in both Caxton's text and the Winchester MS., and there is no evidence that it is merely scribal. It is at least as likely to be Malory's as not. Even if Malory's, it may be due to a phrase in the actual book he was copying. But it does not matter; the effect of a phrase like this in Malory's work as we have it, whether or not in eight parts, is to bind the parts together. The likely reason for the remark, if it is indeed Malory's, is surely that he was thinking forward not particularly to his own translation, if he projected it, but to the "future" event which was part of the whole historical Arthurian sequence, whose cohesion underlies his work. There are a number of other references to "future" events in this first tale (for example, on pages 91, 92, 97, 126, 179–80). Some of these are unquestionably due to "the French book." But as I have emphasized, it is immaterial for the present purpose whether such remarks are original or due to the source, since we are dealing with a work of multiple authorship, not Malory's alone. Whether or not invented or even intended by Malory, the binding effect is there. Thus, granting all that professor Vinaver has shown us of Malory's reducing, dissolving, simplifying power, Malory has not cut the bonds completely. He has at least left in, or put in, those references forward of which I have given examples. In at least one case he has made the reference more explicit than it was in the French, as Professor Vinaver shows us:

> Marlyon warned the kyng covertly that Gwenyvere was nat holsom for hym to take to wyff. For he warned hym that Launcelot scholde love hir, and sche hym agayne (*W* 97).

> [Merlin warned the king secretly that Guinevere was not wholesome for him to take to wife. For he warned him that Lancelot should love her, and she him in return.]

The French original of this is a very obscure hint, which Malory makes perfectly plain—somewhat to the disadvantage, indeed, of Arthur's character. Malory's clarification is not the kind of remark that reveals a modern sense of organic unity in the structure of the "whole book," but it helps to establish, like the other references forward, a sense that we are dealing with a specific tract of experience, a history linked in cause and effect. That these references come so early in the whole historical sequence surely indicates that for Malory the various stories were bound together.

It does not matter that some of the references forward are inaccurate (e.g., that on pp. 179–80): no one can be surprised if an author whose scope is so vast changes the details of his plans. These references are inaccurate inasmuch as they do not agree with the later version produced by Malory himself, because they are translated from the source Malory was following at that moment, the *Suite du Merlin*, and they refer to the Quest of the Grail. From these inaccuracies Professor Vinaver argues

244

Malory's ignorance, when writing this first tale, of the true story of the Grail, or at least of the version he was himself to translate, perhaps years later. Even if Professor Vinaver is right, we need not be driven to denying Malory's consciousness of the total Arthurian context. He cannot have been totally ignorant of the Grail story and its effect on the story of Arthur. At the very least these references he translates would have told him a good deal in outline. And would so devoted a reader of Arthurian tales have remained in ignorance of so well known a story even if, as is not surprising, he was hazy about the details?

Just as there are references forward in the first tale there are references back in the later tales. Some of the most notable are in *The Tale of the Sankgreal* itself, where, for example, Malory, apparently unprompted by his source, deliberately refers back to the story of Balin, which is part of the first tale (*W* 856 ff., especially 862–63). There are similar backward glances in the final *Tale of the Death of King Arthur* (e.g., p. 1198, referring to pp. 265–66). Again, these are more like an historian's references to earlier significant incidents and causes, than an artist's attempt to build up an organic whole. But these connexions have an artistic effect; they give a sense of continuity and also, as it were, of depth. They show the effects of causes remote but not detached. They give that sense of context in human affairs which great literature usually suggests.

Besides these references forward and back there are also specific links between several of the tales which prove that Malory did not think of them as being entirely separate, and which show that he must have intended them to be read in the order in which they have come down to us. Thus, the concluding paragraph, or *explicit*, of the first tale runs:

And this book endyth whereas sir Launcelot and sir Trystrams com to courte. Who that woll make ony more lette hym seke other bookis of kynge Arthure or of sir Launcelot or sir Trystrams: for this was drawyn by a knyght presoner, sir Thomas Malleoré, that God sende hym good recover. Amen EXPLICIT (*W* 180).

[And this book ends where Sir Lancelot and Sir Tristram come to court. Who wishes to compose any more, let him seek other books of King Arthur or of Sir Lancelot or Sir Tristram: for this was composed by a knight prisoner, Sir Thomas Malory, that God may send him good recovery.]

If it is perhaps too much to say quite so definitely as does Professor Vinaver that Malory here "disclaims any intention of writing another Arthurian romance" (*W* xxx), it certainly looks as though he did not expect the opportunity to write more very soon, even though he knew what his sources would be. But before theorizing about this *explicit* one should look at the very first paragraph of the next tale, *Arthur and Lucius,* to compare its very phrasing:

> Hyt befelle whan kyng Arthur had wedded quene Gwenyvere and fulfylled the Rounde Table, and so aftir his mervelous knyghtis and he had venquyshed the moste party of his enemyes, than *sone aftir com sir Launcelot de Lake unto the courte, and sir Trystrams come that tyme also.* . . . (*W* 185: italics mine).

> [It befell that when King Arthur had wedded Queen Guinevere and filled the Round Table, and after his marvelous knights and he had vanquished most of his enemies, then *soon after Sir Lancelot of the Lake came to the court, and Sir Tristram came at that time also.* . . .]

This introductory paragraph clearly gathers up what has preceded and so establishes a chronological development; and what is especially notable is that the phrase about Lancelot and Tristram (which has no counterpart in the French) directly refers to the preceding *explicit*. Malory has created a deliberate link.

It is odd that this deliberate link to some extent seems to contradict the implication in the preceding *explicit* that the author cannot write any more. But Malory clearly worked with the French book in front of him, translating much of the time sentence by sentence, and if we imagine his imprisonment keeping him from the books he needed to continue his work (though he knew, at least roughly, what books they were), then we may have a possible solution to the puzzle. When he was released he was able to find the books he needed for continuation—though, ironically, it may have been a further spell of imprisonment

246

which inflicted on him the necessary leisure. In any event, it is most unusual for a medieval writer to indicate further sources for the continuation—and we may emphasize "continuation"— of his story. That Malory did so suggests that he had some sort of plan for the rest of his work, though it may well have been vague.[4]

There is also a link between the second and third tales. The *explicit* of the second tale says that here is an end of this tale,

And here folowyth afftyr many noble talys of sir Launcelot de Lake (*W* 247).

[And hereafter follow many noble tales of Sir Lancelot of the Lake.]

And so, of course, they do, in the third tale, which takes up the story immediately at the correct point of time: soon after King Arthur's return from Rome, it begins, Sir Lancelot in especial increased marvellously in worship and honour. Therefore, says Malory,

he is the fyrste knyght that the Frey[n]sh booke makyth me [n]cion of aftir kynge Arthure com frome Rome (*W* 253).

[he is the first knight that the French book mentions after King Arthur came from Rome.]

Malory loses no time bringing Lancelot to the fore, telling of the love between him and Guinevere, and mentioning how he saved her from the stake (which happens in both the seventh and eighth tales). It is not clear how far these introductory comments are Malory's own, since no very close source has yet been discovered. Judging from Malory's usual method they are very likely to be entirely his own; but it does not matter. Whether original or not these comments still place the tale in its wider context of the Arthurian story as a whole; and in doing so they establish the present tale as part of that whole. Of course, this kind of connexion is tenuous in certain respects. Professor

---

[4] This is suggested by Professor Lumiansky, "The Question of Unity in Malory's *Morte Darthur*," *Tulane Studies in English*, V (1955), p. 33.

Vinaver is perfectly right to insist on a high degree of autonomy in some of the tales. But the separation is not, could not be, complete.

Between the tale of *Sir Launcelot* and the next of *Sir Gareth* there is no specific link. There is, however, a vague indication of time: it begins:

> In Arthurs dayes, when he held the Rounde Table moste plenoure. . . . (*W* 293).

> [In Arthur's days, when he held the Round Table most full. . . .]

The suggestion here is of the height of the success of the Round Table as an institution. Although there is no specific link with the preceding tale of *Sir Launcelot,* nor any link with the following tale of *Sir Tristram,* the tale of *Sir Gareth* could not come anywhere else than here. The first three tales have already been shown linked together by chronology and by specific references at the beginnings and ends. As will be shown, the fifth tale of *Sir Tristram* leads directly into the sixth, the *Sankgreal,* and that into the seventh and eighth tales. Even if the "separate" tales had circulated in separate manuscripts (for which, significantly, there is not a scrap of evidence) it would have been impossible in collecting them into one book to place the apparently unattached *Sir Gareth* anywhere but in the fourth place. This alone shows the existence of a wider scheme into which the tales must fit. They are related; not independent.

The fifth tale is that of *Sir Tristram,* and one of the objections to considering the tales as a connected series is that Sir Tristram appears as a full-grown man in the previous tale of *Sir Gareth* (and is indeed mentioned even earlier), while his birth and upbringing are not described until this fifth tale. Malory, indeed, is not much interested in giving mere chronology. The beginning of *Sir Tristram,* like the beginning of the preceding tale of *Sir Gareth,* is set in that long, vague period when Arthur was established as the great king of "all the lordshyppis unto Roome" [all the lordships as far as Rome] (*W* 371), and when Lancelot was "named for the mervaylyste knyght of the worlde" [called the most marvelous knight in the world] (*W* 377). This is enough to put the tale in its context of the whole Arthurian story. Tristram's birth and arrival at manhood take place within this general period of the flourishing of the Round Table. This is unrealistic, of course, but no one can claim that romance is bound by the chains of realism. Professor Lumiansky has suggested that we should regard the account of Tristram's birth and so forth as "retrospective narrative."[5] Attractive as this theory is, there seems no evidence for it in the text. It is more likely that Malory regarded the bulky tale of *Sir Tristram* as being in some sense parallel to that of *Sir Gareth*. Or his technique, never very self-aware, was simply not up to the problem he had perhaps unwittingly set himself. He went steadily on, at the beginning of *Sir Tristram*, in a continuous narrative, content to let the wider time-scheme look after itself, since he was here concerned with neither Arthur's rise nor his fall, where chronology was more important.

The Book of Sir Tristram, which is rather more than a third of the whole book, and comes right in the middle, is by general consent the least satisfactory of Malory's tales. If I were contending that there was a modern organic unity of design in Malory's work, the *Tristram* would in itself be enough to refute me. But my contention is more modest; less of a denial of Professor Vinaver's thesis than a modification or complement of it: the tales are structurally connected, and fit into a particular order. Thus, even the *Tristram*, such a stumbling block to attempts to define the general form of the whole book, is connected with the following tale of the Sankgreal, and by virtue of that connexion could occupy no other place in the chain than where it is found.

Towards the end of the *Tristram* comes the story of Lancelot and Elaine. If this story is judged in the context of the *Tristram* alone it is quite irrelevant, Sir Tristram being hardly mentioned. It begins with a hermit prophesying about the Siege Perilous

[5] *Ibid.*

and the winning of the Holy Grail, and then tells how Galahad, the future Grail-hero, was begotten on Elaine by Sir Lancelot, how Guinevere's jealousy sent Lancelot mad, and how he eventually recovered. The Grail itself also appears. All this is quite pointless if the *Tristram* exists for itself alone. The story of Lancelot and Elaine is there to enable us to understand the story of the Grail, which follows almost immediately. There is here a clear structural connexion. It is not Malory's invention; he is following his source. But that does not in any way weaken the effect of the connexion. Moreover, Professor Vinaver points out several interpolations by Malory which emphasize the relationship of the episode to the whole Arthurian Cycle (*W* 793, 794, 796, 832; cf. notes on pp. 1512 and 1518). Surely, had Malory wished completely to separate his tales he would have avoided such interpolations and would have transposed the story of Lancelot and Elaine to the beginning of the Grail Quest where, as simple narrative, it belongs.

Of course, Malory did no such thing. After telling how Galahad was begotten, he returned (following his source) to the tale of Tristram in a brief *Conclusion*. The interweaving is emphasized by La Belle Isode immediately telling Tristram about Lancelot's madness "and how he was holpyn by the holy vessell of the Sankgreall" [and how he was helped by the holy vessel of the Grail]. Then she refers to the great feast to be held at Pentecost next following (which is where the story of the Quest of the Grail will begin), thus making clear the time-sequence where it is important. The end of the *Conclusion* tells how Tristram and Palomides set off for Arthur's court to attend the great feast,

And that same feste in cam sir Galahad that was son unto sir Launcelot du Lake, and sate in the Syge Perelous. And so therewythall they departed and dysceyvirde, all the knyghtys of the Rounde Table.

And than sir Trystram returned unto Joyus Garde, and sir Palomydes folowed aftir the Questynge Beste (*W* 845).

[And at that same feast in came Sir Galahad, who was the son of Sir Lancelot of the Lake, and sat in the Siege Perilous. And so with that they departed and separated, all the knights of the Round Table.

And then Sir Tristram returned to Joyous Garde, and Sir Palomides followed after the Questing Beast.]

This neatly rounds off the tale of Tristram in Malory's accustomed manner, for the tragedy of Tristram was nothing to his purpose: yet even this passage acts as a bridge between the concluding tale and the next. The mention of Galahad and the Siege Perilous throws the interest forward, while it could only have meaning from the previous account of the begetting of Galahad. Granted the autonomy of the *Tristram,* we are yet left with the feeling that however long it may be, it is also a part of a yet longer, more complex story, that of Arthur's Round Table. We have come to a pause, not a full-stop.

The *explicit* which closes the tale, makes the same effect:

Here endyth the secunde boke off syrr Trystram de Lyones, whyche drawyn was oute of Freynshe by sir Thomas Malleorré, knyght, as Jesu be hys helpe. Amen.
But here ys no rehersall of the thirde booke.
But here folowyth the noble tale off the Sankegreall, whyche called ys the holy vessell and the sygnyfycacion of blyssed bloode offe oure Lorde Jesu Cryste, whyche was brought into thys londe by Joseph off Aramathye . . . &c. (*W* 845).

[Here ends the second book of Sir Tristram of Liones, which was drawn from the French by Sir Thomas Malory, knight, may Jesus be his help. Amen.
But here is no recounting of the third book.
But here follows the noble tale of the Holy Grail, which is called the holy vessel and the symbol of the blessed blood of our Lord, Jesus Christ, which was brought into this land by Joseph of Arimathea. . . .]

The *explicit* has some of the oddity which is often found in Malory's prose when he is not dealing with narrative or dialogue. But the absence of the third book is not so odd as it seems, for the third book was itself a version of the Grail story. Malory abandoned it in favour of another version, essentially the same, but less prolix, and less concerned with Tristram. The *explicit,* however, clearly makes another bridge, and *The Tale of the Sankgreal* naturally takes up the narrative at the same feast of Pentecost already mentioned. The continuity is complete.

The Tale of the Sankgreal, sometimes incoherent, occasionally very moving, has many difficulties and puzzles, and it is not always easy to know how to take it. One thing is clear. As Professor Vinaver has shown, it is, unlike its source, essentially an Arthurian tale. It is not anti-chivalric, and Lancelot is the most interesting character (*W* 1522–23). Malory does not agree with his source that the chivalric ideal is anti-Christian. For Malory—and we shall never understand him if we do not understand this—there is no essential incompatibility between the values of Christianity and those of the High Order of Knighthood, of ideal Arthurian chivalry. (Of course he realized that many knights, even Lancelot, fell below this ideal; and he himself seems to a modern reader to be sometimes lacking in moral scruple and insight; for example in the early parts of the *Tristram*.) In the Grail story, therefore, success is largely thought of in terms of the possible success of secular Christian knighthood, and failure again is seen in terms of failure to maintain normal Christian morality. Success and failure are summed up in the achievements of Lancelot. In so far as he succeeds it is because he is brave and good and repents of his sins. His failure is the result mainly of his adultery and consequent disloyalty to Arthur, which blemish his knighthood and eventually bring about the destruction of the king, the Round Table, and all it stood for. In a sense, perhaps, the story of the Grail is debased to an illustration of the quality, both good and bad, of Lancelot, though this would be to take an extreme view, and there is more than that in the tale. But it is certain that Malory rejects, or is not interested in, or does not understand, the transcendent quality of the Grail legend, and of its underlying theology, for he denies their lesson. He has the characteristic English tendency to turn other-worldly and ascetic religion into this-worldly morality. The story of the Grail enabled Malory to work out and emphasize the moral standards which underlie the tragedy towards which the whole Arthurian story moves. This tragedy is related in the two tales which follow *The Tale of the Sank- greal*, and which are as closely linked between themselves as the last but one is to the *Sankgreal*. Once again the continuity and connection is made clear by Malory in his words in the first paragraphs of *The Book of Sir Launcelot and Queen Guinivere*, which immediately follows on the *Sankgreal*:

So aftir the queste of the Sankgreall was fulfylled and all knyghtes that were leffte on lyve were com home agayne unto the Table Rounde—as the BOOKE OF THE SANKGREALL makith mencion—than was there grete joy in the courte. . . .

[So after the quest of the Holy Grail was fulfilled and all the knights that were left alive were come home again to the Round Table—as the BOOK OF THE HOLY GRAIL mentions—then there was great joy in the court. . . .]

Than, as the booke seyth, sir Launcelot began to resorte unto quene Gwenivere agayne and forgate the promyse and the perfeccion that he made in the queste: for, as the booke seyth, *had nat sir Launcelot bene in his prevy thoughtes and in hys myndis so sette inwardly to the quene as he was in semynge outewarde to God, there had no knyght passed hym in the queste of the Sankgreall. But ever his thoughtis prevyly were on the quene.* . . .

[Then, as the book says, Sir Lancelot began to repair to Queen Guin- evere again and forgot the promise and the perfection that he made in the quest: for, as the book says, *had not Sir Lancelot been in his private thoughts and in his mind so inwardly set on the queen as he seemed out- wardly set on God, no knight would have surpassed him in the quest of the Holy Grail. But his thoughts were ever privately on the queen.* . . .]

So hit befelle that sir Launcelot had many resortis of ladyes and damesels which dayly resorted unto hym [that besoughte hym] to be their champion. In all such maters of ryght *sir Launcelot applyed hym dayly to do for the plesure of oure Lorde Jesu Cryst,* and ever as much as he myght he withdrew hym fro the company of quene Gwenyvere for to eschew the sclawndir and noyse (*W* 1045: italics mine).

[So it befell that Sir Lancelot had many supplications from ladies and damsels who daily resorted to him (that besought him) to be their champion. In all such matters of right *Sir Lancelot applied himself daily to work for the pleasure of our Lord Jesus Christ,* and ever as much as he could he withdrew from the company of Queen Guinevere in order to avoid the slander and rumor.]

There could be no clearer example than this of the sense of continuity between the tales, of their connectedness. And this passage also shows clearly the mixture of good and bad which Malory sees in Lancelot, brought out by his partial success, his partial failure, in the quest of the Grail. It may well be that Malory's treatment of the Grail legend is inferior in subtlety and intellectual power to that of his source, but the important thing is that Malory's treatment is different, and must be judged within its own context, which is not that of its source. The context of the Grail legend in Malory's treatment is the whole Arthurian story as treated by him. With his treatment of the Grail, Malory finally won his own limited independence of interpretation. From the end of the Grail story onwards there is hardly any need to argue the essential unity of Malory's great if simple conception. The seventh and eighth tales "form together a coherent whole," as Professor Vinaver himself says (*W* lxxx; cf. xxxi).

The seventh tale comprises five adventures which show Lancelot at the precarious peak of his earthly fame, loving chivalry, "Trouthe and honoure, fredom and curteisie" [Truth and honor, generosity and courtesy]. These adventures culminate in the Healing of Sir Urry; at the end of this great passage, and of the whole tale, comes this final paragraph:

And so I leve here of this tale, and overlepe grete bookis of sir Launcelot. . . . And because I have loste the very mater of Shevalere de Charyot I departe from the tale of sir Launcelot; and here I go unto the morte Arthur, and that caused sir Aggravayne (*W* 1154).

[And so I take leave here of this tale, and overleap great books of Sir Lancelot. . . . And because I have lost the true story of the Knight of the Cart I leave the tale of Sir Lancelot; and from here I go to the death of Arthur, and that was caused by Sir Agravain.]

Malory's reference to "Shevalere de Charyot" is something of a puzzle. Earlier (*W* 1130) he has told us that he has deliberately left off following "La Shyvalere le Charyote," and in the final paragraph of the seventh tale (omitted for clarity in the quotation just made) he has told us briefly what happens in the "grete bookis" he has "overleapt." So he had clearly read the great books, and was deliberately overleaping them. Perhaps when he says he has *lost* "the very mater of Shevalere de Charyot" he means that it has been omitted—lost from the version he wishes to give us, because he is pressing on to more essential matters, as the *explicit* which follows the final paragraph explains:

> And here on the othir syde folowyth *The Moste Pyteuous Tale of the Morte Arthure Saunz Gwerdon* par le Shyvalere Sir Thomas Malleoré, Knyght (*W* 1154).

> [And here on the other side follows *The Most Piteous Tale of the Death of Arthur without Guerdon* by the Chevalier, Sir Thomas Malory, Knight.]

This *explicit* sends us straight on to the final instalment, the eighth and last tale, the *Morte Arthur* itself.[6] There is no specific bridge-passage at the beginning of this last tale, for as Professor Vinaver himself has observed, it forms a coherent whole with the preceding tale. But the first paragraph, about the month of May, ends by showing well enough how Malory conceived the larger movement which underlies the separate adventures:

> so thys season hit befelle in the moneth of May a grete angur and unhappy that stynted nat tylle the *floure of chyvalry of the worlde was destroyed and slayne* (*W* 1161: italics mine).

> [so in this season there befell in the month of May a great anger and unhappiness that ceased not until the *flower of chivalry of the world was destroyed and slain.*]

---

[6] Or as Professor Vinaver entitles it in his separate edition of *The Tale of the Death of King Arthur* (Oxford, 1955).

He has chronicled the rise and glory of the flower of chivalry of the world; now he comes to its grievous destruction.

The next paragraph tells how Agravain and Mordred were the immediate cause of the tragedy: but to understand even this demands our precedent knowledge of the whole long course of Lancelot's love for the Queen, of his greatness and pride, and of the more important greatness of Arthur, which nevertheless depends on Lancelot's loyalty. From this beginning of the eighth tale, of which the foundations have been laid so far back, the story moves forward surely and majestically, perhaps the first true tragedy in English, and one of the most moving. And it closes with a final *explicit*, which hammers home the essential unity of conception that has underlain the *whole book*:

Here is the ende of the *hoole book* of kyng Arthur and of his noble knyghtes of the Rounde Table, that whan they were holé togyders there was ever an hondred and forty. And here is the ende of *The Deth of Arthur* (*W* 1260: italics in line 1 mine).

[Here is the end of the *whole book* of King Arthur and of his noble knights of the Round Table, that when they were wholly together there were a hundred and forty. And here is the end of *The Death of Arthur*.]

Two things are finished; this particular tale, and the whole book of which it is part.

The whole book is bound together in various ways: by the unity of atmosphere and the continuous moral concern; by the chronological continuity of the main events and characters (allowing for some overlapping in the *Launcelot, Gareth,* and *Tristram,* the central books where time is not so important); by significant references back and forward to important characters and events; and by links between the various tales. Some of this binding together is due to the inherent nature of Malory's material, and some of it to Malory's personal contribution. His method has been authoritatively described by Professor Vinaver; Malory has made

(*a*) a rearrangement of episodes consistent with [his] own narrative technique, and (*b*) a series of connecting passages designed to link together the episodes so rearranged (*W* 1575).

But whereas Professor Vinaver would apply this only *within* the eight major sections, we must also apply it to the book as a whole. Malory's method is the same both for the lesser arrangements within the tales, and for the major arrangements of the tales themselves. The smaller sections within the main tales correspond structurally to the major sections within the whole book. Often there are no close links between the subsections of a major tale; but no one doubts that they are parts of a larger whole. The subsections have a high degree of autonomy, just like the major sections.

Analogies for such a loose form as Malory devised are difficult to find, for the very good reason, as Professor Vinaver has shown, that Malory comes at an almost unique moment in the transition from late medieval to early modern methods of storytelling. Probably the closest analogy to Malory's form in English is found in *The Faerie Queene*. Spenser knew Malory's work, and it is possible that he understood Malory's form well enough. *The Faerie Queene* is vastly more subtle and learned than Malory, but it enables us to see how a series of stories may be linked only loosely together without much attempt at organic unity, and yet they must be regarded, as the six complete books of *The Faerie Queene* must be regarded, as one single work of art. Each work has an historical flavour, and each work owes its impression of cohesion to some extent to what may be called extra-aesthetic comments by the author. Thus our feeling about the cohesion of *The Faerie Queene* derives, to some extent, from the Letter to Raleigh, which is external to the poem proper, just as our feeling about the cohesion of *The Morte Darthur* derives to some slight extent from the *explicits*, which might not be regarded, by strict standards, as part of the artistic form.

One is bound to recognize Malory's lack of conscious artistry, his incapacity for abstract thought. But one must also recognize how difficult it was for him to extricate and clarify a coherent pattern from the cyclic tangle of his sources. His triumph lies especially in the last two books. Here the noble simplicity of theme, the moral earnestness, the firm conception of the roles of Lancelot and Arthur and Guinevere, the fertile invention of story and dialogue, the magnificent prose, all unite in a richness of feeling unparalleled in Arthurian literature before or since. Malory's genius is concrete, dramatic, moral; rooted in feeling, not in generalizing intellectual power. The greatness of his achievement lies in these last two tales, but they cannot be severed from the earlier books.

12

THE PLACE OF THE QUEST OF THE
HOLY GRAIL IN THE *MORTE DARTHUR*

P. E. Tucker

1

THIS PAPER WILL SUGGEST THAT THE *Quest of the Grail* IN Malory's works can best be understood as part of the story of Lancelot. As he translated the French *Queste* Malory discovered —almost unwittingly—how he might deal with a feature of Lancelot's character that he disliked, his devotion to Guinevere. His treatment of Lancelot in the *Quest* thus lays down the lines upon which he interprets the story of the *Morte Arthur* proper (i.e. Books VII and VIII in the *Works*), of which Lancelot is the centre; and in demostrating this I hope to show that Malory arrives at a judgement on the conflicting loyalties of love and chivalry in the *Morte Darthur*.

The *Quest* in Malory's English version has commonly seemed as difficult for readers as the French original was for Malory himself, and it is not surprising that criticism has varied so greatly. To Professor Vinaver it seemed "a confused and almost pointless story"[1] compared with the original, and his most recent criticism assesses it mainly as a piece of translation.[2] At the

Reprinted, by permission of the Modern Humanities Research Association, from *Modern Language Review,* XLVIII (1953), 391–97. See also Charles Moorman, "Malory's Treatment of the Sankgreall," *PMLA,* LXXI (1956), 496–509.

[1] *Malory* (Oxford, 1929), p. 84.
[2] *The Works of Malory* (Oxford, 1947), pp. 1524–29.

opposite extreme the late Charles Williams[3] examined Malory's *Quest* in its own right, and tried to trace a link between the opposed ideals of love and religion by elaborating upon the relation between Lancelot and Galahad. This interpretation seems unconvincing because Malory never shows he is aware of any mystical significance in the relationship. I shall try to do justice to Malory's independence, and also try to base my interpretation closely upon the actual passages in which he indicates his meaning, typically slight and awkward as they sometimes are. Malory's main interest in the *Morte Darthur,* and ours, is the story of Lancelot. To discover what part the *Quest* plays in the book we should see what effect it has upon Malory's conception of Lancelot, relating it to what goes before and after.

As regards what goes before, there is one essential point to be made, that Malory is greatly troubled by the French conception of Lancelot as the supreme knight-lover. For Malory knighthood is simply a worthy and honourable status; it is his conception of the highest excellence in a man, and he gives terms like "chivalry" and "worship" a moral significance. Chivalrous adventures are the obligation of noble birth, and they should properly illustrate this ideal of knighthood. But this view of knighthood says nothing of love, whereas in Malory's sources it is scarcely an exaggeration to say that love is the very inspiration of chivalry. This conception can be traced even in the primitive Arthurian court of Geoffrey of Monmouth, it is fundamental in Chrestien de Troyes's romances, and it is still active in the Prose Romances Malory drew upon. *Nullus strenuus miles nisi amet*; *amor facit strenuitatem militiae* [The soldier is not vigorous unless he loves; love produces vigor in the battlefield.] The knightly qualities that Malory stresses in Lancelot, prowess and courtesy, are in his source inspired by Lancelot's love for Guinevere, and his knighthood is devoted to her service. Malory seems to have taken Lancelot as his exemplar of the knightly ideal without realizing how different his conception of chivalry was, and what

[3] In *The Dublin Review,* no. 429, April 1944.

difficulties would arise if he continued translating the *Lancelot-Grail* cycle; he even writes happily in Book III that part of Lancelot's fame comes from his love for Guinevere. But he had already been puzzled in Book I by the part love played in knightly adventures, and in Book III he realizes quite suddenly that he very much dislikes this feature of his sources. When a damsel tells Lancelot he ought as a knight to be a lover, he vehemently repudiates the notion, and the awkwardness of the speech suggests that it expresses Malory's own feelings (pp. 270–71). Malory dislikes the idea that love-service is an integral part of knighthood; how then can he present the later story of Lancelot? In his treatment of Lancelot in the *Quest* he discovered an answer to this problem.

2

The temper of the French *Queste* has been admirably interpreted by A. Pauphilet in his *Études sur la Queste del Saint Graal* (1921). Here it will suffice to recall that it is a rigorously didactic work, and that the writer is chiefly concerned with matters of virtuous conduct. In particular, he condemns the sensuality of courtly love, and the centre of his allegory is the contrast between this sin, as it is exemplified in Lancelot's love for Guinevere, and the virtue of chastity, exemplified in Galahad. In condemning love the writer of the *Queste* condemns the chivalric mode of life as the rest of the *Lancelot-Grail* cycle illustrates it; love and chivalry, intimately linked together, sum up a way of life that is no longer acceptable, the way of "terrestrial chivalry." Malory's reaction to this doctrine is sometimes confusing, for the theological exposition of the French is beyond his grasp, but it is generally dominated by a single straightforward idea. He believes that earthly chivalry embodies an ideal essentially good, and he therefore repeatedly suppresses or modifies passages in which it seems to be condemned. Most of these passages concern Lancelot, and Malory thus gives the impression that he is defending him from the censures of the French writer. Yet in Malory's version Lancelot still undergoes penance and suffers humiliation in his quest, and the reason for this is still his love of Guinevere. Malory thus arrives at a new conception, that Lancelot's life of chivalry is blameworthy only when it is devoted to her service. The following quotation from Lancelot's first confession will illustrate this:

> And than he tolde there the good man all hys lyff, and how he had loved a quene unmesurabely and oute of mesure longe.
>
> "And all my grete dedis of armys that I have done for the moste party was for the quenys sake, and for hir sake wolde I do batayle *were hit ryght other wronge*. And never dud I batayle all only for Goddis sake, but for to wynne worship and to cause me the bettir to be beloved, and litill or nought I thanked never God of hit" (p. 897).

> [And then he told the good man there all his life, and how he had loved a queen immoderately and for an immoderately long time.
>
> "All my great deeds of arms that I have done were for the most part for the queen's sake, and for her sake would I do battle *were it right or wrong*. And I never did battle for God's sake alone, but in order to win glory and to make myself the better to be loved, and little or not at all did I ever thank God for it."]

Here Malory has added to the second sentence, and Professor Vinaver comments:

> From F's [the French writer's] point of view it matters little whether Lancelot fought on the right side or not. By the standards of the *Queste* whatever he did on Guinevere's behalf was part of his sinful life.

This is a true representation of the French, for there the condemnation of Lancelot's love for Guinevere attacks the very basis of his life as a knight, but Malory suggests that his knighthood should be independent of his love for her, and therefore it does matter whether or not he fought with justice. Malory distinguishes between good and bad chivalry by his own standards, and suggests that Lancelot's love for Guinevere mars the perfection of his knighthood—a notion never proposed by the French. This judgement, crude as it seems at first, is the key to his later interpretation of the story of Lancelot.

The same quotation introduces a second feature in that interpretation. Malory makes Lancelot confess that he had often fought not only for Guinevere, "but for to wynne worship and to cause me the bettir to be beloved," and this is the earliest hint of the fault of pride in him. Pride appears as one of the sins of the Round Table fellowship, and of Lancelot in particular, in the French *Queste*, but the author tries to link it with sensuality, and the connexion between the two will not bear very close analysis.[4] Malory here, as often, takes a hint from his source and transforms it for his own purpose: he magnifies Lancelot's sense of his own prowess until it becomes a fault in his knighthood. This notion is brought out in the adventure of the tournament as Malory tries to interpret it. In the French this episode is a piece of symbolism recapitulating Lancelot's progress in the Quest; it is designed to show him how his own sinfulness deceived him until the hermits directed him to the way of Grace. Something of this remains in Malory's version, but ultimately the two interpretations diverge: Malory is more interested in Lancelot's wrong reasons for taking part in the tournament. He says he "thoughte for to helpe there the wayker party *in incresyng of his shevalry*" [intended to help there the weaker party in order to increase his chivalry], and he adds to the interpretation of the Recluse, "And whan thou saw the synners overcom thou enclyned to that party *for bobbaunce and pryde of the worlde*" [And when you saw the sinners overcome, you inclined to that party out of pomp and pride of the world] (pp. 931–35). Here Malory tries to show that Lancelot proudly relies on his prowess alone, careless of other standards. He is censured in the Quest not because the life of chivalry is wrong in itself, but because he had abused it; he fought for Guinevere and for self-glory, and it is comprehensible that this fault should appear again when the Quest is over.

Unlike his source Malory does not completely condemn Lancelot; he insists again and again that he is "the best of ony syn-

---

[4] Cf. Pauphilet, *Études*, p. 40.

full man of the worlde" [the best of any sinful man in the world] (p. 863), and that he has "no pere of ony erthly synfull man" [no peer of any earthly sinful man] (p. 934). This is a double-edged description which sums up for Malory the paradox of Lancelot's quest in both versions, that he at once succeeds and fails in it: he has a vision of the Grail ceremony, but it is only partial. Here the differences between the two versions are subtle, but still definite and important. Lancelot's success in the French must be explained by the penance he undergoes, and his failure by his former sinful life and his deficiency in the final virtue of trust in God—he draws his sword even at the gates of the Grail castle. Malory could understand that Lancelot's achievement was a reward for his penance, and he stresses both these things, but it not unnaturally seemed odd to him that Lancelot should be punished for his past life even after doing penance for it. He therefore interprets his failure thus (in the explanation of a hermit to Gawain):

"For I dare sey, as synfull as ever sir Launcelot hath byn, sith that he wente into the queste of the Sankgreal he slew never man [as Gawain had done] nother nought shall, tylle that he com to Camelot agayne; for he hath takyn upon hym to forsake synne. And nere were that he ys nat stable, but by hys thoughte he ys lyckly to turne agayne, he sholde be nexte to encheve hit sauff sir Galahad, hys sonne; but God knowith hys thought and hys unstablenesse. And yett shall he dye ryght an holy man, and no doute he hath no felow of none erthly synfull man lyvyng" (p. 948).

["For I dare say, as sinful as ever Sir Lancelot has been, since he went on the quest of the Holy Grail he never slew a man (as Gawain had done) and never shall, until he comes to Camelot again; for he has taken upon himself to forsake sin. And were it not that he is unstable, but by his thinking he is likely to turn again, he should be the next to achieve it except for Sir Galahad, his son; but God knows his thought and his instability. And yet he shall die a holy man, and no doubt he has no equal of any earthly sinful man living."]

Lancelot cannot put from his mind "prevy thoughtis" [private thoughts] of Guinevere, as he later tells her (p. 1046), and this is an evidence of the more general trait of instability in his character that causes his failure. His lack of absolutely unwavering resolution is admirably suggested, as Dr. J. A. W. Bennett has pointed out, in a passage that has been quoted to show that Malory makes nonsense of his source. In the French narrative Lancelot, after much wandering, finds himself surrounded by sea and mountain and forest; he resigns himself to prayer and to waiting patiently on the ship when it comes, and this is the culmination of his effort. But Malory writes:

So with thys jantillwoman [the dead sister of Sir Perceval] sir Launcelot was a moneth and more. . . . And so on a nyght he wente to play hym by the watirs syde, for he was somewhat wery of the shippe (pp. 1011–12).

[So with this gentlewoman (the dead sister of Sir Perceval) Sir Lancelot was a month and more. . . . And so one night he went to divert himself by the water's side, for he was somewhat weary of the ship.]

The effort demanded is too much for him. Finally, when Lancelot has returned to Camelot, grateful and a little proud because of what he has achieved in the Quest, there comes the warning that Galahad sends through Bors, marking the transition to the *Morte Arthur* proper:

"My fayre lorde, salew me unto my lorde sir Launcelot, my fadir, and as sone as ye se hym bydde hym remembir of this worlde unstable (pp. 1035–36).

["My fair lord, give my greetings to my lord Sir Lancelot, my father, and as soon as you see him, bid him be mindful of this unstable world."]

The notion that Lancelot is "unstable" was perhaps suggested to Malory by his lack of faith in the French, the full implications of which seem to have escaped him, but the human figure in whose character instability is a fundamental trait is essentially his own creation.

Thus in Malory's version of the *Quest* it is possible to see a new interpretation of the story of Lancelot developing. Malory was already uneasy over the connexion between love and chivalry when he came to the *Quest*. There he found Lancelot condemned as the knight-lover, but being certain that knighthood

265

was a noble ideal, he began to distinguish between good chivalry and bad—the good consisting in "knyghtly dedys and vertuous lyvyng" [knightly deeds and virtuous living] (p. 891), the bad in Lancelot's devoting his service to Guinevere. This notion of "bad chivalry" is further substantiated by suggestions of pride in Lancelot. Malory thus accepts the judgement of his source that Lancelot had not led a perfect life by seeing it in relation to the standard he has himself created. Finally, since Lancelot seemed to endure more humiliation in the Quest than any other knight, his failure there was to be explained by the trait of instability in his character. It has often been observed that this last feature makes a credible and human character of Lancelot, but the judgement on chivalry that Malory proposes is otherwise abstract and dry. I wish now to indicate how in the *Morte Arthur* proper this judgement is worked out again in terms of event and character, restricting myself, however, to features that derive from Malory's interpretation of the *Quest*.

3

The *Morte Arthur* proper (as it is convenient to call Malory's Books VII and VIII) opens with the relapse of Lancelot into his old relations with Guinevere, which Malory, unlike his sources, explains plausibly. Thus the influence of the *Quest* upon his conception of Lancelot appears first in the part played by the trait of instability; but since this has been remarked upon before,[5] no further discussion of it is necessary.

In considering the further influence of the *Quest* I should

[5] Notably by Mr. C. S. Lewis. The most recent discussion of the link Malory has forged here between two of his "books" will be found in the article by Mr. D. S. Brewer, "Form in the 'Morte Darthur,'" in *Medium Ævum*, XXI (1952), 22–23. [See the previous article in this anthology, a restatement of Professor Brewer's *Medium Aevum* article. (Ed.)] Mr. Brewer also points out that the main interest of the *Quest* is in Lancelot, but I am unable to agree when he says that "for Malory, sinlessness—its glory, badge, and symbol—is chastity." Malory seems rather to approve of faithful love when it is virtuous—or so the majority of his own comments on love suggest.

like to take the following passage, already quoted above, as a starting-point:

"And all my grete dedis of armys that I have done for the moste party was for the quenys sake, and for hir sake wolde I do batayle were hit ryght other wronge. And never dud I batayle all only for Goddis sake, but for to wynne worship and to cause me the bettir to be beloved, and litill or nought I thanked never God of hit."

In the *Morte Arthur* proper we see for the first time, because of Malory's limited earlier selection from his sources, how Lancelot devotes his chivalry to the service of Guinevere. This appears first in his repeated rescues of her, which Malory relates to the immediate cause of the quarrel. In the first of these episodes Lancelot is so glad of the chance to win the queen's favour again that he is untroubled by any fear "de se desloiauter"—that is, of fighting in a wrongful cause—as he is in the French account. This time, however, the queen is innocent, but she is not on the second occasion, when Meleagant accuses her; yet Lancelot willingly defies him and kills him for her. The third rescue is a climax, but even before it is reached Malory suggests a judgement of Lancelot's actions, in the most important of his rare comments:

Therefore, lyke as May moneth flowryth and floryshyth in every mannes gardyne, so in lyke wyse lat every man of worshyp florysh hys herte in thys worlde: firste unto God, and nexte unto the joy of them that he promysed hys feythe unto; for there was never worshypfull man nor worshypfull woman but they loved one bettir than another; and worshyp in armys may never be foyled. But first reserve the honoure to God, and secundely thy quarell muste com of thy lady. And such love I calle vertuouse love (p. 1119).

[Therefore, just as the month of May flowers and flourishes in every man's garden, so let every man of honor make his heart flourish in this world: first to God, and next to the joy of those that he promised his loyalty to; for there was never a worshipful man nor worshipful woman but they loved one person better than another; and glory in arms may never be fouled. But first reserve honor for God, and secondly your quarrel must come for your lady. And such love I call virtuous love.]

It is Lancelot and Guinevere who love one another more than

any other person, and Malory cannot help feeling that their fidelity is praiseworthy, just because it is a kind of loyalty. But Lancelot's love cannot be virtuous love, since he now puts Guinevere's "quarell" before everything else. The odd detached phrase "and worshyp in armys may never be foyled" refers surely to the prowess of Lancelot that can never be trampled upon, prowess he repeatedly relies upon, careless of other standards. Bearing this out there is Arthur's reply when Gawain, the third time Guinevere is accused, says he is sure Lancelot "woll make goode for my lady the quene" [will make good for my lady the queen]:

"That I beleve well," seyde kynge Arthur, "but I woll nat that way worke with sir Launcelot, for he trustyth so much uppon hys hondis and hys myght that he doutyth no man. And therefore for my quene he shall nevermore fyght, for she shall have the law" (p. 1175. Not in sources).

["That I well believe," said King Arthur, "but I will not work that way with Sir Lancelot, for he trusts so much in his hands and his strength that he fears no man. And therefore for my queen he shall nevermore fight, for she shall have the law."]

Lancelot's third rescue of Guinevere is the final step in the destruction of true chivalric ideals for the sake of love.

The desire to win worship also plays a part. Lancelot was censured in the *Quest* because he "used wronge warris with vayneglory for the plesure of the worlde" [indulged in wrong wars with vainglory for the pleasure of the world] (p. 928), and in adding this kind of explanation Malory developed the fault of pride in him. The same link between prowess and pride appears in the *Morte Arthur* proper, most obviously in Lancelot's own confessions. After he has been wounded in the tournament of Winchester Bors comes and sympathizes with him, and he replies:

"Overmuche ye sey for the plesure of me whych pleasith me nothynge, for why I have the same isought; for I wolde with pryde have overcom you all. . . ." (pp. 1083–84).

["Too much you say for my pleasure, which pleases me not, because I have sought the same thing; for I would with pride overcome you all. . . ."]

Beside this passage may be set Lancelot's words over the tomb of Arthur and Guinevere:

> "Also whan I remembre me how by my defaute and myn orgule and my pryde that they were bothe layed ful lowe . . . wyt you wel. . . . I myght not susteyne myself" (p. 1256).

> ["Also when I remember how by my imperfection and my vanity and my pride they were both laid quite low . . . know you well. . . . I might not bear myself up."]

Both these passages are Malory's own, and they suggest that for him Lancelot's first action against the Round Table anticipates the second precisely in the pride that helped to cause it. In Lancelot's two great speeches of defiance (pp. 1188, 1198) to Arthur and Gawain the same quality appears, still linked with prowess. Lancelot many times declares that he can prove Guinevere innocent by combat, and he also recalls how much he has done for Arthur and Gawain, insisting that he has deserved well of them. These features might be explained in traditional terms; the first would represent the knight's obligation to defend his lady at all costs, and the second would be a speech of avaunt. This kind of explanation suffices in the story of Tristram and Isode, but hardly in the different context of the Lancelot and Guinevere story as Malory tells it. It is precisely the traditional conduct of a knight-lover that Malory criticizes, and the proud claims of Lancelot here have a hollow ring. His own final confession bears out this interpretation.

There remains to be considered the significance of "And never dud I batayle all only for Goddis sake," and of Malory's later words (also quoted in full above), "But first reserve the honoure to God." Does Malory really establish a connexion between "knyghtly dedys and vertuous lyvyng" and religious standards? At first it does not seem so. At the end of the *Quest* he makes much of the return to Camelot and the newly-strengthened friendship between Lancelot and Bors: the daily life of chivalry has still to be lived. Yet when Lancelot returns he sincerely tries, in Malory's version, to lead a better life, and this means that he defends the

—ladyes and damesels which dayly resorted unto hym that besoughte hym to be their champion. In all such maters of ryght sir Launcelot applyed hym dayly to do for the plesure of oure Lorde Jesu Cryst. . . . (p. 1045).

[ladies and damsels who daily betook themselves to him and besought him to be their champion. In all such matters of right Sir Lancelot applied himself daily to act for the pleasure of our Lord Jesus Christ. . . .]

It is from this life that Lancelot falls away, not from the discipline of the *Quest* itself, and this suggests that Malory derived from the *Quest* the impression that knighthood, as he conceived it, was compatible with Christian morality—a possibility in which his source was uninterested. Malory thus sees Lancelot as under an obligation to make his life as a knight conform with Christian standards of conduct. When he begins to fail, his healing of Sir Urry is a reminder that although he is sinful, he is still the best knight in the world, still in touch with grace when he prays, and the discovery shames him. Only when he fails finally in secular life is the monastic life his refuge. This ending is thus to some extent not conventional but a logical conclusion of the story, a final re-assertion of the standards of the *Quest* when all else fails. And even the final hint of instability is true to Lancelot's character (p. 1253).

Yet Malory's main interest was not in the values of the *Quest,* but in the ideal of chivalry he was sure they sustained in some way. The centre of the *Morte Arthur* proper is the conflict in Lancelot of two loyalties equally great, and the story is told with no didactic intent to diminish the appeal of either. But Malory's sympathies are unmistakable: he sees in the story of Lancelot that the service of love degrades the ideal of " knyghtly dedys and vertuous lyvyng"; and he makes Lancelot himself realise this in the end, when he lies grovelling on the tomb of Arthur and Guinevere in grief, not for the loss of his mistress, but for the destruction of the Round Table chivalry he has brought about. The conception of Lancelot's character through which this interpretation is made possible was evolved in Malory's treatment of the *Quest*.

13

THE DRAMATIC UNITY OF
THE *SECUNDA PASTORUM*

Homer A. Watt

CONSIDERED AS EFFECTIVE DRAMA MANY OF THE ENGLISH
miracle plays are, it must be admitted, pretty sorry stuff. Indeed,
they could hardly be otherwise. The essential story was dictated
by biblical material that did not always offer a dramatic conflict.
In transferring this material from Bible to play the anonymous
authors were concerned primarily with the task of putting brief
episodes into dialogue form and not with that of developing
action, conflict, characters. Where they tried to season the play-
let with contemporary elements, they found themselves cramped
by the necessity of sticking essentially to the biblical episodes. As
a result there is often a lack of unity and economy in the plays,
and the added bits of contemporary realism are foreign to story
and mood. The entire effect, in brief, is agglutinative, as though
the authors were torn between a responsibility to reproduce the
biblical originals and a desire to entertain the audience by odd
items of bickering among characters, monologue acts, and occa-
sional slapstick stuff wedged into the play to provide entertain-

Reprinted, by permission of the New York University Press, from
Essays and Studies in Honor of Carleton Brown (New York, 1940), pp.
158–66. See also Eugene E. Zumwalt, "Irony in the Towneley *Shepherd's
Plays*," *Research Studies of the State College of Washington*, XXVI
(1958), 37–53; and W. M. Manly, "Shepherds and Prophets: Religious
Unity in the Towneley *Secunda Pastorum*," *PMLA*, LXXVIII (1963),
151–55.

ment but totally unrelated to the main biblical action. So Cain's boy in the Towneley play of *The Killing of Abel* is an obvious intruder, as is also Iak Garcio of the first shepherds' play of the same cycle. When, therefore, one of the miracle plays appears on analysis to be an exception, it is a pleasure to demonstrate the extent to which it anticipates those dramatic techniques that emerge in the best work of the Tudor dramatists. Not all of the Tudor playwrights, as a matter of fact, in spite of their acquaintance with classical models, have displayed the technical ability of the "Wakefield Master," anonymous author of the justly praised *Secunda Pastorum* of the Towneley cycle.

Like his dramatic descendants, the Tudor playwrights, the Wakefield Master was under the pressure of tradition, but, like the best of them, he succeeded in subduing the tradition to his dramatic needs. What, in a nativity play, was his dramatic problem? He was committed, certainly, to a dramatic representation of the shepherd story from the second chapter of Luke, and this conmitment he fulfilled as charmingly as has been done in any nativity play. But the Bible story occupies only a climax of one hundred and seventeen lines of a total of seven hundred and fifty-four, and the rest of the play seems to be, at first sight, an unrelated comic interlude. Actually, as will be shown, it is far from being only this. Another traditional pressure upon the Wakefield playwright was that of using not Palestinian shepherds but English contemporary types. But here too he succeeds in merging these diverse elements so as to secure essential dramatic unity. The *Secunda Pastorum*, indeed, will stand up under the strictest structural analysis.

The play has a traditional beginning in which each shepherd comes in grumbling. In these "complaints" there is little that is new. Coll, Gyb, and Daw all complain about the weather; Coll, the old shepherd, sighs about hard times and about the oppression of the poor by the rich; Gyb, the second shepherd, is henpecked, and advises the young men in the audience against marrying in haste lest they repent at leisure; Daw, the boy, has in him the seeds of youthful rebellion, and believes that apprentices are exploited by their masters. The grumblings of the three herdsmen are more effusive and detailed than are those of the shepherds in the *Prima Pastorum* but are not different in kind. In the first nativity play of the cycle the second shephered complains that "poore men ar in the dyke" [poor men are in the ditch] (93) and that in the conflict between master and apprentice he wots not "wheder is gretter, the lad or the master" [which is greater, the lad or the master] (70–71); and the first shepherd, henpecked like Gyb in the second play, quotes with approval the proverb that

> A man may not wyfe
> And also thryfee,
> > And all in a yere.   (97–99)
>
> [A man may not wive
> and also thrive,
> > and all in a year.]

This differs little from Gyb's advice to young men in the *Secunda Pastorum*:

> These men that ar wed / haue not all thare wyll;
> When they ar full hard sted, / thay sygh full styll;   (73–74)
> . . . .
> Bot, yong men, of wowyng, / for God that you boght,
> Be well war of wedyng. . . .   (91–92)
>
> [These men that are wed have not all at their will;
> when they are very hard put, they sigh very quietly . . . .
> But young men, wooing, for God that bought you,
> be well aware of marrying. . . .]

Such plaints, and especially those against social and economic conditions, are probably the expressions in drama of the same verbal rebellion of those who swink which may be found in other contemporary literary forms, such as the debates and the dream allegories. It is just possible, however, that the author of the *Secunda Pastorum* was aware of the foil which they provided for expressions of joy over the golden age that came with the birth of Jesus. His play, certainly, begins on a note of sorrow but ends on a contrasting note of joy.

> It is not as I wold, / for I am al lappyd
> In sorow, (4–5)
>
> [It is not as I wish, for I am all wrapped
> in sorrow.]

mourns Primus Pastor when he first appears. And the exploited shepherd boy expresses at the end of the play the thought of all three that the nativity of Jesus brings better days,

> Lord, well were me / for ones and for ay,
> Myght I knele on my kne / som word for to say
> To that chylde. (685–87)
>
> [Lord, it would be well with me, once and for all,
> might I kneel on my knee to say some word
> to that child.]

Such a formula has the flavor of the typical Elizabethan comedy —sad, unstable beginning and happy ending.

But the dramatic unity of the play is determined by elements even more marked. Of these the most striking appears in the skill with which the author has bound together in a single theme episodes that seem superficially to be unrelated. He does not show, of course, all of Shakespeare's genius in using the dream motif as the flux for diverse elements in *A Midsummer Night's Dream,* but he possessed very evidently some sense of the dramatic value of a single theme to give unity to a play. In the *Secunda Pastorum* his unifying theme is, of course, that of the birth of a child. When the play is so considered, it becomes at once apparent that the Mak-Gyll episode is no unrelated part but is very definitely connected in theme with the conventional nativity scene that follows it. Indeed, Mak's special complaint, upon his first appearance, is that he is like the old woman in the shoe:

> Now wold God I were in heuen, / for there wepe no barnes
> So styll. (193–94)

[Now would to God I were in heaven, for there weep no children
    so endlessly.]

Moreover, his conversation with the shepherds in his first
encounter with them contains frequent allusions to his wife's
unhappy and inconvenient power of reproduction, which keeps
him poor in body and in pocket:

> *1. Pastor.* How fayrs thi wyff? by my hoode, / how farys sho?
> *Mak.* Lyys walteryng, by the roode, / by the fyere, lo!
> And a howse full of brude / she drynkys well to;
> Yll spede othere good / that she wyll do
>   Bot so!
> Etys as fast as she can,
> And ilk yere that commys to man
> She bryngys furth a lakan,
>   And som yeres two.   (253–43)

> [*1. Shepherd.* How fares your wife? By my hood, how fares she?
> *Mak.* Lives rolling about, by the Cross, by the fire, lo!
> And a house full of brew she drinks well, too;
> ill speed other good that she will do
>   except in this way!
> Eats as fast as she can,
> and each year that comes to man
> she brings forth an offering,
>   and some years two.]

The mind of Gyll, too, runs in the same direction. Indeed, in
her plot for hiding the stolen sheep she makes capital of her
known reputation for reproduction:

> *Vxor.* A good bowrde haue I spied, / syn thou can none;
> Here shall we hym hyde / to thay be gone,—
> In my credyll abyde,— / lett me alone,
> And I shall lyg besyde / in chyldbed, and grone.   (332–35)

> [*Wife.* A good trick have I spied, since you know none;
> here shall we hide him until they are gone—
> in my cradle abide—let me alone,
> and I shall lie beside it as in childbed, and groan.]

Later the entire stage business of the pseudonativity shows on
the part of both Mak and Gyll considerable practice in playing

childbed and nursing roles. After Mak first enters, in short, the theme of a childbirth dominates the play to the very conclusion.

The unity of the play that arises out of the nativity theme is enhanced still further by a most remarkable foreshadowing of that contrast of burlesque and serious which is so frequent a device in Elizabethan comedies. It is not to be supposed, of course, that the Wakefield Master knew anything about that juxtaposition of masque and antimasque which created such unity and contrast in the English comedies of two centuries later. It would seem certain, however, that he would have understood and appreciated this device fully, for in the Mak interlude and the conventional nativity scene which follows, the contrast is as well marked as in many of the best of the Elizabethan comedies. In the Mak episode, in fact, it is not the sheep-stealing but the sheep-hiding details which are the more essential to the play, for in these latter appears a perfect burlesque of the charming Christ-child scene that concludes the play. Between the burlesque and the religious episodes the three shepherds provide the character links. Twice a birth is announced to them, and twice they go seeking—once to unearth a fraud, and a second time to worship the new-born Lord. The comparative details are so obvious, once the key is apparent, that pointing them out should hardly be necessary. However, such a comparison reveals the amazing extent to which the Wakefield Master kept in mind throughout his composition of the play the dual episodes of the burlesque and the conventional nativity.

It has been said already that Mak's complaint of his wife's perennial fertility prepares the minds of the three shepherds for his more specific announcement of her latest gift to him. This preparation is not entirely unlike their foreknowledge of the coming of the Christ child:

> *II. Pastor.* We fynde by the prophecy— / let be youre dyn—
> Of Dauid and Isay / and mo then I myn,
> Thay prophecyed by clergy / that in a vyrgyn
> Shuld be lyght and ly, / to slokyn oure syn
> And slake it,

Oure kynde from wo;
ffor Isay sayd so:
Ecce virgo
    Concipiet a chylde that is nakyd.   (674–82)

[*II. Shepherd*. We find by the prophecy—stop your din—
of David and Isaiah and more than I remember,
they prophesied through learning that in a virgin
should be light and life, to quench our sin
    and relieve
our nature from woe;
for Isaiah said so:
Behold a virgin
    shall conceive a child that is naked.]

But no prophets foretell the coming of Mak's heir, and no angel announces his arrival. Mak had planned with his rascally wife to say that she

    . . . was lyght
    Of a knaue childe this nyght,   (337–38)

    [was lightened
    of a knave child this night,]

and he tells the shepherds that the news has come to him in a dream—or rather in a nightmare, for it makes him quite unhappy—:

Now, by Sant Strevyn,
I was flayd with a swevyn,
    My hart out of-sloghe:
I thoght Gyll began to crok / and trauell full sad,
Welner at the fyrst cok, / of a yong lad
ffor to mend oure flok. / Then be I neuer glad;   (383–88)

[Now, by Saint Stephen,
I was flayed with a dream,
    my heart cut out:
I thought Gyll began to croak and travail very gravely,
well nigh at the first cock, of a young lad
in order to increase our flock. Then was I never glad.]

In both the burlesque and the conventional nativity scenes the news of the child's birth comes to the shepherds just after they have slept. In this respect the two scenes are identical; but the arrival of the sheep-baby is absurdly reported by his putative father, whereas the announcement in the Bethlehem scene is in the simple biblical tradition:

> *Angelus cantat "Gloria in exelsis"; postea dicat:*
> *Angelus.* Ryse, hyrd-men heynd! / for now is he borne
> That shall take fro the feynd / that Adam had lorne. (638–39)

> [*The Angel sings "Gloria in excelsis"; afterward he says:*
> *Angel.* Arise, gentle herdsmen! for now is he born
> who shall take from the fiend what Adam had lost.]

In the two sleep episodes, incidentally, one is irresistibly reminded of the burlesque dream of Bottom and the romantic ones of the lovers in *A Midsummer Night's Dream,* and of the similarly contrasting sleep scenes in Lyly's *Endymion.* The sleeping shepherds of Bethlehem the Wakefield Master did not have to invent; his cleverness is apparent in his creation for his Yorkshire trio of a burlesque parallel nap.

The succeeding parallel detail comes with the journeying from the plain where the herdsmen slept to the birthplace. The Yorkshire shepherds are not, to be sure, drawn to Mak's hut by his announcement that his wife has given birth to a man-child, although on their arrival they are at once plunged into a nativity situation. It is to be supposed that the journey to the manger of Jesus at the end of the play is a serious duplication of the burlesque journey to the hut of Mak. Says Daw, after the loss of the sheep has been discovered, and Mak has been suspected of having stolen it:

> Go we theder, I rede, / and ryn on oure feete.
> Shall I neuer ete brede / the sothe to I wytt. (467–68)

> [Go we there, I advise, and run on our feet.
> I shall never eat bread until I know the truth.]

And his master, after the angel's announcement, begs for similar haste:

> To Bedlem he bad / that we shuld gang;
> I am full fard / that we tary to lang. (665–66)

278

[To Bethlehem he bade that we should go;
I am very afraid that we tarry too long.]

Thus twice the three shepherds make a journey to the crib of a newly-born child, probably measuring the distance to their goal in both instances by parading around the pageant-wagon.

There is no indication in the Towneley manuscript that the Bethlehem shepherds were drawn to the stable where the Christ-child lay by a song of the Virgin to her child. But since songs were often sung at a production but not subsequently written in the manuscripts, there is, on the other hand, no certainty that, as the herdsmen approached the holy site, the boy who played Mary did not sing one of the lullabies of Our Lady of the kind that Carleton Brown has put into his volumes of medieval religious lyrics. The Wakefield Master was evidently a trained musician, for not only in the *Secunda Pastorum* but in the *Prima Pastorum* as well (656–59 and 413–14, respectively), he has put into the mouths of the shepherds technical comments on the singing of the angels. It is doubtful if he would have overlooked an opportunity to include a sacred lullaby, especially since it would have provided an excellent foil for Mak's fearful cradle song in the sheep-hiding scene. For in their Yorkshire phase, as it may be called, the music-loving shepherds are almost repelled from Mak's hut by a lullaby that no longer exists, unfortunately, but that was very evidently a hideous and unmelodious burlesque. The gloss of the Early English Text Society edition of the play alludes to this effusion as a "noise," but it was without doubt a song by Mak with his wife groaning a stiff burden from her childbed. For so they had planned it:

> *Vxor.* Harken ay when thay call; / thay will com onone.
> Com and make redy all / and syng by thyn oone;
> Syng lullay thou shall, / for I must grone
> And cry outt by the wall / on Mary and Iohn,
>   ffor sore.   (440–44)

> [*Wife.* Listen ever for when they call; they will come soon.
> Come and make everything ready and sing by yourself;

> you shall sing lullay, for I must groan
> and cry out by the wall to Mary and John,
> > from pain.]

But the shepherds are quick to recognize Mak's deficiencies as a singer:

> *III. Pastor.* Will ye here how thay hak? / Oure syre lyst croyne.
> *I. Pastor.* Hard I neuer none crak / so clere out of toyne; (476–77)

> *III. Shepherd.* Will you hear how they hack? Our Sire wishes to croon.
> *I. Shepherd.* I never heard anyone croak so clear out of tune.]

With so many contrasts in the play it is difficult to think that the author would fail to use this harsh lullaby as a burlesque opposite a sweet song by the Virgin. Incidentally, Gyll's crying out on Mary and John effects an excellent forward link with the conventional nativity.

The Yorkshire shepherds, like the Bethlehem shepherds, find the babe in swaddling clothes (433, 598–99), but warned away by the "parents" they hesitate to approach the cradle. The scene in Mak's hut is divided between the comic business of hunting for the stolen sheep and the fencing with Mak and Gyll over

> > . . . this chylde
> > That lygys in this credyll.　　　　(537–38)

> > [. . . this child
> > that lies in this cradle.]

Failing to find their sheep the herdsmen actually leave the hut but return at the suggestion of the aged Coll:

> > *I. Pastor.* Gaf ye the chyld any-thyng?
> > *II. Pastor.* I trow, not oone farthyng.
> > *III. Pastor.* ffast agane will I flyng,
> > > Abyde ye me there.　　　　(571–74)

> > [*I. Shepherd.* Gave you the child anything?
> > *II. Shepherd.* I trow, not one farthing.
> > *III. Shepherd.* Quickly again will I return,
> > > you wait for me there.]

It is the boy Daw's attempt to press "bot sex pence" [but sixpence] into the hand of the "lytyll day-starne" [little day-star] that leads to the discovery of the fraud and the punishment of the rascally Mak. The link with the nativity episode here is, of course, the gift-giving, in the Mak scene burlesque, in the later episode simple and touching. Daw's term of endearment to Mak's swaddled "infant"—"lytyll day-starne"—is applied, incidentally, by Gyb, the second shepherd, to the Christ-child (727).

One final device employed by the Wakefield Master to give structural unity to the play and also to divide the little drama into definite scenes is the introduction of song. Reference has already been made to the possible contrast of Mak's lullaby and the song of the Virgin, and the biblical original forces the introduction of the "*Gloria in exelsis*" of the Angelus. The three other songs are sung by the shepherds. Of these the second is their attempt to imitate the angel's "*gloria*"—a device employed also in the *Prima Pastorum* (413 ff.). The first is a three-part song —"tenory" [tenor], "tryble" [treble], and "meyne" [middle] (182–89)—used to mark the conclusion of the first scene and the coming of Mak. Finally, the play closes with a "going-out" song by the shepherds, a device exactly similar to that used frequently by the Elizabethan playwrights to mark the ending of a comedy and to clear the stage. The song that the shepherds sang as they left the stable of the Christ-child and brought both burlesque and conventional nativity episodes to an end does not appear in the Towneley manuscript. But Mary's command to the shepherds—"Tell, furth as ye go" [Tell, as you go forth] (744)—and their own feeling—"To syng ar we bun" [To sing are we bound] (753)—indicate clearly that it was no jolly shepherd song that they sang but one of an angel, a star, three simple shepherds, and a babe in a manger. It may have been not unlike the song which the shepherds of the Coventry Corpus Christi nativity play sang as they left Joseph and Mary and the Christ-child:

> Doune from heaven, from heaven so hie,
> Of angeles ther came a great companie,

With mirthe and ioy and great solemnitye,
    They sange terly terlow,
So mereli the sheppards ther pipes can blow.

[Down from heaven, from heaven so high,
of angels there came a great company,
with mirth and joy and great festivity,
    they sang ter-li ter-lo,
so merrily the shepherds their pipes can blow.]

And thus *"Explicit pagina Pastorum"* [The pageant of the Shepherds ends].

14

DOCTRINE AND DRAMATIC STRUCTURE IN *EVERYMAN*

Lawrence V. Ryan

AS THE TITLE PAGES OF THE TWO EARLY EDITIONS PRINTED BY John Skot make clear,[1] *Everyman*, like other examples of its kind, is conceived as a didactic work under a dramatic form: "Here begynneth a treatyse how ye hye fader of heuen sendeth dethe to somon euery creature to come and gyue a counte of theyr lyues in this worlde / and is in maner of a morall playe" [Here begins a treatise on how the High Father of Heaven sends death to summon every creature to come and give account of their lives in this world and is in the manner of a moral play]. Thus, in any judgment of its effectiveness, one must bear this conception in mind. Yet no extended or adequate analysis of the play, from the point of view of the relationship between form and purpose, has so far appeared in print. Most of the com-

Reprinted, by permission, from *Speculum*, XXXII (1957), 722–35, published by the Mediaeval Academy of America. See also Thomas F. Van Laan, *"Everyman:* A Structural Analysis," *PMLA*, LXXVIII (1963), 465–75.

[1] Skot published two editions of *Everyman* at London early in the sixteenth century. A single copy of each edition, known as the Huth (*Short-Title Catalogue* 10605) and Britwell (*STC* 10606) copies, has survived. All quotations, unless otherwise indicated, are taken from the reprint of the Britwell copy made by W. W. Greg for W. Bang's *Materialien zur Kunde des älteren englischen Dramas*, IV (Louvain, 1904).

mentary written over the past half century has concentrated on attempting to establish the priority of composition of *Everyman* or the Flemish morality *Elckerlijc* and on determining the meanings of such pairs of words in the two versions as *kennisse-knowledge, roeken-rood*, and *duecht-good deeds*. As a result, scholars have largely neglected the question of the dramatic structure of *Everyman*. On the other hand, the impression made by this morality on modern audiences as pure drama has served to obscure its original doctrinal purpose. William Poel, who revived it successfully soon after the beginning of the twentieth century, once expressed an opinion which is characteristic of, and possibly helped to shape, the modern reaction:

> I did not myself produce *Everyman* as a religious play. Its theology is indefensible. One can very easily tear it to pieces in that respect. But the whole story, Eastern and not Catholic, in its origin, is beautiful as a piece of art; it offers a hundred opportunities from the point of view of beauty, and it leaves an impression that is fine and chaste.[2]

The approaches of both Poel and the controversialists over the priority of the English-Flemish versions have provided valuable insights to the play, but they fail to get at the essential point about *Everyman*—that is, the relationship between the doctrine that the author wishes to present and the dramatic means he employs to convey that doctrine to his audience.

It is not necessary in studying this relationship to deal with the question whether *Everyman* is a translation or an original work; although it differs from *Elckerlijc* in certain important details, the general structure of the two moralities is very similar. Nor would it be wise to try to convince the modern audience that it ought to react with full sympathy and comprehension to

---

[2] Quoted from a newspaper interview with Poel (London *Daily Chronicle,* 3 September 1913) in Robert Speaight, *William Poel and the Elizabethan Revival* (London, 1954), p. 166. In evaluating these remarks, one must bear in mind Poel's known opposition to any alliance between church and stage, plus his antagonism toward organized religion and toward the Catholic Church in particular.

the lesson presented in the play. But Poel's objection, that its "theology is indefensible" and "can very easily" be torn to pieces, along with his finding more valuable than the clearly presented ideas of the work only a vague sort of fineness and chasteness, is not a valid one and ignores the fact that the doctrinal content is the reason for being of *Everyman*. This article will be an attempt to demonstrate that the theology involved is indispensable, not indefensible, and furthermore, that it gives the play its characters, structure, significance, and even its dramatic impressiveness. Without the theology the artistic merit may not be fully appreciated. The story does not by itself carry the burden; in other words, the real meaning and thus the true and legitimate effect of the work depend not on the action alone, but on a proper comprehension of what the action signifies.

The preacher-playwright of *Everyman* is interested in answering the important question: What must a man do to be saved? His chief problem is to reduce the complex answer to terms of simple dramatic representation without falsifying or obscuring the doctrine. In both respects he achieves success, conveying his teaching through fitting details of "characterization," through simultaneously occurring emotional and doctrinal climaxes, and, most important of all, through the representation of an action which brings into harmony the natural, dramatic, and theological elements of Everyman's experience.

Inherent in the theme are excellent possibilities for subtle irony and surprising turns of fate. For in dramatizing the scheme of salvation according to the orthodox view, the author was faced with two apparent paradoxes. According to Catholic theology, man, having fallen by Adam's original sin, is incapable of saving himself through his own efforts. Only through the graces earned in the redemption by Christ—in which one must believe—is the free gift of salvation made available. After professing his faith, however, one must also continue to coöperate with grace; that is, he must live well in the life of grace in order to achieve heaven. In addition, the benefits of the redemption are passed on to all men through the ministration of Christ's church, of which one must be a member to gain eternal life.[3] Here the paradoxes arise. First, though man is incapable of doing anything by himself to merit salvation and is saved by the Sacrifice on the Cross, yet he is finally judged on the basis of his own good works. The believing Christian must perform good deeds because the precept of charity so commands him and because failure to do so is a grave sin of omission, particularly in a man whose will is sup-

[3] This often reaffirmed doctrine is perhaps most emphatically stated in Pope Boniface VIII's bull "Unam sanctam," 18 November 1302, which begins: "Unam sanctam ecclesiam catholicam et ipsam apostolicam urgente fide credere cogimur et tenere, nosque hanc firmiter credimus et simpliciter confitemur, extra quam nec salus est, nec remissio, peccatorum, etc." [We are forced to believe and maintain with impelling faith the one holy catholic and apostolic church, and we believe this firmly and confess it freely, outside of which there is no salvation nor remission of sins] (*Corpus Juris Canonici,* ed. Aemilius Ludovicus Richter [Leipzig, 1839], II, 1159). A possibility of salvation for virtuous persons who have failed to become members of the true church through no fault of their own is admitted, it must be granted; St. Augustine says, for example, that baptism "impletur invisibiliter, cum ministerium Baptismi non contemptus religionis, sed articulus necessitatis excludit" [is fulfilled invisibly when the administration of Baptism is excluded not by contempt for religion but by an emergency] (*De Baptismo Contra Donatistas,* IV, xxii, 29, in Migne, *Patrologia Latina,* XLIII, 173); and Pope Pius IX declared in 1854 that, while no man can be saved outside the Catholic Church, "tamen pro certo pariter habendum est, qui verae religionis ignorantia laborent, si ea sit invincibilis, nulla ipsos obstringi huiusce rei culpa ante oculos Domini" [it must likewise be held for certain, however, that those who labor under ignorance of the true religion, if the ignorance be invincible, are not bound by any responsibility for that fact before the eyes of God] ("Singulari quidam," 9 December 1854, *Pii IX Pontificis Maximi Acta* [Rome, 1954], I, 624). It is to be remembered, however, that while a possibility of salvation without baptism by water is admitted, no pontiff or council says that anyone may be saved outside the universal church. For all practical purposes, baptism is held to be essential to salvation. This belief is demonstrated by Dante's placing even the most virtuous pagans in limbo, the first circle of hell (*Inferno,* Canto iv). With regard to *Everyman,* it is apparent that the author is concerned only with an audience who are already members of the church. The play is about the means by which one is restored to grace after failing to lead a virtuous life, and it is to be assumed that Everyman is already a baptized Christian.

posed to be in harmony with that of God.[4] As St. James says in his epistle,

Quid proderit, fratres mei, si fidem quis dicat se habere, opera autem non habeat: Numquid poterit fides salvare eum? (James 2:14).

Sicut enim corpus sine spiritu mortuum est, ita et fides sine operibus mortua est (James 2:26).

[What will it profit, my brethren, if a man says he has faith, but does not have works: can the faith save him?

For just as the body without the spirit is dead, so also faith without works is dead.]

That is one difficulty. The second is that while Christ died for all men, only through membership in his church may anyone be saved. This belief in turn poses two problems. It rules out the strictly Calvinistic doctrine of special election. Everyone does receive sufficient grace to save his soul. Nevertheless, even St. Thomas Aquinas admits that why some men are saved and some reprobated is one of the unfathomable mysteries of the divine will.[5] Thus, the author of *Everyman* is careful to show that while

[4] The teaching of the church on this matter is clarified in the condemnation by Pope Clement V and the Council of Vienne, 1311–1312, of the following tenet of the Beghards and Beguines: "Quod se in actibus exercere virtutum est hominis imperfecti, et perfecta anima licentiat a se virtutes" [It is the mark of an imperfect man to exercise himself in acts of virtue, and the perfect soul may be allowed virtues from itself] (*Corpus Juris Canonici,* II, 1100). The doctrine is further supported by Pope Pius V's condemnation, in his bull "Ex omnibus afflictionibus," 1 October 1567, of certain heretical teachings about good works of the theologian Michel du Bay (*Canones et Decreta Sacrosancti Oecumenici Concilii Tridentinii* [Leipzig, 1839], p. 136), and by later condemnations of the doctrines of Miguel de Molinos and the Quietists.

[5] Sed quare hos eligit in gloriam et illos reprobavit, non habit rationem nisi divinam voluntatem. Unde Augustinus dicat (super Joan. tract. 26, non rem. a pr.): *Quare hunc trahat et illum non trahat, noli velle dijudicare, si non vis errare"* [But why he elects some to glory and others he reprobates has no reason except the divine will. Whence Augustine says (Tract. xxvi. in Joan.): *Why he draws this one and not that one seek not to judge if you do not wish to err*] (*Summa Theologica,* I, q. xxiii, art. 5). In another place Aquinas says, "Cum autem Deus hominum qui in eisdem peccatis detinentur hos quidem praeveniens convertat, illos autem sustineat sive permittat secundum ordinem rerum procedere, non

some may not share in its benefits, the redemption was intended for all. Early in the play, God says:

> I hoped well that euery man
> In my glory shulde make his mansyon
> And thereto I had them all electe. (52–54)

> [I hoped well that every man
> should make his mansion in my glory,
> and to that I had them all elected.]

But the author also points out that God's graces in their fulness flow to men only through the church and through the sacraments, which are administered by the clergy. In one speech, Five Wits informs us:

> No remedy we fynde vnder god
> Bute all onely preesthode. (745–46)

> [No remedy we find under God
> except only through the priesthood.]

The problem of presenting these ideas efficiently and without confusion has determined the structure of the morality. *Everyman* goes far beyond the overly simple moral lesson that is likely at first glance to be taken as its theme: "Do good deeds and you will be saved." It offers, in effect, a concise presentation of the orthodox teaching on the matter of man's salvation. For the play

---

est ratio inquirenda quare hos convertat et non illos; hoc enim ex simplici ejus voluntate processit quod, cum omnia fierent ex nihilo, quaedam facta sunt aliis digniora, et sicut ex simplici voluntate procedit artificis ut ex eadem materia similiter disposita quaedam vasa format ad nobiles usus et quaedam ad ignobiles" [And if God, by his prevenient grace, converts some men who are held back by their sins, while, in the ordinary way, he suffers or allows others to continue sinning, there is no reason to ask why he converts some and not others; it comes from his simple will that, if all things were made from nothing, some things are more worthy than others, just as it proceeds from the simple will of the artisan that from the same material similarly conditioned he makes some vessels for noble and some for common uses] (*Summa Contra Gentiles,* III, ch. 161. All quotations from the works of Aquinas are taken from *Opera Omnia secundum impressionem Petri Fiaccadori Parmae 1852–1873* [New York, 1948–1950]).

to be a success, the audience at the end not only must be exposed to but must comprehend the rather involved message revealed step by step through the experience of Everyman.

Structurally, the play turns on two climaxes, growing out of the abandonment of the hero by two theologically and dramatically distinct groups of "friends" in whom he has placed his confidence. Introduced between these two series of desertions are, first, the appearance of Knowledge and Good Deeds, the former character remaining with him until "all is made sure," the latter being the only one to accompany him into the grave; and, second, an episode in which Everyman prepares for death by receiving the last sacraments. An examination of the characters introduced and of the structure shows how both the most effective drama and the clearest revelation of doctrine have been achieved. The action begins with God's sending Death to summon Everyman before the judgment seat. Though one may not make too much of the fact, since there is no reason for another character to be on stage at the time, it is perhaps significant that Death finds his victim walking alone. Dramatically, the aloneness of Everyman in this episode makes him a more pathetic figure. And his isolation is certainly meaningful from the theological standpoint: he is really alone and destitute of help or true friends, because at the moment he has no one to plead for him before God's throne. Having been told by Death, "Se thou make the redy shortely" [See that you make yourself ready shortly] (181), Everyman calls in turn on Fellowship, Kindred, Cousin, and Goods for help, but each one refuses to accompany him on his final pilgrimage.

The names and characterizations of this set of false friends make it plain that Everyman takes the natural course in first seeking help outside himself when faced with his greatest crisis. The pathos of his being abandoned by the creatures he has loved most arouses sympathy, but the author wishes also to teach and remind the audience, even as he solicits their pity, that foolish and sinful men inordinately love transitory things which can

avail them nothing in the end. The first painful step in Everyman's spiritual education and regeneration is his discovery that
excessive love of passing things has placed him in danger of hell-
fire. The characterizations here are done with touches of individ-
uality and ironic humor, for Fellowship, Kindred, and Cousin
make rash promises to stand beside Everyman through all manner of hardship; earthly attachments seem to be man's truest
friends when one has them fully at his command. Fellowship is
rashest of all in his boastful pledge:

> For in fayth and thou go to hell
> I wyll not forsake the by the waye.   (232–33)
>
> [For, in faith, if you go to Hell
> I will not forsake you along the way.]

Then, upon learning the cause of Everyman's sorrow, he shows
his true colors and explains that he will be a constant companion in every kind of sinful doing, but as for making the final
pilgrimage with his friend,

> I wyll not go that lothe iournaye
> Not for the fader that bygate me.   (268–69)
>
> [I will not take that hateful journey,
> not for the father that begot me.]

Kindred and Cousin in their turn raise the hero's hopes with
promises to hold with him in "welth and wo" [weal and woe]
and with him "to liue and dye," but when he explains what he
wants of them, they too depart with lame excuses. Here he learns
that it is not true that "ouer his kynne a man may be holde [*sic*
for *bolde*]" [of his kinsfolk a man may be sure] (326). Finally,
Goods, whom he has loved best of all, tells him unsympatheti-
cally that his inordinate attachment to her has ensnared his soul.

The author, in an improvement over other versions of the
story, is careful to make these false friends appear in a climactic
order according to the increasing danger of each as a distraction
from one's Maker. In *Barlaam and Josaphat,* when the hero is
called to give his reckoning before the king, two of his three

friends desert him while the third remains faithful. These three friends represent, successively, abundance of wealth, wife and child and kindred, and the man's virtues and good deeds. In *The thrie Tailes of the thrie Priests of Peblis*, the appeal is made to riches, kindred and friends, and alms deeds and charity—in that order.[6] The expansion of the number of false friends and the rearrangement of their appearances by the author of *Everyman* constitute a great improvement. First, there is the advantage of dramatic climax gained by substituting a triple for a double refusal. Besides, the writer clearly distinguishes Fellowship from Cousin and Kindred, since he represents a different kind of danger to the soul. Fellowship is willing to help Everyman to "ete & drynke & make good chere Or haunt to women the lusty company" [eat and drink and make good cheer or frequent the pleasant company of women] (272–73). He is likely to lead the hero into sins of the flesh. Cousin and Kindred, however, are dangerous in another way. The hero is likely to misplace his trust in the love and loyalty of his family at a time when he should look to God alone for love and support. Such a mistake would be natural enough because of the close ties that bind members of a family together: "For kynde wyll crepe where it may not go" [For nature will creep where it may not run] (316). Yet none of these false friends is so serious a threat as Goods. The love of human creatures, while it may lead one astray, as too much of it has misled Everyman, is not incompatible with love of God. But no man can "Deo servire, et mammonae" [serve God and Mammon] (Matthew 6:24). Excessive love of worldly goods closes the soul to love of any higher object. These unfaithful

[6] Jacobus de Voragine, "The Life of S. Barlaam," *The Golden Legend,* trans. William Caxton (London, 1900), VII, 94–95; *The thrie Tailes of the thrie Priests of Peblis* (Edinburgh, 1603). Other versions of the story interpret the significance of the three friends in the same way, with the exception of *An Alphabet of Tales,* in which "þe iij frend is almighti God, whilk þatt putt His life & His sawle for His friends when He suffred His passion" [the third friend is Almighty God, who laid down his life and his soul for his friends when he suffered his passion] (ed. Mary McLeod Banks, EETS, 126–27 [London, 1904], I, 42–43).

friends, personifications of external and ephemeral relationships and possessions, promise much, but have finally no solace to offer Everyman. In fact, because of the manner in which the author presents them, it is obvious that they are not only unavailing, but may even be actual hindrances to salvation provided one gives too much attention to them.

The reversal of the pattern of desertion, along with the separation of Fellowship, Kindred, and Cousin into recognizably individualized "characters," not only provides a more realistic and convincing order of climax than that of other versions of the story, but is also dramatically necessary since the episode with Goods is the natural preparation for and transition to the calling forth of Good Deeds.

Left alone after the departure of all these characters, the hero is close to despair. The soliloquy summarizing his discovery of the vanity of his hopes is the first of the two climaxes of the play. Although no remedy seems to be at hand as the speech begins, the time is appropriate for the reversal of fortune, which coincides with the correct theological moment for Everyman to turn at last to something that can save him. The man who loves any creature more than the Creator himself is still a graceless sinner. But now, having been abandoned by all his false loves, Everyman at last remembers his Good Deeds. His turn in this direction is the right one, and it is not mere chance that he makes it. The author has prepared for it through a speech of Goods:

> But yf thou had me loued moderately durynge
> As to the poore gyue parte of me
> Than sholdest thou not in this dolour be
> Nor in this grete sorowe and care.   (431–34)

> [But if you had loved me moderately meanwhile,
> such as giving part of me to the poor,
> then you should not be in this anguish,
> nor in this great sorrow and care.]

The hint that almsgiving, a form of good deeds, would have

been to his true advantage turns the thoughts of Everyman, after he has finished summarizing his disappointments up to this stage, to the one friend who can be of assistance to him.

At this point, however, the author has had to present his doctrine with extreme care. First of all, the church teaches that good works, though they are naturally good and are never to be taken as anything but good, are availing to salvation only to the Christian in the state of grace.[7] Secondly, it is also dogma that man is unable even to begin repentance for his misdeeds unless God supply the first motion in him.[8] God is a wrathful judge, as the opening of the morality indicates, but at the same time he is the merciful Saviour who provides Everyman with the grace to repent. Consequently, Good Deeds is represented as willing to help the hero, but so "sore bounde" [sorely bound] by his sins that she "can not stere" [cannot stir]. There is a moment of dramatic suspense here in order that the audience may grasp the full import of the situation: good deeds in themselves are as

---

[7] "Sicut palmes non potest ferre fructum a semetipso, nisi manserit in vite: sic nec vos, nisi in me manseritis" [As the branch cannot bear fruit by itself unless it remain on the vine, so neither can you unless you abide in me] (John 15:4). In 1415 the Council of Constance condemned John Huss' view that all the works of the unjustified were evil; on the other hand, that good works of themselves do not merit salvation is also made clear in the condemnation of the following teaching of du Bay: "Sicut opus malum ex natura sua est mortis aeternae meritorium, sic bonum opus ex natura sua est vitae aeternae meritorium" [Just as an evil deed by its nature is meritorius for eternal death, so a good deed by its nature is meritorious for eternal life] (Pius V, *loc. cit.*).

[8] "Si quis dixerit, sine praeveniente Spiritus Sancti inspiratione atque eius adiutorio hominem credere, sperare, et diligere aut poenitere posse, sicut oportet, ut ei iustificationis gratia conferatur: anathema sit" [If one should say that without the prevenient inspiration of the Holy Spirit and its assistance man is able to believe, hope, and love, or be penitent, as he should in order that the grace of justification may be conferred, let him be anathema] (Council of Trent, 1547, Session VI, *De iustificatione, Canon* III, *Canones . . . Tridentini*, p. 13). Likewise, Aquinas says "quod homo convertatur ad Deum, hoc non potest esse nisi Deo ipsum convertente" [that a man is turned to God is not possible except by God having turned to him]. (*Summa Theologica,* II: Part i, q. cix, art. 6).

nothing if a man be in the state of sin. What hope, then, since Everyman, since all men, are sinners? Good Deeds provides the answer shortly. She has a sister,

> Called knowledge whiche shall with you abyde
> To helpe you to make that dredefull rekenynge.   (520–21)

> [called knowledge, which shall abide with you
> to help you make that dreadful reckoning.]

A true understanding of the significance of the character Knowledge is crucial to a proper interpretation of the play. Actually, the dialogue shows what she stands for, and the *Elckerlijc-Everyman* controversy has demonstrated that Knowledge here means "contrition" or, better, "acknowledgment of one's sin."[9] Nevertheless, erroneous interpretations of the word persist. Popularly, Knowledge is usually taken as representing comprehension of intellectual truth or (possibly through the influence of the motto of Everyman's Library) learning or merely understanding. But it is evident that the protagonist is not in need of knowledge in the first two senses, and for knowledge in the third sense the author uses the word *cognition* or *intellection*, as when Everyman asks Knowledge to

---

[9] For example, Henry de Vocht, *Everyman: A Comparative Study of Texts and Sources,* Materials for the Study of the Old English Drama, New Series, xx (Louvain, 1947), pp. 57–60, gives extensive evidence from the *OED* to demonstrate that *knowledge* is used in the play in the now obsolete sense of *acknowledgment,* while he denies that the Flemish *kennisse* can be taken in the same sense. In an answer to De Vocht, J. van Mierlo, *Die Prioriteit van Elckerlijc tegenover Everyman Gehandhaafd* (Turnhout, 1948), shows that *kennisse* also can be taken to mean "acknowledgment or awareness of one's inner state of sin." Early in the controversy, Francis A. Wood, *"Elckerlijc-Everyman:* The Question of Priority," *Modern Philology,* viii (1910), 283, asserted that *kennissee* means *contrition* and was wrongly translated in *Everyman* as *knowledge*! The important fact here is not the argument over which of the terms, the English or the Flemish one, is appropriate, but the agreement of these scholars that the character is intended to represent *acknowledgment* of sin.

> gyue me cognycyon
> Where dwelleth that holy man confessyon.[10] (538–39)
>
> [give me knowledge of
> where dwells that holy man, Confession.]

Another error has been to take the character as standing for "faith" or "the grasp of the divine law and the divine plan of the universe."[11] The events of the play, however, show quite certainly that none of these interpretations is correct.

Doctrinally, the character represents the only kind of knowledge that can profit Everyman in his condition—awareness of and acknowledgment of his sin—for she offers to lead him out of his misery by taking him "To confessyon that clensyng ryuere" [To confession, that cleansing river] (536). At this point, such an offer is proper, for Everyman had already made the first tentative acknowledgment of his fault when he said to Goods: "I gaue the that whiche sholde be the lordes aboue" [I gave you that

---

[10] The same passage in Greg's reprint of the Huth copy (Bang's *Materialien*, XXIV [Louvain, 1909]) reads:

> But I praye yon [*sic*] to instructe me by intelleccyon
> Where dwellyth that holy vertue confessyon.
> [But I pray you to instruct me by knowledge
> where dwells that holy virtue, Confession.]

[11] L. A. Cormican, "Morality Tradition and the Interludes," *The Age of Chaucer*, ed. Boris Ford (London, 1954), p. 191. Cormican explains the function of Knowledge in the following way: "Knowledge sets the process of salvation in motion by coming of her own accord to Everyman (faith was a gratuitous gift of God, not attainable by man's striving); she then leads Everyman to Confession, the sacraments of Eucharist and Last Anointing, by which he is prepared for reception into heaven." But it is quite evident that Knowledge comes because Good Deeds has pointed out to Everyman that he ought to recognize and acknowledge his sins. This fact indicates his need, not of faith or understanding, but of repentance. Besides, faith would not necessarily lead one to sacramental confession, whereas a sincere acknowledgment of one's sinfulness would. The sacramental emphasis of the morality is integral and inescapable. It is apparent that the writer was not much concerned about the "faith" of his audience, but that he wanted to drive home to them the point that recognition of their human sinfulness and helplessness should lead them to the sacraments as the normal means by which men receive life-giving grace.

which should be the Lord's above] (458). He is now prepared to repent, but the author takes care to make clear that the motion to repentance has not originated in the sinner himself. Joy begins to fill Everyman's spirit, but with it comes a sense of humility at his own powerlessness. Having just previously recognized, by looking into the book of his own good deeds, that he has nothing to his credit, he says, "Our lorde Iesus helpe me" [Our Lord Jesus help me] (506). This is not a mere ejaculation. As his account now stands, only the mercy and merit of the Saviour can help him. And the motion to repent does come from above, as Everyman now tells us twice. First he says that he is in

> good condycyon . . . in euery thynge
> And am hole content with this good thynge
> Thanked by [be] god my creature.   (524–26)

> [good condition . . . in everything,
> and am wholly content with this good thing,
> thanks be to God my creator.]

A short while later, having confessed his sins, he declares that he will begin his penance, "yf god gyue me grace" [if God gives me grace] (607).

As he carries out his penance, Good Deeds rises from the floor. Up to this moment she has been unable to move, but now that Everyman has fulfilled the requirements of the sacrament—contrition, confession, and satisfaction—he is in the state of grace, and his good works have value for his salvation. Furthermore, carrying out the penance is itself a good work because penance is an act of love (*caritas*) as well as of reparation. Even the flagellation of Everyman helps to strengthen his Good Deeds. Immediately after the penance is completed and the sinner puts on the "garmente of sorowe" [garment of sorrow] (643), Good Deeds and Knowledge introduce to him four "persones of grete myght" [persons of great power]—Beauty, Strength, Discretion, and Five Wits. Again the author's dramatic and pedagogical timing coincide perfectly. Everyman, already made joyous by his confession and the strengthening of his Good Deeds, becomes actually jubilant at the sight of so many friends to assist him on his journey: "lacke I nought" [I lack nothing], he says, naming all of them in turn, "I desyre no more to my besynes" [I desire no more for my business] (680, 683).

The addition of this second set of friends to the traditional story is an innovation of the author and contributes to both the dramatic effectiveness and the clarification of the doctrine toward the exposition of which the entire play is unerringly directed. A second and more surprising climax is prepared by the introduction of these personifications. The hero's exultation is ironic, for upon seeing the grave, all of these counsellors will desert him, even as his false friends had done. Here the intent of the author in creating the new set of characters becomes clear. He brings them in at the moment when Everyman is certainly renewed in sanctifying grace. The new friends, as their names indicate, are properties of Everyman himself, not external things like the first group of companions. They are the natural endowments, good in themselves, that make man the flower of creation and help him to fulfill his natural destiny. But according to Christian teaching man has been called by a free gift of God to a supernatural destiny to which these qualities are unavailing in any way unless, as St. Paul says, men prepare themselves, "induentes novum eum [hominem]" [put on the new one (man)] (Colossians 3:10; Ephesians 4:24). Only after the protagonist, by penitence and forgiveness, has been restored to the life of grace, are the natural powers and qualities sanctified and made effectual for his new life. Once again, the technique of the author is to reveal points of doctrine to the audience in their natural order and as Everyman discovers them through his experience. This incident is also a skilful preparation for the final revelation of the play. The fact that man's unassisted natural powers can not help him toward salvation implies that nothing performed by him without divine aid, even his good works, can bring him to the end for which he was created. But elevated by grace and the supernatural virtues that accompany it, the natural powers and virtues can be exercised to help toward, in fact, must necessarily be exercised properly for one to achieve perfection and salvation.[12]

Still, even in the state of grace the Christian may come to rely too much on these natural powers. The author, having presented the more obvious message in the first climax, proceeds to a more subtle lesson here. There is a danger of Pelagianism in the man who lives well; he may attribute his sanctity to his own efforts rather than to the free gift of God's grace. Dramatically and doctrinally, the author begins now to bring his play to a resolution with the two episodes that finally drive home his point and leave Everyman assured of salvation as he descends into his grave. The first of these is the so-called "digression on priesthood," which is not really a digression at all but a theologically essential and (if properly understood) dramatically appropriate situation. The second is the final desertion of Everyman by all save his Good Deeds.

As the four counsellors "of grete myght" enter, they too pledge themselves to remain with Everyman in his need, but

[12] Concerning the manner in which one should regard and use his natural powers, Aquinas says: "Est igitur naturaliter rectum quod sic procuretur ab homine corpus et inferiores vires animae ut ex hoc et actus rationis et bonum ipsius minime impediatur, magis autem juvetur. Si autem secus acciderit, erit naturaliter peccatum. . . .

"Praeterea, Unicuique naturaliter conveniunt ea quibus tendit in suum finem naturalem; quae autem e contrario se habent sunt ei naturaliter inconvenientia. Ostensum est autem supra quod homo naturaliter ordinatur in Deum sicut in finem. Ea igitur quibus homo inducitur in cognitionem et amorem Dei sunt naturaliter recta; quaecumque vero e contrario se habent sunt naturaliter homini mala" [It is therefore naturally right that the body and the lower powers of the soul should so be cared for by man that to the act of reason and his own good they be not impediments but a great help. If it happens otherwise, however, it will be naturally evil. . . .

Moreover, those things are naturally beneficial to man by which he tends toward his natural end; while those of a contrary nature are naturally not beneficial for him. It has been shown above that man is naturally ordained to God as to the end. These things, therefore, by which man is led to the knowledge and love of God are naturally right; while those of a contrary nature are naturally evil for man] (*Summa Contra Gentiles,* iii, ch. 129).

the promises, while perhaps equivocal, are not rash nor intentionally deceitful as were those of the earlier set of friends. For these characters can not really be false friends, or else Good Deeds and Knowledge would not have presented them to Everyman. Each gives a pledge that is in keeping with his nature (684–93). Strength appropriately will stand by Everyman "in dystres Though thou wolde I batayle fyght on the groude" [in distress, though you wish that I fight the battle on the ground]. Five Wits assures him that "though it were thrugh the worlde rounde We wyll not departe for swete ne soure" [though it were throughout the round world we will not depart for sweet nor sour]. Beauty promises to remain "vnto dethes houre" [until death's hour], and Discretion informs him that "We all gyue you vertuous monycyon That all shall be well" [We all give you virtuous admonition that all shall be well]. None boasts rashly that he will stay with the hero "and thou go to hell" [if you go to Hell], for these qualities do not lie to him; being good in themselves, they give him no ill counsel or misinformation. Nevertheless, irony in the situation is provided by the fact that the somewhat obtuse Everyman does not listen to their speeches attentively, for he evidently supposes that they mean to accompany him into the grave. Thus, at the second climax, their departure, in the natural order in which they would leave a dying man, Beauty first, then Strength, Discretion, and finally Five Wits, dismays Everyman. Again he has been abandoned by the things that have meant most to him: "I loued them better than my good dedes [deeds] alone" he laments (857). The audience, too, is likely to be surprised and moved; for it comes as a blow that these qualities, which help man to realize the perfection of human nature, are in themselves of no consequence before the judgment seat. Most amazing of all is the fact that Knowledge does not accompany one beyond the grave. "O all thynge fayleth saue God alone" [Oh, all things fail except God alone], says Everyman (841), and hears from his one remaining friend that "All fleeth saue good dedes and that am I" [All flee except good deeds, and that am I] (873). At last, through the vicissitudes of experience, the hero has learned his lesson: even the redeemed Christian in the state of grace is capable of forgetting that his natural properties and accidents are in themselves not the instruments of salvation.[13] In themselves, they are merely temporal aids, and they help on the supernatural level only if a man has received the gift of grace. That he is in a state of grace, one demonstrates by his good works, which are acts of love showing that his will is in harmony with the will of God.

The reason for adding this second climax involving a set of characters not found in other versions of the story has been made apparent by the action. The original tale of the man and his three friends is simple and moving, but it is so simple that what the author of *Everyman* understood to be the complete truth about man's salvation could not be represented within its narrow terms. Even in preparing for the first climax of the play with its more obvious lesson, he saw fit to expand the number of episodes and to rearrange them so that the natural order in which Everyman would turn to sources outside himself for help, the theological order in which these externals represent increasing danger to his spiritual welfare, and the order of dramatic logic are made perfectly to coincide. It is disheartening to see the rejection by friends and kindred, but it is the greatest disillusionment of all to learn that wealth, which on earth can buy nearly everything and seems to be man's greatest good, is useless and may be fatal to the soul. This ordering, of course, provides for a smooth and natural transition from the chiding of Everyman by Goods for his neglect of almsgiving to the hero's appeal to his Good Deeds.

---

[13] "In ipsa enim divina visione ostendimus esse hominis beatitudinem, quae vita aeterna dicitur; ad quam sola Dei gratia ducimur et dicimur pervenire, quia talis visio omnem creaturae facultatem excedit, nec est possibile ad eam pervenire nisi divino munere; quae autem sic adveniunt creaturae Dei gratiae deputantur" [We have proved that man's happiness is in that same divine vision that we call eternal life; and we are said to be led there by God's grace alone, because that vision exceeds the power of every creature, nor is it possible to come to it except by a divine gift; so that whatever comes to a creature is attributed to the grace of God] (Aquinas, *ibid.*, III, ch. 52).

But the doctrine is more complex than what the action up to this stage presents to the audience, and the writer was required to find an effective means to dramatize the rest of his message. The action might have been finished off quickly with the confession episode followed by the descent of Everyman and Good Deeds into the grave. Such an ending would have been simple enough to bring about and would have satisfied the formal requirements of dramatic art. It would not, however, have been quite so moving, nor would it have given the audience a fully accurate revelation of what a man must do to be saved. To watch someone receive no help from any external source as he goes to judgment is pathetic enough; to discover the hard truth that one may not even depend on his own powers is a bitter thing. Yet the four counsellors are truly "of grete myght" and are not to be despised or reprehended; they do help Everyman on his earthly journey even if they are unable to enter the grave with him. The author has introduced them to remind the audience of man's utter dependence upon God, for love of whom one must direct all one's powers toward performing the good works that win him mercy on the day of doom.

Nor is Knowledge to be blamed for remaining behind. At the last, Everyman sees why this is so and expresses gratitude for her constant guidance. Acknowledgment of sin is necessary only to the moment of death; after death it is not necessary, since the redeemed sinner, having performed his good works in keeping with the will of God, rejoices in the divine forgiveness and has no need of sorrow for past transgression when judgment is passed upon him.[14] As Dante symbolizes it in the *Purgatorio*, the soul

---

[14] Concerning this matter, Aquinas asserts that "quamvis charitas sit nunc causa dolendi de peccato, tamen sancti in patria erunt ita perfusi guadio, quod dolor in eis locum habere non poterit: et ideo de peccatis non dolebunt, sed potius gaudebunt de divina misericordia, qua eis peccata sunt relaxata" [although charity is now a reason for grief over sin, the saints in heaven will be so filled with joy that sorrow can have no place in them: and consequently they will not grieve for their sins, but they will be able to rejoice over the divine mercy by which they are released from sin] (*Summa Theologica*, III, q. lxxxvii, art. 1).

is first washed in Lethe, the river of forgetfulness of sorrow for past sin, and then in Eunoë, the river of remembrance of good deeds (Cantos xxxi and xxxiii). Knowledge is Everyman's chief guide up to the end. Until death Good Deeds remains in the background, since good works are not given their reward until after death, when the soul has arrived in heaven and the will is certainly and eternally conformed to that of God. Acknowledgment of sin, leading to the sacrament of penance, is thus the first and most important step to salvation, and one must go on acknowledging sin until "all is made sure." Knowledge remains with the hero until she sees "where he is become." She is the only character left on stage at the end, when the angels announce the reception of Everyman into heaven, thus symbolically driving home her significance in the play.

But what may be said about the dramatic value of the "digression on priesthood?" To a modern audience, this may seem like a flaw in an otherwise perfectly realized work of art. But if it does seem so, that is because a modern audience, absorbed in the action for its own sake and preferring to believe that man should depend exclusively on his own powers to work out his salvation, is likely to overlook the sacramental emphasis of the play. The author is very careful (717–18) to state the doctrine that the seven sacraments are "the cure For mannes redempcyon" [the cure, for man's redemption],[15] and he deals specifically with the

---

[15] In affirmation of the general necessity of the sacraments for salvation, the Council of Trent in 1547 issued the following pronouncement: "Si quis dixerit, sacramenta novae legis non esse ad salutem necessaria, sed superflua, et sine eis aut eorum voto per solam fidem homines a Deo gratiam iustificationis adipisci, licet omnia singulis necessaria non sint, anathema sit" [If one should say that the sacraments of the new law are not necessary for salvation, but are superfluous, and that without them or the desire for them men may obtain from God the grace of justification by faith alone, granted that all things are not necessary for each individual, let him be anathema] (Session VII, De sacramentis in genere, Canon IV, *Canones . . . Tridentini*, p. 17). Aquinas likewise says: "Quia vero, sicut jam dictum est, mors Christi est quasi universalis causa humanae salutis, universalem autem causam oportet applicari ad unumquemque effectum, necessarium fuit exhiberi hominibus quaedam

three that are received upon the approach of death—penance, holy eucharist, and extreme unction. Furthermore, the church teaches that the sacrament of penance is necessary for the restoration of grace to the mortal sinner, unless he make an act of perfect contrition for his offenses against God. But Everyman does not have perfect sorrow, since his concern is not that he has offended an all-good and all-loving creator. It is at first motivated only by a desire of avoiding punishment for his sin, and is rather to be called attrition than contrition. Besides, according to church doctrine, even perfect contrition implies an intention of confessing one's sins sacramentally when the opportunity occurs.[16] Hence the need for Knowledge to lead Everyman to *sacramental* confession in order that his Good Deeds may be

---

remedia per quae eis beneficium mortis Christi quodammodo conjungeretur. Hujusmodi autem esse dicuntur Ecclesiae sacramenta" [Because, as has just been said, the death of Christ is a kind of universal cause of human salvation, and since a universal cause needs to be applied to each individual effect, it was necessary to supply man with certain remedies whereby the benefits of the death of Christ might be brought to him in some way. These remedies are called the sacraments of the Church] (*Summa Contra Gentiles,* IV, ch. 56).

[16] Condemned as an error by the Council of Constance in 1418 was the following teaching of John Wiclif: "Si homo fuerit debite contritus, omnis confessio exterior est sibi superflua et inutilis" [If a man shall have been duly contrite for his sins, all exterior confession is superfluous and useless for him] (Ioannes Dominicus Mansi, *Sacrorum Conciliorum Nova, et Amplissima Collectio* [Paris and Leipzig, 1903], XXVII, 1207E). Aquinas gives the positive statement of the church's position on sacramental confession: "Ideo, sicut sine baptismo, in quo operatur passio Christi, non potest esse salus hominibus, ut realiter suscepto vel secundum propositum desiderato (quando necessitas, non contemptus, sacramentum excludit), ita peccantibus post baptismum salus esse non potest, nisi clavibus Ecclesiae se subjiciant, vel actu confitendo et judicium ministrorum Ecclesiae subeundo, vel saltem hujus rei propositum habendo, ut impleatur tempore opportuno" [Consequently, just as without baptism, in which the passion of Christ is operative, there can be no salvation for men, whether it be received really or in desire (when necessity, not contempt, excludes the sacrament), so for those sinning after baptism there can be no salvation unless they submit themselves to the keys of the Church, either by actual confession and acceptance of the judgment of the officials of the Church, or at least by proposing to do these things at the proper time] (*Summa Contra Gentiles,* IV, ch. 72).

able to rise. Next the hero, having become truly contrite through the instruction of Knowledge and the grace of the sacrament, is advised to

> Go to presthode . . .
> And receyue of hym in ony wyse
> The holy sacrament and oyntement togyder (707–09)

> [Go to priesthood . . .
> and receive from him in any way
> the holy sacrament and the anointing together]

that is, holy eucharist and extreme unction. At this point comes the "digression" of Five Wits and Knowledge, during part of which the main character is offstage for the only time in the play. It is the absence of Everyman and the introduction of these speeches immediately before the final climax that trouble persons who criticize the passage as a structural weakness. Yet, if one bears in mind that this is "a treatyse . . . in maner of a morall playe" intended to dramatize Everyman's discovery of the way to eternal bliss, the suitability and even the stage effectiveness of these speeches become clear. The eulogy of priesthood is important at this moment because of the incalculable value to Everyman of penance and the eucharist. Echoing various passages in Scripture, Five Wits tells Everyman of priests that

> God hath to them more power gyuen
> Than to ony aungell that is in heuen
> With .v. wordes he may consecrate
> Goddes body in flesshe and blode to make
> And handeleth his maker bytwene his hande
> The preest byndeth and vnbyndeth all bandes
> Both in erthe and in heuen.[17] (735–41)

[17] Scriptural authority for lines 737–39 is Luke 22:19: "Et accepto pane gratias egit, et fregit, et dedit eis, dicens: Hoc est corpus meum, quod pro vobis datur: hoc facite in meam commemorationem" [And having taken bread, he gave thanks and broke, and gave it to them, saying: This is my body, which is given for you; do this in remembrance of me]. For lines 740–41, the authority is Matthew 16:19: "Et tibi dabo claves regni coelorum. Et quodcumque ligaveris super terram, erit ligatum et in coeli; et quodcumque solveris super terram, erit solutum et in coeli"

[God has given to them more power
than to any angel that is in heaven;
with five words he may consecrate
God's body, make it into flesh and blood,
and he handles his Maker between his hands.
The priest binds and unbinds all bonds
both on earth and in heaven.]

Since normally only the sacrament of penance can restore grace to the mortal sinner, the power of the priest to bind and unbind is obviously crucial in the scheme of salvation. Everyman is also urged to receive the eucharist, for although the church does not hold that the reception of Christ's body and blood is absolutely necessary, there are weighty authorities to emphasize its importance. Christ himself had said, "nisi manducaveritis carnem Filii hominis, et biberitis ejus sanguinem, non habebitis vitam in vobis" [unless you eat the flesh of the Son of Man, and drink his blood, you will not have life in you] (John 6:54). And Aquinas, while he does not say that actual reception of the eucharist is essential, argues that at least the implicit desire to receive it is fundamental to the consummation of the spiritual life.[18] Now the author sends Everyman offstage for twenty-two lines to partake of the last sacraments while Knowledge and Five Wits

---

[And I will give you the keys of the kingdom of heaven. And whatever you shall bind on earth shall be bound also in heaven; and whatever you shall loose on earth shall be loosed also in heaven].

[18] In distinguishing between the necessity of baptism and the necessity of the eucharist, Aquinas says: "Et ideo perceptio baptismi est necessaria ad inchoandam spiritualem vitam, perceptio autem Eucharistiae est necessaria ad consummandam ipsam, non ad hoc quod simpliciter habeatur, sed sufficit eam habere in vota, sicut et finis habetur in desiderio et intentione" [And consequently the reception of baptism is necessary for starting the spiritual life; the reception of the Eucharist, however, is necessary for its consummation, not for its being possessed actually, but it suffices to have it in desire, as an end is possessed in desire and intention] (*Summa Theologica*, III, q. lxxiii, art. 3). The importance of Everyman's reception of the eucharist in his progress toward salvation is thus very great. The same article of the *Summa* concludes with the words: "Eucharistia dicitur sacramentum charitatis, *quae est vinculum perfectionis*" [The Eucharist is called the sacrament of charity, *which is the bond of perfection*].

deliver to the audience a sermon designed to stress the validity of the sacraments regardless of the moral condition of the minister. The very fact that it contains an admonition to the clergy to lead upstanding lives is the clue to the significance of the sermon in the action. If priests give scandal by their conduct, the faithful may stay away from the sacraments and, by so denying themselves access to the means of grace, perhaps lose the opportunity to be saved.

The communion of Everyman is not dramatized, possibly out of a sense of decorum, and the supposedly digressive sermon serves here to express a truth that the hero has learned through his experience. The "digression" is skilfully wrought, even to the point of presenting the lesson chiefly through the speeches of Five Wits, rather than one of the other characters, because "A sacrament is a visible [that is, sensibly evident] sign which imparts grace to our soul."[19] Moreover, the episode is dramatically timely, for it occurs just before the natural powers will be weakened and must depart from Everyman, leaving only the grace received through the sacraments to sustain him and to make his Good Deeds effectual. Thus, when for a moment he again feels abandoned, "O Iesu helpe all hath forsaken me" [Oh Jesus, help; all have forsaken me] (851), he and the audience become ready for the final lesson. Again Good Deeds is ready to come to his aid, but at this final climax she is really able to assist him, having been made efficacious by the infusion of grace which Everyman has received from the sacraments administered by the priest. This, then, is the message of the play which

---

[19] Wilhelm Faerber, *Catechism for the Catholic Parochial Schools of the United States* (St. Louis, 1942), p. 62. Cf. Aquinas, *Summa Theologica*, III, q. lx, art. 4. That the character Five Wits represents the outer, not the inner, senses is evident not only from this passage but also from the earlier promise made to Everyman: "We wyll not departe for swete ne soure" (687). It is appropriate for Five Wits to instruct Everyman in this instance, because "per sacramentorum institutionem homo convenienter suae naturae eruditur per sensibilia" [through the institution of the sacraments, man, consistently with his nature, is instructed through sensible things] (*Summa Theologica*, III, q. lxi, art. 1).

dramatization of Everyman's escape from his original predicament has made clear. In order to be saved not only must a man perform good deeds; he must perform them as a faithful Christian with the aid of the graces that are channeled to him through the church. Though death is the conclusion, the moment is one of release and exaltation, as in Sophocles' *Oedipus at Colonus,* for the meaning of the pattern has been fully revealed to the protagonist as he reaches the end of the tragic experience. Like Oedipus, Everyman discovers that it is better for a man to face reality and to learn what he really is and has, no matter what suffering the discovery may cost him, than to spend his life in pursuing illusions.

A successful play reveals what it has to say through the experience of its characters; all other message is dramatically gratuitous and were better put into some sort of Shavian preface. *Everyman,* conceived primarily to expound doctrine and to inspire to the good life, is powerful in both teaching and moving because in its construction the doctrinal and dramatic orders have been made perfectly to coincide and because what one learns from the play grows naturally out of the action itself. Instead of being "indefensible" and inessential to an appreciation of the work, the theology presented actually determines the structure of the morality and helps to give it the place it admittedly deserves as the most successful thing of its kind in English literature.

15

THE LITERARY STATUS OF THE
ENGLISH POPULAR BALLAD

Arthur K. Moore

SCHOLARS HAVE GENERALLY BEEN INCLINED TO VIEW THE ENG-
lish popular ballad not as an aesthetic object but as a relic of an
early and primitive state of society, in which the literary process
was governed more by instinct than by convention. They have
implicitly denied the existence of a purely literary problem, and
their speculations about the ballad matrix have had the effect
of discouraging criticism of any but an appreciative sort. Yet
excellencies appropriate to learned literature have been incidentally claimed for the ballad, and, in contrast to other forms
of popular art (e.g., lyrical folk song, folk tale, broadside), it
has received expensive notice in anthologies and literary histories. This is not to argue that it deserves less but only to remark
the impropriety of assuming value for what, beyond an occa-
sional explication, has escaped close critical scrutiny.

The ballad doubtless owes its relative immunity from value
judgments to the naturalistic explanation of its origin. Most of
the older scholars probably felt that standards derived from literature of the main cultural stream were largely inapplicable
to songs which, in the best opinion, came ultimately from the
illiterate throng. For some time now, the theory of communal
composition has been in the discard, but discussions of the ballad

Reprinted, by permission of author and editor, from *Comparative Literature*, X (1958), 1–20.

continue to be colored by romantic attitudes toward the ill-defined folk and their creative activity. In important respects the ballad has not been wrenched free of the context in which the eighteenth century placed it by reason of an unconscionably narrow view of literary form. It is my opinion that literature even of the humblest order is completely accessible to criticism and that, accordingly, the ballad, whatever its degree of sophistication, is susceptible to systematic analysis. With the object of clarifying the literary status of the English ballad, I propose to test the obstacles to critical study which by general agreement have been set around it and to consider the achievement of some of those specimens which seem to have very significantly shaped scholarly thinking.

1

The word *ballad* derives from OF *balade*, which in Chaucer's usage as in the French denoted a courtly lyric of fixed form. During the fifteenth century the term was loosely employed and afterward applied somewhat indiscriminately, though perhaps more often than not to more or less popular narrative songs.[1] There is no very ancient authority for the specialized sense standardized by F. J. Child, nor is there any evidence that the Child ballad was ever regarded outside of scholarly circles as *sui generis* [a distinct kind].[2] The contents of his monumental *English and Scottish Popular Ballads* (1882–98)—305 ballads with variants—remained after a long and uncertain sifting process, some notion of which can be gained from an examination of his

[1] Louise Pound, *Poetic Origins and the Ballad* (New York, 1921), pp. 39–46; G. H. Gerould, *The Ballad of Tradition* (Oxford, 1932), pp. 235–38; E. K. Chambers, *English Literature at the Close of the Middle Ages* (Oxford, 1945), pp. 137–39.

[2] William Shenstone in two letters to Percy in 1761 seems first to have insisted on limiting the term "ballad" to narrative songs. Quoted by S. B. Hustvedt, *Ballad Criticism in Scandinavia and Great Britain during the Eighteenth Century* (New York, 1961), pp. 160 f.

earlier collections.[3] He did not live to write an introduction, and the criteria by which the corpus was assembled can only be conjectured. Scholars in this century have commonly agreed (often without independent investigation) that the term "popular ballad," covering Child's exemplars and a few subsequently reported, properly designates a distinct genre.[4] It can hardly be maintained, however, that a ballad genre has been validated, for nowhere are the principles set forth by which these pieces are ordered and contrived and thereby discriminated from other popular narrative songs.[5] In short, this reputed genre yet lacks a serviceably exclusive definition and an unambiguous description of its peculiar art.

The impression is sometimes created that Child might have been able to resolve some of the doubts about the ballad, but what he wrote after a good many years of reflection encourages no such view. His article under "Ballad Poetry"[6] in the *Universal Cyclopaedia* (1900) is with respect to the major issues more intuitional than evidential, and it is wavering besides.[7] His discussion is affected by romantic notions of ancient literature, and the ballad never emerges from the mediaeval shadowland as conceived by the nineteenth century. For him it appears to have been essentially a relic, beautiful but without literary pretensions:

The *popular* ballad, for which our language has no unequivocal name, is a distinct and very important species of poetry. Its historical and natural

---

[3] According to the calculations of Thelma G. James, "The English and Scottish Popular Ballads of Francis J. Child," *JAFL*, XLVI (1933), 51–53, the third and definitive edition of 1882–98 rejects 115 pieces from the first, published under the title *English and Scottish Ballads* (Boston, 1857), and adds 90 pieces, of which 37 were not previously available.

[4] See Gerould, *op. cit.*, pp. 84–86.

[5] In the loosest sense of the term, subsuming many specimens besides Child's, the ballad may possibly be considered a genre; but it has not been shown to constitute a genre in the sense of the classical epic, the Italian sonnet, and other forms controlled more or less by formula. James, *op. cit.*, pp. 57–59, raised the legitimate doubt that a definition could be devised to comprehend all the Child pieces.

[6] Published originally in *Johnson's Cyclopaedia* (1874).

[7] For an attempt to clarify Child's position, see W. M. Hart, "Professor Child and the Ballad," *PMLA*, XXI (1906), 755–807.

place is anterior to the appearance of the poetry of art, to which it has formed a step, and by which it has been regularly displaced, and, in some cases, all but extinguished. Whenever a people in the course of its development reaches a certain intellectual and moral stage, it will feel an impulse to express itself, and the form of expression to which it is first impelled is, as is well known, not prose, but verse, and in fact narrative verse.

Child postulated as the matrix of the ballad a homogeneous community in which "the whole people form an individual." Since the "author counts for nothing" under these conjectured circumstances, the ballad is necessarily distinguished by the "absence of subjectivity and of self-consciousness." Yet he was unwilling to abandon the ballad to a community of illiterates—"the lower orders of a people"—and out of his sense of the fitness of things he contrived an agreeable cultural situation which, unfortunately for his argument, has no demonstrable historical reality:

Nothing, in fact, is more obvious than that many of the ballads of the now most refined nations had their origin in that class whose acts and fortunes they depict—the upper class—though the growth of civilization has driven them from the memory of the highly polished and instructed, and has left them as an exclusive possession to the uneducated. The genuine popular ballad had its rise in a time when the distinctions since brought about by education and other circumstances had practically no existence.

Child's indecisive statement is highly significant; it expresses a measure of allegiance to the old theory of communal composition, which F. B. Gummere was later to elaborate with special reference to the ballad,[8] and at the same time a doubt that ballads could have originated in a throng of dancing and singing

[8] Gummere's exposition of the theory is spread through "The Ballad and Communal Poetry," *Studies and Notes in Philology and Literature,* V (1896), 41–56; *Old English Ballads* (Boston, 1904); *The Popular Ballad* (Boston and New York, 1907); *The Beginnings of Poetry* (New York, 1908). The theory had been largely discredited before Gummere picked it up from German sources, which, in the opinion of Phillips Barry ("Das Volk dichtet nichts," *Bul. of the Folk-Song Society of the Northeast,* No. 7, 1934, p. 4), he wrenched in order to support his argument.

illiterates. He apparently recognized the danger of an upper-class origin to the concept of the ballad as an artless form and almost in the same breath reaffirmed the classless, homogeneous setting. Child's work was in a sense completed by Kittredge, who wrote the introduction to the Cambridge abridgment of the *English and Scottish Popular Ballads* (1904). Kittredge apparently felt nothing of his master's misgivings but spoke strongly for the communal principle, though, to be sure, not for group authorship of extant specimens.

The rise and fall of this theory is not of principal concern here; suffice it to say that Louise Pound among others exposed its absurdities,[9] in the end forcing it out of serious consideration —but, oddly enough, not freeing scholarship of its influence. The important questions were reargued by Gerould, who said all that could be said in defense of Gummere's views against Pound's attack. While finding much to blame in the anticommunalists, he nonetheless executed a perceptible retreat from the more extreme positions maintained by the communalists. His concessions appear, however, to jeopardize the traditional concept of the ballad without much clarifying its origin and status.

Acceptance of the principle of single authorship has meant something less than a complete turnabout. The folk, collectively considered, is a more important factor than the original author, if, as it is widely believed, all of the ballads have been significantly altered in oral tradition by a supposedly beneficial process called communal re-creation.[10] By this view, every ballad is multiple and mutable, consisting of an unascertainable number of versions, all of which may be undergoing change. It is thus futile

[9] A. K. Davis, ed., *Traditional Ballads of Virginia* (Cambridge, Mass., 1929) pp. 4–9, provides a summary account of the controversy.

[10] Fully stated by Barry, "Communal Re-Creation," *BFSSNE*, No. 5 (1933), pp. 4–6, and approved by Gerould, *op. cit.*, pp. 168 f., who, however, used an earlier article by Barry, "An American Homiletic Ballad," *MLN*, XXVIII, 1913), 4 f. On the question of the handling of the ballads by the folk, see the very full discussion of Sergio Baldi, *Studi sulla poesia popolare d'Inghilterra e di Scozia* (Rome, 1949), pp. 42–65.

to speak of an author and impossible to establish a text. Even judgments about individual versions are not entirely feasible, since the ballad is not simply text but a joint product of words, music, and singer which varies with each performance. In this vein Evelyn Kendrick Wells has recently observed:

> It is the product of no one time or person; its author, if ever known, has been lost in the obscurity of the past and in the processes of oral tradition. Its medium is word of mouth rather than print. It goes its way independent of literary influences, carrying for a while the accretions of this or that day and singer, but sloughing them off as it passes to the next. It has no one original text, being freshly created by each successive singer as he makes his own version.[11]

Behind this modified communalism probably lies Gerould's remarkable statement of the ballad's mode of existence, which tends to invalidate the title of the original author to his work:

> The popular ballad . . . has no real existence save when held in memory and sung by those who have learned it from the lips of others. In saying this I am not ignoring the difficult question of its origin . . . but merely emphasizing the primary condition of its being. Strictly speaking, the ballad as it exists is not a ballad save when it is in oral circulation, and certainly not until it has been in oral circulation.[12]

Gerould intended, of course, to support the claims of the folk, but the dense metaphysical integument which he fashioned for that purpose would, if accepted, effectively insulate the ballad against all literary inquiry and indeed against all efforts at understanding. If it cannot be essentially represented in print, it can hardly be apprehended for critical examination. Gerould probably did not mean quite so much, for on occasion he dealt with the ballad as if it belonged to the province of literature and could be discriminated accordingly. He was nonetheless inclined to deny the applicability of any standard save what might be called "balladness," signifying a norm presumed to be implicit in the irrefutable instances.[13]

[11] *The Ballad Tree* (New York, 1950), p. 5.
[12] *Ibid.*, pp. 2 f.
[13] *Ibid.*, p. 35.

The confused status of the ballad today can be explained by reference to the cultural and literary biases of the period which officially discovered it. Percy was in most things a man of his century, with a characteristic tenderness for the past and for the peasant, but also with a view of literature founded in neoclassical theory and practice. A century which revised Shakespeare and rejected Donne could hardly be expected to regard inartificial song seriously as literature, and Percy carefully refrained from making any such claim; yet the primitivism and antiquarianism of the times permitted unbounded enthusiasm for whatever related to ancient men living close to nature. His dedicatory epistle to the Countess of Northumberland presents the ballads "not as labours of art, but as effusions of nature, showing the first efforts of ancient genius";[14] and his Preface, while invoking the taste of ballad lovers like Addison,[15] avoids their critical indiscretions:

In a polished age, like the present, I am sensible that many of these reliques of antiquity will require great allowances to be made for them. Yet have they, for the most part, a pleasing simplicity, and many artless graces, which in the opinion of no mean critics have been thought to compensate for the want of higher beauties, and, if they do not dazzle the imagination, are frequently found to interest the heart.[16]

Later scholars much abused Percy for taking editorial liberties, but none denied that the ballads considered as literature left a great deal to be desired. If less apologetic than Percy, Child actually claimed no more, nor did Kittredge. The latter concluded his Introduction to the Cambridge edition with an infelicitous discussion which evidences a firm intent to claim value for the ballads without stating precisely wherein value resides:

Of the merit of the English and Scottish ballads nothing need be said. It is unhesitatingly admitted by all persons who care for ballads at all.

[14] Thomas Percy, *Reliques of Ancient English Poetry,* ed. H. B. Wheatley (London, 1887), I. 1.
[15] For praising *Chevy Chase* (*Spectator,* Nos. 70, 74) Addison endured considerable ridicule.
[16] Percy, *op. cit.,* I, 8.

There is no occasion to make comparisons as to excellence between these pieces and the poetry of art. Such comparisons are misleading; they tend only to confound the distinctions between two very different categories of literature. The ballads must stand or fall by themselves, not by reason of their likeness or unlikeness to Dante or Shakspere or Milton or Browning. Above all things, they should not be judged indiscriminately or in the lump . . . Finally, the popular ballad, though it may be despised, cannot be ignored by the student of literature. Whatever may be thought of the importance of such verse in its bearing on the origin of poetry in general . . . the ballad, like other forms of popular material, has in the last two centuries exercised a powerful influence on artistic literature, and it will always have to be reckoned with by the literary historian.[17]

This melancholy argument confesses the lack of a sufficient rationale, an original defect of ballad scholarship which to this day has not been repaired.

The followers of Child and Kittredge have not considered the possibility of dissolving Percy's distinction between art poetry and natural poetry, which the critical inflexibility of the eighteenth century dictated,[18] but rather have felt a need to reaffirm it as an integral part of the ballad concept. To allow art to the ballad is to invite troublesome questions about its origin and form, though to deny art is not quite reasonable. Gerould argued that the difference was a matter of consciousness of aesthetic principles. While not denying the existence of principles somewhere in the background of the ballads, he yet minimized to the vanishing point their influence on the composers. His defense of Percy's dichotomy, it must be said, entails an explanation of the creative process in the folk milieu which is highly intuitional, if not mystical.[19] Leach accepted Gerould's distinction and then pressed on to the logical but nonetheless absurd conclusion that the ballads were products of dabbling by the collective illiteracy:

The musician and storyteller on the conscious level intellectualizes his

[17] *English and Scottish Popular Ballads,* ed. H. C. Sargent and G. L. Kittredge (Boston, 1904), pp. xxx f.

[18] See René Wellek, *A History of Modern Criticism: 1750–1950* (New Haven, 1955), I, 126 ff.; M. J. C. Hodgart, *The Ballads* (London, 1950), pp. 159–61.

[19] Gerould, *op. cit.,* pp. 13 f.

material and method by trying them against aesthetic principles already codified and drawn up for him. The folk, on the other hand, accept, reject, modify, augment their songs and stories through unconscious subjective processes; and what one generation accepts, another may change or reject entirely. So we hit on beauty, or pathos, or sense of tragedy not exactly by chance but nearly so.[20]

In the end Leach states, as he must, that the makers of folk song are without art.[21]

Whatever the full explanation of the creative process, there is no reason for thinking it differs fundamentally according to time, place, or social circumstance. It is not evident that learned poets have ever followed rule books slavishly or that unlearned ones have worked without conscious regard for convention. A good deal has been staked on artlessness, which has yet to be plausibly explained. Indeed, the question arises whether this crucial concept is very clear to those who insist upon its validity. For instance, a comment by Wells on a passage of dialogue in *Young Hunting* is something less than coherent: "It is the simplicity of great art, as well as of great artlessness."[22] It is perhaps just as well for the traditional view that artlessness, implying at most an unconscious critical sense in the folk, cannot be substantiated; for the abscence of definite critical controls is incompatible with a ballad genre.

The old idea of natural poetry, which psychologically considered has little to recommend it, is rendered even less tenable in the case of the ballad by a concession made by Gerould and affirmed with damaging elaborations by Leach. They agree, against the opinion of Kittredge and others, that ballads may have been composed on social levels somewhat above the illiterate commonalty and even by minstrels. Percy, it may be recalled, ascribed the ballads to the "ancient English bards and minstrels,"[23] though without much supporting evidence. Kittredge

[20] MacEdward Leach, ed., *The Ballad Book* (New York, 1955), p. 10.
[21] *Ibid.*, p. 33.
[22] Wells, *op. cit.*, p. 91.
[23] Percy, *op. cit.*, I, 7.

argued that minstrels could not have composed them because their repertoires, as far as known, consisted of very different matter.[24] Gerould rather cautiously granted that the makers of ballads may sometimes have been "middle-class folk," even professional minstrels of a rude and illiterate order.[25] Leach expressed the same view, though apparently without Gerould's concern about its implications:

Who are the ballad folk? There is a general impression that they are illiterate hillbillies, wandering around barefoot and smoking corncob pipes. The evidence from numerous records as far back as the Middle Ages points rather to the middle class: small farmers, shoemakers, village schoolteachers, nursemaids, tinkers, wives of small tradesmen, innkeepers, drovers. Among these too are the itinerant singers of songs who go from village to village plying a small trade but concerning themselves largely with singing their stores of songs.[26]

Some of these categories must be reckoned lower class; but, if Leach means what he says, he has fathered the ballads upon a class which produced the bulk of mediaeval literature, including the *Roman de la Rose* and the *Canterbury Tales*, and which from the fourteenth century on was increasingly literate. Not even on the lower side could the middle class be described as artless. Indeed, it may be doubted that any section of mediaeval society was innocent of artificial literature, since knowledge of it depended simply on auditory receptiveness,[27] not literacy. The middle class may have composed ballads, but neither in the Middle Ages nor in the Renaissance was it demonstrably free of the literary taint which has been thought ruinous to balladry. If actually middle class in origin, the ballad can hardly be regarded as a special case, implying an unusual cultural situation and mode of composition.

[24] Sargent and Kittredge, *op. cit.*, p. xxiii.
[25] Gerould, *op. cit.*, pp. 185, 225 f.
[26] Leach, *op. cit.*, pp. 8 f.
[27] Ruth Crosby, "Oral Delivery in the Middle Ages," *Speculum,* XI (1936), 100.

The inordinate concern from Percy to the present with the ballad matrix has been largely owing to the simple conviction that the ballad, while often pleasing, differs in fundamental ways from the verse of more or less learned poets and cannot stand comparison with it. Encumbered by this preconception, scholars have supposed that the ballad could be legitimately prized only as a product of a cultural situation separate and apart from the main stream. This is not to say, of course, that they have had to make excuses to themselves for taking unqualified pleasure in favorite pieces. But it is quite another matter to claim absolute excellence for poetry which appears to fall far below the norms established by major writers. By means of rather shaky inferences a home was found for the ballad in the vast wastes of the Middle Ages, though not in a location that scholarship might visit. The search for origins is not in itself reprehensible, but it has been carried out with something less than scientific objectivity and to the neglect of the ballad as art. The cause was sought before the effect was rightly understood; and perhaps necessarily the supposed matrix, besides lacking historical probability, precluded the possibility of conscious artistry and thus of high achievement. It is not a reproach to Percy that he made no attempt to demonstrate the aesthetic integrity of the ballads; but literary scholars in this century, which in criticism is flexible if anything, cannot pretend to be hampered by neoclassical standards. Criticism was never freer or better equipped than now to determine whether the ballads individually and collectively have value *as* literature as well as *for* literature.

2

Most things relating to the ballad have been violently disputed, but there has been unusual agreement about those specimens especially worthy of inclusion in the golden treasuries of literature. That this should be the case is rather surprising, since literary standards have not been thought applicable to the ballad.[28] It is of course possible that the preference of anthologists has been altogether determined by nonaesthetic criteria. This supposition fails, however, to account for the narrow range of their choices among scores of ballads which demand equal consideration by virtue of metrical arrangement, subject matter, use of authentic conventions, impersonality, and freedom from elegance. The conclusion is hard to resist that in some way literary quality rather than typicalness has recommended them. This inconsistency would perhaps be of little significance except for the likelihood that the influence of the preferred pieces on scholarly thinking has been far out of proportion to their number. In that event, they would invite close study for their central importance to the very concept of the ballad as well as for their probable literary excellence.

It is evident from the anthologies of English literature intended for undergraduate use that scholars have a marked preference for eight of Child's 305 ballads, and in the same versions.[29] *Sir Patrick Spens* (A) seems never to be omitted and *Edward* (B) almost never. *Barbara Allan* (A) and the *Wife of Usher's Well* (A) appear four times in five. The incidence of the *Twa Corbies, Lord Randal* (A), *Johnie Armstrong* (A), and the *Daemon Lover* (A), is about fifty per cent. Others selected with significant frequency—about once in three times—are the *Three Ravens, Mary Hamilton* (A), *Young Waters, Lord Thomas and Fair Annet* (A), *Thomas Rymer* (A), *Kemp Owyne* (A), and the *Twa Sisters* (A). The interest in the last three pieces of this group is perhaps chiefly folkloristic. The *Hunting of the Cheviot (Chevy Chase)* and the *Maid Freed from the Gallows* figure importantly in ballad scholarship but for one reason or another do not often appear in anthologies.

[28] Gerould, *op. cit.*, p. 85, insisted that "we must . . . look with unprejudiced eyes at everything that has the warrant of tradition behind it, whether or not it seems to us 'good' according to any theory of origins or our sophisticated standards of aesthetic taste."

[29] I have based my estimates on thirteen well-known textbooks (e.g., Woods-Watt-Anderson, *The Literature of England*) which are now in print or have been until recently.

While the validity of any useful grouping is likely to be vitiated by marginal instances, the claim can be made with considerable justice that the more famous of these pieces stand somewhat apart in point of internal form. Since none is rich in narrative detail and most are positively deficient, the definition of the ballad as a folk song that tells a story is for this group assuredly inadequate, if not misleading. Telling a story is not the only concern and probably not even the major one. The claim of the ballad to literary merit thus depends to a large extent on pieces which are not, with minor exceptions, pre-eminently narrative. Rather interestingly, in view of the standard definition, no one has argued that they would be the better for telling completer stories; it is perhaps evident that, whatever the method, they do their work well.

Yet the relative sketchiness of the anthology ballads is the source of a difficulty which, though perhaps more apparent than real, requires attention. Inasmuch as time and transmission work substantial and, by the common view, usually unfortunate alterations in the ballad,[30] there is some antecedent probability that even the earliest recorded versions, which anthologists almost always prefer, differ markedly from their originals. It stands to reason that a ballad caught up after a century or two of oral transmission will register a loss of detail, if of nothing more serious, and in any case will have suffered as art. Accordingly, the ballads in question here may represent varying degrees of deterioration from originals which, if available, would provoke contempt for their derivatives. Although there is not much concrete evidence to oppose this view, it rests ultimately on the unwarranted assumption that most extant ballads traveled far—some even from the Middle Ages—before lodging in print. But, however ancient their story content, the ballads themselves are not, except in a small handful of instances, demonstrably mediaeval,

[30] See J. R. Moore, "The Influence of Transmission on the English Ballads," *MLR*, XI (1916), 408.

and very few antedate the seventeenth century.[31] Most of the favored anthology pieces cannot be dated earlier than the eighteenth century, and none recalls extant mediaeval song in style. Indeed, the authentic mediaeval specimens, which might be expected to show balladry at its best, are as a group neither rich in detail nor remarkable as literature. While the most admired ballads as now known probably differ from their originals, it would be absurd to postulate for them a long and generally deleterious oral career prior to the earliest recordings. In any event, the literary value of a ballad is properly measured only by its aesthetic achievement; how it reached its available state or states, though important for cultural history, is ultimately of no concern to criticism. Close analysis tends to show that in the main the anthology versions require no literary allowances to be made for them and thus provide no basis for assuming superior, or even longer, originals.

It is possible to describe the method of the popular ballads as narrative, dramatic, or even lyrical, but none of these terms or any combination of them (e.g., dramatic narrative, lyrical-dramatic narrative)[32] is of much use to criticism. Some years ago M. J. C. Hodgart proposed to supply the lack of a serviceable term with "montage."[33] Whether generally applicable to the ballads or not, the term permits a valuable insight into the method of the ones at issue here. At the center of most of these pieces is a commonplace (and usually tragic) predicament set around by scenes sufficient to define it and at the same time to outline, often very vaguely, a story of considerable magnitude. The matter, shaped up from various angles of representation, tends to point away from the particular situation and toward a general meaning, and it is upon the higher level that

---

[31] Pound, "On the Dating of the English and Scottish Ballads," *PMLA*, XLVII (1932), 15, argues persuasively that the great period of ballad making was after the Renaissance.

[32] Leach, *op. cit.*, p. 5; W. J. Entwistle, *European Balladry* (Oxford, 1939), p. 18.

[33] Hodgart, *op. cit.*, p. 27, acknowledges his debt to S. Eisenstein's *The Film Sense* (1943), in which parts of *Paradise Lost* are studied as montage.

these ballads have their greatest interest. They are most significantly symbolic structures; and to speak of them as narrative, dramatic, or lyrical is to call to mind poetry of different management. W. K. Wimsatt, Jr., has written, "But the best story poems may be analyzed, I believe, as metaphors without expressed tenors, as symbols which speak for themselves."[34] His example—*La Belle Dame Sans Merci*—is incontrovertible, though its aesthetic appears to differ from that of the symbolistic popular ballads. Wimsatt does not state the criteria by which the best story poems are to be sorted out, but he would probably agree that little is to be gained by analyzing as symbolic structures those fairly long and detailed ballads in which the story seems to be everything or nearly so. Child's collection assuredly abounds in innocent narratives (e.g., *Young Beichan*) and dramatic exchanges (e.g., *Riddles Wisely Expounded*), and possibly only a minority actually demand metaphoric extension. This is not to imply, however, that only the popular anthology pieces are eligible for such treatment or that others are any the less the products of conscious and individual artistry.

The most famous version of *Sir Patrick Spens*, though decidedly fragmentary as narrative, leaves a distinct impression of achieved art. The literary result considered, it can hardly be thought accidental that the spectacular circumstances surrounding the foundering of the ship are neglected and that acts and scenes of an unessential order are held up to view. The very poverty of local detail sets a limit on narrative interest, while the obviously symbolic import of much of the content points the whole experience ineluctably toward an abstract level of meaning. Indeed, *Sir Patrick Spens* insists so powerfully on being something more than a story of death at sea that its otherness densely overspreads the simple relation. At the center of the ballad is an ironic situation—the king sitting "in Dumferling toune" [in Dunfermline town] appears to honor Sir Patrick by choosing him to undertake an important voyage which, on

[34] *The Verbal Icon* (Lexington, Ky., 1954), p. 80.

account of the season, is unlikely to turn out well. The poet exploits the mixed feeling with which the sailor quite naturally reads his orders from the king:

> The first line that Sir Patrick red,
> A loud lauch lauched he;
> The next line that Sir Patrick red,
> The teir blinded his ee.

> [The first line that Sir Patrick read,
> a loud laugh laughed he;
> the next line that Sir Patrick read,
> the tear blinded his eye.]

Spens must needs laugh and weep at a command which is, the conditions for sailing considered, utterly absurd and yet full of dark fatality for him. An ominous weather forecast spoken by a crewman supports his pessimistic appraisal of the situation and removes all doubt about the result:

> "Late late yestreen I saw the new moone,
> Wi the auld moone in hir arme,
> And I feir, I feir, my deir master,
> That we will cum to harme."

> ["Late, late last evening I saw the new moon,
> with the old moon in her arms,
> and I fear, I fear, my dear master,
> that we will come to harm."]

With his poem largely secured by this exciting symbol, the poet might have been expected to proceed in a conventional way to the tragic conclusion, but he elected to risk a novel tactic. What follows is then, not a step-by-step narration culminating in the sinking of the ship, but a series of scenes which ironically announce the outcome and cast shadow after shadow across the experience:

> O our Scots nobles were richt laith
> To weet their cork-heild schoone;
> Bot lang owre a' the play wer playd,
> Thair hats they swam aboone.

[Oh our Scots nobles were quite loath
    to wet their cork-heeled shoes;
but long before all the play was played,
    their hats they swam about.]

O lang, lang may their ladies sit,
    Wi thair fans into their hand,
Or eir they se Sir Patrick Spence
    Cum sailing to the land.

[Oh long, long may their ladies sit,
    with their fans in their hands,
before they see Sir Patrick Spence
    come sailing to the land.]

O lang, lang may the ladies stand,
    Wi thair gold kems in thair hair,
Waiting for thair ain deir lords,
    For they'll se thame na mair.

[Oh long, long may the ladies stand,
    with their gold combs in their hair,
waiting for their own dear lords,
    for they'll see them no more.]

Haf owre, haf owre to Aberdour,
    It's fiftie fadom deip,
And thair lies guid Sir Patrick Spence,
    Wi the Scots lords at his feit.

[Half over, half over to Aberdour,
    it's fifty fathom deep,
and there lies good Sir Patrick Spence,
    with the Scots lords at his feet.]

The effect of the poet's shift is to lower the pitch and to generalize the tragedy; the particular disaster, which is of a sort most poignantly meaningful to seafaring peoples, tends to merge with the multitude of other fatal misadventures dogging the footsteps of mankind. The scenes contemplated by the poet, besides fleshing out the narrative slightly, reveal human beings taking pathetic and somewhat irrelevant postures in the face of circumstances beyond their power to control. The Scottish nobles are said to be concerned with emblems of rank and wealth—their cork-heeled shoes—when life itself is in jeopardy. The wives, waiting helplessly on shore with fans and gold combs in their hands, recreate and suffer the last agonies of their men. And "guid" Sir Patrick, arranged at the bottom of the sea with the Scottish lords at his feet, receives such honor as position confers but an honor which no man would rush to claim. Several questions about the tragedy remain unanswered but make no demand for answers, since larger considerations overshadow the particular event. By using an ironical angle of vision, and avoiding detail closely related to the calamitous moment, the poet blocks off the pathetic level of experiencing the tragedy and compels his audience to brood over the fatal forces which in one form or another overtake all men.

The achievement of *Sir Patrick Spens* is approached, though hardly equalled, by some other ballads which use much the same formula. In *Young Waters* the observations are relevant and moving but not overwhelmingly portentous; their focus is rather the particular tragic instance than the moral design of a world in which a young man can be executed for no other offense than his own handsomeness. It is significant of little more than personal distress for the victim to remark:

> "Aft I have ridden thro Stirling town
>   In the wind bot and the weit;
> Bot I neir rade thro Stirling town
>   Wi fetters at my feet."

> ["Often have I ridden through Sterling town
>   in both the wind and the wet;
> but I never rode through Sterling town
>   with fetters on my feet."]

Such a statement, obvious and even trivial, is of course two-layered; but it makes no large demands and folds quietly into the story. *Mary Hamilton* tends in the opposite direction despite a series of sentimental gestures toward the close. In its best part the ballad has as much tension as *Sir Patrick Spens* and as much symbolic force. There are few passages in Child's collection more powerful than Mary's reply to the "auld queen" [old queen], who has accused her of murdering the infant got on her by the "hichest Stewart of a' " [highest Stewart of all]:

> "I winna put on my robes o black,
>   Nor yet my robes o brown;
> But I'll put on my robes o white,
>   To shine through Edinbro town."

> ["I will not put on my robes of black,
>   nor yet my robes of brown;
> but I'll put on my robes of white,
>   to shine through Edinborough town."]

Although weakened by the concluding matter—Mary's drinking healths to her "weil-wishers" [well-wishers] and her unexceptional reflections on her parents—the ballad refuses to be taken at either the literal or the moral level and constantly intimates the hopeless struggle of a valiant spirit against a universe of evil consequences.

The fragmentary *Wife of Usher's Well* bears certain formal resemblances to the ballads previously discussed, but it is less obviously manipulated than any of them. Whereas the scenes sifted out by the author of *Sir Patrick Spens* betray very artful discrimination and ironic twisting, those of the *Wife of Usher's Well* have a central importance and, moreover, seem to speak pretty much for themselves. Since the tragic situation is basically ironical, the poet has only to report the circumstances in order to create a powerful impression. It is noteworthy, however, that his extreme detachment tends to call attention to the cruel universe which surrounds the hapless wife. Word comes to the woman of the death of her sons, presumably by drowning, and in her distress she pronounces a terrible curse:

> "I wish the wind may never cease,
>   Nor fashes [fishes] in the flood,
> Till my three sons come hame to me,
>   In earthly flesh and blood."

The curse appears to effectuate the return of the sons, but the audience learns a grim fact unknown to the mother, that the birch of which their hats were made grew "at the gates o Paradise." The Prodigal Son was not more cordially entertained than the unsubstantial sons of the deluded wife:

> "Blow up the fire, my maidens,
>   Bring water from the well;
> For a' [all] my house shall feast this night,
>   Since my three sons are well."

> And she has made to them a bed,
>   She's made it large and wide,
> And she's taen [taken] her mantle her about,
>   Sat down at the bed-side.

Cock's crow brings the inevitable revelation; as usual in such cases the revenants must return to the grave or abide a "sair pain" [sore pain]. The distress of the mother is not reported and need not be. The ballad finally speaks most significantly not of a woman whose cursing earned a terrible punishment but of the vanity of human wishes. Its success is owing to an attitude so remote and restrained as to create a positive deficit of compassion and accordingly a very naked symbolization of the human predicament of the *Wife of Usher's Well* can be measured by the *Daemon Lover*, which, though involving a revenant and an even more sensational action, is nothing more than a sentimentalized ghost story.

Laying stress on strategy, as I have done, supposes conscious authorship and thus affronts the notion that the ballads evolved without expert guidance. If every ballad, as in the standard view, registers the impress of several hands, the question of the author's attitude is very nearly an impertinence. Understandably, older scholars often felt impelled to doubt the authenticity of specimens strongly intimating a sophisticated point of view, though admitting the most attractive of these to the canon on the assumption that they were originally honest folk songs. Apparently from principle, the importance of the ballad speaker has been implicitly denied, and his varying angles of representation have been lumped without much discrimination under objectivity. While the ballads are of course objective, they are not for that naive reportage; indeed, the anthology pieces are patently artificial structures, evidencing conscious shaping from definable angles. The simple-seeming *Wife of Usher's Well* is no less a work of conscious art than *Sir Patrick Spens*, which has been suspected of learned handling. Although *Barbara Allan* has not been questioned on this count, it is instinct with compassion and selective of detail to the point of serious incompleteness. What may have originated as a grim account of malefic image making or similar witchery[35] has been culled for tender moments, and these have been organized to obtain a sentimental response. Although telling a poor story, this ballad unmistakably commemorates tragic love and thus by contrivance succeeds at an abstract level. The same general theme is embodied much more fully in *Lord Thomas and Fair Annet* and *Fair Margaret and Sweet William*; but in contrast to *Barbara Allan* these insist strongly on a higher meaning only in versions embellished with that widely used symbol of true love, the intertwined briar and rose.

The *Three Ravens* with its speaking birds and dense symbolism also suggests rather more contriving than natural poetry would allow, while its superlative congener, the *Twa Corbies*, indisputably declares the hand of a conscious artist. Child could not bring himself to accept the latter, though he had evidence that it was every bit as traditional as the other, if not so old. He printed it with the inconclusive remark that it sounded "something like a cynical variation of the tender little English ballad" —meaning the *Three Ravens*. "Cynical variation" is apparently intended to leave the impression that some version of the *Three Ravens* suffered, at least in ballad quality, from sophisticated handling.

What led Child to reject the *Twa Corbies* was probably not

[35] A mere conjecture. There is some suggestion of a causal connection between the man's illness and Barbara Allan's resentment of the slight.

so much its tone as its sheer perfection; such metrical felicity and freedom from irrelevancy were hardly to be expected in folk song. The older ballad is no less artificial, and it ends with a frank intrusion, "God send euery gentleman, / Such haukes, such hounds, and such a leman" ["haukes" - hawks; "leman" - lover]; but a certain roughness and incoherency appear to vouch for its subliterary origin and career. The *Twa Corbies* is less detailed and less exciting in content but more complex in meaning. Literally considered, it announces the practical interest of a pair of scavengers in a dead and deserted knight. Most significantly, it is a kind of *Earth Song*, grimmer for lacking Christian reference and more plausible for being a symbolic structure rather than a rhetorical and dialectical exercise. Much of the power of the ballad comes through its evaluation of the knight from a scavenger's angle of vision and thus in nonhuman terms. The victim's desertion by hawk, hound, and lady—all emblematic of worldly felicity—is immediately significant of faithlessness and perhaps in the last instance of treachery, but the scene is thereby symbolically emptied of civilized values. Accordingly, the social amenities which tend to soften the fact of death are precluded, and the knight is seen simply—and terrifyingly—as an article of consumption, a mere incident in cosmic process which by various means returns all organic matter to that state whence it came. This commonplace of nature becomes excruciatingly evident when one of the corbies specifies the "bonny blue een" [bonny blue eyes] and the "gowden hair" [golden hair] as the first parts to be utilized. The same bird concludes the poem with a solemn observation, which is, the situation considered, positively bizarre:

> "Mony a one for him makes mane,
> But nane sall ken where he is gane;
> Oer his white banes, when they are bare,
> The wind sall blaw for evermair."

> ["Many a one for him makes moan,
> but none shall know where he has gone;

330

  over his white bones, when they are bare,
  the wind shall blow forevermore."]

 The speaker of the poem—the "I" of the first line—does not return and need not; for the experience finds its significant level of meaning in the last stanza.

 Edward and *Lord Randal* leave as strong an impression of conscious art as the *Twa Corbies,* but probably have been saved from suspicion because of their conspicuous use of incremental repetition. Gummere professed to see in this device an archetypal feature and staked a good deal on it.[36] Yet in both of these ballads incremental repetition plainly subserves a structural principle which cannot be accounted for by an improvising throng—namely, the climactic ordering of parts. In *Edward* the mother's questions about the victim of her son's bloody sword elicit increasingly grave responses—hawk, horse, and then father. Lord Randal's meeting with his "true-love," his eating fried eels, and his mortal illness gradually show a causal relationship, and each new disclosure casts a deeper shadow across the central experience. When the principal has at last made known his predicament (patricide in *Edward,* poisoning in *Lord Randal*), he proclaims the extent of his temporal loss in a last testament, the parts of which are arranged in an ascending scale of interest culminating in a terrible curse. These symmetrical ballads cannot be easily faulted, nor can their excellence be plausibly explained by the process of communal creation or even re-creation.

 The foregoing discussion permits the observation that the best of the ballads show some significant resemblances. They appear to share a moral universe which is not certainly Christian and probably not primitive. Though of uncertain design, it vaguely recalls the world of *King Lear*, in which evil circumstances harass the just and the unjust alike. The characters appear to be resigned to their fate; and, if they allow themselves a comment,

---

 [36] *The Popular Ballad,* pp. 117–34. For dissenting arguments, see Pound, *Poetic Origins,* pp. 121–35, and Gerould, *op. cit.,* pp. 105–107.

it is commonly irony born of hopelessness. At the center in each case is a rather simple tragic situation which can be known essentially from a very sketchy relation. Ordinarily, a good deal of the story is left to inference, and not all the information directly provided is of first importance to it. Only a slight impression of linear movement is created because the circumstances held up to view tend to work centripetally on an anguished moment, which is, strictly considered, only a short dramatic interval in the narrative continuum. Concrete particulars are chosen for their logical relevance to the central predicament and somewhat too for their symbolic force, as, for example, the "cork-heild schoone" which the Scottish nobles of *Sir Patrick Spens* were reluctant to wet. The contracted focus is regulated by the angle of representation and finally validated by the symbol which evolves. The measure of success is not story interest—indeed, most of the good ballads fail signally on this count—but abstract meaning or meanings. It is fair to say, I believe, that the quality of the experience developed by these ballads is more appropriate to lyrics of an objective kind than to narratives.

My examination of the anthology ballads points to the conclusion that their art is conscious and successful. To claim so much for them is not, however, to imply that they are equally successful or that even the very best deserve the status of monuments. Kittredge obfuscated the issue of achievement by invoking some of the greatest names in literature,[37] whose major work obviously lies several degrees of magnitude beyond any of the ballads. Their proper place is with the shorter, more or less narrative poems, of which the language affords a multitude between *Robene and Makyne* and *Sister Helen*; and in this broad category they appear to no disadvantage. These ballads are admittedly conspicuous for their lack of elegance and for their freedom from the influence of the schools. Their rhetoric is not classical, and their diction, though hardly colloquial, is

[37] *Ibid.,* p. xxxi.

assuredly not Latinate. But they are not on that account inartificial or inferior. So much formal contriving evidences an art which, though as yet imperfectly understood, is assuredly highly disciplined.[38]

A moment's reflection will show that to claim distinctive form and superior excellence for the anthology ballads is to create a number of difficulties. Unless highly unlikely results are to be ascribed to communal re-creation, the existence of single and successful craftsmanship must be recognized for them and at no great distance from the earliest dates of record. An alternative is to consider as sophisticated adaptations the specimens which have been thought most worthy of notice; but ineptness would then become a test of genuineness. If the authenticity of the anthology pieces is granted and at the same time their exceptional ordering, the definition of a popular ballad as a folk song which tells a story has very limited usefulness. If the ballad is by origin mediaeval and if, as Wells states, the Robin Hood exemplars provide a "norm of style by which we may judge other ballads,"[39] the anthology pieces clearly belong elsewhere; for neither in idiom nor in internal form do they recall indisputably early ballads. To be sure, the quality ballads are not *sui generis*, however similar some of them may be, but in their

[38] I have left music out of account from a conviction that the ballads, though unquestionably written to be sung, exist primarily as poems. This is in no way to deny that a given ballad benefits from a melody which unobtrusively confirms its tone or that the music has technical interest, if not much independent value. The fact that ballads have remained fairly intact and coherent in oral tradition is strong evidence that their accompaniment has always been sufficiently subdued to allow easy communication. Yet most of the ballads invite musical utterance; and, while not literally writing their own music, they suggest it, within broad limits, by rhythm and tone. *Barbara Allan,* for example, has attracted several dolefully romantic tunes. It would be absurd to discount the power of music to deepen the kind of tragic experience which ballads most successfully communicate, but it would be equally absurd to argue that music is necessary to their success. Many a valued ballad survives without music, while the music which attaches to some others of quality, including *Sir Patrick Spens,* is unimpressive, if not unworthy.

[39] *Ibid.,* p. 11.

exceptionalness they suggest reasonable objections to viewing Child's collection as a genre in any useful sense of the word.

It is unlikely that the term "popular ballad" can be validated even for very general use. The cultural circumstances under which Child's exemplars and others thought comparable[40] were produced cannot be known with any certainty and thus cannot warrant the attributive "popular" with respect to origins. Though doubtless popular by destination, they are not by that fact distinguishable from numerous other story poems.[41] It is not even feasible to limit "popular" to those pieces which have been transmuted in oral tradition, since this distinction assumes a restricted form. Unqualified "ballad," ringed though it is with sociological connotations, must be retained, in the absence of a better term, to designate the whole class of short story poems in common measure and variations thereof.

If the popular ballad is then nothing definable, what principles of selection could have guided Child? A definite answer is of course impossible,[42] but it is a fair guess that he cast a net wide enough to include all but the most elegant story poems in common measure and couplets and then thinned his catch by imposing rather vague socioliterary requirements. He was apparently disposed to accept any specimen which recalled by its meter and stylistic devices[43] the more famous ballads in the

[40] Gerould, *op. cit.,* pp. 28–31, denied the inclusiveness of Child's collection, and Leach, ed., *The Ballad Book,* has anthologized specimens rejected by Child.

[41] Baldi, p. 42, asserts: "Non credo che sia possibile documentare per quegli anni altro senso della parola 'popolare' se non quello di 'rinvenuto fra il popolo'; né dimostrare che il popolo fosse allora visto altrimenti che il fedele e passivo depositario di un'arte dimenticata dalle classi colte" [I do not believe it possible to document for those years another sense of the word "popular" if not that of "return among the people"; nor to demonstrate that the people were then seen as other than the faithful and passive depository of an art forgotten by the cultivated classes].

[42] See Gerould, *op. cit.,* pp. 27 f.

[43] E.g., understatement, questions and answers, alliterative formulas, incremental repetition.

early collections, whether or not there was much structural similarity. He was apparently disposed to reject whatever evidenced learning or the more objectionable features of the broadsides, especially sentimentality and intimacy of presentation. But he seems never to have settled upon the minimum requirements of a popular ballad, and there is no rational principle by which all of his selections can be associated. Critically considered, his collection is a mélange, diverse both as to matter and as to method. Although a model of editorial reliability and a storehouse of valuable information, it is not as a unit significant for literature.

Judged by the poems which wear the label, the ballad is an external form hospitable to narrative matter of any sort and indifferent to its management. This is not a very satisfactory definition, but further delimitation, whether by sociological or literary criteria, invites vitiating exceptions. Yet the ballad loses nothing by being at once more numerous and less definite than Child imagined; it is a form of social expression highly interesting in many of its exemplars for folklore and social anthropology, and nonetheless literature of intrinsic merit. Systematic study remains as feasible as ever, for numerous groupings are logically justified with respect to social use and structure.[44] It is perhaps needful to remark, however, that what is no more precisely definable than the ballad form cannot reasonably be traced back to the French *carole*[45] and the eleventh-century dancers of Kölbigk.[46] Furthermore, sociological data, though often necessary to the understanding of the ballads, cannot properly be invoked for purposes of classifying or evaluating them as literature.

[44] Many poems loosely classifiable as ballads are most properly to be considered under other headings, e.g., romance, *chanson d'aventure* [song of adventure], epic.

[45] W. P. Ker, *Collected Essays,* ed. Charles Whibley (London, 1925), II, 101–104; Chambers, *op. cit.,* p. 184.

[46] See Gerould, pp. 207–10; Wells, p. 203; Edward Schröder, "Die Tänzer von Kölbigk, *Zeitschrift für Kirchengeschichte,* XVII (1896–97), 151.

Critical analysis appears just now to be the most useful approach to the ballads. More definite answers to questions relating to origin, age, priority of competing versions, and transmission seemingly cannot be given, and purely historical scholarship in any case is not competent to deliver the ultimate value judgments needed to decide their literary status. The brief explications attempted in the preceding section suggest that attention to internal form, besides demonstrating the achievement of individual ballads, can lead to the recognition of new and less ambiguous groupings. Traditional classifications, usually according to subject and rhetorical furniture, have tended to create false impressions of uniformity and thus have had the effect of closing up lines of questioning most likely to reveal the intricacies of ballad structure. The art of the ballads is often of a respectably high order and accordingly deserving of serious critical study unfettered either by genetic fallacies or by historical relativism. This view appears to be shared by a number of recent anthologists, who in their discussions of individual ballads simply ignore the theoretical restraints on criticism which this article has considered and, as I believe, substantially removed.